William Henry Davenport Adams

Heroes of the Cross

Studies in the Biography of Saints, Martyrs and Christian Pioneers

William Henry Davenport Adams

Heroes of the Cross

Studies in the Biography of Saints, Martyrs and Christian Pioneers

ISBN/EAN: 9783744664653

Printed in Europe, USA, Canada, Australia, Japan

Cover: Foto ©Lupo / pixelio.de

More available books at **www.hansebooks.com**

HEROES OF THE CROSS

OR,

STUDIES IN THE BIOGRAPHY OF SAINTS, MARTYRS, AND CHRISTIAN PIONEERS

BY

W. H. DAVENPORT ADAMS

"Consider thou the example of the Saints on all sides: what have they not done in order to love GOD, and lead a devout life?"—S. FRANCIS DE SALES.

> "Fair camp in arms of peaceful fortitude,
> And no ungentle warfare, in one band
> Together knit of holy brotherhood,—
> One Faith, one Hope, one Leader, sternly trained,
> Far from earth's noise, to learn the eternal song,
> And gain the conquest of a heavenly land."
> ISAAC WILLIAMS, *from the Parisian Breviary.*

LONDON:

J. MASTERS AND CO., 78, NEW BOND STREET.

MDCCCLXXX.

LONDON :
J. MASTERS AND CO., PRINTERS,
ALBION BUILDINGS, BARTHOLOMEW CLOSE, E.C.

PREFACE.

THE title of this volume indicates its character: it is a record of the lives of certain men and women who have fought the good fight with zeal and constancy; true Heroes of the Cross, never swerving in their loyalty to the Standard they embraced. Enthusiasts these, whom the world laughs at or ignores, but whose self-denying labours have largely added to the sum of human happiness. Victors, whose successes are not always apparent to or understood by the critical historian or the so-called philosopher, but who have won "the crown" in right of their ardour and their courage, their humility and their long-suffering. We give freely of our admiration to brilliant soldiers and able statesmen; but is it less due to the religious reformer or the earnest confessor, who, in the service of CHRIST and for the welfare of his fellows, is prompt to endure all things, to strive and toil and wait, and to seal a life's testimony by a martyr's death? Biography has been defined as teaching by example. But what better examples can we hope to find than those of men who have shown the highest devotion, the purest generosity, the profoundest self-sacrifice? The enthusiasm of a Bernard; the simple piety of a Francis de Sales; the practical philanthropy of a Vincent de Paul; the self-forgetfulness of a Martyn or a Patteson; the fervour of a Francis Xavier; can we fail to profit by the contemplation of such Christian graces? We may not be able to raise ourselves up to so lofty a level as they attained: but seeing what they achieved and endured, how they were tried and how they prevailed, we may take heart to meet with calmness and patience our own smaller troubles and temptations, and run the race set before us with a clean conscience and a braver spirit. We may seek to imitate them, not in the grandeur of their works, or in the wonderful sanctity of their lives, but in their forgetfulness of self, their trustfulness, their meekness, their charity, and, above all, in their obedience to the voice of duty, their submission to the will of GOD.

In selecting my examples, I have studied, first, variety, and second, novelty. As to the first point, I have brought together sketches of an English bishop, the founder of a great religious order, the mediæval orator whose eloquence moved masses of men with eager sympathy, the great reformer of Florence, a scholar missionary, an English matron, a Jesuit missionary. Resembling one another in their devout enthusiasm, they will be found to differ vastly in intellectual and moral characteristics, so that each presents a distinct type of the Christian life. With regard to the second point, I claim that this volume includes a number of biographies founded upon authorities not easily accessible to the general reader; some of which are by no means so well known as seems desirable and profitable; and that they have never before been presented in so compact and available a form. This is specially true of the chapters devoted to the great men of the mediæval Church. I would add that all have been prepared under a strong sense of responsibility; and with a desire to render them suitable for perusal in families, and by the younger members of the Anglican communion. For this purpose, controversial topics have been carefully avoided, and references to dogmatic difficulties made as brief as possible. I hope a note of true Catholicity will be found in every page. Upon the lives and characters, and upon the gifts and graces, of the Christian heroes whom I have sought to commemorate, it has been my delight to dwell, and not upon their religious systems. But while I have refrained from theological bitterness, and from that violent language against the Roman Church which, in some quarters, is considered a mark of true Protestantism, I must own that, throughout, I have written from the standpoint of an English Churchman, and in entire and unhesitating sympathy with the teaching of the Church of England.

W. H. D. A.

CONTENTS.

	PAGE

I.
S. COLUMBA: APOSTLE OF CALEDONIA. 521—597 . . . 1

II.
S. BERNARD OF CLAIRVAUX: THE "MAN OF GOD." 1091—1153 51

III.
S. FRANCIS OF ASSISI: FOUNDER OF THE FRANCISCANS. 1182—1226 105

IV.
S. CATHARINE OF SIENA: "LA BEATA POPOLANA." 1347—1380. 153

V.
GIROLAMO SAVONAROLA: THE REFORMER OF FLORENCE. 1452—1498 199

VI.
S. FRANCIS XAVIER: THE APOSTLE OF THE INDIES. 1506—1552 285

VII.
ANNE ASKEW: AN ENGLISH MARTYR. 1520—1546 . . 323

VIII.
S. Francis de Sales: Bishop of Geneva. 1567—1622 . 349

IX.
S. Vincent de Paul: the Religious Philanthropist. 1576—1660 385

X.
Henry Martyn: Scholar and Missionary. 1781—1812 . 415

XI.
John Coleridge Patteson: Missionary Bishop of Melanesia. 1827—1871 441

S. COLUMBA:

APOSTLE OF CALEDONIA.

> "Isle of Columba's Cell,
> Where Christian piety's soul-cheering spark,
> (Kindled from Heaven between the light and dark
> Of time) shone like the morning star."
> WORDSWORTH.

[*Authorities* :—"Life of S. Columba," by Adamnan, edited by Dr. Reeves, 1857; Montalembert, "Les Moines d'Occident," 1863; Book of Deer, edited by Dr. John Stuart; Cosmo Innes, "Scotland in the Middle Ages;" Thomas Innes, "Civil and Ecclesiastical History of Scotland;" "Life of S. Columba," by Dr. John Smith, 1798; Lanigan, "Ecclesiastical History of Ireland;" Dr. G. Grub, "Ecclesiastical History of Scotland;" J. Hill Burton, "History of Scotland;" Bp. Forbes (of Brechin), "Kalendar of Scottish Saints;" Butler, "Lives of the Saints;" Abp. Ussher, "Ecclesiastical Antiquities;" Duke of Argyll, "Iona," &c.]

S. COLUMBA.

CHAPTER I.

FROM the beginning of the fifth century, the claim advanced by the Bishops of Rome to a spiritual Primacy, and to the supreme government of the Universal Church, seems to have been very generally acknowledged by the Christian world. The conception of this tremendous claim was due to the aspiring genius of Pope Innocent;[1] it was afterwards adopted and partially developed by Leo the Great; it became a reality during the pontificate of S. Gregory. The last named was a contemporary of the saint of Iona, the Apostle of Western Scotland, the great and holy Columba; or, rather, the latter's sun rose above the horizon as that of S. Gregory began to sink below it; yet neither before the age of Columba, nor during his lifetime, was the power of Rome acknowledged either in Britain or Ireland. The allegiance which the Continental nations vowed to the chair of S. Peter was never conceded by the early British Church. Not less resolute in the assertion of her independence was the Church of Ireland, distinguished as she was by the number and devoutness of her holy men. Ireland was called, and not unjustly, *Insula Sanctorum*, the Isle of Saints;[2] but it was not the Island of Rome, and its saints

---

[1] Dean Milman, "Latin Christianity," ii. c. 1.
[2] "In the age following S. Patrick," says Camden, "Ireland was termed *Sanctorum Patria*, and the Scotch monks in Ireland and Britain were eminent for their holiness and learning, and sent many holy men into all parts of Europe."

refused to recognise the Roman authority. Nor, until the eleventh century, did Rome admit into the Kalendar of Saints the name of a single Irish bishop, priest, or monk.

In the sixth century Ireland was greatly in advance of her sister-isle in general culture and religious fervour. Her Church was "the burning and shining light of the Western World;" like the bright beacon of some rock-planted lighthouse, which flings its warning and helpful radiance over a wild waste of waters, it sent forth a pure and sacred glow to illuminate the dark places of heathendom. The English scholars were jealous of the superior fame of Ireland as the home of learning. She had her churches and almshouses, and she had also her colleges, schools and libraries. Bæda informs us that many of the nobles, and of the lower ranks of the English nation, repaired thither for purposes of study,[1] or to lead a calm and spiritual life. She had also her monastic system, a system peculiar to herself, and a system which differed widely from that afterwards established by the Mediæval Founders. Her monasteries were numerous, and wherever they were situated they became centres of civilisation and of the highest moral influence. While the Eastern monks or anchorites made a condition of passive meditation the secret of a devout life, and dispersed into the solitudes of the desert to satisfy their aspirations by stern self-discipline and rigid asceticism, the Irish monks adopted the doctrine afterwards formulated by S. Bernard in the well-known phrase, "Laborare est orare," and thought that they did nothing well unless it was done for the good of their fellow-men. They prayed frequently and fasted oft, but they did not deny themselves the sweet pleasures of a domestic life, and many families, all probably belonging to one particular tribe, were united in these remarkable communities. It may almost be said that they set the type and pattern of what may be called Christian Socialism. Their members shared all things in common; they worked, they prayed together; if threatened by an enemy, they rose with one consent against him. They acknowledged the rule of a superior, whose authority seems generally to have been hereditary, and with whom they may well have been connected by the ties of blood; so that each convert combined the features both of

[1] Bæda, iii. 27.

a clannish and a monastic organisation. And though I see no reason to suppose that their members were counted by hundreds, and tens of hundreds, as some authorities assert, yet it is probable that each community was of considerable strength, and it is certain that in each were represented all classes of the population. There were priests among them, of course, and there were also writers and caligraphers, musicians, painters, and carvers; men who could wield the pen, and men who could handle the plough. Over all ruled one supreme personage, exercising a kind of theocratic rule, prince and priest, abbot and legislator, as powerful as much from the force of his character or his natural genius, as from the traditional sanctity of his position.

But, besides the Abbot, each monastic colony had its Bishop or Bishops,[1] an ecclesiastical anomaly, which has sadly perplexed historians, and proved the subject of a fertile and ingenious controversy. Let me frankly confess that I see no grounds for believing that the Celtic Bishops exercised any territorial jurisdiction. They were Bishops without dioceses; missionary Bishops; whose chief object seems to have been to continue the succession, and ordain priests. Whether they were subject to the rule of the monasteries with which their names are connected, it seems impossible to determine; they may simply have held themselves aloof as representing the Universal Church. All that can be safely asserted is, the impossibility of denying, in the face of undisputed tradition and authentic testimony, the existence of the Episcopal order in the monastic communities of Ireland.

It might reasonably be supposed that the lively fancy of the Celt would not fail to divert itself with so congenial a subject as the Irish Saints. It took this glorious army, and arrayed it in martial order, dividing it into three great battalions: the first, led by the Patron Saint of Erin, was wholly composed of Bishops, Roman, British, Frankish, and Irish-Scottish, and shone with the radiance of the sun; the second, commanded by S. Columba, and consisting exclusively of priests, glowed like the moon; and the third, under the guidance of S. Colman and S. Aidan, numbering

[1] Dr. Todd, "Life of S. Patrick," pp. 171, 172.

both Bishops, priests, and hermits, glittered like stars. Imitating Montalembert, I may point among this numerous host to two or three of its most illustrious names. As for instance, the much-wandering S. Brendan, whose voyages in search of the Earthly Paradise, half real, half allegorical, exercised no inconsiderable influence on the mind of Christopher Columbus, and may have stimulated that spirit of adventure which opened up to Europe the wonders of the New World: and S. Kevin, whose memory still haunts the shore of wild Glendalough, and who, it is said, could count by millions the beatified souls whom he had led to the Celestial Gate. S. Finnian, too, the founder of the great monastic school of Clonmel: S. Comgall, who established that glorious Bangor on the stormy Irish coast, of which such remarkable traditions have been handed down to us: S. Dega, who was a skilful workman in iron and copper, and a notable caligrapher, transcribing no fewer than three hundred copies of the Gospels: and lastly, S. Mochuda, who was famous for his love of music, and desired above all things to sing in melodious strains the praise of GOD.

Such were some of the holy Evangelists sent forth from the Irish monastic communities, but not one of them remains so conspicuous in history, not one of them accomplished so noble a work, as he who, bred up in the school of Clonard, became the abbot-ruler of Iona, and the Apostle of Caledonia.

Columba was born on the 7th of December, 520, or 521, at Gartan, in the county of Donegal.[1] By his father, Fedhlimidh, he was descended from the great King Niall of the Nine Hostages; his mother, Eithne, belonged to one of the royal houses of Leinster. The slab of stone on which, according to tradition, she bore him, is still pointed out by the Irish peasantry, who assert that if a person pass a night upon that stone, he will be cured for ever of a too keen longing in exile for his beloved fatherland.

After Columba attained to greatness, it was considered right and proper that his birth should be invested with

[1] The primary authorities for his age are, Cummenus Albus, or Comyn the Fair, seventh Abbot of Iona, (657—669,) and Adamnan, ninth Abbot, (690—703.) The work of the latter has been carefully and learnedly edited by Dr. W. Reeves.

marvellous attributes, and accordingly his biographer records a dream which occurred to his mother some time before the birth of her child of promise. An angel appeared to her, and displayed a veil (*peplum*), on which were embroidered flowers of the greatest variety, and wonderful richness of colouring. Immediately, as she gazed, the veil was borne afar by the wind, and as it streamed away, it unfolded itself to a great length, so that it overspread valley, and forest, and mountain. Then the angel spake: "Thou art about to bring forth a son that shall blossom in all sweetness, who shall be numbered among the prophets of GOD, and is the predestined leader of numberless souls to the Heavenly Country."

It is supposed that Columba passed his boyhood in the neighbourhood of his birthplace. It was the boyhood of one marked out for a sublime mission. While receiving instruction from the priest who had baptized him, he was constantly favoured with miraculous manifestations. His guardian angel watched over him sedulously. On one occasion the youthful saint was invited to choose the virtues he most preferred, and he chose Chastity and Wisdom. Straightway, three damsels of exceeding loveliness stood before him, flung their white arms about his neck, and embraced him. He repulsed them angrily. "What, then, dost thou not know us? We are three sisters, and our Father gives us to thee for thy brides." "Who is your Father?" "Our Father is GOD, is JESUS CHRIST, the LORD and SAVIOUR of the world." "And what are your names?" "Virginity, Wisdom, Prophecy, and we are come to love thee with an incorruptible love, and to abide by thee for ever."[1]

When of a fitting age he was sent to Moville,[2] where he made rapid progress under the fostering care of S. Finnian, and was admitted to the diaconate. Thence he betook himself to Leinster, to study under Gemman, a famous bard, who probably developed his latent love of poetry. His theological course was completed under S. Finnian of Clonard, who ruled wisely and prosperously over a monastic community of considerable importance.

A strange story is connected with Columba's residence under the roof of Gemman. The bard and the youth were

[1] This is one of the post-Adamnan legends. See O'Donnell, i. 36.
[2] Adamnan, lib. ii. c. 1.

seated out of doors at a short distance from each other, reading, when they saw afar a young girl pursued by a robber. The young girl at the same time caught sight of them, and hastened to seek the bard's protection. Gemman, much disturbed, summoned Columba to assist him in defending the maiden, who vainly sought to conceal herself under their long robes. The robber, on coming up, took no heed of her protectors, but slew her with his lance, and departed, leaving her dead body at their feet. "How long," exclaimed Gemman, "will GOD leave unpunished this crime which so dishonours us?" "For this moment only," answered Columba, "for as the soul of this innocent creature ascends to Heaven, so will her murderer's soul go down to hell." Scarcely had he uttered these words, before the assassin fell dead.[1]

Columba received priestly orders at the hand of Etchen, the "Bishop" in Clonfad, and completed his preparation for his mission in the monastery at Glasnavidan, now Glasnevin, near Dublin. When the plague dispersed this community in 544 he returned to the north; and, about two years afterwards, founded a religious house at Tyrconnel. If the statement be accurate, it conveys a striking proof of the influence he had already attained, owing partly perhaps to his royal lineage, as well as to his singular piety, and remarkable intellectual powers. For the next sixteen years, if his biographers may be credited, he devoted himself specially to the foundation of religious houses, and no fewer than thirty-seven afterwards professed to trace their existence to his labours. Of these the most important were Durrow, (Dair-mach,) and Derry, (Doir-chalgaich,) both taking their names from the oak forests in the heart of which they were planted. Derry seems to have received his special favour and affection. It was his favourite residence; the deep shadows of the surrounding woods, and the shimmer of the neighbouring sea, having, no doubt, a magical charm for his sensitive imagination. Later in life it held a foremost place in his memory, and suggested to him one of the simple but touching songs which attest his poetical genius. This song appears to have been handed down to another generation, and in time to have assumed the following form:

[1] Adamnan, ii. 25.

"Were all the wealth of Scotia[1] mine,
From its centre to its borders,
I would give all for one little cell
In my beautiful Derry.
For its calm and for its purity,
For the white angels that sweep
In hosts from one end to the other,
I love my beautiful Derry.
For its calm and for its purity,
For Heaven's angels that come and go,
I love my beautiful Derry.

"My Derry, my fair oak grove,
My loved little cell and dwelling,
O GOD in the heavens above,
Let him who profanes it be cursed!
Beloved are Durrow and Derry.
Beloved is Raphoe the pure,
Beloved the fertile Drumherne,
Beloved are Sords and Kells![2]
But dearer and fairer to me,
The salt sea where the sea-gulls cry,
When I come to Derry from far;
Yes, dearer and fairer to me,
   Dearer to me!"[3]

It is not one of the least attractive of the aspects under which S. Columba appears to us, this, as claiming a place among the ancient minstrels of Ireland. And he was not only a poet, but, like all true poets, had a warm and generous regard for every son of song. In his monastic commonwealths the bards were ever welcome; and nowhere more welcome than in the religious house which he erected on an islet in Loch Key. With his own fervid love of poetry he seems to have inspired its monks, for we are told that they complained bitterly if he suffered any wandering minstrel to depart without entertaining them by the melodies of his harp and voice. We may imagine the pleasant converse that took place between Columba and these favoured guests: how they would discourse on high and holy themes, on the beauty of the star-sown heavens and the wonder of the lone grey ocean; and how that Columba would at times recite

---

[1] The ancient name of Ireland.
[2] Raphoe, Drumherne, Sords and Kells were Monasteries founded by Columba.
[3] Dr. Reeves, "Adamnan," pp. 288, 289.

his own pathetic and flowing verse, now in Greek, now in Latin, receiving modestly the praises of his delighted auditors.

When we remember that Columba was also an unwearied traveller and a great warrior, for he fought in at least three considerable battles, we cannot but own that he stands before us as a remarkable and unique character. His activity was not inferior to his versatility. Rest, that is, the lethargic rest which consists simply in inaction, was foreign to his nature. He was always at work; mind and body were incessantly on the strain. He was the controlling spirit of numerous large communities; he had duties to discharge in connection with his princely position; from north to south, from east to west, he moved with fiery zeal, he read largely, and as we have seen, he composed; he sang to the harp; as a priest, the servant of GOD, he was indefatigable; he translated numerous copies of the Psalms and Gospels. How did he find time or energy for labour so multifarious and so incessant? Poet, missionary, traveller, warrior, ruler; in his life-time he played many parts, and played each well. More correctly speaking, he played *no* part, for he *was* all that he appeared to be. Burning with an unquenchable enthusiasm, he spared not himself for the sake of his fellow-men; and in every phase of his many-sided character we see plainly that his activity was maintained and directed by the boundless love with which he was inspired; a boundless love for his GOD and SAVIOUR showing itself, as in its highest manifestation, and as such love must always show itself, in a holy desire to further the best interests of humanity, and to bring the heathen world within the range of the sweet and blessed influences of the Cross.

It was in the summer of 563 that this Hero of the Cross, with twelve followers, forsook his native land and its happy colonies of devout workers, and crossed to the west coast of Britain.

We nowhere learn with certainty the motives that inclined him to this arduous enterprise. It is true that historians put forward two reasons; that he was inspired by an unconquerable longing to preach the Gospel to the Northern Picts, and that he left Ireland on account of a contention with his former master, S. Finnian of Moville. But neither seems to us sufficient.

With reference to the first hypothesis, we may point out its assumption that the Saint could find no more work to do for CHRIST in his own country, or that he preferred the salvation of the barbarians to that of his own people. It does not seem that either supposition is tenable. Before we can estimate the value of the second hypothesis, we must ascertain the particulars of the alleged misunderstanding.

We are told that Columba, while on a visit to S. Finnian, contrived to make a secret copy of that master's Psalter, which we may imagine to have been embellished with rare caligraphical devices, by shutting himself up at night in the church or oratory where it was deposited. He was discovered at his task by some belated wanderer, who carried the information to S. Finnian. Books in those days were regarded with jealous devotion by their possessors; and Finnian, enraged at an act which seemed to him one of theft, demanded the finished copy, on the plea that an unauthorised copy belongs by right to the owner of the original, inasmuch as the transcription is the offspring of the original book.

Columba, however, refused to yield, and the point at issue was referred to the arbitration of Diarmaid, or Dermot, who is described as the *basileus* or chief king of Ireland, and as sprung from the same royal race as Columba himself. His judgment was conveyed in a pithy phrase which passed into a proverb, *La gach Roin a Roinin*, "To every sea-cow her sea-calf," and ordered the copy to be given up to S. Finnian. Columba waxed indignant:—"The sentence is unrighteous," he exclaimed, "and I will revenge myself." Shortly afterwards Curnan, a son of the King of Connaught, pursued for having committed an act of homicide, fled to Columba for sanctuary, but was seized by Diarmaid's orders, and put to death. This violation of the ecclesiastical sanctity attaching to his person, as the founder and lord of so many religious settlements, increased Columba's anger, and kindled the fire of a disposition naturally quick and impetuous. "I will denounce thee, wicked king," he exclaimed, "to my brethren and kindred, who will listen to my voice, and punish thee, sword in hand. Nor shalt thou see my face again until GOD, the great Judge, has subdued thy pride. As thou hast scorned me to-day before thy clans and chiefs, so will GOD scorn thee on the day of battle before thine enemies."

To escape the king's vengeance, Columba retired to his own province, and as he travelled alone over the desolate plains and the rugged hills, he endeavoured to soothe himself with the consolation of the harp. It was then that he composed his celebrated "Song of Trust," a relic of the Irish poetry, the authenticity of which there seems no reason to doubt.[1] It runs as follows:—

> "Alone am I on the mountain,
> O royal Sun, prosper my path,
> And then I shall have nothing to fear.
> Were I guarded by six thousand,
> Though they might defend my skin,
> When the hour of death is fixed,
> Were I guarded by six thousand,
> In no fortress would I be safe,
> Even in a Church the wicked are slain,
> Even in a lake-surrounded isle;
> But GOD's elect are secure,
> Though in the battle-front
> No man can kill me before my day,
> Even had we closed in combat;
> And no man can save my life
> When the death-hour has come.
> My life!
> As GOD wills, so let it be:
> Nought can be taken from it;
> Nought can be added to it:
> The lot which GOD has fixed
> Ere a man dies must be lived out.
> He who seeks more, were he a prince,
> Shall not a mite obtain.
> A guard!
> A guard may guide him on his way;
> But can he defend
> Against the touch of death?
> Forget thy poverty awhile;
> Think of the world's hospitality.
> The Son of Mary will prosper thee,
> And every guest shall have his share.
> Many a time
> What is spent returns to the bounteous hand,
> And that which is retained
> Not the less has passed away.
> O living GOD!
> Alas for him who evil works!
> That which he expects not befalls him,

[1] Adamnan, "Life of S. Columba," edited by Dr. Reeves.

That which he hopes for glides from his hand.
There is no *Sreod*[1] that can tell our fate,
Nor flight of birds upon the branch,
Nor trunk of gnarled oak.

* * * * *

Better is He in Whom we trust,
The King Who has made us all,
Who will not leave me to-night without refuge.
I worship not the music of the birds,
Nor fortune, nor the love of son or wife;
My Inspiration is CHRIST, the Son of GOD,
The Son of Mary, that great Abbot,
The FATHER, the SON, the HOLY SPIRIT.
My lands are with the King of kings;
My order is at Kells and at Moone."[2]

Thus sang Columba on his weary way; and the same song, it is said, will protect all who repeat it while they travel.

Having reached his native province, Columba soon succeeded in forming a confederacy against King Diarmaid; and the Hy-Nialls of the North, assisted by the King of Connaught, declared war against the Hy-Nialls of the South. The latter, under Diarmaid, accepted the challenge, and encountered their adversaries in battle at Culdreimhne, or Cool-Drevny, where they suffered a severe defeat. The victory is ascribed by the annalists to the influence of Columba, who, with fasting and prayer, besought Heaven to undertake the punishment of the unjust king. How far his fasts and prayers availed we may not conjecture; but it is probable that his war-songs were not less inspiring or successful than those of Tyrtæus, and that the example of his personal courage was not without effect.

So soon as the ecclesiastical rulers of the Isle of Saints were apprised of this great battle, and of Columba's share in it, they met in synod at Teilte (now Teltown), condemned him for the crime of shedding blood, and pronounced against him sentence of excommunication. If we may believe the chroniclers, this was not the soldier-priest's first offence, his restless and impetuous temperament having involved him in many of the forays and expeditions of his clan; the sen-

---

[1] *Sreod*, a Druidical term, signifying "an omen."
[2] Moone in Kildare, where S. Columba's abbatial cross is still preserved.

tence, therefore, was not wholly undeserved. Columba, however, made haste to protest against it, and appeared before the Synod. Here a splendid opportunity is afforded to the old chronicler of embellishing his simple narrative with the *purpureus pannus* of a miraculous incident, and he does not forget to avail himself of it. To record the Saint's presence at Teilte was not enough: he adds that Abbot Brendan, the founder of the monastery of Birr, immediately on seeing him, went up to him, and embraced him. And when asked how he could give the kiss of peace to a blood-guilty man, he replied:—" Ye would do as I have done, and ye would never have excommunicated him, could ye see what I see, a pillar of fire going before him, and angels accompanying him. I dare not stand aloof from one whom GOD has predestined to lead an entire people to everlasting life." No marvel that the sentence of excommunication was cancelled and Columba dismissed, with an exhortation to gain to CHRIST as many heathen souls as the number of Christians who had perished on the red field of Culdreimhne.[1]

It was then, says Montalembert, that his soul seems first to have been troubled, and that remorse sowed in it the seeds at once of a startling conversion and of his future Apostolic mission; seeds which were encouraged to ripen by the wise counsel and gentle remonstrance of his friends. But it is the belief of less credulous writers that in the battle of Culdreimhne Columba had no share, apart from the anxiety he would naturally feel for the welfare of his kinsmen. And, therefore, as we have seen, these authorities attribute his departure from Ireland to his desire to undertake the instruction of the Christian subjects of Conal, King of the Dalriadic Scots, and the conversion of the Picts of the North. For myself, I do not presume to reject the whole of the narrative, notwithstanding the ob-

---

[1] The Latin Psalter, the alleged origin of this strange warfare, became, under the name of the *Cathac*, or " Fighter," a national relic of the O'Donnell clan, to which Columba belonged. It was carried in all their battles as an omen of victory. For some years it has been deposited in the Museum of the Royal Irish Academy, but it was recently photo-zincographed for the great work on the " National Manuscripts of Ireland," published under the auspices of the Treasury.

viously doubtful character of many details. There are gleams in Adamnan's sober pages of the soldier-spirit of his hero, and the burden of all the traditions that have come down to us is to the effect that, whether his exile from Ireland was voluntary or compulsory, it originated in connection with some deed of violence. The melancholy pervading his songs points, perhaps, to a similar conclusion; and it may be conjectured that some such incidents as the Battle of Culdreimhne and the Synod of Teilte, by awakening his conscience and quickening in him a sense of exceeding sinfulness, accomplished the sanctification of his character, previously marred by so many faults.

And so it came to pass that S. Columba, with his twelve attendants, took leave of the green shores he loved so deeply, and sailed across the sea, taking a north-easterly course. If doomed to live an exile from his native land it must be in some asylum so far distant from it that its outlines could not loom against the horizon to keep ever open in his heart the wound that bled so freshly. Bitter enough was that dreary voyage! As the hide-bound coracle[1] tossed upon the waves, each hour seemed doubly long that kept before his eyes the vision of the well-known, well-loved coast. He came at last to the wild group of islands which Nature seems to have torn from the cliffs and promontories of Argyll. In one of these he resolved to fix his abode, and thence he would send abroad his missionaries to raise the banner of the Cross among the heathen Picts. Which should it be? Not Islay; it was too large for his small company, and too near the fatherland. Not Jura; only the gloomiest anchorite would choose it for the scene of his penitential tears. Should it be Oronsay? The legend tells us that Columba actually disembarked there, but on climbing the lofty hills, could still see the thin blue rim across the distant ocean that spoke of home. Northward, then, still northward, the brown sail swelled before the breeze; and he was swiftly borne onward to the isle which has ever since been identified with his name; the isle which he has surrounded with an atmosphere of sanctity, romance, and poetry, the rugged, wave-worn Hy, I-colm-kille, or Iona.

[1] *Curraghs*, or boats made of a wooden framework, covered with skins, are still in use on the Irish coast.

Through a labyrinth of rocks his boat glided into a creek known to this day as *Port' a Churraich*, the Port of the Coracle; a small inlet, fenced round by steep rocks of gneiss, and lined with a margin of richly-coloured pebbles of green serpentine, green quartz, and blood-red felspar. Columba immediately disembarked, and mounted the nearest eminence. Looking to the west and the south he beheld only the melancholy waters, and then he knew that the home-land was far away. Hence, this hill has ever since been marked by a cairn, known to the Gael as *Cairn cul ri Erin*, or the Cairn with its back turned on Erin. With his back turned upon Erin, Columba felt he might hope for rest, and he resolved to fix his residence on the lonely island to which the Hand of GOD had so wonderfully guided him over the western sea.

CHAPTER II.

I PAUSE for a moment in my narrative to glance at the natural characteristics of Iona and its surrounding archipelago.

The description drawn by the eloquent pen of Montalembert is well known. He speaks of the aspect of the island as something sad and gloomy almost to sullenness. Not a tree, he says, has been able to resist either the withering wind or the destroying hand of man. Only three miles in length by two miles in breadth, low and level, encircled by grey rocks which scarcely rise above the level of the sea, and overshadowed by the high and sombre peaks of the great island of Mull, it is deficient even in that austere beauty which the neighbouring isles and shores borrow from their lofty basaltic cliffs, or from the conical-crested hills, whose perpendicular sides are incessantly beaten by the waters of the Atlantic, hurrying onward to plunge into the sea-worn and loud-resounding caverns. Upon the narrow surface of the island white patches of land alternate with scanty pastures, a few poor crops, and the dreary moors which supply the inhabitants with peat. Yet poor as is this culture, it is everywhere narrowed and impeded by the gneiss which continually crops up, and in some places extends into a singular labyrinth of rocks.

Of the Hebridean Archipelago the great Frenchman's picture is painted in equally dark colours. Nothing, he declares, can be less attractive at the first glance than that grave and solemn nature, which is picturesque without charm and grand without grace. We traverse, he says, a maze of bare and sterile islands, sown, like so many extinct volcanoes, on the dull and angry waters, which are sometimes vexed by swift currents and perilous whirlpools. Except on rare occasions when the pale northern sun gives a temporary life to those shores, the eye roams over a dreary tract of sea, relieved at intervals by the foaming crests of the long billows, or by the white roll of the tide, here dashing against low reefs of rock, and there against massive cliffs, with a wail which fills the silence. Through the continuous fogs and rains of that rude climate are occasionally visible the summits of mountain-chains, with steep and naked declivities descending to the sea, where their base is washed by the ever-plunging surf. The gloom of the landscape is broken only by that peculiar configuration of the coast which Tacitus has sketched with so much vividness of phrase :—" Nusquam latius dominari mare, multum fluminum huc atque illuc ferre, nec littore tenus adcrescere aut resorberi, sed influere penitus atque ambire, etiam jugis atque montibus inseri velut in suo."[1] As in the Norwegian fiords, ocean gashes and hollows cut the island shores into a myriad of creeks and bays and gulfs, of seemingly unfathomable depth, and narrow as they are profound :—

"Mare, quo latus ingens
Dant scopuli, et multa litus se valle receptat."[2]

Their various and varying outlines it would be impossible to describe, as they wind, serpent-like, into the hearts of the mountains. Rugged peninsulas, terminating in pointed headlands, or rising into cloud-capped peaks; isthmuses so narrow that from their central ridge the sea is visible on either hand; straits so pent up between converging walls of rock that the eye shrinks from penetrating their deep shadows; huge ramparts of basalt or granite, scarred with the

[1] Tacitus, "Agricola," x.   [2] Persius, "Satiræ," vi.

traces of the elemental war; caverns, as at Staffa, lofty as the loftiest cathedral nave, and lined by stately rows of prismatic columns; everywhere, in short, a singularly diversified combination of sea and land, but a combination in which the sea is dominant, and never ceases to assert its supremacy.[1]

Such, indeed, is one of the phases under which that wild Western Archipelago presents itself to the observer. But if it have its gloom, it has also its brightness; if it have its terrors, it has also its attractions. And thus would one write of it who had seen it in the early radiance of a summer-morn, when a rare glow touches the shining waves, and lights up the aspiring mountain-tops until they become so many altars of fire, at which the ancient Magians might fitly have done homage to the sun. Thus would one write of it who has seen it in the warm haze of a summer-noon, when every outline is softened by the tremulous lustre, and a singular sense of calm pervades the air, and there is no more ripple on the sea than on a field of corn when lightly stirred by the passing wind. And thus would one write of it who has seen it in the rich glories of a summer-sunset, when land and sea are aflame with vivid purples, and gold, and emeralds; when the mountains are bathed in a deep strange light, which seems a reflection of the celestial splendour; when the contrasts of colour are so intense, and so many, and so sudden in their changes, and so magical in their effects, that the mind is overpowered by the splendid phantasmagoria, and loses itself in dreams of another and a purer world, into the surpassing glories of which it appears to have obtained a fugitive insight.

Columba was a poet, and to a poet Iona was enchanted land. It has been well remarked that its claims depend on a wonderful union of the three greatest powers in nature—the sky, the sea, the mountains.[2] Only those who have visited the western coast of Scotland know the full force and magic of this combination; the marvellous influence of a sky which is incessantly varying its character; the majesty of a sea remarkable for its long rolling billows, its startling accesses of fury, its intervals of strange and almost

[1] Montalembert, "Les Moines d'Occident," liv. ix. c. 2.
[2] Dr. Lindsay Alexander, "Iona," c. i.

eëry calm; and the sublime grandeur of mountains which rise up sheer from the bosom of the waters, and are so rugged and scarred and broken that they might be taken for the ruins of an elder world which, in some dread convulsion, had perished beneath the deep. It is impossible to believe that Columba was insensible to all these forms and appearances of mingled beauty and awfulness. We may even conjecture that the reports of them had been carried to his ear by some of the daring mariners who then maintained a communication between the Scots of Ireland, and the Scots of Argyll, and that they attracted him to Iona when he went forth on his voyage of exile. At least they may have determined him, when once he had reached the island, to make it his permanent residence. Iona would also commend itself to him on account of its seclusion and tranquillity; a seclusion and a tranquillity which would be very dear to Columba at this turning point of his career. At all events, we know that he fixed his abode on the wave-worn rock of which he obtained a gift from Conal Mac Comgail, king of the Dalriadic Scots.

No fewer than thirty names has the island received. *I* or *Hy*, in vogue among the natives, means simply "an island;" *Iona*, the "island of waves," or according to another interpretation, "Holy Island;" and *I-colm-kille*, the "island of Colm of the Cells," (*cellæ*, or churches,) are the three best known, but of these the second, Iona, is the one in general acceptation.

And it is to "Iona" that our thoughts revert when we would trace the early growth of the Scottish Church, and it is under the name of "Iona" that the "illustrious island" retains a place in our fondest memories. As Iona it has been depicted by artists and celebrated by poets; has attracted the footsteps of reverent pilgrims from all parts of the civilized world; and as Iona has drawn from the austere lips of the moralist of the "Rambler" the well-known eulogium :—" To abstract the mind from all local emotion would be impossible, if it were endeavoured; and would be foolish, if it were possible. Whatever withdraws us from the power of our senses, whatever makes the past, the distant or the future predominate over the present, advances us in the dignity of thinking beings. Far from me and my friends be such frigid philosophy as may conduct us indifferent or unmoved over any ground which has been dignified by wisdom, bravery, or virtue. That man is little to be envied whose patriotism would not gain force upon the plains of Marathon, or whose piety would not grow warmer among the ruins of Iona."[1]

It was here that Columba founded his cell and monastery; a rude building of planks thatched with reeds, situated on a slightly elevated ground, and surrounded by huts of similar construction, in which his disciples dwelt. Here he devoted himself to the evangelising pursuits of his noble life: occasionally assisting his monks in their agricultural operations; more often engaged in the study of Holy Scripture, in the transcription of the sacred text, in long and solitary meditations, and in converse upon things human and divine with the numerous guests who soon began to flock to his island sanctuary. Hither came the restless, the penitent, the unhappy, to seek counsel and enjoy repose; so that a considerable community before long had gathered round the great missionary's dwelling.

Adamnan records a curious narrative of a dialogue which passed between Columba and one of these wayfarers,—a narrative not only curious but suggestive, as throwing some light on the spiritual feelings of Columba's age. Being informed one day that a stranger had arrived from Ireland, the saint repaired to the *hospitium* to ascertain his news, and learn something of his past history. The new comer informed him that it was his desire, in exile, and bound by monastic vows, to repent of his misdeeds. To test his sincerity, Columba drew a sombre picture of the austerities and rigid obligations of the monastic life. "I am prepared," was the reply, "to undergo the severest and most humiliating conditions thou canst impose upon me." Then having confessed, he swore on his knees to perform whatever penance he was commanded. "It is well," said Columba; "now rise and begone; thou must first labour and repent in yonder island of Tiree for seven years, and after that I will see thee again." "But how," continued the sufferer, "am I to expiate a perjury of which I have not yet spoken? Before I left my country I slew a poor man;

[1] Samuel Johnson, "A Visit to the Hebrides." (1773.)

I was in fetters, and about to suffer the penalty of death for my crime, when a worthy kinsman rescued me by paying the blood-money. I swore that I would serve him all the rest of my life; but after some days of service I deserted him,—and here I am, notwithstanding my vow."

On hearing this avowal, Columba added, that until the seven years of penance had expired, the perjurer could not be admitted to the Paschal Communion.

When the period had elapsed, Columba received him benignantly, administered the Sacrament, and sent him back to Ireland to his patron, carrying an ivory-handled sword for his ransom. The patron, however, refused the ransom sent by the "holy Columba." He was "unworthy of it;" and loosening the girdle from his waist, he gave the penitent both pardon and freedom. The latter remained at home until after the death of his parents, when he joyfully returned to Iona, bringing with him the ivory-handled sword. "Henceforth," said Columba, "thou shalt be called *Libran*,[1] for thou art free, and released from every tie." And he was permitted to take the monastic vows. But when he was ordered to set out for Tiree, to spend his years away from Columba's inspiring presence, Libran's strength gave way, and he fell on his knees bitterly weeping. The Abbot could not alter his sentence, but he did what he could to mitigate it. "Thou must live far from me,—it cannot be otherwise; but thou shalt die in one of my monasteries, and shalt rise again with my monks, and share with them the joys of Heaven."

Such is the story of Libran,—Libran de Arundineto, as Adamnan calls him; and however inaccurate it may be in its details, it shows us, first, the remarkable character of the influence which S. Columba exercised; second, the wide knowledge of his sanctity which had spread abroad; and third, the vigorous precautions he took to prevent unworthy candidates gaining admission to his monastic brotherhood. These precautions, I may add, were rendered imperative by the increasing number of applicants. Daily, nay, hourly, as Columba and his disciples mused, or read, or worked in the quiet of their cells, or carried on their labours in the fields, they were disturbed by the shouts which reached

[1] From *Liberandus?*

them from the neighbouring shores of Mull. Then the boat was launched, and ferried across the strait. The strangers embarked, and arriving in Iona, sought physical help as well as spiritual, food and medicine for the body, as well as food and medicine for the soul. Many having obtained the ready assistance they sought, departed again to make known the goodness and generosity of Columba in all directions; others stayed and drank in the truths of CHRIST's religion, and in due time were admitted as monks, or sent abroad to strive and suffer as missionaries.

It is said that he allowed no woman to enter Iona, but as he did not enjoin celibacy upon his followers, he set apart a neighbouring island as a residence for their wives, which is still called *Edian nam ban*, "the Woman's Isle." A grotesque tradition pretends that sows were also excluded, on the ground that "where there was a sow, there too would be a woman; and that where there was a woman, there must be mischief;" a maxim which reminds us of the cynical question of the Eastern monarch when he was informed of any disaster, "Who is she?" as if a woman must necessarily be at the bottom of it. We may dismiss the exaggeration as a puerile fancy.

Surrounded by his devoted followers, Columba lived and laboured; his settlement consisting of a church or oratory, with an altar and niches; an *hospitium*, or residence for strangers; cells or huts for himself and his monks; an open place or area, probably in the centre of the enclosure; and a barn or granary, in which was stored the annual harvest. At dawn and eve the community were summoned to their religious duties by the chiming of a bell, whose clear notes as they floated out to sea must often have stirred a devout impulse in the heart of the wave-tossed mariner. Here for four and thirty years Columba lived and laboured, diversifying his island work by evangelising missions on the mainland and among the neighbouring islands, and by visits to Ireland, when the first bitterness of exile had passed away.

His earliest mission was to the Dalriadic Scots, who occupied the coast of Argyll, at a distance of thirty miles from Iona. They were Irish by origin, and, like all the Irish, Christians by name. But until Columba visited them, they possessed no ecclesiastical organisation, and the preaching of S. Ninian and S. Palladius had left as few traces among them as among the Southern Picts. He soon however awakened the religious spirit among this fervent race. No one indeed could be better qualified for the enterprise he had undertaken. He was an enthusiast, and enthusiasm is the lever with which worlds are moved. He possessed those qualifications of person and address which are so powerful with the multitude; a voice sonorous but sweet, a majestic yet genial deportment, a comely countenance, a tall and handsome figure. It was known that his practice harmonised with his teaching, and that when he exhorted his hearers to live a pure, a truthful, and a Christian life, he asked them only to achieve a conquest which he had already accomplished in himself. His success, therefore, was a foregone conclusion; and after spending two years among the mountains and glens, and on the borders of the misty lochs of Argyll, he was free to carry the Cross of CHRIST into another region.

According to the best authorities, it was in A.D. 565 that he began to preach the Gospel to the Northern Picts. They were idolaters,—so much is certain,—though it is not known what were the peculiarities of their gods or modes of worship. They were savages, and owed their name, it is said, to their custom of painting their bodies in various colours before they went into battle. They were free, for the mighty barrier of the Grampians had repulsed even the torrent of Roman invasion, and the courage of the fierce Northern race had baffled the genius of Agricola.

Into the romantic but desert territories inhabited by the Picts, Columba appears to have penetrated through the great valley of lakes which strikes across the Highlands in a south-west and north-east direction, breaking up the range of grey mountains that shuts off Northern from Southern Scotland. The water-way provided by the succession of lochs that fills this valley, lochs linked together by a bright chain of silver-shining streams, was readily accessible to the light coracles employed by Columba and his disciples. Crossing the beautiful expanse of Loch Ness, he descended the river that flows from it into the Northern Sea, and near whose ample estuary brightens the cathedral city of Inverness. Doubtlessly the passage was long and painful, but this Hero of the Cross triumphed over every difficulty. On arriving at the capital of the Pictish King Bruidh or Bruide, son of Mailchon, who ruled from the Forth to the Pentland Firth, the gates of the royal fortress (Craig-Phadrick) were churlishly closed against him. Columba, we are told, made the sign of the cross, touched the rude timber with his hand, and immediately the gates rolled back,[1] admitting him and his followers into the royal presence. The latter, stricken with awe, rose up to do this powerful visitor reverence, addressed him in humble language, and thenceforth became his servant.

Columba made many converts among the Picts; but despite the royal friendship, he was greatly impeded in his holy work by the hostility of the priests or soothsayers, whom the chroniclers strangely designate *Magi*. The sanctity which the Druids of England attached to the groves and trees was here ascribed to streams and fountains, some of which were reputed to be favourable, and others injurious to man, a superstition suggested probably by the natural properties of the waters. Against this superstition Columba waged continual war, openly drinking of the springs which the Magi had affirmed to be fatal unto death. They did not, however, venture upon direct violence against him; their devices were of a less perilous kind. One day, when he and his monks issued out of the royal fortress to chant vespers, the Magi, to prevent the sacred sounds from reaching the ears of the people, raised aloud their own barbarous songs and incantations, but Columba straightway sang the forty-fifth Psalm, "Eructavit cor meum verbum bonum," with so sonorous a voice as to silence his adversaries, and make the bystanders, including the king himself, tremble with awe.

Besides chanting and preaching, and constant deeds of charity and love, Columba enforced the influence of his mission, if his biographer may be credited, by working miracles. A Pict, who with his wife and family had embraced Christianity, was sorely grieved by the serious illness of one of his sons, which the Magi hastened to represent as a proof of the power of their gods, and a punishment for

---

[1] "Tunc manum pulsans contra ostia, quæ continuo sponte, retro retrusis fortiter seris, cum omni celeritate aperta sunt."—Adamnan, i. 35.

the father's apostasy. On hearing of his follower's trial, Columba repaired to his house, to find that the youth had just expired. After breathing words of consolation in the ears of the sorrowing parents, he passed, unattended, into the chamber where the dead child lay. There he flung himself on his knees, and, bathed in tears, prayed long and earnestly: then, standing erect, he exclaimed: " In the Name of the LORD JESUS CHRIST, return to life, and arise!" As he spoke, the soul returned to the body of the child,— who, it is probable, had been lying in a trance. The saint assisted him to quit his couch, led him into the adjoining apartment, and gave him back to his parents. Thus did he show, according to Adamnan, that he possessed the power of working miracles, as Elijah and Elisha possessed, or S. Peter, and S. Paul, and S. John.

I think we may accept the incident as authentic, without believing that any miraculous element entered into it. It is easy of explanation, as I have already hinted, without raising Columba to an equal rank with the Prophets of the Old or the Apostles of the New Dispensation. I am bound, however, to acknowledge that a very respectable modern authority attributes to him this remarkable power. Mr. Thomas Innes considers[1] that, as the saint was called upon to labour among a people fortified in their prejudices against truth by their Druids or magicians, " a set of men inspired and animated by the devil, and in great credit and authority with this people," through their "charms, enchantments, and false wonders," he could best prove his mission and establish his authority by working miracles which appealed to the senses, and rose above the common course of nature. But if we accept such an argument, we must surely extend it to the Roman missionaries, and recognise the truth of all the marvels stored up in the Roman hagiology. Further; why has the exercise of so grand a power absolutely ceased? It is as necessary against the heathendom of Africans and Melanesians as it was against the heathendom of the Picts; and S. Columba differed in no wise from Bishop Patteson except in the greater force and strength of his character, and the wider scope of his Evangelising work. He stands forth so conspicuous a servant of the Master, and so suc-

[1] Innes, "Civil and Ecclesiastical History," p. 195.

cessful a pioneer of the truth, that he needs no adventitious conditions to command our interest and excite our admiration. And his life will teach us a deeper and truer lesson if we strip it entirely of the phenomenal, and look upon it simply as the life of a man like unto ourselves in all but his profounder enthusiasm, his wider sympathies, his loftier spirit, his more absorbing and self-sacrificing devotion.

The principal opponent of his work among the Picts seems to have been the Magus or Druid, Broïchan, the king's foster-father. Much that savours of the miraculous is mixed up with the narrative of the contest between them. For example, Columba desired to obtain the freedom of a young female slave, a countrywoman of his own, who was held in servitude by Broïchan; but had the mortification to find his petition scornfully rejected. "Be it so," he said, at last; "but know, Broïchan, that if thou refusest to liberate thy captive, thou shalt die before I leave this province." And so saying he left the castle, and proceeded towards that river Ness which figures in Pictish history as conspicuously as the Nile in the annals of Egypt. Before he had gone far, however, he was overtaken by two messengers from the king, to tell him that Broïchan had met with a calamity, was dying, and to save his life would liberate the slave. Thereupon Columba picked up a pebble from the river-bank, blessed it, and gave it to two of his monks, with the instruction that the sick man must drink freely of water in which this pebble had been steeped. The king's messengers and the monks returned to the castle, and the latter, in exchange for Columba's stone of healing, received the liberated handmaiden ("liberata famula"), who was sent back to her native country.

Broïchan recovered his health, and with it, his animosity against the Apostle. Resorting to his familiar spirits for help, he covered the waters of Loch Ness, on the day fixed for Columba's return to Iona, with a dense mist, and raised against him a strong contrary wind. Nothing dismayed, Columba embarked, and ordered his mariners to hoist the sail; when, to the confusion of the Druids and the amazement of the people, the boat sped southward as merrily and as speedily as if impelled by a favourable breeze.[1]

[1] Adamnan, ii. 34.

In his enterprise of converting the Picts, Columba was greatly assisted by his disciples, who, fired by their master's enthusiasm, visited the remotest isles of Ocean, or penetrated into the wildest glens, in order to proclaim the faith of CHRIST. We must remember that at this period Northern Scotland was very sparsely inhabited; and the numbers of the Picts were not so large as to render impossible or improbable their conversion by one energetic teacher and a few faithful followers. The real difficulty of the task would consist in the savage character of the country, rendering travelling both laborious and painful, and the still more savage character of the people, long nursed in a wild and sanguinary creed. But over every obstacle their devout perseverance triumphed, and far and wide they pursued their twofold work of civilisation and evangelisation. The numerous monastic communities which they planted exercised, undoubtedly, a favourable influence on the social condition of the Picts; accustoming their members to an orderly and peaceful mode of life, to agricultural pursuits, to the recognition of fixed laws; and preparing the way to a still further development of civilisation. In this direction the good accomplished by S. Columba was considerable; and it is not too much to say, perhaps, that he did more than any of the Pictish kings towards that fusion of the Picts and Scots into one nation which forms the starting-point of all authentic Scottish history.

CHAPTER III.

BY means of that curious and venerable record of the remote past known as the *Book of Deer*,[1] we obtain an insight into the process by which S. Columba established his monastic colonies.

We are told that the saint and his disciple, Drostan, arrived, in the course of their missionary wanderings, on the

---

[1] The *Book of Deer* was edited, for the Scottish Society of Antiquaries, with a scholarly preface, by the late Dr. John Stuart.

rocky shores of the Bay of Aberdeen; and that, soon after their coming, the *mormaer*, or ruler, of the principality of Buchan made an offering to them of the "city" or settlement of Aberdeen in perpetuity. As there was a not inconsiderable population inhabiting the sea-shore and adjoining district, Columba accepted the gift, and building a few huts, with a church, founded "a monastery."[1]

Then he proceeded to another of the mormaer's "cities," the situation of which was so pleasant to the poetic eye of the apostle that he asked it in gift, but his request was declined. Here, of course, a miracle comes in. The mormaer's son immediately fell sick to death, and was rescued only by the prayers of Columba at the earnest entreaty of the penitent chief, who then presented him with the land he had previously refused.

On this land huts of stone or wattle were quickly raised as before, and thus sprang into existence the celebrated monastery of Deer.

In the monastic record the story runs as follows:

"Columcille, and Drostán, son of Cosgrach, his pupil, came from Hí, as GOD had shown to them, unto Abbordoboir, and Bede the Pict was mormaer of Buchan before them, and it was he that gave them that town in freedom for ever from mormaer and toisach. They came after that to the other town, and it was pleasing to Columcille, because it was full of GOD's grace, and he asked of the mormaer, to wit Bede, that he should give it to him; and he did not give it; and a son of his took an illness after [or in consequence of] refusing the clerics, and he was nearly dead [*literally*, he was dead if it were but a little]. After this the mormaer went to entreat the clerics that they should make prayer for the son, that health should come to him.... They made the prayer, and health came to him. After

---

[1] "In later times the parish church of Aberdour was dedicated to S. Drostan. It was placed by the brink of a gorge, on a ledge or table-land overlooking the brow of the Dour, at a spot about 150 yards distant from the shore of the Moray Firth. In the beginning of the sixteenth century, the bones of the saint were here preserved in a stone chest, and many cures were effected by means of them. In the face of the rock, near where the stream falls into the sea, is a clear and powerful spring of water, known as S. Drostan's Well."—Dr. Stuart, *Preface to the Book of Deer*, pp. iv., v.

that Columcille gave to Drostán that town, and blessed it, and left it as [his] will, 'whosoever shall come against it, let him not be many-yeared [or] victorious.' Drostán's tears came on parting from Columcille. Said Columcille : ' Let Déar [Tear] be its name henceforth.' "[1]

The site of Deer,[2] as Dr. Stuart remarks, would have much in it to attract the susceptible nature of S. Columba. With rich pastures washed by the ripple of the river, and the deep shadows of the oak trees clothing the surrounding heights; the scene could scarcely fail to remind him of his own well-loved monastery of Durrow, with its woods and grassy levels, in which, as he himself tells us, he was wont to listen to the murmur of the winds and the flute-like notes of the joyous ouzel.

It is always stated that in the Columbite monasteries the rules of obedience and asceticism were strictly enforced ; but they applied, we imagine, only to those members charged with religious duties. Among them the spirit of their daily life was indeed austere. As Mr. Hill Burton observes,[3] its austerity is indirectly shown by the nature of the relaxations allowed in accordance with the dictates of hospitality. If a stranger arrived on a fast day, a *consolatio cibi*, or slight repast of bread and milk, was allowed to break in upon the prolonged abstinence. The duties exacted by the monks were exceedingly arduous ; the punishments inflicted, very rigorous ; yet that, on the whole, the sway of Columba was gentle though firm, and tender though exact, we may infer, not only from what we know of his character, but from the love and reverence with which he was regarded.

How marvellous the contrast between the Iona of the present and the Iona of the Columban age ! Barren and poverty-stricken, and lying, as it were, on the outskirts of

---

[1] The word *Deer*, however, seems really to be identical with *Daire*, "oak-groves ;" and it is to be noted that Columba was partial to founding his communities in the shelter of the great oak-forests, as here, at Deer ; and at Durrow and Derry in Ireland.

[2] The "Book of Deer," which is still in existence, would seem to have been transcribed by one of the Pictish monks early in the ninth century. It contains the Gospel of John complete, portions of the other Evangelists, and numerous memoranda in Gaelic of grants made by the Celtic chiefs of Buchan, written by a different hand, and at a different date.

[3] Burton, "History of Scotland," i. 253.

British civilization, it is visited in the summer season only by curious tourists, or by pilgrims desirous of paying their homage to a great man's memory. But in the sixth century it was the scene of a busy cultivation; horses, cattle and sheep throve upon its pastures, a large community lived almost entirely upon its produce; a small flotilla of barks and coracles continually hovered about its shores; and illustrious strangers, both civilians and ecclesiastics, repaired to it in such numbers as almost to rival the Miltonic picture of Imperial Rome.[1]

> "See
> What conflux issuing forth, or entering in, . . .
> Of embassies from regions far remote."

About A.D. 571 or 574, died Conal, King of the Dalriadic Scots. At the time of his death, Columba was in the island of Hinba, and in a vision an angel appeared to him three times in succession, showing him the "glass book"[2] of the ordination or consecration of kings. Reading in its pages, he found it written that he was to place the crown on the brow of Aidan, nephew of Conal, and son of King Gauran. This was not pleasing to the Saint, as he preferred Aidan's brother, Eogenan. But each night came the angel with the mystic book, and each night he smote the saint with a whip, saying :—" Know for certain that I am sent to thee by GOD, in order that thou mayest ordain Aidan to the kingdom, according to the words which thou hast read." So that at last Columba was forced to obey, and returning to Iona, he was met by Aidan, and he laid his hands upon him, and blessed him, and foretold the fortunes of his dynasty.

How much of the fabulous mingles with this narrative it is impossible to say, but I cannot attribute to its incidents the importance claimed for them by some enthusiastic writers. Montalembert, for instance, gravely asserts that Columba thus claimed, in respect to the Scottish or Dalriadic kingdom, the same authority with which the Abbots of Armagh, as successors of S. Patrick, were already invested in respect to the "kings" of Ireland. Dr. Lingard with equal gravity

---

[1] Milton, "Paradise Regained," iv. 61—67.
[2] The Vitreux Codex, so called because it was enclosed in a glass or crystal cover.

discusses the question whether the Byzantine Emperors borrowed the rite of coronation from the petty princes of Britain and Ireland, and concludes that, on the contrary, the British chiefs, after their separation from the Empire, caused themselves to be crowned with the same ceremonies which they knew to have been adopted by their former masters. The fact is, Columba and Aidan are more likely to have remembered the example of Saul and Samuel than any Roman or Eastern precedent; if, indeed, it is not more probable that the ceremony was simply an acknowledgment of the king's right by an ecclesiastic who had obtained a wholly abnormal and an extraordinary amount of popular influence.

I have already referred to Columba's occasional visits to Ireland, after he had conquered the first bitterness of exile. His last, and most remarkable, took place in 590, when he attended the Great Council of Drumceatt,[1] in Derry. He was accompanied by King Aidan, and one of his objects was to compose a difference which had arisen between that sovereign and Aidh, or Aidus, king of Ireland. The assembly sat for fourteen weeks, and included the two sovereigns, the nobles and great men, and the bishops and abbots of the country. The first question before them was the preservation of the privileges of a community scarcely less influential than the clerical order, namely, the Irish Bards, those men to whom the nation owed so much both as poets and historians, who did so much for the national genius, who kept alive in the hearts of the people the flame of patriotism. In the old days the poet exercised a power that none could afford to despise. He *made* history. His songs were the only channels through which the deeds of the warrior or statesman could be transmitted to posterity. Only through his songs could the prince secure the good repute of his contemporaries. Only through his songs could valour be dignified and endurance consecrated, could cowardice be shamed, and folly chastised. Such a position was necessarily attended by many evils, the chief of which was, a tendency to the abuse of the immunities it conferred. And so the Bards had provoked against them that force of " public opinion " which exists in every community, and in

[1] Said to be derived from *Dorsum cetæ*, "the Whale's back."

every community, sooner or later, proves strong enough to check the tyrant and the oppressor. Relying upon this force, King Aidh proposed that the order should be abolished, and, doubtless, would have carried his proposal but for the poetical sympathies of Columba. Coloniser, ruler, evangelist, priest! he was all these, but he was something more. By right of genius he belonged to the great Bardic order, and he stood forward to plead the cause of those whom he took to his heart as brethren.

The measure of his personal influence is shown by the fact that he succeeded. He represented that wise men should not pull up the wheat with the tares; that the exile and destruction of the poets would be the death of History, the extinction of antiquity, the crushing out of national life. His arguments so far prevailed that the council agreed to confirm the traditional privileges of the order; but on condition that the number of its members was limited, and that they were placed under certain regulations to be drawn up by Columba himself.

The Bards knew that they had been saved by the apostle, and they manifested their gratitude by exalting him in their strains. It is fair to conclude, perhaps, that they fully repaid the service he had rendered them, and that not a little of his fame is due to the pious particularity with which they chronicled his virtues and his achievements. According to a strange legend, the good saint was temporarily led astray by the intoxication of this delightful incense. Dallan Forgaill, the third chief of the Bards, having composed a song in honour of their preserver, proceeded to sing it in his presence. A flush of gratified pride passed over the saint's countenance. It was observed, however, by Baithen, one of the twelve disciples, who boldly reproved him, and told him that he could see a cloud of demons hovering around his head. Columba wisely profited by the rebuke so sharply administered; and reminding Dallan that only after men are dead do we engrave their names upon brass, he forbade a repetition of the eulogium. It was not therefore until after his decease that the celebrated *Ambhra*, or "Praise of S. Columb," became generally known. Then it was taken up into the memory of the people both in Ireland and Scotland, and acquired in time such a sanctity that men came to regard it as a spell or talisman, and to believe that whoever knew it by heart and sang it devoutly would die a happy death. Nay, more, if one sang it daily, one would certainly be saved,—an evil superstition which, according to the legend, was miraculously exposed. For a priest of Armagh, who lived an evil life, and desired, as many do, to obtain salvation without the exercise of self-sacrifice, hastened to learn the wonder-working Ambhra. Alas, as fast as he learned he forgot one half. He made a pilgrimage to Columba's tomb, and quoted, and prayed, and repeated his lesson over and over again, with no other result than always to forget the first portion while he committed to memory the second.

We return to Drumceatt. After the question of the Bards had been decided, the Council discussed the relations existing between the "King of Ireland" and the King of the Dalriadic Scots. Here, too, the personal influence of S. Columba secured a peaceful issue, and Aidh agreed to renounce all claims of superiority over the settlers in Alba. It would seem that Columba advised the assembly to refer the matter to the learned S. Colman, and that the latter decided in favour of British Dalriada.[1]

We see, then, that at this great Council, our Hero of the Cross, the Apostle of Caledonia, received from the princes and prelates of Ireland every token of reverence and affection; while he, on his part, was never weary of finding opportunities to inculcate the Gospel lessons of charity, peace, and concord. On its dissolution, he undertook a tour of inspection, visiting the clan-monasteries he had founded, or those in which he was interested by the associations of his early life. We can imagine with what joy he paced once again the leafy glades of the oak-forests of Durrow and Derry! He travelled also to Clonmacnoise, where the monks, with the Abbot Aritherus at their head, came forth to meet him in solemn procession, filling the air with the sweet grave sounds of litany and psalm. They prostrated themselves on the ground at his feet; then rose at his bidding, and lavished caresses upon him: after which they escorted him to the Abbot's hut, screening him from the

---

[1] Reeves, "Adamnan," p. lxxvi.; O'Donnell, bk. iii. c. 2—10.

crowd that pressed upon his footsteps by a rampart of green boughs and branches, borne by four men.

On this journey a miracle occurred, which may here be narrated in illustration of the tendency of the old hagiographers to adapt the wonders wrought by our LORD to the circumstances of their respective heroes. At one of his own monasteries, where Columba halted, a poor scholar, mean of aspect and hesitating of speech, who was employed in the meanest labours of the community, wound through the throng, and stealthily drawing near the great Abbot, touched the hem of his robe unseen, as the Canaanitish woman touched her Redeemer's garment. Columba, perceiving that a virtue had gone out of him, turned round, and throwing his arm about the youth's neck, kissed him. "Away, little fool!" shouted the spectators. "Not so," exclaimed Columba; and addressing the pale-faced scholar, "My son," he said, "open thy mouth, and show thy tongue," (*O fili, aperi os, et porrige linguam.*) Trembling, he obeyed. The Abbot made the sign of the cross upon his tongue, and added: "Let none henceforth despise this child, who appears to you so fit to be a mock. Daily shall he increase in wisdom and virtue; and he shall yet be numbered with the greatest among you; for to this tongue will GOD give the gift of eloquence and wholesome learning." The prediction was fulfilled, and S. Eman is still an honoured name in the ancient Kalendar.

After Columba's return to Iona, he continued to watch over the well-being of the monasteries he had founded, and to maintain with them a constant correspondence. Here, again, his biographer would have us believe he was miraculously assisted. One day, says Adamnan, he suddenly paused in his labours in his island-cell, and cried aloud, "Help, help!" (*Auxiliare, auxiliare!*) Two of the brethren, who chanced to be standing on the threshold, asked him wherefore he called, and to whom he addressed himself. He explained that he was speaking to the guardian angel of the community, bidding him hasten to the rescue of a man who had fallen from the summit of the round tower at Durrow. That he would arrive in time to save him he nothing doubted; such was his estimation of the indescribable swiftness of the angelic flight, which he compared to that of lightning.

On a misty and dreary day in Iona, when the sun hung heavy with clouds, the Abbot was observed to burst into tears. He was asked to explain the cause of his distress. "Ah, my son, I do not weep without reason; for at this very hour I see my beloved monks of Durrow condemned by their Abbot Laiorannus to fatigue themselves by building up the high tower of their monastery." Happily, charity is contagious, and at that very hour, as was afterwards ascertained, the Abbot of Durrow felt burning within him a new flame of compassion, and awakening to a sense of his unnecessary severity, he bade his monks desist from their toil, and seek refreshment and repose.

The reader will wonder, perhaps, why I repeat these illustrations of the childlike credulity of S. Columba's biographer; and whether I require of him to believe Adamnan as fully as Adamnan appears to have believed *his* informants, and the traditions which he received? I have already said that I see no reason for admitting in S. Columba the existence of any miraculous gifts; but then these stories, whatever may be their folly or improbability, are valuable so far as they show the breadth and depth of the impression which Columba produced upon his contemporaries. Had not Columba been "a king of men," strong to govern and apt to teach; had he not possessed a spirit of heroic devotion and irresistible ardour, these legends would never have been originated, or would never have passed current; their obvious falsehood would have caused their rejection. In our own time, for instance, we have seen an attempt made to impose upon the world a Napoleonic legend, which artist and historian strove their utmost to popularise; but facts have been too strong for them, criticism has been too searching, and the world refuses to see in the ambitious Consul and aggressive Emperor, that all-seeing, all-knowing, and magnificent hero who shines on the glittering page of Thiers and the canvas of Horace Vernet. But such was not the case with S. Columba. His life was so pre-eminently a life of holy work, his character was so pre-eminently that of a Christian teacher, that there was a natural readiness in the minds of men to accept any stories or traditions which seemed to bring out that life and character into bolder relief.

And here I may observe that *one* fact is established by the very legends Adamnan takes so much delight in recording; namely, that S. Columba was no Roman ecclesiastic. That he was, in a certain sense, the founder of Episcopacy in Scotland, and that the Episcopal Church of that country may rightly trace back her lineage to this remarkable man, I hold to be an incontrovertible fact. That he considered no ordination valid unless conferred by the hands of the Bishop, is proved by numerous details of his history. Yet we must not suppose that he was a Scottish Churchman after the orthodox type. He lived in an age and under conditions not favourable to the developement of an exact ecclesiastical organisation. He was not a Bishop himself, but he planted Bishops in his monasteries, whose sole function however, seems to have been the transmission of the succession, for they certainly did not occupy their fitting position as spiritual fathers and rulers in the Church Catholic. Columba was divinely commissioned to accomplish a special work at a special time, and if he accomplished that work apart from the Church system then prevailing in the civilised West, who shall blame him? Enough for us to know, without presuming to fix his exact place in the ancient hierarchy, or to seek to bring the Church in Iona into close parallelism with the Church of Rome or of Alexandria, that he diffused the light of GOD'S truth through the wildernesses of Caledonia, and gave an impulse to its civilisation which it never afterwards lost.

CHAPTER IV.

"But he dies—the saintly Sower—
  Lo! 'tis the Holy Morn:
With joyful praise he seeth
  The garnered wealth of corn.
'They shall not lack,' he crieth;
  'The children shall be blest;
Though the long Sabbath calleth
  The Father unto rest!'

Then gently they uplift him,
  And lo! a little space—
An infinite sweet rapture
  Doth lighten in his face;

> And well they know he seeth
> The coming great Reward!
> The glory of the Blessèd;
> The vision of the LORD!"
>
> S. J. STONE, M.A.

THE life and works of this Hero of the Cross present so many points of interest, and are so suggestive of lessons to the Christian reader, that I have not scrupled to dwell upon them at considerable length. I feel unwilling, indeed, to take my leave of this indefatigable pioneer of Christianity and civilisation, as one shrinks from parting with a friend whose virtues have grown upon one's knowledge during bright years of increasing intercourse. I feel unwilling to quit the Sacred Island which was hallowed by his presence, where he showed how pure and precious a life may be lived by him who seeks with singleness of purpose ever to do the Master's will. For I cannot but say, with Montalembert, that it is not merely the Apostle or monastic founder who stands out before us so distinctly and so grandly among the dim shadows of the past; beyond and besides this, it is the Christian, who carried into practice the truths he taught; who was the friend, the benefactor, the brother of all men; the brave and generous defender of the feeble, the laborious, and the poor; who occupied himself not only with the soul's welfare but also with the rights and interests and daily comforts of his fellows; in whom the force of an intense sympathy was revealed by a wise and continued interposition against all wickedness and oppression.

I have referred to the missionary voyages of S. Columba and his monks. When we remember that in rude boats of osier and hides they crossed the stormy waters which separate Scotland from Ireland, and navigated the wild dark creeks that ramify among the Western Archipelago, we cannot but admire their steadfast courage. It seems allowable, also, to conjecture that their nautical skill, such skill as springs from observation and experience, must have been considerable. Of the tumultuous ocean-currents and violent gales they had no fear; but they quailed at times before the appearance of the large whales and sharks which then frequented the Hebridean waters; or were alarmed by hosts of marine creatures ("bestiolæ") which attached themselves to the keel and sides of their boats, and threatened to pierce the skins that covered the rude framework. On a certain occasion, S. Baithen, afterwards Columba's successor, fell in with a shark or whale or one of the cetacean tribe; but, reflecting that he had received the abbot's blessing, he boldly continued his course, and was rewarded for his confidence by seeing the monster disappear beneath the waves. "After all," he exclaimed, "both this monster and myself are in the power of GOD!"[1]

In one of these voyages an incident occurred which, to this day, is commemorated in the armorial bearings of the ancient see of the Isles. A storm arose; the waters ran heavily, and frequently dashed their foamy crests over the missionary bark—that new Argo, bound on a holier quest than the adventurous ship of mythologic story. Columba hastened to assist his companions in baling out the water. "What you are now doing," they said, "is useless; but do you pray for us, that we may not perish." The saint went forward to the prow, and raised his hands and heart to heaven. Straightway the gale subsided.[2]

As there is good reason to believe that Columba was a skilful navigator, who had carefully studied the phenomena of the winds and currents; so is there reason to believe that he had no inconsiderable knowledge of agriculture, and understood the cultivation of cereals and fruit-trees. Some of the legends which have come down to us would seem also to prove that he was an adept in the treatment of ordinary diseases, and experienced in the properties of herbs. When we read of his sending the blessed Bread to a devout maiden who, in returning from Mass, had broken her leg; of his curing ophthalmia by salt which his benediction had in like manner rendered healing; of his restoring others to health by the mere invocation of the Holy Name, we see in these miraculous stories only the natural expression of the wonder created among the common people by the success of his modes of treatment. Doubtless,

---

[1] A fine speech, worthy of being remembered along with the noble saying of Sir Humphrey Gilbert, who, when his ship was on the point of foundering, cheerily said:—"Courage, my men; we are as near heaven by sea as by land."

[2] Adamnan, bk. ii. c. 11.

they were simple enough; but then, in those days, blood was pure, and frames were hardy, and men who lived laboriously and abstemiously were probably exempt from the virulent maladies that afflict a more corrupt and enervating state of civilisation.

It has been well said, that to heal the sick, to succour the poor, and to comfort the afflicted, was S. Columba's daily task; that no grief was too trivial, no estate of life too humble for his sympathy.[1] One day, while he was visiting an island on the Irish coast, a pilot came into his presence with a melancholy tale that his wife had conceived an aversion for him. The good Abbot immediately sent for her, and reminded her of the duties which the Divine Law has imposed upon the married state. "Whatever thou mayest order, however irksome it may be," she answered, "I will do it; except this one thing, that I should live with Lazarus. I refuse not to take charge of his household; or I will undertake a pilgrimage to Jerusalem; or, if such be thy will, I will cross the sea, and retire into a nunnery."

Columba replied that, so long as her husband lived, neither nunnery nor pilgrimage was lawful; and he advised that all three of them, fasting, should unite in prayer to GOD,—namely, the wife, the husband, and himself.

"Oh," said the woman, "I know that thou canst obtain from GOD that which seems impossible to others."

Whereupon they did as the Abbot counselled, and all night long Columba implored his Master to restore happiness to the divided twain. On the following morning, he said to the woman, softly: "And now, tell me, to what nunnery do you think of emigrating to-day?"

"To none," she answered; "him whom I hated yesterday, to-day I love; for my heart, in the night, though how I know not, has been transformed in me from loathing to affection."

And the story ends like a fairy tale; for the good couple lived happily ever afterwards.[2]

Columba now drew near the close of his noble life. Conscious of the coming change, he devoted even more time

---

[1] Dr. Grub, "Ecclesiastical History of Scotland," i. 62.
[2] Adamnan, bk. iii., c. 20.

than before to religious meditation; fasting oft, watching oft, praying always. His biographers tell us that he redoubled his austerities, and ascribe to him some self-imposed penances which it would have been impossible for his weakened frame to bear. Many marvels announced to the monks that they were on the point of losing their great Abbot. The lonely cell which he had built for himself on a neighbouring island was illuminated nightly by a strange mysterious lustre, which streamed far out upon the sea, and the voice of Columba was often heard uplifted in unknown canticles. Remaining three days and three nights without food, he issued forth, after this surprising vigil, rejoicing that he had discovered the meaning of certain texts of Holy Writ, to which he had never before obtained a key. Returning to Iona, and spending according to wont the greater part of every night in prayer, his monks saw with wonder that a miraculous light continually surrounded him, as if he had been transfigured. One winter's eve, a young man who was afterwards fourth of the Abbots of Iona, abode in the church while the others slept. Suddenly, the saint entered, preceded by a golden glory ("aurea lux"), which fell from the vaulted roof, and spread into every corner of the building, even into the little oratory where Veignous, terrified, sought concealment.[1] All who passed by the sacred building, while the good Abbot was engaged in his devotions, could not fail to see this singular gleam and glow, which burst upon them like fire from heaven. And one of the young monks, curious to know whether the same radiance filled the Abbot's cell, rose in the night, though it was contrary to orders, and groped his way to the door; but, looking in, was blinded by "excess of light," and fled.

There is a glen in the west of the island—over whose rocky walls hung in wreaths and festoons the ivy with which the monks wove together the wattled sides of their rude huts—still called the "Glen of the Temple," that leads to an arable level, known now, as in Columba's time, by the name of Machar, or the "Sandy Plain." Out of the midst of this plain rise two green hills. One morning, the saint said to his attendants: "Let no one follow me to-day, for I would be alone;" and so saying, he betook himself to

[1] Dean Stanley, "Church of Scotland," p. 28.

the solitude of Machar. A monk, however, impelled by curiosity, or, it may be, fearing lest some accident might befall his infirm superior, followed him, and climbing a rocky bluff which juts into the plain, like a promontory into the green sea, he saw Columba on the larger of the two hills, surrounded by a company of angels in white raiment. After the lapse of nearly thirteen hundred years, that eminence is still known as *Cnoc Angel*, the " Knoll of the Angels."[1]

Thus heralded by signs and wonders, the last days came.
And it happened that two of the monks—an Irishman and a Saxon—two of those who were admitted to his most intimate confidence,—sitting, one day, in their master's cell, saw that he changed countenance ; that first a glow passed over his face, as if he had experienced a sudden access of joy ; and then, a gloom and pallor, as if he were plunged in overwhelming sorrow. They pressed him with tender inquiries : What ailed him ? what had affected him ? He remained silent. They fell at his feet, and, with tears, implored him not to distress his children by concealing the mysteries which had evidently been revealed to him. " Dear children," he answered, after a pause, " I was fain not to grieve you. But know, that it is thirty years to-day since I began my pilgrimage in Caledonia. Long have I prayed GOD that with this thirtieth year my exile might terminate, and I might be recalled to the heavenly country. When you saw me so joyous, it was because I could see the angels who came in quest of my soul. But, suddenly they halted ; yonder, on that rock across our island-strait, as if they would gladly have approached, but were prevented—prevented, because the LORD hath given less heed to my fervent prayer than to that of the many churches which have prayed for me, and have obtained that I should linger in this body for four more years. This is the reason of my sorrow. But in four years I shall die without the wretchedness of any previous illness ; in four years the holy angels will return for me, and I shall take my blissful flight with them towards the LORD."[2]

---

[1] Also called " the Great Hill of the Fairies." See Reeves, p. 257.
[2] Adamnan, bk. iii., c. 22.

That some such vision may have risen on the mind of an aged saint, oppressed with years, and spent with work and watchfulness and austerity, is not impossible. Similar predictions of death, moreover, are not uncommon; nor is their fulfilment. But whether the miracle be an illusion of Columba's own, or a fancy of his biographer's, evolved out of some romantic tradition, the four years passed, and it became plain that the old man's departure was close at hand. The balmy winds of later May were blowing over the western sea, and Columba desired to visit the green corn-fields, and take his leave of the monks who were there at work. Too feeble to walk, he was conveyed in a car drawn by oxen. Conversing with his faithful labourers, he said:—"I much wished to die on Easter Day, and my wish was granted; but then I was fain to tarry a little longer, that the joyous festival might not be changed into a season of gloom for you." They wept bitterly, for they knew they should see his face no more, and they felt like children about to be parted from a loved and loving father; but with wise and hopeful words he comforted them. And turning towards the east, he bestowed his blessing on the island and its people.

On the following Saturday, supported by his faithful companion, Diermit or Diarmaid, he proceeded to bless the granary belonging to the monastery. Seeing two large heaps of corn piled up, the produce of the last harvest, he exclaimed, "I rejoice to see that my children, if I leave them this year, will not suffer from want." "Why, beloved father," inquired Diarmaid, "why oppress us by thus talking of your death?" "I have a little secret to tell thee, if on thy knees thou wilt promise to reveal it to no one till I am away. To-day is Saturday, which in Holy Writ, is called *Sabbath* or *Rest.* And truly to me it *is* a Sabbath, for it is the last day of my life, the day on which I shall cease from my labours. On this very night I shall go the way of my fathers. It is my LORD JESUS CHRIST Who deigns to invite me; and it is He Who hath made known that my summons will come to-night."

Then he began his return journey to the monastery; but growing weary, he sat down for awhile, near a wayside cross,[1] at the foot of a slight ascent. And while he rested, the old white horse which had carried the daily supply of milk to the monastery for many a year, came up to his aged master, laid his head on his shoulder, and seemed to weep tears of farewell. Diarmaid would have driven him away, but Columba said :—" The horse loves me ; leave him with me ; let him weep for my departure. The Creator has revealed to this poor animal what He has hidden from me, a reasonable man." And he pronounced a blessing upon the faithful beast.

Resuming his journey, he slowly ascended an eminence, the Tor-Abb, from the summit of which he could see all that bright and varied panorama of isles and ocean and cloud-capped mountains he loved so well. As he gazed, a rush of thought and emotion swept over his soul, and he broke out into prophetic words which have been literally fulfilled.

"This place, apparently so small and obscure," he cried, "shall be largely honoured, not only by the Scottish kings and their people, but by the chiefs of barbarous nations and their subjects, and it shall be held in reverence even by the devout men of other churches."

After this he returned to his cell, and for some time was occupied in his favourite work of transcribing the Psalms. On coming to the 39th, and the ninth verse, " Inquirentes autem Dominum non deficient omni bono," (" They who seek the LORD shall want no manner of thing that is good,") he suddenly laid aside his pen :—

"I must stop here," said he, "let Baithen write what follows."

His biographers do not forget to remind us of the applicability of the Psalmist's words to the dying saint ; and they point to the following verse, " Come, ye children, and hearken unto me : I will teach you the fear of the LORD," as not less suitable to the character of Baithen, whom Columba had thus indicated as his successor.

The saint then repaired to the church,[2] where he attended

---

[1] The spot is supposed to be marked by the monument known as Mc Lean's Cross.
[2] The reader will understand that Columba's church and monastery were alike of the rudest construction, built of oaken planks, and thatched

Vespers. Returning to his cell, he lay for some time on his bed with its stone pillow, which, in Adamnan's time, was still preserved beside his tomb, and proceeded to give his final directions that Diarmaid might communicate them to his disciples:—

"Dear children, these are my last words. Live in peace and charity one with another; and if so ye live, following the example of the saints, GOD, Who comforts the just and strengthens the good, will help you, and I, dwelling with Him, will intercede for you, and you shall obtain of Him not only what is necessary for this life in all abundance, but also those everlasting joys reserved for all who keep His law."

Such were the last words of S. Columba.

For awhile he lay in silence; all through the solemn night he lay, communing with Him Whom he had striven so earnestly to serve; but, in the dim misty dawn, when the matin-bell rung for the Sunday festival, he arose, and hastening before the others, entered the church alone. The building, as the brethren approached, seemed to be filled with a dazzling radiance, which, however, passed away before Diarmaid reached the spot. Groping in the darkness, for the lights had not yet arrived, the monk exclaimed, plaintively:—
"Where art thou, O my father?" There was no reply, but he found the saint prostrate before the holy altar, and placing himself at his side, he raised the venerable head upon his knees. A crowd of weeping monks, holding their rude lanterns, gathered quietly round those central figures, and turned eagerly towards the well-known face, over which was so swiftly stealing the grey shadow of death. Once more his eyes were opened; with that strange, wistful, inquiring gaze we all have seen in the eyes of the dying: that gaze which seems to pierce the mysterious veil, and to recognise the beckoning angel-hands beyond. For a moment they

---

with reeds, after what Bede calls the *mos Scottorum*, or Scottish manner. Adamnan speaks of S. Columba as sending forth his monks to gather "bundles of twigs," to build their hospice. The difference between the churches and the monastic tents seems to have been that the former were constructed, not of basket-work, but of squared timber; "they were log-houses, not wigwams." See the late Joseph Robertson's interesting article on "Scottish Abbeys and Cathedrals" in *Quarterly Review*, Vol. lxxxv. pp. 110—112.

rested on the brethren with a look of love and serene happiness, while, with Diarmaid's assistance, Columba raised his right hand, and made the sign of Blessing. His arm fell powerless; a soft sigh escaped his lips; and the Apostle of Caledonia was no more. But his face remained sweet and tranquil, and bright with a holy joy, like that of a sleeper who in his sleep has been favoured with a vision of the golden gates of Heaven.[1]

It was early on the morning of Sunday, the 9th of June, in the year of grace 597, that Columba closed his career, being then in the 76th year of his age.[2]

CHAPTER V.

WHILE matins were sung, the body of the great missionary remained in the church which he had founded. Afterwards it was removed to the cell which had witnessed his fasts, his vigils, and his prayers; the brethren chanting psalms as they wound along the weary way. For three days and three nights it lay (so to speak) "in state," clothed in priestly robes, and surrounded by many lights; while from all parts came men and women to gaze on the cold white face they had learned in life to love and reverence. Finally, shrouded in snowy linen, it was laid in the grave, the stone pillow on which the saint had been accustomed to repose being set up beside it as a memorial.

I have already indicated the conception I have been led to form of the character of this Hero of the Cross; but it may interest the reader if I here reproduce the view entertained by one well fitted to sympathise with his enthusiasm, and to comprehend the importance of his mission, the illus-

---

[1] "Et post sanctam benedictionem taliter significatam, continuo spiritum exhalavit. Facies rubens, et mirum in modum angelica visione exhilarata, in tantum remansit ut non quasi mortui, sed dormientis videretur viventis."—Adamnan, iii. 23.

[2] The best authorities all agree that this was the date of S. Columba's decease.

trious Montalembert.[1] In no part of his great work, for great it is, in spite of occasional extravagance and a sometimes injurious partiality, does he seem to write with more consciousness of pleasure than when he is tracing the various stages of the career, or dwelling on the virtues and heroic qualities of S. Columba. And when the story is told, his admiration reaches its climax. This great Apostle, he exclaims, in a troublous time and an unknown country, exhibited all that is grandest and purest, and, it must be added, all that is most easily forgotten in human genius, the gift of ruling the souls of others by ruling himself. Thus he proceeds to picture the tall old man, with his fine and regular features, his powerful yet melodious voice, the Irish tonsure high on his head, and his long grey hair falling behind; and he shows him to us, seated at the prow of his coracle, steering through the misty archipelago and winding lochs of north-western Scotland, and carrying from isle to isle, and from shore to shore, Light, Justice, Truth, the life of the conscience, and the sunshine of the soul.

We may learn a lesson by studying the mysteries of that grand nature, and its gradual education from youth to old age. No more than his namesake of Luxeuil, the Burgundian missionary-monk, was he a *Columba* or Dove. Certainly, in his earlier life, it was in gentleness that he was most deficient. He responded eagerly to the unrest and battle-spirit of his age; was profoundly influenced by the strife and discord of his country. We may say of him that he was born a soldier, with all a soldier's daring, generosity, and high temper; and to the last, happily for Caledonia, he remained a soldier—*insulanus miles*, as Adamnan calls him—only instead of warring against his fellow-men, and lifting the banner of his tribe, he warred against the hosts of the Devil under the banner of the Lamb. But, indeed, is not every missionary, every true priest, a Hero of the Cross, a warrior of the Church? Needs he not a warrior's fire, a warrior's patient fortitude, and a warrior's lofty sense of duty?

Columba, says Montalembert, was marked by contradictions and contrasts; he was tender yet irritable, rough yet courteous, cold yet compassionate, caressing yet imperious,

---

[1] Montalembert, "Les Moines d'Occident," livre ix., c. 7.

loving in his gratitude, yet prone to revenge; not a perfect man by any means, yet a man of noble nature; influenced by pity as well as by wrath, and mastered, above all other passions, by those two which burn most brightly in the clearest soul,—a love of country, and a love of the beautiful. By no means given to melancholy when he had conquered his life's one great sorrow, his banishment from Ireland; by no means partial, except in his later days, to solitary meditation, but trained by prayer and self-conquest to wonderful gifts of evangelical exposition; scornful of rest—that is, of the rest of indolence—and never wearying of intellectual or physical toil; endowed with a supreme natural eloquence, and with a voice so sonorous and penetrating that it was afterwards regarded as one of the most wonderful gifts he had received from GOD; truthful, loyal, original and powerful in words as well as in deeds; in cloister and mission and council, on land and on sea, among his own people and among the Picts, always and everywhere inspired by a wide charity and a burning devotion,—such was Columba! He was seaman, soldier, orator, poet, ruler, monk, apostle. To us, looking back across the waste of time, he appears a man as extraordinary as he was loveable, in whom we perceive, notwithstanding the misty shadows of tradition and the shifting lights of legend, the pure, upright, peerless servant of GOD; a man worthy of all our honour and all our admiration, for his was that true piety which will conquer the human weakness, the sinful instinct, the warring passion, and glow all the more brightly for the fiery ordeal through which it had passed.

I cannot conclude this sketch of Columba without some brief notice of his island-home. It contains few memorials of the saint himself, but many of the Church which he established. The ecclesiastical edifices, however, while marking the site of his settlement, belong to a later period. The most venerable is S. Odhrain's, or Oran's, Chapel; built, according to some authorities, by Queen Margaret, about 1080, but, according to others, dating from the thirteenth century: a quaint, low, and now unroofed building, 60 ft. in length and 22 ft. in width. On the south side lies the *Reilig Oran*, or "Burial Place of Oran," in which for generations were buried the illustrious dead. King Duncan, as Shakespeare tells us, was

> "Carried to Colm's Kill,
> The sacred storehouse of his predecessors,
> And guardian of their bones."

The memorial slabs are very numerous, and mostly interesting: some are carved with knots, flowers, plants, figures of recumbent warriors, and various emblems and devices. Beneath them sleep many a zealous priest, many a wild sea-rover, nobles and knights, and the old chieftains of the isles.

Apart from these details, the spot is worthy of a pilgrimage, for it is unquestionably the site of the little wattled church in which S. Columba breathed his last. There are some things, as the Duke of Argyll remarks, for which tradition may be safely trusted. "The succession of generations among men," he says, "has been compared to the leaves of the forest; but, unlike forest-leaves, which all die about one time, and reappear at another time after a long interval that cuts off the seeming continuity of life, the generations of mankind are renewed from day to day and from year to year; so that the young hold fast the memories of the old, and that which was dear to the fathers is dear to the children also." Hence it is not possible to believe that the site of S. Columba's altar could ever have been forgotten. The monks, if no others, would have been careful to perpetuate its recollection. And Queen Margaret would assuredly raise her own chapel in the midst of such sacred associations.

Close beyond the Reilig Odhrain, a little to the northeast, and nearly opposite to the western part of the cathedral church, rises a rocky eminence, covered with green turf, which is scarcely less precious as a shrine to the pilgrim-enthusiast. From its isolated position; from its neighbourhood to S. Odhrain's Chapel and the ancient burial-place; and from the glorious prospect which it commands of sea and mountain, of the green fields beneath, of the shining Sound, and the blue line of distant coast, we may well believe that the Tor-Abb, or "Abbot's Knoll," must have been a favourite place of resort with all the generations of men who have lived and worshipped on the Holy Isle.

How often from this natural beacon-tower will the brethren have watched for their Abbot's returning bark, as it glided over the shining waters to the sound of litany and psalm! How often will Columba himself have stood here in solitary meditation, drinking in with the inner sense all the singular glories of form and colour that lighted up the surrounding landscape and seascape—rose-tints of summer morning shooting across the eastern sky; warm glow of summer noon shimmering with a sunny haze round the far-off peaks; and purple, emerald, and golden lustres kindling in the west as the orb of day dropped down below the rim of waters! From the same spot he will often have noticed the approach of stranger vessels, bringing holy men to sit at his feet and listen to his genial wisdom, or penitent sinners yearning to quench the fire of remorse that burned in their hearts with the gentle dew of his counsels and his prayers! And, at a later date, how often the watcher on the Tor-Abb would see " the beautiful galleys of the olden time" sailing up the silent channel with their freight of royal or noble dead, intended to be laid in the bosom of the sacred island—strangely peaceful ending of many a stormy career! A grassy mound near the present landing-place is pointed out as the natural bier on which the corpse rested when first brought ashore. Thence it was carried, in solemn procession, along the *Strail-na-Marbh*, or "Street of the Dead," to its grave in the Reilig Odhrain.

The Chapel of the Nunnery, which belonged to a religious house of Augustinian canonesses, is another interesting ruin. There is also the Temple Ronaig, now a mere shell, which Mr. Skene considers to have been the ancient parish church of the island. It was dedicated to S. Ronan, the hermit of Eilan Rona, who died in 736. The principal ruin, however, is that of the Abbey-church or Cathedral, which exhibits a cruciform ground-plan, with an extreme length of 160 feet; breadth of nave and aisles, 24 feet; length of transepts, 70 feet; length of choir, 60 feet. In front of the principal enclosure stands S. Martin's Cross, a monolith of red granite, fourteen feet high, richly wrought with the quaint Runic sculpture.

But the interest of Iona lies not in its ruins, not in its natural features, but altogether in its human associations.

For the stranger who has seen the grand old cathedrals and ruined abbeys of England, or even those of Scotland—Melrose, and Jedburgh, and Dunfermline, its ecclesiastical edifices will have little attraction. He may even wish, perhaps, that they were altogether removed, so that he might the more easily and fully recognise the island as the Home of S. Columba. The "Port of the Coracle," the "Abbot's Knoll," the "Sandy Plain," the "Cairn of Farewell,"—would not these suffice to carry his memory back into the misty past? And if not a stone remained to remind him of the work which the great Abbot began, would his sympathies be any the feebler? Would he not have before him those more glorious and everlasting memorials of the poet-saint, the sea, and the isles, and the mountains? Would not the prediction which Columba is said to have uttered, just as surely be fulfilled?

"Huic loco, quamlibet angusto et vili, non tantum Scotorum Reges, cum populis, sed etiam barbararum et exterarum gentium Regnatores, cum plebibus sibi subjectis, grandem et non mediocrem conferent honorem: a sanctis quoque etiam aliarum Ecclesiarum non mediocris veneratio conferetur."

S. BERNARD OF CLAIRVAUX:

"THE MAN OF GOD."

"A man so devout, so holy, and so pure, that he is to be commended and preferred before all the fathers."—LUTHER.

[*Authorities:*—Full details of the life of S. Bernard will be found in the chronicles included in the Abbé Migne's edition of his Works. See also Charles de Rémusat, "Abélard" (1845); Acta Sanctorum; Neander's "Life of S. Bernard;" Dean Milman, "History of Latin Christianity;" Canon Robertson, "History of the Christian Church;" J. C. Morison, "Life and Times of S. Bernard;" Michelet, "Histoire de France," (3rd Vol.); Fuller, "Holy War;" Wilkins, Gieseler, &c.]

S. BERNARD OF CLAIRVAUX.

CHAPTER I.

IN the castle of Fontaines, near Dijon, in Burgundy, to Tesselin, a brave Burgundian Knight, by his wife, Alith or Aletta, was born, in the year 1091, a son whom they christened Bernard.

He was happy in his parents. Tesselin was not only brave but gentle, a great lover of the poor, a champion of justice, a servant of GOD. His wife was a very noble woman; foremost in all works of charity, and distinguished by her lowliness of mind and ardour of piety. She bore to Tesselin seven children, six sons and a daughter; and she dedicated them all to the LORD. After receiving at home the rudiments of education, and profiting by the bright example set before him, Bernard was sent to the church of Châtillon as a preparation for the priesthood. There he fulfilled the promise which had already raised his mother's hopes. Studious and reserved, he showed a marked inclination for a contemplative life,[1] yet he was not without literary ambition, and he entered freely into competition with his fellows in scholastic exercises. And we may well conceive that the fervent military spirit which he inherited from his father was not wholly dormant; that it would be kindled by the tales which could not fail to reach Châtillon of that grand movement of the First Crusade,

[1] "Mire cogitativus."—S. Bernard (ii. 1063).

led by Godfrey of Bouillon, Tasso's hero, for the delivery of the Holy Land from the supremacy of the Crescent, in which the Duke of Burgundy, his father's suzerain, perished. He could not be uninfluenced by that chivalry of the Cross which was then giving a new direction to the enterprise and thought of Europe.

He was still in his boyhood when his mother died (1105.) It was her custom to celebrate the festival of S. Ambrose, patron of the church at Fontaines, by assembling beneath her roof a number of clergy; and to the glory of GOD, the Blessed Virgin, and the patron-saint, solemnly refreshing them with food and wine. A few days before the festival of 1105, it was revealed to her that she would die on that anniversary, and on the vigil she was seized with a violent fever. Next morning, she desired that the Holy Sacrament might be administered to her; and strengthened by the Body and Blood of her LORD, she bade the guests sit down to the feast she had provided. While they were at table, she sent for her eldest son Guido, and requested him, when they had eaten and drunk, to bring them to her chamber. As they stood around her bed, she announced her approaching departure, and entreated their prayers. They immediately began to chant a litany, Alith making the responses till her latest breath. At the words, " By Thy cross and passion, Good LORD, deliver us," she made the sign of the cross, and passed away.

His mother's death left Bernard free to determine his own career. At first he yielded to the social influences around him, and, like other young men of good family, engaged in military exercises and worldly pleasures; but this restless, feverish life was alien to his contemplative nature, and often in the hours of silent thought he seemed to hear the chime of convent bells, and the voice of his beloved mother, calling him to a nobler vocation. When his friends and brothers observed his leaning towards a monastic life, they endeavoured to divert him from it by engaging him in the study of Dialectics, then made popular by William of Champeaux and Peter Abelard. For a time this diversion stayed his spiritual growth; but even in his most engrossing mental labour he still saw the image of his mother warning him that she had bred and educated him in a higher and holier hope.[1] On one occasion, he was proceeding to join his brothers who, under the Duke of Burgundy, were besieging the Castle of Granci, when this idea took firm possession of his mind. He seemed to hear his mother reproaching him for his worldliness and his selfish love of knowledge for selfish ends. Coming to a church by the wayside, he could not refrain from entering it, and there a sudden enthusiasm of devotion filled his soul; he wept and prayed; and lifting his hands to heaven, poured forth his heart like water in the presence of his LORD. From that day he never wavered in his resolve to assume the monastic habit, though he did not conquer his worldly tendencies without a struggle. He had to fight that battle which every man must fight and win before he can become a soldier of the Cross. "I am not ashamed to confess," he says, "that often, and particularly at the beginning of my conversion, I experienced great hardness of heart, and an extreme coldness. I sought after Him Whom my soul was fain to love; Him in Whom my chilled spirit might repose and rekindle itself. But no succour came; no heavenly rays to dissolve the strong ice which bound up all the spiritual senses, or to revive the sweetness and serenity of the spiritual Spring; and thus my soul continued weak and languid, a prey to grief, almost to despair, and murmuring internally. Who is able to abide His Winter? Then, all at once, perhaps by the first word or at the first sight of a devout-minded person, sometimes at the simple recollection of one dead or absent, the HOLY SPIRIT would begin to breathe, and the ice-bound waters to flow; and day and night, tears would be my meat."

It has been said that the instinct which leads us eagerly to impart to others the spiritual truth which has seized upon our own mind; the impulse to preach, to exhort, to labour, to convert; is one of the most beautiful in our nature. With Bernard it was very strong; and having thrown off the fetters of the world, he keenly desired that his brothers and kinsmen should rejoice in an equal freedom. With many of them he was successful; with his uncle, "a worthy man and powerful in the world," Gaudry, lord of Touillon; and with all his brothers, except Gerard, the second. He, a

[1] "Conquerentem quia non ad ejusmodi nugacitatem tam tenere educaverat, non in hac spe erudierat eum."—S. Bernard, ii. 1066.

gallant knight ("*miles strenuus*"), who had won renown with his spear, was inclined to laugh at Bernard's ardour, and regarded as an impulse of levity the conduct of his brothers. "Ah!" said Bernard, with his keen insight into character, "it is suffering alone, my brother, that will bring thee understanding." And placing his finger on his brother's side, he added :—"The day will come and come quickly, when a lance shall pierce thy side, and make a way to thy heart for that counsel of salvation which thou dost now despise. And thou shalt greatly fear, but in no wise perish." The prediction, before long, was fulfilled. Surrounded and overthrown in a skirmish, Gerard was carried off prisoner, with a spear-thrust in his side. "I turn monk," he exclaimed, "O monk of Citeaux!" and on effecting his escape, he devoted himself to GOD.

Soon afterwards, Bernard assembled his converts in church, when, as they entered, the preacher was reading the words :—" GOD is faithful, and He that hath begun a good work in you, the same will perform it unto the day of JESUS CHRIST." This text he accepted as an encouragement to persevere in the course on which he had entered, and putting on " the new man," he displayed a constant anxiety for the safety of souls. With so much vigour and such persuasive earnestness did he preach, that mothers hid their sons, wives their husbands, companions their friends, lest they should be borne along upon the full stream of his eloquence. Having gathered about him, at length, a company of thirty chosen spirits, he withdrew with them into seclusion at Châtillon, so as to allow time for their resolution to mature, and for the arrangement and disposal of their secular concerns. This preparation lasted about six months; and then, in the year 1113, and in the twenty-third of his age, Bernard led them to the gate of the monastery of Citeaux, the head and source of the Cistercian community, already famous for the rigid austerity with which it was conducted. Founded by Robert de Molême, it was intended to revive the strict rule of S. Benedict; but under Abbot Stephen Harding, its discipline had become so severe, as even in the religious world to beget a very general feeling of aversion. The monks ate but one meal a day, and had to sing psalms and work in the fields, for twelve years, before even that was permitted them. They never tasted meat, fish, fat, or eggs, and only rarely partook of milk. Their dress, limited to three garments, was made of the coarsest wool. Their couch was harder than the hardest pallet on which the weary peasant rested his limbs. Nothing of the "beauty of holiness" embellished their church or its services. Everywhere was self-denial, poverty, the sternest simplicity. Of recent years, to their voluntary privations had been added a scarcity almost approaching to a famine,—followed by an epidemic, which among men weakened by fastings and mortifications, swept like a scourge.

Whoever desired to join the community at Citeaux, was required to wait four days before he was taken to the Chapter in presence of the assembled brethren. On the fifth he was admitted; and having prostrated himself before the lectern, was asked of the Abbot what he wanted. He replied:—"GOD's mercy and yours." The Abbot bade him rise, explained to him the severity of the rule, and again demanded his intention. If the applicant still persisted, he said:—"May GOD Who hath begun a good work in thee Himself accomplish it." For three days this ceremony was repeated, and after the third repetition the applicant was admitted into the cells of the novices, and entered at once upon his year of probation.

The daily order of a Cistercian monastery was as follows:— The great bell rang at two in the morning; and the monks, immediately rising, hastened from their dormitory, along the dark still cloisters, to the church. There a faint glimmer of light was diffused by a single lamp. After a brief private prayer they began matins, which lasted for two hours. Lauds did not commence until dawn, and thus, at all events in winter-time, the monks secured for themselves a considerable interval, which they could employ in reading, writing, or meditation. Various religious exercises occupied them until nine, when they went forth to work in the fields. At two o'clock they dined; at nightfall the bell called them to vespers; at six or eight, according to the season, they finished the day with compline, and then retired to the dormitory. Thus their daily life furnished a practical illustration of S. Bernard's own famous maxim, *Laborare est orare.* By their agricultural toil, they did much towards the cultivation and fertilisation of large districts of barrenness, and recommended the plough and the harrow to a community long accustomed to give all honour to the sword.

> " ' Here Man more purely lives, less oft doth fall,
> More promptly rises, walks with stricter heed,
> More safely rests, dies happier, is freed
> Earlier from cleansing fires, and gains withal
> A brighter crown.'¹—On yon Cistercian wall
> *That* confident assurance may be read:
> And, to like shelter, from the world have fled
> Increasing multitudes. The potent call
> Doubtless shall cheat full oft the heart's desires;
> Yet, while the rugged liege on pliant knee
> Vows to rapt Fancy humble fealty,
> A gentler life spreads round the holy spires;
> Where'er they rise, the sylvan waste retires,
> And aëry harvests crown the fertile lea."
>
> WORDSWORTH.

But austere as was the Cistercian rule, it did not satisfy the enthusiastic soul of Bernard. He was so possessed with the love of his SAVIOUR that he knew not how to give it due expression except by rigorous chastisement of that body which seemed to him to come between the SAVIOUR and himself. He resolved on conquering the senses, on subduing them to the service of CHRIST. The time given to sleep he regarded as lost; and the time occupied by the visits of friends; for it was time taken from the contemplation of Divine things. He ceased to have any desire for food, and by his excessive abstemiousness induced so great a sickness of the stomach that he could scarcely retain any aliment, and what he ate seemed less to sustain life than to defer death.² When his physical weakness withheld him from sharing the manual labour of the monks, he betook himself to other and more menial offices, that he might supply by humility his deficiency of strength. In all this self-sacrifice we recognise a principle most admirable; but

---

[1] "Bonum est nos hic esse, quia homo vivit purius, cadit rarius, surgit velocius, incedit cautius, quiescit securius, moritur felicius, purgatur citius, præmiatur copiosius."—*S. Bernard.* This sentence was usually inscribed in some conspicuous part of the Cistercian houses.

[2] "Non tam ad vitam sustentandam quam ad differendam mortem." —Op., ii., 1071.

we recognise too, an unwise manifestation of it. The body is not, as the monk of Citeaux regarded it, the enemy of the soul, or else its slave; it needs discipline, but not torture; it is, or should be, the temple of the HOLY GHOST; and to preserve a just balance between the moral and the physical nature should be the object of every Christian.

Bernard was saved from degenerating into a mere ascetic, measuring his piety by the amount of physical pain he endured, through his warm love of Nature. Like Columba, he had a passion for the woods and the mountains; there was joy for him in the colour and outline of a fine landscape; his heart opened to the singing of the brook in the leafy valley. His sympathies were with Nature in its divine calm and rest; his observant and keen intelligence drew mystic lessons from its external facts. Writing to a friend and disciple, he says: —"Trust to one who has been taught by experience. You will find something far greater in the woods than in books. Stones and trees will teach you lessons which no masters will teach you. Think you not that you can suck honey from the rock, and oil from the flinty stone? Do not the mountains drop sweetness, and the hills flow with milk and honey, and the valleys stand thick with corn?" (Experto crede: aliquid amplius inveneris in silvis quam in libris. Ligna et lapides docebunt te quod a magistris audire non possis. An non putas posse te sugere mel de petrâ, oleumque de saxo durissimo? An non montes stillant dulcedinem, et colles fluunt lac et mel, et valles abundant frumento?)[1] In after years he was wont to confess that any knowledge which he possessed of the things of CHRIST, and any facility in the exposition of Holy Scripture, was due to his hours of prayer and meditation among the woods and in the fields, with none but the oaks and beeches for his teachers. Theology and Nature: these were his only subjects of intellectual meditation. As yet the revival of learning had not awakened the European mind, and of the glorious literature of Greece and Rome he was almost wholly ignorant. The Bible, and the writings of the Fathers, and the book of Nature,—these were the sources of his knowledge, and from these his powerful and original genius drew rich stores of thought and imagery.

[1] S. Bernard, Epist. 106.

In 1114 Bernard completed his profession, according to the established form. In the presence of the Chapter he made final disposal of whatever worldly goods he possessed. His head was shorn, and the hair burnt by the sacristan in a piscina reserved for the purpose. Advancing to the presbytery steps, he read the form of profession, made over it the sign of the cross, and reverently bowing, approached the altar. He placed his profession on the right side of it, which he kissed, and again bowing, retired to the steps. The Abbot, standing on the same side of the altar, removed from it the parchment, while the novice on his hands and knees implored pardon, thrice uttering the words:— "Receive me, O LORD." The whole congregation answered with "Gloria Patri," and the cantor began the psalm, "Have mercy on me, O GOD," which was chanted by the two choirs alternately. The novice then humbled himself at the Abbot's feet, and afterwards did the same before the Prior, and successively before all the religious present, even going into the retro-chorus, and prostrating himself before the sick, if any there were. Towards the close of the psalm, the Abbot, carrying his crozier, moved towards the novice, and bade him rise. A cowl was blessed and sprinkled with holy water; and the Abbot, stripping the novice of his secular garments, clothed him with the monastic habit. The Credo was said, and the novice having become a monk, he was admitted into the choir.[1]

The rumour of the sanctity of the new brother spread far and wide, and attracted so many votaries to Citeaux that the convent could not furnish accommodation for its inmates. Two additional cloisters were built, and these proving insufficient, a colony of monks was sent out to establish a new monastery. In this way arose the Abbey of La Ferté, under Bertrand, and that of Pontigny, which, before many years had elapsed, was to afford shelter to Thomas Becket. In 1115 a third exodus was found indispensable, and of this emigration Bernard, notwithstanding his unripe manhood, was appointed leader. With twelve monks he set out for Clairvaux,[2] a deep woodland valley in

[1] Usus Ordin. Cisterc., c. 103, cit. by Morison.
[2] "When Bernard and his twelve monks silently took their departure from the church, you might have seen tears in the eyes of all

the Bishopric of Langres, formerly known as the Valley of Wormwood, (*Vallis Absinthialis*,) but since that plant had been extirpated, justifying its new name by the brightness of its picturesque scenery, through which a pure fresh streamlet rippled. "It is formed," says a writer, "of two hills of equal height, one to the north, the other to the south of the valley. These hills extend towards a third eminence, by which it is divided into two long and narrow gorges at the western extremity. On the east it loses itself in a fertile plain, watered by the river Aube. The rays of the sun are thus darted full on the valley during the morning, while the slopes on the north and south, which recede as they bend eastward, receive them during the remainder of the day; the light being thus continually reflected from the hills above, no part of the valley, except that covered by the forest, is in shadow till the fall of eve, when the western hills completely hide the setting sun."

There Bernard and his monks took up their abode, and with their own hands raised a rude dwelling, which was long preserved by the pious veneration of successive generations. Chapel, dormitory, and refectory were all included in one fabric, and sheltered by a common roof. The windows were scarcely wider than a man's hand: the bare earth served for floor. Above the room in which the monks partook of their coarse fare was the dormitory. It was reached by a ladder. The beds were made in the form of wooden troughs, each just long enough and wide enough for a man to lie down in. An opening hewn out with an axe in one of the sides, allowed egress and ingress. The inside was strewn with chaff, twigs, dry leaves, which, with the woodwork, also formed the covering. At the summit of the stair or ladder was the Abbot's cell. Its dimensions were of the scantiest, and these were reduced by the loss of one corner,

present, while nothing was to be heard but the voices of those who were singing the hymns; nor could even these brethren repress their sobs, in spite of that sense of religion which led them to make the most strenuous efforts to command their feelings. Those who remained and those who departed were all involved in one common sorrow, till the procession reached that gate which was to open for some, and to close upon the rest."—*Annales Cisterc.*, p. 79. La Ferté and Pontigny, founded in 1113 and 1114, and Clairvaux and Morimont, founded in 1115, were called " Les quatres filles de Citeaux."

through which access was obtained to the apartment below. A framework of boards was so placed over the flight of steps as to serve for a bed; two rough-hewn logs of wood were the pillows. The roof was low and slanting, so that near the wall it was impossible not alone to stand, but to sit upright. Such was Clairvaux.

The monks seem to have been settled in this rude abode early in September. For the coming winter, however, they had no store laid by. During the summer their fare had been a compound of leaves intermixed with coarse grain. In the winter they would have to live upon roots and beech-nuts. To the want of sufficient food was added the lack of clothes and shoes. Other privations pressed upon them as the season advanced, and at last their supply of salt was exhausted. Then Bernard called to him one of the brethren :—" Guibert," he said, " saddle the ass, go to the fair, and buy for us some salt." Guibert answered :—" Where is the money?" " Believe me," rejoined Bernard, " I know not the time when I had gold or silver. He Who holds my wallet and my treasures is above." " But if I go empty-handed, I shall return empty-handed." " Nevertheless, my son, go in peace. Our Great Treasurer will be with thee in the way, and will grant thee all for which I send thee." Guibert received his Abbot's benediction and went forth, though still doubtful of the success of his errand. On his way, however, " the GOD of all consolation was pleased to assist him;" for being accosted by a priest, he told him on what business he was bound, and drew so sad a picture of the sufferings of the convent, that the priest, moved with compassion, took him to his own house, gave him half a bushel of salt, and fifty *solidi*. Thereupon, rejoicing, Guibert hastened back to Clairvaux. " I tell thee, my son," said Bernard, when apprised of his success, " that no one thing is so indispensable to a Christian as faith. Have faith, therefore, and it will be well with thee all the days of thy life."

Suffering from hunger, cold, and other evils, the monks murmured bitterly. They were prepared for poverty, but not for starvation, and declared that they must return to Citeaux. Bernard endeavoured to revive their trust in GOD, and when in this he failed, he betook himself to

earnest prayer. Presently was heard a voice from heaven :—
"Arise, Bernard, thy prayer is granted thee." "What
didst thou ask of the LORD?" said the monks. "Wait,
and ye shall see, ye of little faith," was the reply; and immediately
came a stranger to the convent, who gave the
Abbot ten livres.

Reassured by these instances of Divine favour, and influenced
by Bernard's loftiness of character and heroic
patience, the monks ceased their complaints, and with the
year 1116 an era of prosperity and peace dawned upon the
little colony of Clairvaux. In order to receive abbatial
ordination, Bernard repaired to the Bishop of Chalons, the
celebrated William of Champeaux, whose cordial friendship
and admiration was secured by his noble qualities. The
Bishop observing that Bernard's excessive austerities and
arduous duties had endangered his health, obtained from
the Cistercian Chapter leave to manage and control him for
a twelvemonth. Having caused a cottage to be built outside
the conventual precincts, he ordered Bernard to dwell
in it, relieving him of all care and responsibility of monastic
government, and regulating his dietary on reasonable
principles. Unfortunately he left him in charge of a man
wholly unworthy of and unfitted for such a trust. It was
about this time he was visited by William of St. Thierry,
afterwards his friend and biographer, and his account of
this visit is singularly interesting :—

"I found him in his hut," he says, "relieved from the
presidency of the convent by the orders of the Bishop and
the Chapter, and he was then at leisure for himself and GOD,
and exulting as if he already tasted the delights of Paradise.
When I entered that chamber, and contemplated the place
and its inhabitant, I call GOD to witness that I was overcome
with a feeling of veneration, as if I had been approaching
the altar of GOD. On conversing with him, I found such a
force and yet such a sweetness in his speech, that I conceived
a strong desire to stay with him, and share his poverty; so
that if I could have chosen my lot among all that the world
has to offer, I should have desired no other than that of
remaining always with this man of GOD, as his servant.
After he had given us a cordial welcome, we inquired how
he did, and how he liked his new mode of life. 'Excellent

well,' he replied, with his usual benign smile; 'formerly reasonable beings submitted to my rule, but now, by the just judgment of GOD, I am obliged to submit myself to a man devoid of reason.' This he said concerning an ignorant rustic, to whose care he had been committed, and who boasted he could cure him of the infirmity from which he was suffering. As we sat at meat with him, I thought how carefully so precious an invalid should be tended, but when we saw him served, by this doctor's orders, with food which a healthy man in the extremity of his hunger, would hardly touch, we could scarcely respect our vow of silence, and were on the point of assailing this empiric as a sacrilegious homicide. But he who suffered from this treatment was wholly indifferent, and approved of everything that was placed before him."

William of S. Thierry proceeds to describe Clairvaux:—
"At the first glance," he says, "as you entered it by descending the hill, you could see it was a temple of GOD; and the still, silent valley bespoke, in the modest simplicity of its buildings, the unfeigned humility of CHRIST's poor. Moreover, in this valley full of men, where no person was permitted to be idle, where all were occupied with their allotted tasks, a silence, deep as that of night, prevailed. The sounds of labour, or the chants of the brethren in the choral service, were the only exception. The order of this silence, and the fame that went forth of it, struck such a reverence even into secular persons that they dreaded breaking it, I will not say by idle or wicked conversation, but even by pertinent remarks. The solitude also of the place, shut in between dense forests and a narrow gorge of neighbouring hills, in a certain sense recalled the cave of our father, S. Benedict, so that while they strove to imitate his life, they had also some resemblance to him in the loneliness of their habitation."

Notwithstanding the ignorance of his medical superintendent, Bernard recovered his health, and resumed his duties as Abbot. He did not again indeed lead that life of absolute seclusion and excessive severity which he had formerly practised; he himself was conscious of its unwisdom,[1]

[1] Yet it is probably true, that the effect of his passionate eloquence and firm conviction were considerably enhanced by his pallid face and

and perceived that its only result had been to unfit him for labouring in CHRIST's service;[1] but he entered upon a career of vigorous effort and exertion. He endeavoured to improve, by his sermons, the minds of those with whom he came in contact, and to inspire them with his own hatred of worldliness and the world; or he sought to influence them in conversation by his subtle and various eloquence, which, with quick insight, he adapted to the character and circumstances of every individual. He began also his wide and impassioned correspondence, which presents us with the best because the truest portrait of his mind and heart, his intellect and imagination, his strength and weakness. Everybody solicited his advice on every subject; on the details of private affairs, as well as on the concerns of Church and State. And in these letters we find him severely censuring the disorders and corruptions of the Church, and exhorting her priests to live a life worthy of their high vocation. We find him persistently labouring for the dignity and extension of his order; earnestly interceding with the great for those who were suffering through their injustice; and always protesting against wrong-doing and oppression. We find him defending the interests of the Church against Popes, and the independence of the Church against sovereigns. And we find him exhorting all his correspondents to throw aside the garments of sin, and to clothe themselves in white raiment purified by the blood of the Lamb.

It was about this time (1120,) that Bernard composed four Homilies on the words of S. Luke:—"The angel Gabriel was sent from GOD." A modern writer criticises them as curious in many ways. "The crudity, not to say horribleness, of some of the ideas; the ambitious and gaudy rhetoric; the conspicuous absence of high spiritual thought, make them interesting as evidence of what Bernard was,

emaciated form, which testified to the ascetic sanctity of his life in a manner easily understanded of the people.

[1] The severity of his discipline had almost crushed out his natural senses, so that, for many days together, he ate blood, supposing it to be butter, and drank oil without knowing it from water. He could not tell whether the roof of the novices' chamber was or was not vaulted; whether there were two or three windows at the east end of the church; and for a whole day he walked along the shore of Lake Leman without recognising the water.

as contrasted with what he became." His intellect, as yet, had not acquired its full developement, had not wholly thrown off the super-sensitiveness begotten by solitary meditation and physical weakness. His force of character, however, impressed very strongly the minds of those who were admitted to his company, and contributed with his sanctity of life and ardour of devotion to induce a belief in his possession of miraculous power. In 1122 he was again visited at Clairvaux by William of S. Thierry, who was suffering from a dangerous illness. While at Clairvaux, he recovered; and of course his recovery was a miracle, wrought by Bernard. "It happened," he says, "that, as Septuagesima Sunday approached, on the Saturday night previous, I had improved in health so much that I could get out of bed alone, and even go in and out of doors without assistance. I began, therefore, to arrange for returning home, which, when Bernard heard of, he at once forbade, and prohibited all hope of, or attempt to return before Quinquagesima. I obeyed readily, as both my inclination and debility led me to acquiesce. Up to Septuagesima I had been eating meat; he had ordered it as necessary for me; now I wished to leave it off, but he would not consent. However, in this I would not yield; neither his advice, request, nor command influenced me, and so we parted on that Saturday night, he in silence to compline, I to my bed. When, lo, my malady revived in all its strength and fury, and with such violence seized me, and all through the night with such malignity tortured me, above all my strength, above all my endurance, that, despairing of life, I thought only to live till the morning, so that I might once more speak with the man of GOD. After this miserable night I sent for him, and he came; not with his usual countenance of pity, but rather of reproof. At last, smiling, he said; 'Well, will you eat to-day?' I had already attributed my affliction to my previous disobedience, and I answered, 'Whatever you choose to order.' 'Rest still then,' he enjoined, 'you will not die this time,' and went away; and at once all pain went with him, except that exhausted by the night's sufferings, I could scarcely rise from my bed the whole day. But what manner of pain was that? I never recollect anything like it in my life. However, the day after I was whole, and recovered my strength, and in a few days, with the blessing and favour of my good host, I returned to my own people."

More striking illustrations of his miraculous powers are recorded by his biographers. It could not be otherwise, considering the temper of the age in which he lived; an age which regarded the contention between the Powers of Good and Evil as something which every man could see and know by external evidence; which looked upon the world as the playground or battlefield of demons, engaged in frustrating the purposes of Divine Providence; and believed that every pious man, by virtue of his piety, could openly triumph over them and refute and expose them. "Poor, feeble man," to use Mr. Morison's language, "had to pick his way in the midst of them; on either side of his path, at all hours of sleeping or waking, his mind and his heart were the desired prize of one or the other. The deliberately wicked man was given over for the time, in full property, to the fiend. The good, the deeply holy man, was surrounded by choirs of angels; and the devils were supposed almost to howl at his approach. He was changed, he was another creature to their believing eyes; he was in direct correspondence with GOD; the breath of the Divine Love had robed him in beauty. Could there be any difficulty in thinking that to such an one—one on whom the smile of the Eternal was supposed to rest; one whose thoughts moved, like the angels in Jacob's dream, to and fro between earth and heaven; one whose future glory in the kingdom of the just was well assured—would it have been possible to doubt that to such an one the forms and things of this miserable, accursed earth would give a swift obedience as of servants to their lord? Could inert matter, which even the very devils were able to work upon, resist a holy man full of the Spirit of GOD? Must not the earthly give way to the Heavenly? Must not CHRIST be the conqueror of Satan?"[1]

That Bernard was gifted with extraordinary Christian graces, and a piety beyond the piety even of most religious men, was very evident to his contemporaries; and therefore they ascribed to him the power of working miracles. It could not be otherwise; it was, in fact, an obvious syllogism.

[1] Morison, p. 69.

To the saints was granted the privilege of baffling the devils and reversing their work. Bernard was a saint among saints; hence he possessed the privilege in a pre-eminent degree—in such a degree that his kinsmen feared lest it should fill him with unworthy exaltation; so that both his uncle Gulderic, and his brother Guido, were incessantly engaged in humbling him. They were two thorns in the flesh, ordained by GOD to prevent him from being exalted above measure. They excited him with harsh words; they underestimated his good deeds; they affected to depreciate or ignore his signs and wonders. In company with the Bishop of Langres, Bernard and his brother Guido were passing the Château Landres, in the territory of Sens, when a certain youth, afflicted with an ulcer in his foot, earnestly besought Bernard to touch and bless him. Bernard made the sign of the cross, and immediately the lame was healed. Returning that way a few days afterwards, they found him whole and well. Guido, however, could not be restrained, even by the miracle, from rebuking his brother, and taxing him with presumption for having touched the lad, so anxious was he in his fraternal love![1]

Among the miracles attributed to him are the following:— A knight who had suffered terribly for eighteen months from an attack of quartan fever, was instantly cured by Bernard with a piece of consecrated bread. Gerard, the venerable Bishop of Limoges, told of a young man related to himself who had received a mortal wound in the head: as he lay foaming and unconscious, a small mouthful of bread, blessed by the man of GOD, was placed between his lips, and within that very hour he was healed. When Walter of Montmirail, whose uncle became a monk at Clairvaux, was about three months old, his mother received Bernard as a guest. Thankful that she was honoured by having so worthy a man under her roof, she presented her infant to receive his blessing. As was his wont, the man of GOD began to speak of the salvation of their souls to those around him; while the mother, with her babe in his lap, sat at his feet. But, as he spoke, he now and then stretched

[1] "Cæterum sæpe dictus beati viri frater ne ipso quidem poterat compesci miraculo, quominus increparet eum, et præsumptionis argueret, quod acquieverit tangere hominem."—S. Bernard, ii. 1081.

forth his hand, and the infant strove to seize it. When it had made several attempts, its action was at last observed ; and, as they all marvelled, the child was allowed to have its way. With the deepest reverence it took the saint's hand between both its tiny palms, lifted it to its mouth, and kissed it : and this, not once only, but as often as it was permitted.

Even in the smallest matters great things occurred through the power of Bernard's sanctity. When he dedicated the church of Joigny, it happened that the place was filled by an incredible number of flies, so that their humming and incessant flying about were an intolerable nuisance to everybody present. As no remedy could be devised, Bernard said:— "I excommunicate them," and in the morning they were all found dead. They covered the whole pavement, and were shovelled out with spades ; so that the church was cleared of them. On another occasion, as Bernard was returning from Chalons, he and his companions were greatly retarded in their progress by a storm of wind and rain. Some few of them, however, pushed in advance; and in time, as owing to the intense cold the usual attention was not given to each other's movements, he was left almost alone. Now, the horse of one of the two who kept by his side, contrived, by some accident, to steal away, and galloped across the open plain. In vain did they endeavour to catch him ; and the cold making any further delay for this purpose inexpedient, "Let us pray," said S. Bernard ; and, kneeling down with the brother who remained by him, they were scarcely able to repeat the LORD'S Prayer, before the horse in all meekness returned, stood still before Bernard, and was restored to his rider.

In 1125, monastic business, or some other object, induced Bernard to visit the monastery of La Grande Chartreuse, founded by S. Bruno some forty years before. The prior was one Guigo, who had for awhile been corresponding with "the man of GOD," and rejoiced to find that Bernard in the flesh was in all things equal to Bernard in his wonderful letters. There was only one exception ; namely, that the saddle on which the Cistercian abbot had ridden to La Grande Chartreuse, was a thing costly and luxurious, and as such unworthy of a disciple of S. Benedict. But it turned out that the trappings were not his own, but, with the horse, had been lent to him by his uncle, a Cluniac monk, and that Bernard, absorbed in devout meditation, had never noticed them, and knew not of what they were composed.

Bernard also visited Paris at this time; and an anecdote of his visit furnishes a vivid illustration of his character. During his stay in the crowded, dirty, and ill-built city which was then the capital of the French kingdom, Bernard lodged with an archdeacon, and was thrown into the company of several persons, who invited him to go into the schools and lecture there. He consented; but instead of discoursing on the philosophical puzzles and subtleties to which the students were accustomed, he spoke of the Christian philosophy; and recommended a contempt of the world and worldly pleasures, and the practice of poverty for the sake of CHRIST. The students did not receive his exhortations with willingness; and Bernard, much dispirited, returned to the house of his friend, and throwing himself on his knees began to pray, and with such intensity of devotion that he wept abundantly, with sobs and groans that were heard outside his chamber. On inquiring what could be the cause of grief so passionate, the archdeacon was told by a monk well acquainted with Bernard, that "that wonderful man, glowing with the fire of charity, and wholly absorbed in GOD, cared for nothing in the world save only to recall the wandering to the ways of Truth, and to gain their souls to CHRIST; and because he had just sown the word of life in the schools, and gathered no fruit in the conversion of the clerks, therefore he thought GOD was angry with him. Hence," said the monk, " this storm of groans and this outpouring of tears; wherefore I fully anticipate that to-morrow's large harvest will compensate for to-day's sterility."

The monk's expectation was fulfilled; for when Bernard preached on the following day, all the students listened devoutly, and several of them expressed their intention of assuming the religious life. Bernard accordingly resolved to take them at once to Clairvaux; they were brands snatched from the burning, and he could not afford to lose them. Accordingly he set out from Paris, and at nightfall reached S. Denys. But, next day, when everybody was prepared to continue the homeward journey, Bernard said to them :—" No; we must return to Paris, where still linger some who belong to us, some whom it behoves us to include in this the LORD's fold, so that there may be one fold and one Shepherd." As they drew near Paris, they saw three clerks at a distance, coming towards them. "GOD has helped us," exclaimed the saint; "behold, yonder are the clerks for whom I returned." When they approached, and recognised Bernard, they rejoiced with a great joy, saying :—"O most blessed father, you have come to us who desired you much. For it had been our intention to follow you, and we hardly hoped to overtake you." "I knew it, beloved," he replied; "we will now travel together, and by GOD's grace I will lead you on your journey." Then they went on their way; and they persevered under the discipline of his rule all the remainder of their days.[1]

CHAPTER II.

AS yet Bernard was no more than a monk; a monk among monks, if you like; renowned for his sanctity, and generally felt to be a man of strong and dominant intellect; but still, a secluded monk, dwelling in a mean monastery in a remote Burgundian valley. It was through his multifarious and incessant correspondence that he was laying the foundation of that influence and authority, which, before long, was to terminate a dangerous schism in the Church, to silence a formidable heretic, and to inspire, if it did not originate, the Second Crusade. I have said that in his correspondence we get a clue to Bernard's character; and it certainly shows us a man of rare powers of mind, with a singular knowledge of the human heart, a burning hatred of wrong, a warm sympathy with the oppressed, a sagacity that is seldom at fault, and a judgment that is almost always cool, calm and impartial. A vassal of Count Thibaut of Champagne, named Humbert, had been falsely accused, and condemned to prove his innocence by a judicial combat. Failing in this, he was deprived of his fief, which necessarily reduced his wife and

[1] S. Bernard, Op., ii., 1202.

children to want, was thrown into prison, and had his eyes put out. Bernard immediately wrote to Count Thibaut, urging that whatever might have been Humbert's crime, it was not just that his wife and children should suffer. The letter produced no effect, and Bernard wrote again in a tone of indignant reproof :—"Had I asked of thee, gold, silver, or the like, I am fully persuaded that I should have obtained my request; in truth, I have already experienced your liberality, unasked. Why then am I counted unworthy to obtain from you the only favour I *have* asked, and asked not in my own but GOD's name; not for my own sake, but far more for yours? Know you not that 'with what measure ye mete, it shall be measured to you again?' Know you not that it is as easy, ay, a thousand times easier for GOD to cast you out of the heavenly inheritance, than for you to eject Humbert from his patrimony? Cases there are indeed, in which the guilt is so manifest, that justice leaves no room for the exercise of mercy; but even then you must take vengeance in sorrow and trembling, impelled by necessity and judicial duty rather than by any desire of gratifying yourself." Bernard's importunity had at last its due effect. Count Thibaut was induced to investigate the case, and being convinced of Humbert's innocence, reinstated him in his original position. Incidents such as these are not infrequent in Bernard's letters, and he is always to be found throwing his influence on the side of the weak and suffering.

The candour and stern simplicity with which he could administer a reproof, appears in his letters to Ogerius, who had resigned his pastoral post in order to become a monk. Bernard was always angered by what seemed to him a gross dereliction of duty, the abandonment of a post in which a man might be useful to his fellow-men. So he wrote to Ogerius :—"Is it not true that you preferred your own ease to the welfare of others? I am glad you enjoy your calm of rest; but do you not enjoy it too much? Every good thing which pleases us so much that we love it, even when it is not expedient or lawful, ceases for that very reason to be good." He then proceeds to offer some good advice :—
"Be simple among the brethren, devout before GOD, subject to your superior, obedient to your elders, kindly to your juniors, pleasing to the angels, useful in speech, lowly in heart,

gentle to all. Be careful, lest having once been placed in authority, you think yourself entitled to honour, but rather show yourself the more humble to all as one among many. And another danger may arise to you from this quarter, of which I would wish to give you warning. We are all of us so fickle, that what we wished for yesterday, we refuse to-day, and what we refuse to-day, we shall desire to-morrow. Now, if it should happen, through the Devil's suggestion, that a regret for your lost authority assault your mind, for all that you have manfully despised you would then childishly yearn. What before was so distasteful, would then be invested with fresh charms, the dignity of position, the charge of the house, the despatch of business, the obedience of servants, your own liberty, your power over others; so that you will almost repent having given up what it was painful to keep. If this most evil temptation seduce you, even for an hour, it will not be without grave injury to your soul."

S. Bernard first appears on the European stage in 1127. It would seem that Louis had forcibly deprived the Archbishop of Paris and his clergy of a portion of their goods ; in displeasure, according to Bernard, at their reformation of life and conduct, which had led them to abandon the royal court and its gaieties, and endeavour to discharge their high duties with a conscientiousness they had never before displayed. The Archbishop, in conjunction with the Archbishop of Sens, retaliated by placing the kingdom under interdict, and then they fled to Citeaux. Stephen, the illustrious Abbot of Citeaux, immediately addressed a remonstrance to the king urging him to restore what he had unjustly seized, and offering his good services as a mediator between him and the prelate he had wronged. Louis was much moved by the Abbot's earnest appeal, and would probably have yielded to it, when Pope Honorius suddenly raised the interdict, and thus humiliated and disgraced the two Archbishops. His conduct drew from S. Bernard a keen reproach. "Tristes vidimus, tristes et loquimur, honorem ecclesiæ, Honorii tempore non minime læsum." "Sadly we have seen, and sadly we assert, that the honour of the Church has been not a little damaged in the time of Honorius."[1]

[1] S. Bernard, Op., Epist. xcvi.

To the king, Bernard was not less direct in his plain speaking; "Your obstinacy," he said, "will be punished by the death of your eldest son Philip, for last night I saw you in a dream, you, with your younger son, Louis, fall at the feet of the two prelates whom you have set at nought; whence I infer that the death of your first-born is at hand, and will compel you to implore the favour of the Church which you now oppress, to allow you to set your son Louis in his place." Three years later Prince Philip died, (1130,) and the monks of Clairvaux claimed that his death was a fulfilment of their Abbot's prophecy.

Bernard's "Apology," as it is called, to the Abbot William of S. Thierry, belongs to this year of activity, 1127. It was provoked by the worldly grandeur and worldly laxity of the monks of Cluny, who are painted vigorously, but in unfavourable colours, and are solemnly reproved for their devotion to the pleasures of the senses. "I am astonished," he writes, "to see among monks such excess in eating, in drinking, in clothes, in bed-covering, in horse-trappings, in buildings. Economy is now stigmatized as avarice, soberness as austerity, silence as sullenness. On the other hand, laxity is called discretion, extravagance liberality, talkativeness affability, silly laughter a happy wit, pomp and luxury in horses and clothing, respectability; superfluous attention to the building is called cleanliness; and when you countenance one another in these trifles, that forsooth is charity." He sternly condemns the sumptuous decoration of the Cluniac churches:—
"so ingeniously do ye lay out your money, that it returns with a manifold increase. It is spent that it may be doubled, and plenty is born of profusion. By the exhibition of wonderful and costly vanities, men are excited to give rather than to pray. Some beautiful picture of a saint is shown, and the brighter its colouring the greater is the holiness attributed to it : men run eager to kiss; they are invited to give, and the beautiful is more admired than the sacred is revered. In the churches are placed, not *coronæ*, but wheels studded with gems and surrounded by lights, which are not less glittering than the precious stones inserted among them.[1] Instead of candlesticks, we see great and heavy trees of brass, wonderfully

---

[1] "Ponuntur in ecclesia gemmatæ non coronæ sed rotæ circumseptæ lampadibus, sed non minus fulgentes insertis lapidibus."

fashioned by the skill of the artificer, and radiant as much through their jewels as through their own lights.[1] What do you imagine to be the object of all this? The repentance of the contrite, or the admiration of the spectators? O vanity of vanities! but not greater vanity than folly."

This boldness of reproof, this independence of thought, and this fervid flowing eloquence drew upon Bernard the attention of his contemporaries, and gradually a conviction arose that the age had at last produced the man who was capable of guiding and controlling it. From the seclusion of Clairvaux he was called, in 1128, to the Council of Troyes, where he took a prominent part in organising the religious military Order of the Knights Templars. The rapid extension of this Order was greatly promoted by his influence and recommendation; and at a later period, he was induced by Hugo-a-Paganis, the first Grand Master of the Temple, to compose a treatise in praise of the "new warfare" (Liber de laude Novæ Militiæ Militis Templi), which is instinct with the characteristics of his genius, in its weakness as in its strength:—"This," he exclaims, "is a new mode of warfare, unknown to former ages: an incessant struggle of a twofold nature; on the one side, against flesh and blood, and on the other, against spiritual wickedness in high places; a most marvellous struggle, for which both the inner and the outer man alike take up the sword. These knights live, and fight, and triumph most gloriously for CHRIST, and still more gloriously do they die, for Him, the martyr's death." He contrasts these soldiers of the Cross with the soldiers of the world. "What a surprising error it is, what madness, O ye Knights, to fight at such cost and labour for no wages except those of death or sin! Ye clothe your horses with silken trappings; ye flaunt gay cloaks over your breastplates of steel; ye paint your spears and shields and saddles; ye deck your spurs and bridles with gold and silver and jewels; and in this radiant pomp, with an amazing and incredible madness, ye rush upon death. Have ye not learned from experience that these qualities are specially needed by a knight; that he must be

---

[1] "Cernimus et pro candelabris arbores quasdam erectas multo aeris pondere, miro artificis opere fabricatas, nec magis coruscantes superpositis lucernis quam suis gemmis."

bold and vigilant, quick in his movements, and prompt to strike?"

In February, 1130, died Pope Honorius II. Then was seen the scandal of a double election, a majority of the Cardinals raising to the vacant throne Cardinal Gregory with the title of Innocent II., the minority electing Peter Leonis with the title of Anacletus II. The latter was at first so far successful, through a dextrous employment of both gold and iron, as to compel Innocent II. to fly from Rome, and seek refuge in France. At Cluny he was received with a splendid welcome, and there he remained while Louis VI. summoned a council at Etampes to inquire into and decide upon his claims, as compared with those of Anacletus. Bernard was specially invited to the council by the king and the chief bishops. He left Clairvaux in a depressed and uncertain mood; but on the way he was favoured with a vision, in which he saw a large church, filled with people singing harmoniously in praise of GOD, and this gave him new vigour. After fasting and prayer the council proceeded to business, and unanimously resolved that as the business concerned GOD it should be referred to "the man of GOD," and that by his judgment they should abide. Bernard then examined into the circumstances of the double election, and more particularly into the respective merits of the competitors. When he opened his mouth, he was supposed to speak by the inspiration of the HOLY GHOST, and he unreservedly pronounced in favour of Innocent. The Council accepted this conclusion, and with praises to GOD, and vows of fealty to Innocent, broke up.

The King immediately despatched Suger, Abbot of S. Denys, with words of greeting to his new spiritual father; and at Saint Benoit-sur-Loire met him in person, with the Queen and the royal children. Bowing his "oft-crowned head," he knelt at the feet of the pontiff, and pledged to him his affectionate and faithful service. At Chartres appeared Henry I. of England, with a brilliant train of prelates and nobles. He was undecided which Pope to prefer, but his clergy were fain that he should acknowledge Anacletus. Into his presence, however, Bernard made his way, and his fiery eloquence and strength of character decided Henry's choice. "Are you afraid," said Bernard, "that you may sin by yielding obedience to Innocent? Think how you may answer to GOD for your *other* sins, and let *this* sin rest on me."[1] Henry then acknowledged Innocent, and made him many magnificent presents.

Secure in the support of the two great rulers of Western Europe, Innocent proceeded to test the disposition of Lothair, the German Emperor. Accompanied by Bernard, and attended by cardinals and bishops, he repaired to the monastery of Morigny, where he remained three days, and met with Peter Abelard, the hero of the sad romance that is for ever associated with the name of the impassioned Heloise. Thence the brilliant company travelled to Liége (March 22, 1131), where Lothair received the Pope with profoundest reverence, holding the rein of his horse as he ambled through the bannered streets; and in return was crowned by Innocent's hands, along with his wife Richenza, in the cathedral. He promised to march into Italy and seat the Pope in S. Stephen's chair; but in consideration of this direct assistance, asked that the privilege of episcopal investiture, which Henry V. had surrendered by the concordat of Worms, should be restored to the Imperial crown. To the Romans present this demand foreshadowed great and certain evils; they trembled when it was put forward; but they were on the point of yielding when Bernard boldly stood forward, and revived their sinking courage. He addressed the Emperor with the utmost freedom, and plied him with such arguments of force that Lothair abandoned his position, and without further demur admitted Innocent's claims. With bared head, and on foot, he made his way through the crowd to the Pope on his white palfrey, and with one hand took the rein, while in the other he held a wand, as symbolic of protection to his acknowledged lord.

Returning into France, Pope Innocent celebrated Easter at S. Denys. On the vigil of that "Queen of Festivals" he passed the night in prayer, and with the first streak of dawn, repaired to the church, accompanied by all his retinue. There they made the preparations usual at Rome. On the Pope's head was placed the *phrygium*,'or helmet-shaped cap circled with gold, and then, sitting on a cream-white palfrey,

[1] "Cogita quomodo de aliis peccatis tuis respondeas Deo, istud mihi relinque, in me sit hoc peccatum."—S. Bernard, ii. 1094.

which glittered with costly trappings, he was led forth. His clergy and officials preceded him, two abreast, on horseback, singing a triumphal chant. The barons and noble feudatories of the abbey attended on foot, and led the Pope's palfrey by the rein; while others went in advance, and distributed largesse among the crowd. The road was strewn with willows, and along the side gorgeous hangings fluttered on a line of posts. An immense multitude thronged to see the sight; including even the Jews of Paris, who offered to their arch-persecutor a copy of their law covered by a veil. "May GOD Almighty," was the Pope's epigrammatic reply, "remove the veil which is on your hearts!" In this fashion he proceeded to the church of the Holy Manger, which shone resplendent with golden coronæ and precious stones. And the Abbot Suger and the Pope having offered up mass, the whole company retired to the cloister, to partake of a splendid banquet.

In strange contrast with this brilliant scene was Innocent's reception at Clairvaux, which he afterwards visited. "CHRIST'S poor" received him with no display of purple and fine linen, with no blare of trumpet or flutter of banners; but carrying a cross of stone, and chanting psalms in subdued accents. The Pope and his attendant bishops were moved to tears by this austere spectacle, but the monks themselves fixed their eyes upon the ground, looking neither to the right nor to the left. The rude stone church, with its naked walls, the refectory with its cold earthen floor, the simple fare of the monks, who, if a fish were placed on the table, reserved it for the Pope, astonished the visitors; and we can well believe that the Romans saw nothing to desire. The solemn service of the choir was grievously disturbed by a monk who suddenly exclaimed, "I am the CHRIST!" but we are told that the demon who instigated this outbreak was quickly silenced by the exhortations of S. Bernard.

Innocent spent upwards of a twelvemonth in France, and his entertainment began to be felt as a heavy burden. He was a Pope without revenues, and he was accompanied by a large gathering of bishops and courtiers. In October, 1131, he held a grand council at Reims, which was attended by thirteen archbishops, and two hundred and sixty-three bishops. Louis VI. was present in person; the Emperor

Lothair, Henry I. of England, and the Kings of Aragon and Castile, were represented by ambassador-prelates. The extraordinary influence which Bernard's strong mind and firm will had obtained over Innocent was here perceived; though the Pope in public preferred to consult his cardinals, he was always guided by the opinion which he had previously obtained from the Abbot of Clairvaux in private. In April, 1132, he crossed the Alps into Italy, pausing at Lyons to shower favours on Clairvaux and on the Cistercians as a body, including an entire immunity from tithes. He was still accompanied by Bernard, without whose counsel he was powerless, and to whose enthusiastic support he owed everything. Escorted by Lothair, with a body of 2000 horse, he entered Rome; but Anacletus still held a considerable portion of the sacred city, relying on the troops furnished by Roger, the Norman Duke of Sicily. The climate compelled the Emperor to retire; and soon afterwards Innocent was forced to abandon the field to his rival, and seek shelter at Pisa. Bernard, ever active on his behalf, for he had identified his cause with that of right and justice, addressed a note of rejoicing to the Pisans :—
" Pisa is chosen to take the place of Rome, and before all the cities of the earth to become the seat of the Apostolic dignity. Nor is this the result of chance, nor by the decree of man, but it hath been willed by the divine providence and favour of GOD, Who thus spake unto Innocent the Anointed :—' Choose Pisa for thy dwelling-place, and I will pour My blessing on that city, and the wickedness of the Sicilian tyrant shall not prevail against her. His menaces shall not shake her steadfastness; neither shall she be seduced by his gifts, nor beguiled by the subtlety of his cunning. O Pisa! Pisa! thou shalt be envied by all cities, for the sake of the glory shed on thee by the presence of him who is thy father, and the father of Christendom, the primate of the world, the judge of the earth.' "

At Pisa, in May, 1136, a great council was held, when Anacletus was excommunicated, and sentence of deposition delivered against his partisans. Bernard was here the principal figure. He was treated with the greatest deference, and his voice really governed the decisions; but the honours with which he was loaded did not shake his calm self-reliance or disturb his composure. From Pisa he repaired to Milan, that through his mediation its citizens might be reconciled with the Pope and the Emperor. At his approach the city poured forth its thousands and tens of thousands to do him honour. They contended with one another for the privilege of touching him; they drew out threads from his tunic, to be preserved as relics or employed as remedies for the sick. Bread and water were brought from a distance for his blessing, which was supposed to endue them with a sacramental virtue; and many miracles were wrought, partly through his own sanctity, and partly through the absolute faith which the people reposed in him. The reform which he accomplished was not the least wonderful of these! All gold and silver ornaments were removed from the churches, and shut up in chests, as being offensive to the man of GOD; men and women put on sackcloth and coarse woollen garments, and submitted to have their hair shorn, in token of their repentance. The fame of these things soon spread over the surrounding countries, and from all parts men came to be healed of their diseases, or to see the saint by whom such great deeds were performed.

The Milanese conceived so great an affection for the "man of GOD" that they solicited him to accept their archbishopric. Bernard, however, perceived that he could do better and higher work as a simple monk, than as an ecclesiastical dignitary; that his influence would be greater, and his time more fully at his command. "To-morrow," he said to the crowd that pressed around him, "I will mount my horse, and if it carry me out of your city, I shall conclude that I may not accede to your request; but if, on the other hand, it should refuse to bear me beyond the walls, I will then agree to become your archbishop." Bernard's horse responded to Bernard's inclination, and did *not* refuse to bear him beyond the walls of the old Lombard capital. Thereupon, he took his departure from Milan, and travelled through the territories of Pavia and Cremona, in order to negotiate terms of peace between them and Milan, and secure the release of the Milanese prisoners. A new archbishop, Robald, was soon afterwards elected; and the influence of Bernard proved sufficient to extort from the Milanese their consent to his acceptance of the *pallium* from Pope Innocent. This surrender of the ancient privilege of their church, which they had hitherto jealously preserved, is a striking testimony to the power he personally wielded.

Having thus successfully striven to compose the dissensions and heal the wounds of the Church in Italy, Bernard set out on his return to Clairvaux, of which he had seen but little in four busy years. The news of his coming spread before him; and on his crossing the Alps, crowds of shepherds and peasants came down from their heights to greet him, and receive his blessing (1135). Soon after his arrival at Clairvaux, he undertook the rebuilding of the monastery, which was no longer capable of containing the numbers who sought admission within its walls. At first he felt a natural hesitation. "Remember," he said to his monks, " remember the labour and cost of our present house; with what infinite pains did we at last succeed in constructing the aqueducts which supply our offices and workshops with water; and what will be said of us if we now destroy our own work? We shall be counted fools, and rightly, for we have no money. Let us not forget the warning of the Gospel, that 'he who would build a tower, must first sit down and count the cost.'" The brethren replied:—" You must either repulse those who are sent to you by GOD, or you must build lodgings for them; and surely it would be a miserable thing if through fear of the expense we opposed any obstacles to the development of GOD's work." This consideration decided him; and the labour of building was begun. Abundant offerings poured in from all parts. Many labourers were hired; many gave their services without payment. The monks themselves plied axe and hammer lustily; while some squared the stone, others felled the timber, and others raised the walls. The waters of the river were distributed into several channels, which were made to feed the various mills. "The fullers and the millers, the tanners and the carpenters, and other artificers erected the machines and appliances necessary to their respective trades; and the obedient water, brought by subterranean pipes throughout the offices, afforded a plentiful and gushing spring wherever it was wanted. At last, having fulfilled its various duties, it retired to its original bed, and swelled to its ancient size. The walls were completed with unexpected celerity, enclosing the whole extent of the spacious monastery. The abbey rose from the earth; and, as if animated by a spirit of life, the new church seemed to grow and increase."[1]

Bernard was soon called from his peaceful duties at Clairvaux to act again on a wider stage. Gerard, Bishop of Angoulême, had been employed by several popes as legate for Aquitaine and the adjoining provinces of Spain. When the schism took place, he espoused the cause of Innocent; but that pope having refused to renew his legation, he joined the party of Anacletus, and was rewarded with a fresh commission. In his efforts to engage the support of Henry of England, and of the princes of Spain and Brittany, for Anacletus, he had failed; but he was more successful with William IX., Count of Aquitaine, and, with his consent and assistance, he filled the see of Bourges, and various abbacies and benefices, with his own partisans, men whose sole recommendation was that of noble birth. The learned and devout Geoffrey, Bishop of Chartres, was Pope Innocent's legate, and he now applied to Bernard to join him in reclaiming Count William from the error of his ways. They all met at Parthenay, where Bernard found it easy to engage the Count in the cause of Innocent, as he neither understood the merits of the dispute, nor cared for one competitor more than the other; but he found him resolute not to restore the bishops and abbots ejected by Gerard, protesting that they had deeply offended him, and moreover that he had solemnly sworn never to forgive them. Bernard abandoned all attempt at argument, and repaired to the church to celebrate mass. The Count, as a schismatic and excommunicate, durst not assist at the ceremony, and remained standing outside the door; until Bernard came forth with a stern countenance, and flashing eyes, and an air of solemn command which had in it something more than human.[2] Holding the consecrated host in his hands, he addressed the Count in awful words: "Often have we solicited thee, and thou hast treated us, the servants of GOD, with contempt. Lo, here cometh to thee the Blessed

[1] J. C. Morison, "Life and Times of S. Bernard," pp. 188, 189.
[2] "Jam non se agens ut hominem."—S. Bernard, ii. 38.

Son of the Virgin, He Who is the Head and the LORD of the Church which thou persecutest. Behold thy Judge, at Whose Name every knee is bowed both in heaven and in earth, the Judge into Whose hands thou must one day surrender thy soul. Wilt thou reject Him too, as thou hast rejected His servants?" A breathless silence fell upon the spectators, who, with tears, and with inward prayer, awaited some miraculous sign from heaven. Overpowered by Bernard's enthusiasm, and believing that in his hands at that very moment rested his LORD and Judge, the Count, stricken in every limb, fell suddenly to the ground. His knights hastened to lift him up, but he could neither see nor speak, and foaming at the mouth, he again fell with his face upon the grass. Bernard then approached, touched him with his foot, and bade him arise and receive the command of GOD. "Here," he said, "is the Bishop of Poitiers, whom you have driven from his church; go and be reconciled to him with the kiss of peace. Lead him back to the episcopal throne from which you wrongfully expelled him. Give glory to GOD instead of contumely, and exhort all the separatists in your dominions to return to the unity of the Church." The Count could not speak, but he heard and obeyed; and Bernard's mission was fulfilled. Bishop Gerard of Angoulême, it is true, persisted in his schism; but he was soon afterwards found lifeless in his bed, having died excommunicate, and without the last Sacraments.

Bernard once more returned to Clairvaux; where, in a bower garlanded by wreaths of pease-blossoms, erected in the most secluded angle of the Bright Valley, he gave himself up for hours to meditation on divine things. To the monks he preached daily or almost daily; at morning, noon, or evening, as his own avocations or those of the monks permitted; always with a fervid eloquence and a profound earnestness that touched the souls of his hearers. It was at this time he composed and delivered his famous sermons on the Canticles; making that mystic book the text of his discourse, because he was so deeply convinced of the force of divine love as a motive of action. We have space only for a few brief extracts.

"Remember that no spirit can by itself reach unto our minds, that is, supposing it to have no assistance from our body or its own. No spirit can so mingle with us, and be poured into us, that we become in consequence either good or learned. No angel, no spirit can comprehend me; none can I comprehend in this manner. Even angels themselves cannot seize each other's thoughts, without bodily organs. This prerogative is reserved for the highest, the unbounded Spirit, Who alone, when He imparts knowledge either to angel or man, needs not that we should have ears to hear, or that we should have a mouth to speak. By Himself He is poured in; by Himself He is made manifest. Pure Himself, He is understood by the pure. He alone needs nothing; alone is sufficient to Himself and to all by His sole omnipotent will."

"I must not pass over in silence those spiritual feet of GOD, which, in the first place, it behoves the penitent to kiss in a spiritual manner. I well know your curiosity, which does not willingly allow anything obscure to pass by it; nor indeed is it a contemptible thing to know what are those feet which the Scripture so frequently mentions in connection with GOD. Sometimes He is spoken of as standing on them, as 'We will worship in the place where Thy feet have stood.' Sometimes as walking, as 'I will dwell in them and will walk in them.' Sometimes even as running, as 'He rejoiceth as a strong man to run a race.' If it appear right to the Apostle to call the head of CHRIST GOD, it appears to me as not unnatural to consider His feet as representing Man; one of which I shall name mercy, and the other judgment. Those two words are known to you, and the Scripture repeats them in many places. On those feet, fitly moving under one divine head, CHRIST, born of a woman, He Who was invisible under the law, then made Emmanuel ('GOD with us'), was seen on the earth, and conversed with men."

"As regards creatures devoid of sense and reason, who can doubt that GOD needs them much less? but when they concur in the performance of a good work, then it appears how all things serve Him Who can justly say: 'The world is Mine, and the fulness thereof.' Assuredly, seeing that He knows the means best adapted to ends, He does not in the service of His creatures seek efficacy, but suitability."

The repute of his eloquence as well as of his sanctity drew

men from all parts of Christendom to the leafy shades and secret tranquillity of Clairvaux. There they could find rest from action, and peace in a world of tumult, and by the holy example of the man of GOD could confirm themselves in their feeble endeavour after the truth. They felt emotions never felt before, and were conscious of thoughts such as had never before elevated their minds, while they listened to the flood of glowing words that poured from his hallowed lips, or marked the purity and devotion of his daily life. But for Bernard himself there was neither rest nor tranquillity. The Church depended for its right government on the monk of Clairvaux. And not only was his advice urgently requested by bishops, and abbots and ecclesiastics of all ranks, but by princes and rulers, who desired the benefit of his calm judgment and penetrating sagacity. He was equal to every need. His counsel always suited the occasion, and was always what the applicant had required. He could direct the Head of the Church, reprove an archbishop, or give sound advice to a young abbot. Nowhere does he appear to greater advantage than in his frank and cordial letters to his humbler correspondents, and from this advice to the young abbot we gladly quote some admirable sentences, which show that the Monk of Clairvaux was a man of wide sympathies as well as of masculine intelligence.

"Do not," he says, "put forward the empty excuse of your rawness or want of experience; for barren modesty is more pleasing, nor is that humility praiseworthy which passes the bounds of moderation. Attend to your work; drive out bashfulness by a sense of duty, and act as a master. You are young, yet you are a debtor; you must know you were a debtor from the day you were bound. Will youth be an excuse to a creditor for the loss of his profits? Does the usurer expect no interest at the beginning of his loan? But, say you, I am not sufficient for these things. As if your offering were not accepted from what you have, and not from what you have not! Be prepared to answer for the single talent committed to your charge, and take no thought for the rest. 'If thou hast much, give plenteously; if thou hast little, do thy diligence gladly to give of that little.' For he that is unjust in the least is unjust also in much. Give all, as assuredly you shall pay to the uttermost farthing; but, of a truth, out of what you possess, not out of what you possess not.

"Take heed to give to your words the voice of power. You ask, what is that? It is, that your works harmonize with your words, or rather your words with your works; that you be careful to *do* before you *teach*. It is a most beautiful and salutary order of things that you should first bear the burden you place on others, and learn from yourself how men should be ruled. Otherwise the wise man will mock you, as that lazy one to whom it is labour to lift his hand to his mouth. The Apostle also will reprove you, saying: 'Thou who teachest another, teachest thou not thyself?' ... That speech, also, which is full of life and power, is an example of work, as it makes easy what it speaks persuasively, while it shows that can be done which it advises. Understand, therefore, to the quieting of your conscience, that in these two commandments, *i.e.*, of precept and example, the whole of your duty resides. You, however, if you be wise, will add a third, namely, a zeal for prayer, to complete that treble repetition of the Gospel in reference to 'feeding the sheep.' You will know that no sacrament of that Trinity is in any wise broken by you, if you feed them by word, by example, and by the fruit of holy prayers. Now abideth speech, example, prayer, these three; but the greatest of these is prayer. For although, as has been said, the strength of speech is work, yet prayer wins grace and efficacy for both work and speech."[1]

CHAPTER III.

IN 1137 Bernard was called again to Italy, where the affairs of the Papacy were still in a disturbed condition. Roger II., who had been crowned King of Sicily by Anacletus, continued to support his cause; but otherwise the partisans of the anti-pope had lost heart, and were most of

[1] J. C. Morison, "Life and Times of S. Bernard," pp. 228, 229.

them inclined to a reconciliation with Innocent. They hesitated through various moral and political considerations; either they were afraid of losing the dignities and emoluments to which Anacletus had promoted them, or they held themselves bound by the oath they had taken. Bernard met the former difficulty by promising his good offices with the Pope; to the latter he opposed certain arguments, ingenious rather than conclusive, which proved of sufficient efficacy in cases where the reasoning faculty was aided by the will. Having succeeded so well with many of the antipope's adherents, Bernard resolved to attempt to detach King Roger from the alliance. The Emperor Lothair, with the aid of the fleets of Genoa and Pisa, had wrested from him all his conquests on the mainland, but differences had arisen between him and Innocent, and the Imperial forces were on their homeward march when Bernard entered on his task of mediation. He was met by Roger with a proposal that seemed fair enough : he was willing, he said, to hear both sides, and suggested that their representatives should, in his presence, expound their respective claims, on the understanding that he would acknowledge Innocent's authority if the arguments in his favour preponderated. The offer was accepted. Anacletus put forward Peter of Pisa, who was renowned for his dialectical skill and knowledge of jurisprudence. Bernard appeared for Innocent. The combat took place at Salerno, before Roger and his court. Peter of Pisa opened with a rhetorical speech, in which he exhausted all the resources of his casuistry. When it came to Bernard's turn, he spoke with his usual directness and force :—

"I know, Peter, that you are a wise and learned man, and I would that a better cause and a more honourable business engaged your attention; for had you truth and reason on your side, your eloquence would prevail over every other. As for myself, a rustic, more used to spade and hoe than to public declamations, were it not that the faith requires me to speak, I should observe the silence prescribed by my rule. Charity, however, forces me to speak, inasmuch as Peter, the son of Leo, protected by King Roger, rends and divides that vesture of the LORD which neither the Jew nor the heathen presumed to rend.

There is one Faith, one LORD, one Baptism; neither do we know two Lords, two faiths, two baptisms. To begin from antiquity,—there was but one ark at the time of the Flood; in this ark eight souls were saved; all the rest of the world, as many as were outside the ark, perished. No one will deny that this ark was a type of the Church. Lately, another ark has been built, and as there are now two, one must be false, and must sink in the depths of the sea. If the ark which Peter rules be of GOD, it follows that that in which Innocent governs must perish. Therefore the Eastern Church will perish, and the Western also. France, Germany, Spain, England, and the barbarous countries will perish in the waters. The monastic orders of the Camaldoli, the Carthusians, the Cluniacs, the Cistercians, the Præmonstrants, and innumerable other congregations of servants and handmaidens of the LORD; it is inevitable that they all sink to the bottom of the sea. The bishops, and abbots, and princes of the Church, with millstones fastened to their necks, will plunge headlong into the depths. Roger alone, out of all the lords of the earth, will enter Peter's ark, and while all the rest perish, he alone will be saved. GOD forbid that the religion of the whole world should perish, and that the ambition of Peter, whose life has been such as is known to all, should obtain the kingdom of heaven."

Overcome by Bernard's earnestness, and feeling perhaps a secret conviction that the cause of Anacletus was lost, Peter of Pisa embraced Bernard, yielded to his appeal, and accompanying him to Rome, made his submission to Innocent. Roger did not so readily succumb, being desirous to secure the possession of certain lands which he had occupied in the neighbourhood of Beneventum and Monte Cassino. The schism, however, was virtually at an end; and this through the personal influence of one man. Soon afterwards Anacletus died, and though another anti-pope was set up, and named Victor IV., he speedily resigned the hollow dignity. Repairing by night to Bernard's lodging, he threw off his insignia, abandoned his pretensions, and was led by the Abbot to pay homage to the triumphant Innocent. Thus was once more restored the unity of the Church; the mystical vesture was again made whole. Bernard, to whom this holy and happy work was due, was everywhere honoured as the peacemaker, and could not make his appearance in public without being escorted by vast processions of men and women. With his usual humility he hastened to escape from these grateful demonstrations, and returning to the still shades of Clairvaux, quietly resumed his exposition of the Canticles. (June, 1138.)

A heavy blow soon afterwards fell upon him in the death of his brother Gerard, whose virtues and graces he has commemorated in a funeral sermon of singular and solemn beauty. " My very heart left me," he exclaimed, "when he was taken away, through whom my meditations in GOD were made free. But I did violence to my mind, and I have dissembled until now, lest it should appear that faith was conquered by emotion. While others wept, I, as you perhaps took note, shed not a tear until he was laid in his grave. Clad in my priestly robes, I pronounced with my lips the usual prayers; with my own hands, according to the usual custom, I cast the earthy dust on the body of my brother, soon itself to be resolved into dust. Those who watched me wept, and wondered why I wept not also, for their pity was less for him than for me, for me who had lost him. . . . . But I could not command my grief, though I could control my tears. As it is written : 'I was afflicted, and I kept silence.' But the suppressed anguish struck deeper root within, and has become more bitter, as I perceive, from not being allowed expression."

From domestic sorrows, however, he was called away by the excitement of controversy. Towards the close of the year 1139, his attention was directed to a Compendium of Theology[1] recently issued by the celebrated Abelard, the errors in which were thus summed up by William of S. Thierry :—" 1. That he (Abelard) defines faith as the estimation of things not seen. 2. That he declares the names of FATHER, SON, and HOLY GHOST to be improperly applied to GOD, and that this is a description of the fulness of the Highest Good. 3. That the FATHER is full Power, the SON a certain Power, the HOLY SPIRIT no power. 4. That the HOLY SPIRIT is not the substance of the FATHER and of

[1] His "Introductio ad Theologiam."

the SON, as the SON is of the substance of the FATHER. 5. That the HOLY SPIRIT is the soul of the world. 6. That by free will, without the assistance of grace, we can will and act rightly. 7. That CHRIST did not take flesh and suffer, in order to deliver us from subjection to Satan. 8. That CHRIST, GOD and Man, is not the third Person in the Trinity. 9. That in the Sacrament of the Altar, the form of the former substance remains in the air. 10. That diabolical suggestions are made to men through physic. 11. That from Adam we do not contract the fault of original sin, but its punishment. 12. That there is no sin, except in consenting unto sin, and in the contempt of GOD. 13. That sin is not committed by concupiscence and delectation and ignorance, and what is thus committed, is not sin, but nature." Bernard occupied himself until the Easter of 1140 in examining these allegations, and came to the conclusion that they endangered the purity of the faith once for all delivered to us by the saints. There was, indeed, between himself and Abelard a direct antithesis. As the latter was the very type of intellectual unrest, so was Bernard the type of intellectual repose. Bernard believed, and was content; Abelard believed, and questioned. Bernard surrendered himself to serene meditation; Abelard was the victim of incessant inquiry. The former considered only what was practical; the latter delighted in speculation. The contrast in their lives had been not less marked than in their characters, for Abelard's had been as stormy, passionate, and irregular as Bernard's had been tranquil, harmonious, and orderly. We can therefore readily understand, (as Canon Robertson remarks,[1]) that the active and devout churchman was ready to suspect a man so different from himself as the bold, rhetorical schoolman, who rejoiced in paradoxes and hazardous conjectures. "He felt instinctively that there was danger, not so much in this or that individual point of his teaching, as in the general character of a method which seemed likely to imperil the orthodoxy of the Church." It was the natural dread of the dogmatic theologian for the theological speculator and free inquirer.

Bernard, therefore, summoned all his powers, all his

[1] Robertson, "History of the Christian Church," v. 117.

energies to denounce the sacrilegious disturber of the Church's peace. He addressed impassioned appeals to the Pope, and Cardinals, against his several monstrous errors and his general hostility to the established faith. He agreed to confront him openly[1] at a council which the Archbishop of Sens had summoned to meet in his archiepiscopal city, on the occasion of the translation of the relics of its patron-saint, (Whitsuntide, 1140.) The King of France was present, and a great number of bishops and ecclesiastics; and thither went Abelard with a long retinue of disciples, and Bernard attended only by two or three monks. The two foremost men of the age, the representatives of the two great antagonistic schools of thought, stood face to face, and began that obstinate contention between Religion and Science, which even in our own time has not come to a termination. The first day of the council was occupied in the inspection and adoration of the sacred relics. On the second the question of Abelard's heresies was taken up. The king, girt round by his knights and nobles, and the Archbishop of Sens, attended by his suffragans, in full pontifical pomp, met in S. Stephen's Church. Between the double row of warriors and courtiers, bishops, priests, and monks, the famous scholar strode into the centre of the sacred building. There, opposite to him, in a pulpit, which existed down to the epoch of the French Revolution, stood the Abbot of Clairvaux, the one man whose influence extended over a wider world than his own. He held in his hand the incriminated book of Abelard, and read, or caused to be read, the passages which he had marked as erroneous and dangerous. The reading had scarcely begun when Abelard, discouraged, it is supposed, by the hostile faces around him, or sensible of the overwhelming influence of his adversary, rose suddenly, and to the disappointment and surprise of the audience, appealed to the Pope. Such an appeal, before sentence, was unusual and contrary to the law of the Church; but the bishops remembered the depth of the Papal jealousy, and forbore to excite a prejudice in favour of the appellant by condemning his person. They continued,

[1] At first, however, with reluctance, in the belief that he was no competent antagonist for a skilled dialectitian like Abelard, who had been "a man of war from his youth."

however, to discuss the propositions imputed to him, and fourteen out of the seventeen they pronounced heretical and false.[1] This condemnation they reported to the Pope, requesting him to confirm it, and to prohibit Abelard from teaching; and Bernard wrote to the Pope and the Cardinals in similar terms. "His yet unpractised hearers," he says, "mere tyros, but newly weaned from the milk of logic, and as yet scarcely capable of receiving even the elements of the faith, he leads into the mysteries of the Holy Trinity, to that which, shrouded in darkness, hides itself from human eyes; and not only in the schools, but in the public places, and in the streets, the Catholic faith, the conception of the Virgin, the sacrament of the Altar, the incomprehensible mystery of the Trinity, are made subjects for disputation, not for the learned alone, but for boys, for ignorant men, and for fools. He has taken measures also for transmitting his poisonous doctrines to posterity, to the injury of all future generations. The faith of the simple-minded is derided; the highest themes are degraded by bold and audacious questions; and our fathers are held up to laughter, and contempt, because they considered it wiser to dismiss these questions than to attempt their solution. There are no bounds to the presumption of human reason; it leaves nothing to faith,

---

[1] Berenger of Poitiers, in his "Apology for Abelard," draws an amusing satirical picture of the conclave at Sens. It must not, of course, be accepted as even approximating to the truth. He treats Bernard as "a mere idol of the multitude, as a man gifted with a plentiful flow of words, but destitute of liberal culture and of solid abilities; as one who by the solemnity of his manner imposed the tritest truisms on his votaries as if they were profound oracles. He ridicules his reputation for miraculous power; he tells him that his proceedings against Abelard were prompted by a spirit of bigotry, jealousy, and vindictiveness, rendered more odious by his professions of sanctity and charity. Of the opinions imputed to his master, he maintains that some were never held by Abelard, and that the rest, if rightly interpreted, are true and catholic. The book, he says, was brought under consideration at Sens when the bishops had dined, and was read amidst their jests and laughter, while the wine was doing its work on them. Any expression which was above their understanding excited their rage and curses. As the reading went on, one after another became drowsy; and when they were asked whether they condemned his doctrines, they answered in their sleep without being able fully to pronounce their words."—Robertson, *History of the Christian Church*, v. 119.

and wills that men should not see anything through a glass darkly, but all things face to face. Better had it been for him if, in accordance with the title of his work," (his treatise on Ethics entitled 'Nosce Teipsum,') "he had *known himself:* for he treats of sin and virtue without moral rectitude; of the sacraments of the Church without faith; of the mystery of the Trinity without simplicity, and without unction."

Abelard found no favour at Rome. At Lyons, when on his way thither, he was met with the information that Innocent, without waiting for his defence, had condemned him absolutely, and sentenced him to seclusion in a monastery. In this sore strait he found a good Samaritan in the person of Peter, Abbot of Cluny, who, while he abhorred Abelard's heresies, admired his genius, respected his frankness, and pitied his misfortunes. He offered him an asylum at Cluny, which was gladly accepted; and there, with the sanction of the Pope, Abelard spent the few remaining years of his stormy life in repose. Through the good offices of the Abbots of Cluny and Citeaux he was reconciled to Bernard, and in a confession which he drew up, he expressed his acceptance of the Catholic faith, and disowned some of the doctrines imputed to him, "the words in part, and the meaning altogether." He died in 1142.

An eloquent writer, referring to Bernard's various works, pronounces him to be one of the great active minds of his age; commanding kings, compelling nations, swaying the minds of all with whom he came in contact; in a word, one of the statesmen of history. And certain it is that, had he never lived, the twelfth century, so far as we can judge, would have assumed a totally different aspect. It is now the fashion with the modern philosophical school to underrate the influence of a great man upon his age; yet the reality and extent of that influence is demonstrated by history itself. No doubt the power of a great man largely consists in this, that he represents and embodies the tendencies, intellectual and moral, of his time, and is its exponent as well as its director. Such was the case with S. Bernard, in whom we see the highest manifestation of the great need of the twelfth century, the need of a higher spiritual life, the need of a profounder recognition of the unstability of things human and the permanency of things divine. But while Bernard was a statesman, a ruler of men, an adviser of kings and princes, he was also, and pre-eminently, a monk. " He was, by intuition and inclination, a prayerful monk, doubtful and anxious about the state of his soul, striving to work out his salvation with fear and trembling here on earth. The highest good he knew of, the ideal of Christian faith as he had been taught it—this was what inflamed his heart, nerved his will, and braced his energies of mind and body to the extremest tension. To him and to his contemporaries this ideal was realised in the life of a pious monk. And a pious monk it was his desire above all things to be; that he failed to obtain the perfection at which he aimed, no one would have been more ready to acknowledge than himself. But that he also succeeded better than most, is proved by the almost concurrent testimony of his own and after ages."[1]

In a sketch like the present, however, we must necessarily regard him chiefly in those aspects of his character with which history deals; but we may record that, in 1142, he pronounced against the dogma of the Immaculate Conception of the Virgin, a dogma which has recently been accepted by the Roman Church as an article of faith. In the following year his immense influence was exerted in effecting a reconciliation between Louis VII. of France and Thibaut, Count of Champagne; and in procuring the deposition, by Pope Eugenius III.,[2] of Archbishop William of York, whom he considered to have been wrongfully intruded into that see. We pass on to consider the illustrious Abbot in the last great work of his laborious life, in the part which he had in initiating and organising the Second Crusade. It was in December, 1144, that Zenghis, the Mohammedan prince of Mosul and Aleppo, made himself master of the Christian city of Edessa. Its capture was followed by a terrible massacre of the Christian inhabitants, which was checked by the command of Zenghis, and a number of captives were sold as slaves. Shortly afterwards Zenghis was assassinated; and during the absence of his son Noureddin, the Christians recovered Edessa through an agreement with the Armenian inhabitants. But they had held it

[1] J. C. Morison, " Life and Times of S. Bernard," pp. 367, 368.
[2] Eugenius III. was consecrated Pope on the 18th of February, 1145.

only a few days, when Noureddin invested it with an overwhelming force, captured it with great slaughter, and after plundering it of everything valuable, razed it to the ground. That the city of King Abgarus, who was supposed to have been the honoured recipient of a letter from the SAVIOUR Himself; the city where the miraculously-impressed image of the SAVIOUR's countenance had for centuries been preserved, and had acted as a talisman and safeguard against the attacks of the infidel; that the city where the Apostle S. Thaddeus had preached, and where his remains and those of S. Thomas, the Apostle of the Indies, reposed in their consecrated shrines; that the city where the lamp of Christianity had burned with glorious lustre when all the rest of Syria lay in the darkness of Mohammedanism; that this city of precious memories and associations should have fallen into the hands of unbelievers, was a sore grief and trouble to Western Christendom. Moreover, the warriors of the Crescent were pressing forward with ruthless vigour, and the Latins, unless they were speedily succoured, would soon be driven out of the Holy Land. In these circumstances, Pope Eugenius resolved upon a new Crusade; and on the 1st of December, 1145, he addressed to the King, nobles, and people of France, a letter, calling upon them to take up the Cross, and engage in a Holy War.[1] Louis VII., then in his twenty-second year, was by no means indisposed to gratify the Pope's wishes. The capture of Vitry, three years before, when a terrible massacre of the innocent population had taken place, rested heavily on his conscience. He felt himself partly bound by a promise which his brother Philip had been prevented from fulfilling; and, doubtlessly, he was also stimulated by a desire to emulate the achievements and rival the renown of the heroes of the First Crusade. At the Christmas festival of 1145, he summoned to

---

[1] To those who responded to his appeal the Pope offered the same privileges which Urban II. had bestowed upon the first Crusaders: remission of sins for all directly engaged in the expedition; the protection of the Church for their families and property; no suits were to be brought against them until their return; those who were in debt were released from payment of interest; while the possessors of fiefs were allowed to pledge them in order to raise money for defraying the costs of the war.—Robertson, v. 132.

Bourges his knights and nobles, and the dignitaries of the Church, and declared to them his wish to engage in the recovery of the Holy Land from the Infidel. The Bishop of Langres, who had recently returned from Palestine, was present, and drew a graphic picture of the miseries which the Christians were suffering at the hands of their Moslem oppressors. Louis asked Bernard for his counsel and guidance; but was informed that the wishes of the Holy See must first be ascertained. The Pope replied by a long letter of encouragement and exhortation, and delegated to Bernard the office of preaching the Second Crusade. This preliminary settled, the King summoned a general meeting of nobles and prelates, knights and monks, at Vezelin for the following Easter. As neither the market-place nor the abbey church could hold the multitude that assembled, they were ranged along the declivity of the hill which overlooks the valley of the Eure; while on the summit was raised a platform of wood for the reception of Bernard and the King. Pale, worn with disease and the unresting toil of many years, the Monk stood there, with every eye riveted upon him; the enthusiasm which possessed him being visible in the flashing glances and the glow that irradiated the furrowed countenance. His fiery eloquence swayed the thousands before him to his will. Enthusiastic shouts arose of "The Cross! the Cross!" and Bernard scattered among the people a large heap of crosses which had been brought for the purpose. When these were exhausted, he tore up his monk's cowl to satisfy the eager hands stretched towards him; and so long as he remained in the town he did nothing but make crosses.

At Chartres, whither he next repaired, he was named leader of the Crusade; but he was too sagacious not to know his unfitness for a military post,[1] and he could not but remember the lamentable failure of Peter the Hermit. He continued, however, with a zeal and devotion which triumphed over disease, to preach a Holy War throughout France and a great part of Germany. His success was without bounds. Wherever he went, thousands followed him, singing and praying; at Friburg, Basle, Constance,

[1] "There is more need in the Holy Land," he said, "of fighting soldiers than of chanting monks."

Spires, Cologne, Frankfort, Mayence. The whole male population seemed prepared to assume the cross. Cities and castles were emptied; and Bernard tells us that the old prophecy of "seven women taking hold of one man" was almost fulfilled among those who remained at home.[1] At Frankfort, where he endeavoured to persuade the Emperor Conrad III. to join the expedition, Bernard nearly lost his life in the press. Conrad did his best to keep back the excited, eager crowd, but finding the effort too much for him, he threw aside his cloak, seized the abbot in his robust arms, and conveyed him to a place of safety.

The renown of Bernard, and his reputation for working miracles, had spread all over Germany; and as he ascended the Rhine, thousands flocked to greet him, bringing with them the lame, and sick, and blind, that he might heal them. He disavowed all credit on account of his miracles, but he believed in their reality, and regarded them as confirming his mission; so that his enthusiasm was raised to the highest degree, as was that of the crowds who waited upon him. The Bishop of Constance kept a diary of what he saw with his own eyes: every day, he says, the man of GOD wrought *some* miracles, and on occasions as many as twenty. A sufferer was brought to him; he made the sign of the Cross over the part affected, and the cure was complete. The church bells rang full merrily; and a chorus of voices was heard singing:—" CHRIST, have mercy on us; *Kyrie eleison*, all the saints help us." At Cambray, a boy, deaf and dumb from his mother's womb, sat down beside the bishop. The bishop presented him to S. Bernard, and in the self-same hour he both spoke and heard. "A boy blind from his birth, whose eyes were covered with a white substance,—if indeed, eyes they could be called, which had neither colour, nor vision, nor even so much as the usual cavity,—received his sight from the imposition of Bernard's hand. We ascertained the fact," says the Bishop, "by numerous proofs, hardly believing our senses, that in such eyes as his any sight could reside."

" On another day we came to Molesme, the monastery

---

[1] "Vacuantur urbes et castella, et pene jam non inveniunt quem apprehendant septem mulieres virum unum, adeo ubique viduæ vivis remanent viris."—Epist. 247.

whence went forth those of our fathers who founded the order of Citeaux. It was on Wednesday, and the monks received the man of GOD with great devotion. When he was seated in the Guest-house, a certain man, blind with one eye, came in, and kneeling, begged his mercy. With his holy fingers Bernard made the sign of the cross, and touched the blind eye, and immediately it received sight, and the man returned thanks to GOD. About an hour afterwards, as dusk came on, the holy man went out to lay hands on the sick who were waiting at the door. The first to be cured was a boy blind with the right eye, who, on closing the left eye, with which alone he had seen previously, discerned all things clearly, and told at once what anything was which we showed to him. And again, at the same place, a little girl who had a weakness in the feet, and had been lame from her birth, was healed by the imposition of hands: and her mother rejoiced abundantly that now, for the first time, she saw the child standing and walking."[1]

As in the throe of excitement and fanaticism preceding the First Crusade, so again in the tumultuous preparation for the Second, the Jews became the victims of a sanguinary persecution, and their slaughter was openly advised by an ignorant monk, named Rudolf. With a courageous tolerance, worthy of his noble character, Bernard set himself to stay the outbreak of cruelty, and openly withstood the monk Rudolf at Mayence. He summoned him to his presence, rebuked him for his evil conduct, and finally persuaded him to return to his monastery. But the people of Mayence took umbrage at the departure of their favourite, and at Bernard's interposition in behalf of the Jews. They threatened to rise in revolt against him. Instead of being surrounded, as was usually the case, by an admiring and reverential crowd, he was hemmed in by a mob of angry fanatics. His calm intrepidity, however, did not desert him, and that wonderfully eloquent voice of his soothed them into submissive penitence.

As Bernard was ignorant of German, his discourses were interpreted to the multitude. They lost, no doubt, in the process of translation; still such was their effect, when emphasized by his gestures, his looks, his very tones, that

[1] S. Bernard, Op., ii., 1858—9, transl. by Morison.

every heart was touched; and even the phlegmatic Germans beat their breasts, and shed tears, and tore the saint's clothes in order that they might take up the cross. At Spires he met again with the Emperor Conrad (December 27,) and pressed upon him so earnestly the duty of rescuing the Holy Sepulchre from the infidels, that he undertook to consult his advisers, and to give an answer on the morrow. Bernard proceeded to celebrate mass, and the Divine Spirit began to stimulate him, so that he declared (though no one had asked him) that it was better not to pass the day without a sermon. He spoke with his wonted fervour and directness; and towards the close, turning suddenly towards the Emperor, addressed him in a powerful apostrophe. He represented him as standing before the judgment-seat, and as called by CHRIST to give an account for all the benefits he had received. Then, expatiating on the pomp and circumstances of royalty, he enumerated all the Emperor's riches, dignities, possessions, councillors, intellectual gifts, and bodily strength. The "miracle of miracles," as Bernard styles it, was wrought. "Never," as quaint old Fuller says, "could so much steel have been drawn into the East, had not this good man's persuasions been the loadstone." The Emperor, overpowered by the contrast between what GOD had done for him and he had *not* done for GOD, exclaimed, with tears :—" I acknowledge the gifts of the Divine favour; neither in the future shall I be found ungrateful for them. I am prepared to serve Him, seeing that CHRIST has thus admonished me." The Emperor's words drew forth an exultant shout from the crowd; and Bernard, from the high altar, investing him with the cross, gave him the standard which he was to bear at the head of the warriors of Christendom.

Thus Louis of France and Conrad of Germany became leaders of the Second Crusade.

CHAPTER IV.

IT is not within our province to trace the history of the Second Crusade. In this, her new contest with Asia, Europe was again unsuccessful; and of the four hundred thousand warriors who followed Louis and Conrad to the field of war, few returned to their native lands. The disastrous result of an enterprise undertaken by Bernard's advice not unnaturally proved unfavourable to his influence and reputation. He was accused as the author of all the calamities it had involved. He had preached it, had urged men to join in it, had foretold its success: was he not a false prophet? His reply was conclusive:—No, for he had announced that it was to be undertaken as a work of GOD, whereas the princes and knights who had engaged in it had thought only of their own glory, had been guilty of the most shameful vices, had proved themselves ignorant of military art and the management of men, and had shown by their scandalous lives that they were unworthy of being used as instruments in GOD's service. In the apologetic letter or defence, which he addressed to Pope Eugenius, he said:—"Let us call to mind GOD's dealings of old time, if perchance we may find consolation in them. I speak of things of which none are ignorant, yet which no one will choose to know; for thus it is with the heart of man, that what he knoweth when he hath no need of it, he forgetteth when it might be useful to him. Moses, when he brought his people out of Egypt, promised them a better land; for otherwise that earthly-minded people would not have followed him. He brought them out there, but to the *promised* land he brought them not; and yet the last and unlooked for result is not to be ascribed to the rashness of the leader, who acted by GOD's command, and through GOD's assistance, He confirming the work by miracle. But you will say it was a stiff-necked people, rebelling against the LORD and His servant Moses. Yea, verily, they *were* unbelieving and rebellious. But what are these men? Ask themselves."

The latter years of Bernard's life were devoted, though

with many interruptions, to the completion of his chief literary work, *De Consideratione*, "The Book of Consideration," which he addressed to his friend and disciple, Pope Eugenius.[1] It was designed to place before him a graphic description of his high vocation as the follower of S. Peter; to indicate the abuses and corruptions that had gradually crept into the Papal system; to exhort him to root them out, and to rely upon the spiritual influence of the Papacy alone. It also aimed to withdraw his mind from earthly things by an elaborate analysis of the means through which the soul may attain to the loftiest elevation of which it is capable. Bernard complains of the manifold engagements which absorbed the time of the Popes; of their being employed to decide upon suits which were rather secular than ecclesiastical, and fell under the laws of Justinian rather than under those of CHRIST. Such occupations prevented the Pope from investigating the truth and meditating upon holy things; and Bernard advised him to get rid of them as far as possible by devolving some part of his jurisdiction upon others, by cutting short the speeches and artifices of lawyers, and by discouraging unnecessary and trivial appeals to Rome. With all his old eloquence he pointed out the dangers of pride and love of rule, and he declared that the splendour of the Papacy was copied, not from S. Peter, but from Constantine; that the Roman Church ought not to be the mistress of other churches, but their mother; the Pope, not the lord of other bishops, but their brother. He strongly condemned the frequent exemption of abbots from episcopal rule, and of bishops from obedience to their metropolitan. In language as energetic as was afterwards used by the hottest Reformer he condemned the greed, profligacy, and arrogance of the Papal Court. He warned Eugenius to exercise great care in his choice of officials and confidants, to cultivate justice and impartiality, and to advance resolutely, though gradually, towards a reformation of the prevalent abuses.[2] In this book, the saint of Clairvaux, as Robertson remarks, by the unreserved plainness of his language and by the weight of his authority, supplied a potent weapon which, from age to age, was continually employed

[1] It was written at the Pope's request.
[2] Robertson, "History of the Christian Church," ii. 155—157.

by those who desired to reform the Church and the court of Rome. Luther spoke of it as "omni pontifici memoriter noscendus." In many respects it anticipated Luther, and had succeeding Popes acted on its advice and warnings, Luther's work might not have been needed, or at all events would have been more limited in its scope and less destructive in its effect. Indeed (says Morison), to any who can look below the surface, to any who can see through the varying costume which each successive age throws over the deeper characteristics of human nature, there will appear much in the Abbot of Clairvaux to remind them of the great Saxon Reformer. The same ardour, not to say hastiness of temper; the same bold and manly disregard of consequences in denouncing sin and falsehood; the same heroic intrepidity; the same real humility and gentleness under all their divine wrath.

Passing over Bernard's repression of certain heresies which arose in Languedoc, and his confutation of Gilbert de la Poirée, Bishop of Poitiers, who, following in the steps of Abelard, wandered into the paths of speculative inquiry, and broached heterodox views of the Trinity, we come to the close of our brief record. For some time the state of the saint's health had been daily growing more precarious. Such was the debilitated condition of his stomach that he could take no solid food, and even liquids gave him pain. He slept little; his legs and feet were enormously swollen; and he suffered from a distressing physical weakness, which confined him almost entirely to his bed. Yet his mind retained its vigour; he carried on an extensive correspondence; and his exhortations to his monks were numerous and earnest. With that practical broad sympathy which was one of the marked features of his character, he rose from his sick bed, and proceeded on a painful journey to Metz, to effect a settlement of the sanguinary contention between its burghers and the nobles of the country. It was fitting that the last public appearance of this zealous lover of peace and preacher of charity should be as a peace-maker and a benefactor. But on his return his disease attacked him with redoubled violence, and every day brought him nearer to the grave. He was not unwilling that it should be so. He felt that his work in life was done, and a sense of loneliness came upon him as one by one his friends preceded him; Suger first (1151),—then Count Thibaut of Champagne (1152),—and, lastly, his beloved disciple, Pope Eugenius (July, 1153). A slight improvement in his condition taking place, which he attributed with his usual lively faith to the prayers of his sorrowful monks, he exclaimed :— "Why do you thus detain a miserable man? You are the stronger, you prevail against me. Spare me, spare me, let me depart." Gradually he lost his interest in public affairs; that intellect, which for a quarter of a century, had made its mark upon Europe, sank into repose. When the Bishop of Langres came to visit him, he found that the dying saint could not give his attention to any secular concerns. " Marvel not," said Bernard; "for clearly I am not of this world."[1]

His friends, and the community which he had governed with so much gentle wisdom, were loth to say farewell, and with tears and prayers implored him not to leave them. Their deep affliction touched him, and for a moment he seemed to hesitate. Only for a moment. Lifting up his dove-like eyes,[2] he said :—" Thy will be done."

And so he passed away, at the age of sixty-three, in the year 1153, on the 20th of August; "ascending," in the words of a contemporary chronicler, " from the Bright Valley to the Mount of Eternal Brightness." He was buried without ostentation in the conventual church, some relics of S. Thaddeus, which had been recently brought from Jerusalem, being laid, as he had desired, upon his breast. In 1174 he was admitted by Pope Alexander III. to the honour of canonization; and in 1830 Pope Pius VIII. confirmed to him the title of " Doctor."

[1] " Tunc vero ipse flens cum flentibus."—Vit. Bern., p. 1179.
[2] "Columbinos oculos." All the chroniclers refer to the "dove-like simplicity and angelic purity" which shone in his eyes. S. Bernard was above the middle stature, of a singularly meagre frame, of a clear and fresh complexion, with a beard slightly inclining to red.

S. FRANCIS OF ASSISI:

FOUNDER OF THE FRANCISCANS.

"The wondrous life
Of the meek man of GOD . . .
Seraphic all
In fervency."
DANTE. *Parad.* xi. 25.

[*Authorities*:—The contemporary biographies, by Cardinal Bonaventura, Thomas of Celano, and the *Tres Socii* (Three Companions, Fra Ruffino, Fra Leo, and Fra Angelo,) will be found in the Bollandist *Acta Sanctorum*. Of next importance are the "Annals of the Order," by Lucas Wadding. Recently, the career and character of Francis have been exhaustively treated by Karl Hase, in his "Franz von Assisi." See also Dean Milman's "History of Latin Christianity," and Canon Robertson's "History of the Christian Church," as well as Mrs. Oliphant's eloquent and sympathetic biography, "Francis of Assisi," in which, however, she makes too much use of her skill as a novelist. Reference may also be made to Montalembert's "Vie de S. Elisabeth d'Hongrie," and Ozanam's "Les Poëtes Franciscains," Prof. Brewer, "Monumenta Franciscana"(both Series,) and Hallam, "Middle Ages."]

S. FRANCIS OF ASSISI.

CHAPTER I.

A WELL-TO-DO merchant of Assisi, one of the Bernardini, returning from a journey in France to his native town, some time in the summer of 1182, found that, during his absence, a son had been born to him, whom his mother had named Giovanni. Out of affection for the country in which he made his wealth, Bernardino caused the babe to be baptised by the name of Francesco. According to the biographers, his birth had been predicted by the Erythrean Sibyl, and typified in the Old Testament. In his Apocalypse S. John had described him as "an angel ascending from the east ;" he and S. Dominic were the two staves, "Beauty and Bands," figured in the prophecy of Zechariah; and to increase the similarities between his nativity and that of our LORD, it is said that his mother, at the instigation of an unknown visitor, removed to a stable shortly before she gave birth to the marvellous child.

Francesco, or Francis, received the rudiments of education from the clergy of the parish of S. Giorgio ; that is, he learned a little Latin, and more French, the Provençal French in which the troubadours wrote their love-songs. Speedily called to assist his father in his trade, which in those days was not considered dishonourable, Francis entered into it with sufficient energy; but he had all a young man's love of gaiety and splendour, of handsome clothes, of music and song, and merry friends. To those friends he gave gorgeous banquets, and the wooded shades of Umbria resounded with their light laughter. But there was nothing sinful in his merriment; it was simply the exuberance of a happy youth; and it was observed that at times a strain of pensiveness entered into it; he seemed suddenly to pause and ask himself that question which at one time or other agitates the heart of each of us, Is life worth living? It was in this mood that he would have his fine clothes lined with stuff of the coarsest texture, compounding, as it were, with his conscience for indulging in worldly things which a lofty spirit ought to despise. He was very generous to the poor; and no beggar ever asked him for alms in vain: so that when the neighbours churlishly said of him, that he was more like the son of a prince than Pietro Bernardino's son, his mother was not without justification for answering:—"If he lives like the son of a prince now, he shall hereafter be a child of GOD."

In one of the petty wars which so frequently broke out between Perugia and Assisi, Francis, bravely fighting in defence of his city, was taken prisoner, and lay in captivity for a twelvemonth.[1] His natural buoyancy served him well during this dreary period; and he sustained the courage of his companions in misfortune by his constant air of cheerfulness and unselfishness of temper. (A.D. 1206.) Returning to Assisi, he resumed his butterfly life, winning the golden opinions of the citizens, in spite of themselves, by his many graces of character. At the age of twenty-five, however, he was seized with a severe illness, which proved to be the turning-point of his career. He recovered from it to look at life and the world and nature with different eyes; to see them from a different view-point; to feel that there were mysteries in his own being of which he had hitherto been unconscious. His former pursuits grew distasteful; he cared neither for pleasure nor money-making; he wanted a higher aim, a loftier purpose. Looking about for a new vocation, he bethought himself of being a soldier; the activity of the career would divert his thoughts; of its chances he might avail himself to make a reputation. At that time, a citizen of Assisi was levying a company of adventurers to march with him into Apulia, to support the claim of Count Gauthier de

[1] Hase, *Franz v. Assisi*, p. 21; Tres Socii (in *Acta SS.*) p. 4.

Brienne, "the gentle count," to the throne of Sicily. The thought occurred to Francis that he would do well to enlist under this banner. While revolving it in his mind, he went out one day, again ruffling it in his brave attire, and fell in with a certain soldier of honour and courage, but poor and miserably clad. His generous ardour was aroused immediately; he stripped himself of his bravery, and with sympathetic hands forced it upon the poor soldier, thus discharging a double office of pity by clothing the shame of a noble cavalier and relieving a poor man's penury.

That same night Francis had a vision, in which a stately palace rose before him; a stately palace with a capacious armoury; and in that armoury, every kind of weapon, battle-axe, and sword, and spear, but each marked with the sign of the cross; while 'all the walls were bright with banners and military trophies. For whom could this great place of arms be prepared? A voice answered him:—"For thee and for thy soldiers." Then, at dawn of day, Francis sprang from his couch: blithe of heart, for had not GOD shown him the way he was to go? He quickly donned his armour, and mounted his horse, and like Don Quixote went forth to defend the right and sustain the oppressed. As he rode through the streets, his fellow-citizens looked upon the light that shone over his countenance, and asked him what good fortune had befallen him. "I shall yet be a great prince," he answered, and he spurred his horse, set his lance at rest, and with his sword by his side, crossed the threshold of the unknown. Modern sceptics will deride this young enthusiast for his confident belief that GOD had deigned to point out to him his fit career. The nineteenth century is, as we well know, far in advance, intellectually as materially, of the twelfth; and young men, now-a-days, are slow to believe in direct communion with GOD, or indeed, in the Divine intervention; but are they happier, or do they do greater things, than Francis of Assisi?

Over hill and plain rode the young warrior until he reached Spoleto. There he again fell ill; and in one of his feverish visions he became aware that a voice was questioning him. "Francis," it asked, "which can do the greater good? the Master or the servant?" He seems to have felt no alarm at the strange interruption of his sleep, but to have answered calmly:—"Certes, the Master." "Why dost thou leave the Master for the servant, the Prince for his follower?" "LORD, what wilt Thou have me do?" "Return to thy country," said the voice, "and then it will be told thee what to do; for thou hast mistaken the interpretation of the vision with which GOD favoured His creature." We may well suppose that Francis underwent a sharp struggle before he could make up his mind to obey this mysterious command. It was no light thing for a young cavalier to abandon his hopes, to put aside his high ambition, and, after setting forth so proudly, with the eyes of a whole community upon him, to return without honour won, without bringing back a token from even one foughten field. But he humbled himself, and turned his horse's head towards Assisi, and rode homeward over hill and plain, to take up his place once more in his father's household. Doubtless this was hard to bear; but harder still the pause, the inaction, the suspense that followed. Not at once was he told "what to do." And so he resumed his old avocations, and joined again in his old pleasures; though not with the old energy in the one case, nor the old delight in the other. Sometimes he broke out into an excess of gaiety; more often he was grave, silent, self-absorbed. On a certain occasion, after presiding over a merry revel, he sallied forth, with his companions, into the hush and calm of the starry night. Immediately he was silent, he who had until then been loudest of laughter and wildest of jest. "What ails thee, Francesco?" cried one of his friends, struck by the sudden change. "He is thinking of a wife!" exclaimed another, jovially. "Ay," said Francesco, "of a wife nobler, fairer, richer than any your imagination can conceive." The biographers who relate this incident cannot agree whether the wife thus mystically hinted at was Religion or Poverty. It was probably the latter; for from his earliest years he had strongly, and one may almost say strangely, sympathized with the poor; had been deeply, painfully struck by the width of the gulf between them and those of his own position. And especially had he felt and sorrowed for those poorest of the poor, those most miserable of GOD'S creatures, the leprosy-stricken, who were then regarded with a dread and an abhorrence rising almost to frenzy. So Francesco chose

Poverty as his bride, and his life will show us that he found in her an exceeding beauty and an inexhaustible treasure.

Meanwhile, he was groping about as in a mist to discover the true landmarks of his course. It was by slow and gradual stages that GOD led him into his destined vocation. One day, while out riding, he met a leper. Remembering that if he would be a soldier of CHRIST he must first conquer himself, he dismounted from his horse, and overcoming the first instinctive impulse of aversion, went forward to embrace the sufferer; when he stretched out his hand for alms, he kissed it, filled it with money, and blessed him. Again he threw himself in the saddle, and continued his journey; but looking back over the plain, what was his astonishment!—the leper had disappeared. Then he became aware that the supposed leper was CHRIST, Who had thus tested the young man's faith.[1]

Shortly afterwards he went to Rome on his father's business, and wandering into S. Peter's, was struck with the smallness of the offerings laid upon its altars. Flaming up with generous indignation, he flung his purse in "at the window,"—that is, in at the opening of one of the side chapels,—so that it fell upon the pavement with a crash, to the great amazement of priests and worshippers. Rapidly retiring, he stepped forth into the piazza, fevered with thoughts which his impetuous brain could not stay to analyse. There he saw the beggars sitting in the sun and waiting for the alms of the devout,—as they sit and wait to this day,—and again smitten by the sharp contrast between things as they were and as they should be, he despoiled himself of his costly garments, and exchanged them for a beggar's rags; and in these he sat upon the great broad steps of the cathedral, and begged until evening came.

From this time he would seem to have dedicated himself and his life to the Cross, to have united the religion of faith with the religion of good works. The life of our LORD made a profound impression upon his imagination, and all his hopes, and desires, and aspirations centred in the possibility of a close and real imitation of it. He was so penetrated by a sense of the humility of CHRIST, His marvellous generosity, His exquisite tenderness, His unbounded love,

[1] Bonaventura, *Vit. S. Francisci.*

that he could never withdraw himself from the contemplation of a subject which he found to be inexhaustible. He realized every incident in that sublime history as few of the most ardent souls have realized it; was present, so to speak, at His birth in the manger, at His teaching in the Temple, at His raising of Lazarus from the grave-sleep, at His agony in the night-shadows of Gethsemane, at His suffering on "the bitter tree," at His resurrection from the new sepulchre in the rock, and at that last awful scene when He ascended into Heaven to sit down on the right hand of GOD the FATHER Almighty. It was to him no cold form of words, no narrative to be criticised and harmonised, but a great grand LIFE, to be admired, adored, loved, and imitated.

Kneeling one day in the lonely ruins of the Church of S. Damian, to Francis a voice spake and said: "Francis, seest thou not the shattered condition of My House? Go then, and restore it for Me." "With a glad heart, dear LORD," answered Francis, thankful that at last a mission was vouchsafed unto him, and seeing not that the House, the Temple for which CHRIST died was no sanctuary "built with hands," but the Holy Catholic and Apostolic Church.

Seeking out the priest who had charge of the mouldering fane, he gave him all the money he had in his purse, that he might keep a lamp perpetually burning at the foot of the image of CHRIST Crucified. Then he hastened home to raise funds sufficient for the due execution of the work entrusted to him. Without pausing to consider the rights of property, or it may be in a belief that he was justly entitled to a share of his father's wealth, he loaded his horse with as many bales of cloth as he could carry, started for the fair of Foligno, and there disposed of the goods and his horse also. With eager feet he returned to Assisi, hastened to S. Damian's, and placed the money in the priest's hands. Astonished at the amount, the priest questioned him how he came by it; and on hearing the particulars, declined to receive what it was not in the donor's right to give. He consented, however, to allow the young man, who was disappointed, grieved, and ashamed, a prey to conflicting emotions, to remain with him.

Meanwhile, his father, having discovered his loss, was not unnaturally indignant, and, accompanied by his neighbours, proceeded to S. Damian's to recover both his money and his son. Francis took refuge in a dark cave or cellar, where for several days he lingered in want and misery. At length he resolved to confront his father; and pursued by the populace with threats, and jeers, and even stones, he, who had once been their brilliant favourite, ragged and exhausted, crawled along the streets to his home. He met with a cold welcome. Pietro Bernadone, availing himself of the absolute authority with which the Italian law armed the parent, shut him up in a prison, until, one day, during the father's absence, his mother's fond heart went out towards him, and she loosed his fetters, and set him free. The result was that both father and son carried their complaint to the Bishop of Assisi, who advised Francis to restore the money, to have faith in GOD, and rest confident that He would supply him with all that was necessary for the work of His Church. Restore the money! ay, that he would; and to the father who had hunted him down with vengeance rather than justice, he would restore everything that he could pretend to claim, even the clothes he wore. He threw off his garments as he spoke, and it was then seen that, unknown to any one, he had been wearing a hair-shirt, as an act of self-inflicted penance. "I call all present to witness," he said, "that up to this time I have reverenced Pietro Bernadone as my father, but henceforth I am the servant of GOD. I have given back to him the money which he sought with so much violence, and even the clothes I have had from him. Henceforth I will no more say, 'My father Pietro Bernadone,' but, 'My FATHER Which art in Heaven.'" Deeply moved, the Bishop covered the young man's nakedness with his own episcopal mantle, and Bernadone, who had forfeited the sympathies of the crowd, went home with his money and his son's clothes, but without his son.

As for Francis, a labourer's rude garb was procured for him, and thus attired, he betook himself to the leafless woods,—it was wintertime,—where he wandered about awhile, happy though homeless, and singing in the gay Provençal tongue his thanksgiving to GOD Who had released him from the bondage of the world. He fell in with robbers, who, when they found he had nothing to give them, flung him into a snow-drift; he only sang the louder. For a time he discharged the most menial offices in a monastery. At Gubbio he received from an old friend a hermit's trappings, —the short tunic, the leathern girdle, the staff and slippers. With devout fervour he dedicated himself for some time in the hospital at Gubbio to the miserable lepers, washing their feet, dressing their sores, and, it is said, working among them some miraculous cures.[1] As Milman remarks, the moral miracle of his charity towards them is a more certain and a more affecting proof of his true Christianity of heart. S. Francis himself says :—" When I was in the bondage of sin, it was bitter to me and loathsome *to see and look upon* persons infected with leprosy; but that blessed LORD brought me among them, and I did mercy with them, and I departing from them, what before seemed bitter and loathsome, was turned and changed to me into great sweetness and comfort both of body and soul."

As S. Francis bestowed so much of his holy care upon the lepers, it is desirable that I should say something respecting the condition of that unhappy class, which even Christianity condemned to seclusion from the rest of mankind. The disease of leprosy, originating in the East, had been brought into the West by the Crusaders, and in the thirteenth century it devastated Europe like a scourge. The extent to which it prevailed is indicated by the number of lazar-houses that were then erected. Loathsome and terribly infectious, none were exempt from its ravages, and the imperfect medical science of those days was able neither to cure nor alleviate it. "Once a leper, always a leper. Political economy could devise no precautions; none, except the most necessary, as the most cruel, the dismemberment of the infected limb. The leper was driven from home and occupation, from family and township; he was disqualified from approaching house or city; deprived of all civil rights; incapacitated from making a will; excom-

---

[1] On one occasion he healed a leper with a kiss :—" Nescio quidnam horum magis sit admirandum, an humilitatis profunditas in osculo tam benigno, an virtutis præclaritas in miraculo tam stupendo."—S. Bonaventura, *Vit. S. Fran.* (Acta SS.)

municated from the Church. The political economist of the thirteenth century had skill enough to accomplish thus much, no more; leprosy, like pauperism, was made penal; but the bitterest penalty that man could inflict did not extinguish lepers or paupers, they still continued to cumber the face of GOD's earth, to the discomfiture of the mediæval economist and his political regulations."[1] It was among this miserable people that, as we shall see, S. Francis and his followers laboured most assiduously, not indeed in the spirit of the political economist, but in that of the religious enthusiast,—the Hero of the Cross.

After a period of sharp probation, Francis returned to Assisi, and employed himself in the work of restoring the church of S. Damian. He went through the streets of the city begging stones:—"Whoever will give me one stone shall have one prayer; whoever two, two prayers; whoever three stones, three prayers." Many mocked; but, calm and unmoved, he carried the stones on his shoulders to the place of building, and the church began to rise to the sound of his joyful hymns and holy songs. Then a reaction took place, and the men who had jeered and gibed, sprang forward to assist. Francis steadily worked on, allowing himself little time for rest or sleep, and refusing all food which he did not obtain by begging. His father, wounded in his respectability, and mad with rage at the young man who had formerly borne himself as the son of a prince, but now toiled with his hands like a common labourer, and lived upon alms,—reproached him harshly, and cursed him. He took a beggar of the lowest class, and said:—"Be thou my father, and give me thy blessing." The Priest of S. Damian, knowing that he had been accustomed to dainty fare, "had been fond of syrups and confectionery, and had abstained from common food," and fearing lest his bodily strength should give way for want of sufficient sustenance, cunningly provided him with a few simple delicacies. At first, in his absorption, the enthusiast knew not of what he was partaking, but suddenly awaking to the fact, he gravely rebuked the mistaken kindness of his friend, and seizing a dish, hurried into the town, begged from his neighbours their driest scraps, and returning, sat down to the unsavoury meal. At first his

[1] Prof. Brewer, *Monumenta Franciscana*, Int. pp. xxi. xxii.

appetite recoiled from it, but he conquered the disgust, ate and blessed GOD, and was able to say that no meal had ever pleased him better. Was this madness? No, the highest, truest wisdom. For the work Francis had undertaken the most absolute conquest of self was indispensable. Half measures could not be permitted, for in such lies always the possibility of retrogression. And, moreover, he could hope to conquer the world only by showing how complete had been this business of renunciation. No great reform was ever accomplished by moderate men. You cannot convince a drunkard of the error of his ways while you still continue to take a prudent glass. And Francis could not have preached the nothingness of worldly enjoyments while he himself partook of them in ever so small a degree.

The zeal of Francis was successful in accomplishing the restoration not only of the church of S. Damian, but also of the churches of S. Peter and S. Maria degli Angeli (or the Portiuncula,) the latter of which thenceforth afforded him a shelter. Up to this time he had remained a layman, neither seeking orders nor desiring the monk's cowl, but in his own way working out his salvation with fear and trembling. One day in 1208, when hearing mass in the Portiuncula, a text fell upon his ear, which supplied him with the watchword he had long been waiting for. It ran :—" Provide neither gold, nor silver, nor brass in your purses ; neither scrip for your journey, neither two coats, neither shoes, nor yet staves." He recognised it at once as a call from Heaven : and on leaving the church, threw away his wallet, his staff, and his shoes, clothed himself in the coarsest dark grey tunic, bound it round him with a cord, and set forth on the holy work of calling sinners to repentance. Does not the reader see him at this great epoch of his life ? A man of something less than middle stature, with an oval face and a full low forehead : dark clear eyes shining lustrously under straight eyebrows ; thick dark hair, and a straight but delicate nose ; modest yet noble lips, which parted frequently with a winning smile ; close-set, even, and white teeth : a voice soft yet keen, and capable of sounding notes of warning or denunciation ; a black beard not very fully grown. His neck was thin, but the well-shaped head was firmly set upon square shoulders ;

the arms were short; the hands thin, with long fingers; the feet small. As might be supposed, the figure was spare, almost attenuated, but the skin had the delicacy of that of a woman. Such was Francis of Assisi, when he started upon his mission in the year 1208; a man of no great robustness, yet with a wonderful faculty of endurance; a man who could work laboriously, though he ate and slept little; a man whom a wonderful love of CHRIST and CHRIST's creatures seemed to inspire with almost superhuman energy.

His words smote like fire, penetrating the heart; for like all men who have lived to sway great bodies of men, and to effect great reforms or changes, like Bernard and Savonarola, and Luther and Wesley, like Pym and Chatham, and Cobden and Gladstone, he was gifted with a strong and persuasive eloquence. In an age peculiarly susceptible to fresh impulses, it could not but be that the enthusiasm of Francis should prove contagious, that his strange ardent piety should kindle zeal. Round this bare-footed, ill-clad Assisan, who came among men like a new Elijah, disciples began to gather; disciples unquestioning, loyal, filled with an almost blind adoration. The first, according to S. Bonaventura, was a noble, rich, and learned citizen, Messer Bernardo di Quintavalle. The second was Pietro de Catanio, a Canon of the Cathedral of Assisi. Then came a citizen named Egidio, and in quick succession, Sabatius, Morito, and Giovanni de Capello. The seventh was Philip, who is described as a sweet and mellifluous preacher. With these seven Francis retired to a lonely spot in the bend of the river that flowed by Assisi, a spot called *Rivo Torto*, and proceeded to seek a rule for their guidance. Thrice upon the altar he opened the Gospels, and read three texts in reverence for the Holy Trinity: first, "If thou wilt be perfect, sell all thou hast, and give to the poor," (S. Matt. xix. 21;) second, "Take nothing for your journey," (S. Mark vi. 8;) third, "If any one will come after Me, let him take up his cross and follow Me," (S. Matt. xvi. 24.) Having thus furnished them with a divine commission, he sent them out by twos into the neighbouring country, east and west, north and south, as if to partition the world. "Go," he said, "proclaim peace to men; preach repentance for the remission of sins. Be patient in tribulations, watchful in prayer, strong in labour, moderate in speech, grave in conversation, thankful for benefits." And to each, as he took leave of him, he added, "Cast thy care upon the LORD, and He will sustain thee."

So they went forth as they were commanded; went forth like their master, bare-footed, without staff or wallet; and gave their message to all who had ears to hear. Some laughed, some sneered, all wondered; but when their preaching failed their example was not wholly fruitless, and this direct representation of the blessedness of Poverty struck home to many hearts. After awhile the disciples re-assembled at Rivo Torto, and four were added to their number,—Masseo, Ginepro, Elias of Cortona, (a man of bold intellect, who eventually became vicar of Francis, and his successor,) and Leo, the "Pecorello," or "little sheep," renowned for his simplicity, his faithfulness, his deep attachment to his leader. As Francis looked round upon them, and saw that they represented all classes, the rich and poor, the mean and noble, the lettered and unlettered, his mind awoke to a conception of the grandeur of the work on which he had unconsciously entered. Rising from his brief sleep one night, he stole forth into the silence and the darkness, so overwhelmed with thoughts of the future that he could only say—"GOD be merciful to me a sinner;" when suddenly the load was lightened, the cloud disappeared, and a vision was revealed to him of the vastness of the harvest he would be permitted to reap. He returned to his brethren, and sought their sympathy. "Be comforted, beloved," said he, "and rejoice in GOD, and let us not be sad because we are few; for GOD hath shown to me that you shall increase to a great multitude, and shall continue to increase to the end of the world. I see crowds thronging to me from every quarter: French, Spaniards, Germans, and English, each in their different tongues, and all encouraging one another." Perhaps none of the brethren understood, or put much faith in the prophecy, except Elias of Cortona, through his keen intellectual perceptions, and Leo the Pecorello, through his affections; but they saw that their Master was glad, and they rejoiced in his gladness. As for Francis, he resolved on instituting a new Order, for which he chose, characteristically, the name of *Frati Minori*, the "Minor Brothers," or "Lesser Brothers," and he drew up for it a Rule, which at first filled twenty-seven chapters, each containing twenty-seven precepts, by which his followers, and all who hereafter joined the Order, were to be bound. Its three main principles were, Chastity, Poverty, Obedience. As to the first, they were forbidden, except a few who might safely do so from age or austerity of character, and then only to urge penitence or give spiritual counsel, to speak to a woman alone. As for the second, they were to give their goods to the poor, to renounce all possessions, and all property, even in the clothes they wore, the cord which girt them, and the breviary they studied. They were to look upon money as something dangerous and infected; might on no account receive it in alms, except for a poor brother. They were forbidden to ride so long as they had strength to walk. They were charged literally to fulfil the precept, if stricken on one cheek, to offer the other, if despoiled of a portion of their dress, to give up the rest. As for the third principle, Obedience the most implicit was insisted upon; but not simply as coercive and obligatory, it was to be a prompt, trustful, affectionate obedience; and the bond of the new brotherhood was to be the profoundest mutual love.

The work which the Rule prescribed for the Brotherhood was to preach. Like S. John the Baptist, they were to go forth into the wilderness of the world, and proclaim the coming of the kingdom, to call men to repentance, and to gladden stricken hearts with the tidings of the remission of sins. The brethren of other communities might till the land, or cultivate the arts and foster letters; safe from the storm and unrest of the time, and happy in the enjoyment of a gracious and graceful ease; but the Lesser Brethren were required to take up the Cross of CHRIST, and go in and out among men, endeavouring to rescue the oppressed, to comfort the weary, to reclaim the erring, to succour the feeble. They were to follow in the steps of CHRIST; and in CHRIST's name, and for CHRIST's sake, to proclaim the glad tidings of the Gospel. From this holy toil they were to be distracted by no selfish considerations, no anxiety for the morrow, nay, nor even for the day; they were to live on the alms of the faithful, taking no thought of how they should be fed, or wherewithal they should be clothed. To sleep at night under arches, or in the porches of deserted churches, among lepers and outcasts, the mean and the vile; to beg their bread from door to door; to set an example of piety and humility; this was the Rule which Francis enjoined on his disciples. " If I had as much wisdom as Solomon," he said, " and happened to find the poorest, simplest priests in the world, I would not preach in their parishes contrary to their will." Francis had had large experience of the social conditions of his age, and the extent to which these conditions pressed upon the poor: and his Rule was founded upon that experience. He designed to show Christianity to the poor as *their* religion; to hold forth the Gospel as a Gospel for the weak and oppressed; and he sent among them teachers qualified to teach, but as ill-clad and ill-fed as themselves. The Frati Minori were poor missionaries preaching to the poor, and dependent upon their sympathies, deriving their strength from this very dependence. They found their chief sphere of work in the towns; and in the towns they planted themselves in the worst, the most squalid, the most neglected quarters, building monasteries which differed in but few respects from the rude dwellings among which they were placed. In the *Speculum Vitæ* are recorded S. Francis's own directions on the point :—

"Said S. Francis to Bonaventura, who had given the friars a farm to build a convent near Siena :—' Shall I tell you how the settlement of the friars ought to be built? When the brethren go to a city where they have no dwelling-place, and find some one willing to give them so much land as is sufficient for a building, a garden, and the like, they must above all things, be cautious not to grasp at more than is necessary, always having regard to holy poverty, and that good example which they are bound on all occasions to exhibit. When,' he continued, ' they have a competent piece of ground, they are to go to the bishop of the city, and certify the fact to him. 'My lord, such an one for the love of GOD and the salvation of his soul, is willing to give us a competent piece of ground to build a dwelling-place. We come, therefore, to you, because as you are the father and lord of all the flock committed to you, so you will be lord of all of us who settle there. We wish with your blessing to begin our building.' Having obtained his blessing, they shall go and make a deep ditch all round the land whereon they propose to build, and a good fence instead of a wall, as an emblem of their poverty. Then they shall build poor cottages of mud and wood, and some few cells for the friars to pray in and labour in for the eschewing of idleness. They shall have small churches and not large ones, either for preaching or on any other pretence. And if ever prelates or clerks, or religious or secular men visit the brethren, their poor houses, cells, and churches, shall prove to them the best sermons, and they shall be more edified by these things than by words.'"[1]

So clearly did S. Francis perceive that the success of his disciples would be largely bound up with their poverty, and this a real and pinching poverty, not a sham and an affectation, that he took the most stringent precautions against abuse. He ordained that they should not only be poorly lodged, but poorly clothed, and poorly fed. They could not sell the offerings they received, and they were forbidden to receive more than their actual necessities required, such as meal, salt, figs, and apples, wood for fuel, milk or stale beer. However rough the road, or inclement the weather, they paced along the miry streets and unpaved roads, bare-footed and bare-headed, and in gowns of the coarsest cloth. You might trace them by the imprints of their torn and bleeding feet. "If the Gospel net, woven out of purple and fine linen, had hitherto rather scared than caught the fish it was intended to enclose, the founder of the Mendicant Orders took care it should be as coarse and homespun as poverty itself could make it."[2]

I have already referred to the saint's compassion upon the leper. This he dictated to his Order; whoever desired admission into it, whether of noble or ignoble birth, was commanded to wait upon leprous patients. We read in the *Speculum Vitæ*, how he appointed the friars of his order, scattered throughout the world, diligently to attend the lepers, wherever they could be found. And they followed this injunction with the greatest promptitude; though, to the last, the Master was more zealous than his disciples. "There was in a certain place, a leper so impatient, froward, and impious, that everybody supposed him to be possessed by an evil spirit. All who served him he abused with terrible oaths

[1] Speculum Vitæ, p. i. 10.
[2] Prof. Brewer, *Monumenta Franciscana*, Pref. p. xix.

and imprecations, often proceeding to blows, and what was still more fearful, he uttered the direst blasphemy against CHRIST and His most holy Mother, and the holy angels. The friars endured his ill-usage patiently; but they could not tolerate his blasphemies; they felt they ought not to do so, and therefore they resolved to abandon the leper to his fate; having first taken counsel with S. Francis. Brother Francis thereupon visited the leper, and upon entering the room said to him in the usual salutation :—'The LORD give thee peace, brother!' 'What peace,' exclaimed the leper, 'can I have, who am entirely diseased?' 'Pains that torment the body,' replied S. Francis, 'turn to the salvation of the soul if they are borne patiently.' 'And how can I endure patiently,' answered the leper, 'since my pains are unintermitting, unresting, night and day? Besides, my sufferings are increased by the vexation I endure from the friars you have appointed to wait upon me. There is not one of them who serves me as he ought.' S. Francis saw that the man was troubled by a malignant spirit, and went away and prayed to GOD for him. Then returning, he said :—'Since others satisfy you not, let me try.' 'You may if you like; but what can you do more than others?' 'I am ready to do whatever you will.' 'Then wash me,' replied the leper, 'for I cannot endure myself. The stench of my wounds is intolerable.' Then S. Francis ordered water to be warmed with sweet herbs; and, stripping the leper, began to wash him with his own hands, whilst a friar standing by poured water upon him."

Another anecdote is related in illustration of the strength of his sympathy with these unfortunates :—[1]

"Visiting, on one occasion, the house of S. Mary de Portiuncula, he found a simple friar named James, to whom he had entrusted the office of tending the lepers. Seeing the friar consorting with a leper on the road from the hospital to the church of S. Mary, S. Francis rebuked him, saying, that he ought not to conduct his Christian brethren, the lepers, in that manner, as it was not becoming to him or to them. For though S. Francis was willing that his friars should serve the lepers, he did not like to have them taken out of the hospital when the plague was upon them; as men

[1] Speculum Vitæ, Part i. p. 56.

could not endure to see them. He had scarcely uttered the words when his conscience smote him, he thinking that the leper had coloured at his remark; therefore, wishing to make satisfaction to GOD and the leper, he confessed his guilt to Peter Calaneus, the minister-general, and begged him to confirm the penance he intended to impose upon himself. Then said S. Francis, This is my penance; to eat out of the same dish with this Christian brother. When all were seated at table, a single dish was placed between S. Francis and the leper. He was a leper all over, disgusting for his ulcers; especially as his fingers were covered with sores and blood; insomuch that as he dipped his fingers in the dish and carried the morsels to his mouth, the gore and blood dripped into the dish. As the friars looked on they were greatly grieved and pained at the sight. But for the reverence they bore him, not one dared utter a word."

When Dean Milman says that Francis tended the lepers sometimes "with more than necessary affectionateness," he may possibly be referring to this anecdote, by which many, no doubt, like Francis's brethren, may be "grieved and pained;" but as desperate diseases need desperate remedies, so the attitude assumed by Christianity towards the unhappy leper could be modified only by a great act of self-control and compassion on the part of the advocate of a tenderer and more tolerant system. Before men would learn their duty it was indispensable that an example should be set which could not be misunderstood.

The effect of the Franciscan policy upon the neglected masses of the population was widely and permanently beneficial. The influence exercised was much greater than it would have been if it had emanated directly from the clergy, or even from that body which it sought to improve. " Lessons of patience and endurance," says Professor Brewer, "fell with greater persuasion and tenderness from the lips of men who were living and voluntary examples of what they taught. Dressed in a long robe of coarse cloth, surmounted by a mantle of the same material, bare-headed, bare-footed, begging his bread from house to house, the voluntary poverty of the friar removed the scandal under which Christianity laboured from the excesses and the superfluities of its privileged teachers."

For the same reason Francis rejected the pomp of ritual and the pride of learning. He ordered that the Franciscan services should be conducted with simplicity, that there should be no elaborate musical demonstration. Himself a poet of no mean order, it is hardly correct to say, as Milman says, that he despised and prohibited human learning; but he knew that dialectic exercises and theological displays were unfitted for the poor among whom he desired his disciples to labour. It was by this feeling he was actuated when to a novice who showed some reluctance in parting with his books he said, that his books, valued by the young man at £50, must not be allowed to corrupt the gospel which enjoined upon the friars to have nothing of their own. From another he took away even a psalter, telling him that, if that were allowed him, he would next wish for a breviary, and then for other books, until he became a great doctor of the chair, and imperiously ordered his humble companion to fetch the volumes he required.[1]

---

[1] This novice had obtained the licence of the general minister to have a psalter, but could not be satisfied without the Father's permission. Francis replied:—"Charles the Emperor, Roland and Oliver, and all the paladins, and all other stalwart men in battle, pursued infidels to the death with great sweat and labour, and gained their memorable victories. The holy martyrs died in the fight for the faith of CHRIST. But now-a-days there are folks who, by the mere vaunt of their exploits, seek for glory and honour among men; and so there are some among you who take more pleasure in writing and preaching about the works of the saints than in imitating their labours." Some days after, as he was seated by the fire, the novice came to him, repeating his request. Said Francis to him:—"When you have got a psalter, then you'll want a breviary, and when you have got a breviary you will sit in your chair as great as a lord, and you will say to your brother, 'Friar, fetch me my breviary.'" Saying this with some warmth, he took ashes from the hearth, and laying them on his head, rubbed his hand round and round, as if he had been washing his head, exclaiming, while the novice looked on astonied:—"I am your breviary, I am your breviary." And then he continued:—"Brother, I too was once tempted as you are by the possession of books; and wishing to know the LORD's will in this matter, I took the Gospels and prayed to Him that He would show me His will in the first passage to which I should turn. And when I had finished my prayer, and opened the book, I chanced upon these words:—'To you it is given to know the mysteries of the kingdom of GOD; but to others in parables.' How many gape after knowledge! How much happier he who has made himself barren for the love of GOD." Some days later this persistent novice returned to the subject

That these precautions originated in no abstract dislike of, or contempt for letters, is proved by his affirming at a general chapter, when asked whether men of learning might be admitted into the Order, that they might, inasmuch as learning was not without its uses. His real object was, to secure that his priests did not give up their time to works of meditation, which must necessarily have interfered with those active labours of love and mercy in which they could best imitate the example of their LORD. "Many friars," he said, "who bestow all their time and thought on the acquisition of philosophy, forsaking their proper vocation, and wandering in mind and body from the way of prayer and humility, when they have preached to the people, and have turned some to repentance, are inflated and conceited at the result, as if it were their own and not another's work. Whereas it happens not unfrequently that all they have done is to preach to their own prejudice and condemnation. In the conversion of men they have really done nothing; they have been no more than the instruments of those by whom the LORD has truly reaped the fruit."

That his friars should preach in language easily understanded of the people; that they should preach the great truths of the Gospel without any admixture of theological subtleties; that they should preach with such force and fervour as to compel the indifferent, and with such plainness and simplicity as to draw the ignorant, to listen; such was the great object of Francis, and he set aside whatever might interfere with its realisation. Other Orders might foster

---

in the church of the Portiuncula, when the holy man replied, apparently with some abruptness:—"Go and do as the minister tells you." As the novice went on his way, S. Francis, recollecting himself, ran after him, crying aloud:—"Stop, brother, stop." And when he had overtaken him:—"Return with me," he said, "to the spot where I said to you, 'Do with the psalter as the minister told you.'" And, returning to the spot, he bent his knee before the novice, saying:— "*Mea culpa*, brother, *mea culpa*. Whoever will be a Friar Minor must possess nothing more than his habit, or carry shoes if necessary." And this was always his answer to persons consulting him on the subject. "A man's knowledge," he said, "is equal to his works; he only prays well who works well (*tantum religiosus est bonus orator quantum est bonus operator*). For a tree is known by its fruits."— Wadding, i. 346, cit. Robertson and Prof. Brewer.

illustrious scholars and keep alive the lamp of learning; it was well that they should; but *his* Order was instituted for a different purpose, to save souls, and to mitigate the poor man's sorrows. He wanted men with a profound knowledge of the human heart; not with a profound knowledge of the scholastic philosophy. It was to a life of active charity, and not to a life of lettered leisure, that he called his followers. They were to go to and fro until in the darkest corners and the most squalid hovels the word of the LORD had free course and was glorified.

We have seen how vividly Francis realised to himself the life of our LORD upon earth, how he endeavoured to conform himself to His example and precepts. Hence it was that his genius specially took hold of the *practical* side of Christianity; that he laboured not only to make men believe, but to *live* as if they believed. Hence, as Mr. Maurice has pointed out, his anxiety, and the anxiety of his followers, to exalt the Virgin Mother, to dwell upon her perfect womanhood, her tenderness, her beauty, her maternal sympathy, her sympathy with the human sorrows which she herself had experienced. And in this way S. Francis became a great social reformer, communicating a decided impulse to European civilization. "He insisted," as Professor Brewer points out, "on the humanity of the SON of GOD; he dwelt on His poverty and sufferings as a man. He exalted the condition of woman by exalting the Virgin Mother. He insisted on her spotless purity, on her maternal authority and dignity, on her mysterious fellowship with her Son, on her joys and sorrows." No doubt the tendency was carried to an excess. His anxiety to bring out the human character of her history led the friar to give greater prominence to the childhood than to the manhood of CHRIST, to attribute too special an elevation and dignity to the parent, to raise the Mother at the expense of the SON. No doubt, too, the favour with which these doctrines were received tempted the clergy to carry them to extravagant lengths and to degrade them by gross images and representations: yet the work done was, on the whole, a noble work, and in itself would justify our admiration of the Worker.

Of the sound sense, the genial sagacity, the practical wisdom of S. Francis I might easily multiply illustrations.

Though rigidly ascetic in his own life, he was no friend to asceticism, and in his Rule retained only the ordinary vigils and fasts of the Church. He did not advocate an excessive mortification of the body, and in his later years regretted the abnormal austerities which had weakened his own powers. The flesh was to be subdued to the spirit, but not to be rendered incapable of serving and supporting it. The servant of GOD was to eat, sleep, and drink with discretion, so that his bodily energies might always be equal to the efficient discharge of his daily duties. Nor did S. Francis approve of a religion of gloom. He loved a cheerful countenance and a cheerful heart. He reproved one of his friars for assuming a sad and gloomy aspect, because of his offences. " It is enough," he said, "that your sorrow should be known between you and your GOD. Pray for His mercy to spare you, and restore that cheerfulness to your soul which you have lost by your own demerits." He was no lover of long prayers ; his own were as brief as they were earnest. He seems to have held that there was no time in life for indulgence in the mere formalities of religion ; an active, a zealous, a rational, and a cheerful piety was the piety he recommended.

This side of his character—there was another, as we shall see—is well exhibited in his directions for the choice of a Minister-General of the Order. They have something of that shrewdness which we find in the advice of Polonius to his son, though necessarily of a more elevated tone :—[1]

"A minister-general," he writes, "ought to be of irreproachable life, of great discretion, spotless character, and free from partiality, lest by showing too great an affection for one party he bring a scandal on the whole. He must be studious in prayer, apportioning certain hours for his own soul, and others to his flock. He must begin the day with mass, and with devout obedience commend himself therein and his flock to the Divine protection. After prayers he is to present himself to his brethren, and standing in the midst of them, he is to hear the questions of all, and reply to all, and provide for all, with charity, patience, and kindness. He is not to be an accepter of persons ; not to care

[1] Monumenta Franciscana, xxxiii., xxxiv.

less for the simple and uninformed than for the learned and the wise. If he has the gift of knowledge, he is all the more to show himself a pattern of piety and simplicity, of patience and humility. Let him foster virtue in himself and others, not ceasing to preach it assiduously, attracting others more by his example than his words. Let him anathematise money, the chief corruptor of our profession and perfection; and, therefore, as an example to be followed by all, let him have no purse and no coffers. His habit and one little book shall content him; a pen-case, seal, and writing materials, shall be his associates. He is not to be an accumulator of books; not very intent upon reading, for fear that he should derogate from his office the time he devotes to study. He shall piously comfort the afflicted, lest, as he is their ultimate refuge in trouble, if they find not relief and remedy from him, the disease of desperation should grow too strong for them. To win the perverse and proud to meekness, let him humble himself, and abate somewhat of his own right to gain a soul. To the runaways of his Order let him open the bowels of mercy, as to sheep that have been lost; let him never refuse to pardon them, well knowing that their temptations are very strong, and if the LORD permitted him to be tried his fall perchance might be worse than theirs. As the vicar of CHRIST, I would have him honoured with devout reverence by all, and that provision be made for him by all, and in all things with all benevolence, in proportion to the exigence of his need and the suitableness of our state. He ought not to be exalted by the honours and favours shown to him more than he is delighted by injuries, nor should he suffer dignities to affect his manners, except for the better. If ever he require more ample or generous fare, let him not take it in secret, but openly. To him it appertains to discern the secret conscience, and elicit the truth from hidden veins. Therefore, let him regard all accusations with suspicion at first, until the truth shall be known by diligent inquiry. Let him give no heed to gossipers, and particularly suspect all accusations proceeding from such persons, and be slow to credit them. Let him not from desire of retaining popularity, refuse or relax the forms of justice and equity; nor, on the other hand, let him suffer souls to perish from overmuch rigour; let not torpor arise from excessive kindness, nor the relaxation of discipline from over-indulgence; and so let him be feared by all who love, and loved by all who fear him."

CHAPTER II.

THE Rule laid down, and the Order instituted, Francis and his companions resolved on visiting Rome, and obtaining the sanction of the Pope. They travelled on foot, without purse or wallet, having first elected Brother Bernard as "a kind of Vicar of JESUS CHRIST" to whom they promised entire obedience; and cheering the journey with songs of praise, they slept at night in deserted churches, and by day subsisted on the alms of the charitable. On the way they met a knight in arms whom they received into their company, thus making it up to the mystical number of Twelve. " Angelo," said S. Francis, to the novice; "instead of that baldric thou shalt gird thee with a cord; instead of thy sword thou shalt take the cross of CHRIST; for thy knightly spurs, mud and mire."

Innocent III. was walking on the terrace of the Lateran, when a mendicant, in a coarse shepherd's dress, presented himself, and began to describe his project for converting the world to Christianity by poverty and humility. The haughty Pope hastily dismissed the intruder; but, according to the legend, his dreams that night made him sensible of his error. He saw, in the first, a palm tree gradually grow up at his feet until it attained a goodly height, and as he gazed, wondering what the vision meant, a divine revelation impressed upon his mind that the palm tree signified the poor man whom he had that day driven from his presence. In his other dream, he saw the great church of S. John Lateran, toppling to the earth, when it was suddenly arrested and sustained by the same poor man in the shepherd's dress. In the morning he sent to inquire for the stranger, who was found in the Hospital of S. Antony close at hand. The true explanation of the legend is, that Innocent, a man of

K

keen intellectual insight, had remarked in the stranger no ordinary power of enthusiasm and imagination; or that S. Francis obtained the interposition of John of S. Paul's, the Cardinal Bishop of S. Sabina, to whom he had been recommended by the Bishop of Assisi.

The Rule was submitted by Innocent to the consideration of the Cardinals, by a majority of whom it seems to have been regarded as impossible for human strength to observe; whereupon John of S. Paul's exclaimed: "To suppose that anything is difficult or impossible with GOD is to blaspheme CHRIST and His gospel." The Pope, however, was also of opinion that the discipline was too severe, and saying that he would consider of it, a second time dismissed the reformer. On their next interview Francis approached him with a parable:—" There was once," he said, " a rich and mighty king who married a very beautiful woman, living in a desert, and greatly delighted in her, and had by her children who bore his image. When her sons grew up their mother said to them,—' Be not ashamed, my sons; you are the children of a king.' And having supplied them with all necessaries, she sent them to the royal court. When they appeared before the king he admired their beauty, and, seeing in them some likeness to himself, inquired:—' Whose sons are ye?' They answered that they were the sons of a poor woman dwelling in the desert; whereupon the king, rejoicing, said:—' Fear not, ye are my sons; and if I nourish strangers at my table, how much more shall I not nourish you, who are my lawful children?'" The poor but beautiful woman, living in the world-wilderness, was Poverty, the widowed spouse of JESUS CHRIST; the poor brethren in the shepherds' tunics of the new Order were her sons, and the sons of the Heavenly King. Innocent, if he did not appreciate the parable, appreciated the imaginative power of the man who spoke it, and he granted a provisional confirmation of the Order. "Go, in the name of the LORD," he said, "and in His strength preach repentance to all men. And when He has multiplied you in numbers and grace, come back to me, and I will grant to you greater gifts, and entrust you with greater privileges." He recommended that the brethren should receive the tonsure, so that, though not priests, they might be esteemed clerks; he gave them his blessing, and dismissed them, unconscious, perhaps, of the influence which, through this new Order, the Church would acquire over the democracy of mediæval Europe, but doubtlessly perceiving that it had acquired an instrument of considerable power. (A.D. 1210.)

Here we may recall the sketch of S. Francis's history, down to this date, which Dante has presented in the 11th canto of the " Paradiso " :—

> " A dame,[1] to whom none openeth pleasure's gate
> More than to death, was, 'gainst his father's will,
> His stripling choice ; and he did make her his
> Before the spiritual court, by nuptial bonds,
> And in his father's sight ; from day to day,
> Thus loved her more devoutly. She, bereaved
> Of her first husband,[2] slighted and obscure,
> Thousand and hundred years and more remain'd
> Without a single suitor, till he came.
> Nor aught avail'd that, with Amyclas,[3] she
> Was found unmoved at rumour of his voice,[4]
> Who shook the world : nor aught her constant boldness
> Whereby with CHRIST she mounted on the cross,
> When Mary stayed beneath. But not to deal
> Thus closely with thee longer, take at large
> The lovers' titles—Poverty and Francis.
> Their concord and glad looks, wonder and love,
> And sweet regard gave birth to holy thoughts,
> So much that venerable Bernard first
> Did bare his feet, and, in pursuit of peace
> So heavenly, ran, yet deemed his footing slow.
> O hidden riches ! O prolific good !
> Egidius bares him next, and next Sylvester,
> And follow, both, the bridegroom : so the bride
> Can please them. Thenceforth goes he on his way
> The father and the master, with his spouse,
> And with that family, whom now the cord
> Girt humbly ; nor did abjectness of heart
> Weigh down his eyelids, for that he was son
> Of Pietro Bernardone, and by men
> In wondrous sort despised. But royally
> His hard intention he to Innocent
> Set forth, and, from him, first received the seal
> On his religion."

[1] Poverty.   [2] JESUS CHRIST.
[3] The poor fisherman to whom Lucan refers in his "Pharsalia," bk. v. l. 531.
[4] Julius Cæsar.

After visiting the tombs of the Apostles, the brethren of the new order of the Frati Minori set out on their homeward journey, singing as they went, with joyful hearts. They re-assembled in their old place of meeting at Rivo Torto, and there abode for some months, living upon the poorest, scantiest fare, but never abating their calm and cheerful courage. It was at this time, perhaps, that the brethren, who, it will be remembered, were laymen, unaccustomed to repeat the offices of the Church, applied to their master for a form of prayer. That which Francis gave them was characteristically brief: the *Pater Noster* and the *Adoramus Te Christe* ("We adore Thee, O CHRIST, in all Thy Churches which are in all the world, and we bless Thee because by Thy holy cross Thou hast redeemed the world.") From Rivo Torto they removed to their leader's well-loved home and haunt, the Portiuncula, which, with a plot of ground adjoining, was given to him by the owners, the Benedictine convent of Monte Subiaco, and became the cradle and nursery of the famous Franciscan Order.

Preaching and praying, begging alms of which they gave freely to the poor, tending the sick, consoling the bereaved, carrying succour to the oppressed, Francis and his disciples pursued their daily work with an enthusiasm which never flagged. Their numbers increased daily; their influence increased daily. There were no longer any jeers or hootings or stones; but as they passed by, blessings and prayers followed them, and those bare-footed men in their modest shepherds' dresses were reverenced as saints. "Because they possessed nothing earthly, loved nothing earthly, and feared to lose nothing earthly, they were secure in all places; troubled by no alarms, disturbed by no anxieties, they lived, with peaceful minds, waiting without care for the coming day or the night's lodging." Such are the words of Bonaventura; and they set forth a life of simple, honest, unquestioning faith, such as few men have ever lived since CHRIST first preached the doctrine of self-renunciation.

As the head of an Order whose renown was swift-spreading over Christendom, Francis was frequently the guest of the high and noble of the earth; but under no circumstances could he be induced to depart from the strict letter of his Rule. He sat down at the profuse table; and he ate and drank in perfect courtesy, but was careful so to season the viands that they should afford no indulgence to the palate. With that picturesqueness of phrase peculiar to him, he would say:—" Brother Ash is pure," and over the rich and savoury dish would sprinkle ashes, and eat cheerfully, conversing with his usual smiling affability. Or sometimes, he took the glass of water by his side, and as if it were an ordinary thing, emptied it on his plate, never seeking to draw attention to what he was doing. This practical illustration of his sincerity was absolutely necessary in an age when the wits and poets made merry over the excessive liking of the clergy for the flesh-pots of Egypt. Once, when ill, he was persuaded to partake of some chicken; but, as soon as he recovered, his conscience smote him, that he should have pampered his appetite while many of GOD'S creatures were perishing for want of food. He desired one of the brethren, therefore, to lead him, with a rope round his neck, to the gate of Assisi, and there proclaim the enormity of his offence. "Behold," he said, "the glutton who eats the flesh of fowls, though you know it not." Practice such as this was more eloquent than any precept. The excitable Italian crowd were melted to tears; they read in the spectacle a lesson to themselves. "What idolaters are we," they exclaimed, "that we should spend our lives in shedding blood, and fill both soul and body with drunkenness and luxury !" The poor were all the better for the self-denial that prevailed in Assisi until, at all events, the moral of Francis's abasement was forgotten.

So rapid was the increase of the new Order that it became necessary in 1212 to hold a Chapter, and thenceforward these assemblies were of annual occurrence. In the same year an incident took place which led to the institution of a Second Order. Milman remarks that the passionate fervour of the preaching, the mystic tenderness, the austere demeanour of Francis and his disciples could not but work rapidly and profoundly among his female hearers. It would be more correct to say, perhaps, that the practical character of the religion they preached, and their affectionate concern for the poor and feeble, appealed irresistibly to woman's charitable sympathies. One of the earliest and most distinguished of these converts was Clara or Chiara, the daughter of a noble family called Scifa, who from her earliest years had glowed with the love of CHRIST, and recoiled from the world and worldly things. She became known to Francis, who sought to lead her out of the darkness into the light. On the night of Palm Sunday she stole from her father's house, fearing his opposition, and " in honourable company" made her way to the little church of the Portiuncula. We could wish that this had not been done with the saint's sanction, for assuredly CHRIST does not teach the neglect of household duties or domestic ties; but we must remember that he would look at the matter from a very different stand-point to any which we now occupy. So the maiden put aside her ornaments, sacrificed her long tresses, and assumed the rough brown woollen gown and cord which were to be thereafter her distinctive attire. This ceremonial would seem to have occurred about midnight. "The little church streaming light out of all its windows into the external blackness, and the girl with her heart beating, with her long locks falling under the scissors, among that crowd of brown-frocked brethren, some one or two wistful women, servants or dependants, looking on—what a curious mixture of stealth and solemnity, light and darkness, there is in this midnight scene! She had come in the dark, with her attendants, through the fresh spring air and the rustle of the silent woods, escaping like a captive from her father's house. She did not choose, we are told, to use the ordinary door, but cleared with her own hands one which had been blocked up by stones and wood—probably a door unused and partly built up, according to the fashion of the country, that the living might not pass where the dead had gone. When the ceremony was over, and Clara had wrapped her girlish figure in the Franciscan habit, the founder of the Order went out with her again into the night to conduct her to the nearest female convent of the Benedictines [that of S. Damian], where she could remain with decorum and safety."[1]

Of Clara it is said that, except to receive the blessing of the Pope, she never once lifted her eyelids so that the colour of her eyes could be seen. She became the first mother or superior of the Poor Ladies of S. Damian, or as

[1] Mrs. Oliphant, "S. Francis of Assisi," p. 94.

they were afterwards called, the Poor Clares or Claresses. The life of these sisters has been described as one long dreary penance; but we may well doubt whether they felt it so. Certainly their vocation would never have suited an active, impatient, curious spirit; for even in their services there was an element of monotony. The sisters who could read were to read "the Hours," but without chanting; and those unable to read were not to learn. Their life was one of waiting. They stood aside and prayed; prayed for the support of their brethren, prayed for the salvation of a world too busy to give a thought to GOD's Hereafter.

Francis next set forth to subdue the world, to preach the cross to mankind. While his Order was extending in all directions, was spreading its branches throughout Christendom, he resolved, for himself, to go forth among the peoples lying in darkness, and to carry the lamp of life into the night of Mohammedanism. With one companion he set out for Syria, but contrary winds drove him to Illyria, and thence he was compelled to return to Ancona. It was then near the time for the second Chapter of the Order, and Francis deemed it advisable to be present at its deliberations. After these were concluded, he again departed on his chivalrous enterprise; but confining himself at first to a mission to the Moors of Spain. Again he was baffled in his aim. He seems to have reached Lusitania, but he got no further, and illness forced him to return to Assisi early in 1214. In the following year Pope Innocent held the fourth great Lateran Council, at which S. Francis met Dominic, the founder of the famous Dominican Order, and obtained a formal recognition of his Rule. The Chapter held in the following June disclosed a wonderful increase of the numbers of the brethren, and it was found necessary to ordain provincial masters in Spain, Provence, France, and Germany. In 1219 the brotherhood mustered 5000 strong.

We may pause here a moment to glance at the distinctive features of S. Francis's character. What strikes us specially is his exceeding gentleness. S. Bernard could be impetuous, even vehement; S. Dominic had an element almost of cruelty, certainly of rigour, in his temper; but Francis was always patient, always urbane, always seeking the happiness of others. Next we must comment upon that sympathy with the poor which burned so deeply and lastingly in his heart, that it inspired him to idealise and spiritualise Poverty; she was his bride; he devoted himself to her service. So keen was his compassion for the poor that he would not rest until he was one of the poorest. "The bread given in alms," he would say, "is holy and blessed bread; it is sanctified by the praise and love of the Almighty." Once, when asked by what virtue men become dearest to CHRIST, he replied:—"Know, beloved, that Poverty is the special way to salvation; for it is the food of humility and the root of perfection. It is the treasure of which we read in the Scripture, that it was hidden in a field: to buy which a man should sell all that he hath, and in comparison with which, all that can be given for its purchase is to be accounted nothing. And he who would to this height attain must lay aside not only worldly prudence, but even all knowledge of letters, that thus stripped of all externals he may come to see what is the power of the LORD."

Out of this contempt of wealth and idealisation of poverty naturally sprang his heroic charity, a charity which in its boundlessness of self-denial puts to shame all our modern notions of benevolence. As everything was the gift of GOD, it seemed to Francis a matter of course that it should be shared with GOD's creatures. Meeting a poor wretch, half-naked, with only a few rags to screen him from the cold, he immediately thrust his mantle upon him:—"I had it but as a loan," he said, "until I found some one in greater need of it than myself." But he was charitable in something more than material things. If he had the ready hand, he had also the generous soul. He loved not to speak ill of any, nor to hear ill of any. No harsh judgments dropped from his lips; he nourished no unkind suspicions. There was not a touch of selfishness in his disposition; not a particle of envy. He was asked by one of the brethren how it was that, amid all his cares and responsibilities, he preserved his blitheness and genial composure:—"When I am tempted to sadness or slothfulness," he replied, "I look at the cheerful bearing of my companions, and, observing their spiritual joy and happiness, I shake off the temptation and the idle sorrow, and am full of gladness within and gaiety without." He loved to see all around him happy, and was unsparing in his efforts to promote and preserve their happiness.

The gentleness of his nature showed itself in his love of animals. For the birds he had a very strong affection; but he could not endure to see any beast ill-treated. To lambs and larks he was specially partial, as the images of the Lamb of GOD and the Cherubim. There can be no question that he was a great orator, if to sway and stir and control the passions of a multitude be a sign of oratory; and all great orators must possess something of the poet's imagination, something of the poet's faculty of tracing similitudes, something of his power of presenting the picturesque side of things. His ordinary language had a poetical force and vivacity, as in his saying, when the surgeon was about to cauterise him :—" Fire, my brother, be thou discreet and gentle to me." His metrical compositions are the irregular strains of an improvisatore, chanted from a full heart, without any preparatory study. Mrs. Oliphant has translated one of them, and we reproduce her version because it fairly represents its innate vigour and feeling as well as its want of form :—

" Highest Omnipotent good LORD,
   Glory and honour to Thy Name adored,
     And praise and every blessing,
     Of everything Thou art the source,
   No man is worthy to pronounce Thy Name.

" Praised by His creatures all,
   Praised be the LORD my GOD,
   By Messer Sun, my brother above all,
   Who by his rays lights us and lights the day—
   Radiant is she, with his great splendour stored,
     Thy glory, LORD, confessing.

" By Sister Moon and Stars my LORD is praised,
   When clear and fair they in the heavens are raised.

" By Brother Wind, my LORD, Thy praise is said,
   By air, and clouds, and the blue sky o'erhead,
   By which Thy creatures all are kept and fed.

" By one most useful, humble, precious, chaste,
   By Sister Water, O my LORD, Thou art praised.

> " And praisèd is my LORD
> By Brother Fire—he who lights up the night—
> Jocund, robust is he, and strong and bright.
>
> " Praisèd art Thou, my LORD, by Mother Earth—
> Thou Who sustainest her, and governest,
> And to her flowers, fruit, herbs, dost colour give and birth."

This "Song of the Sun," or, as it is sometimes called, "Song of the Creatures," was one of the earliest poems written in the Italian vernacular. Francis had spent forty nights in exhausting vigils, and had an ecstasy, at the conclusion of which he called to one of his brethren to take a pen and write, and then dictated to him this rude lyrical outburst, which was afterwards used by the Franciscans as a daily hymn. It is a song of thanksgiving; wild, irregular, broken, if you will; but full of a force and fervour which seize upon the attention. He added two more verses on separate occasions; one, when a quarrel had arisen between the magistrates and the Bishop of Assisi, which was ended by the chanting of these peaceful strains; and the other, after he had had a vision, in which he had learned that he would pass away into his rest before long :—

> "And praisèd is my LORD
> By those who, for Thy love, can pardon give,
> And bear the weakness and the wrongs of men.
> Blessed are those who suffer thus in peace,
> By Thee, the Highest, to be crowned in heaven.
>
> " Praised by our sister Death, my LORD, art Thou,
> From whom no living man escapes.
> Who die in mortal sin have mortal woe ;
> But blessed they who die doing Thy will,—
> The second death can strike at them no blow.
>
> " Praises, and thanks, and blessing to my Master be :
> Serve ye Him all, with great humility."

Montalembert speaks of the saint's poetry in language of eloquent but extravagant praise. On the other hand, Dean Milman seems scarcely to do justice to it. He speaks of it[1] as nothing more than a long passionate ejaculation of love to the Redeemer in rude metre, which has not even the

---

[1] Dean Milman, "Hist. Lat. Christianity."

order and completeness of a hymn. "It is a sort of plaintive variation on one simple melody; an echo of the same tender words, multiplied again and again, it might be fancied, by the voices in the cloister walls." It is surely something more and better than this. Very short, says Ozanam, but all his soul is to be found in it! There you see the man as he was, with his deep love of nature; his fraternal friendship for all GOD's creatures; his inexhaustible charity, and his all-absorbing devotion to his LORD. "It comes to us like a breath from that Eden of Umbria, where the sky is so bright, the earth so full of flowers. The language has all the simplicity of a new-born idiom; the rhythm shows all the inexperience of an immature poetry, which satisfies indulgent ears with little effort. Sometimes, instead of rhyme, the poet is content with a single assonance; sometimes it occurs only at the beginning and end of a stanza. The fastidious critic will not easily recognize in it the rules and conditions of a lyrical composition. It is nothing but a cry; but it is the cry of an infant poetry, destined to grow and make itself heard throughout the world."

Several hymns are ascribed to S. Francis; one or two doubtfully; the others are marked by all the characteristics which are discernible in the Canticle. Among the early vernacular poets of Italy we cannot refrain from giving to the founder of the *Frati Minori* the highest place.

> " O Love, O Love, which thus hast wounded me,
> No other name than Love can I proclaim;
> O Love, O Love, let me be joined to Thee!
> Love only sets my heart aflame.
> O Love, O Love, Thou so possessest me,
> My heart flows fast at Thy dear Name;
> My strength would be all pain above,
> Were I not with Thee, O Love!
> O Love, for courtesy,
> Make me to die of Love!"[1]

[1] Mrs. Oliphant, "S. Francis of Assisi," p. 238.

CHAPTER III.

AFTER the great Chapter of 1219, the Chapter Storearum,[1] as it is called in Franciscan annals, Francis revived his dreams of a crusade against Mohammedanism. More fortunate than on the previous occasion, he reached the Egyptian coast, and at Damietta found the army of the Crusaders encamped, opposed to the Moslem host of the Sultan, Malek-al-Kamed. He made a vain effort to compose the quarrels which divided and weakened the Christian leaders, and when he failed, predicted their defeat. He knew that in union was strength. With one companion he proceeded on his own enterprise of conquest, crossed the Nile, and boldly confronted the spears of the Arabs, though the Sultan had set the price of a gold bezant on any Christian head. As he went, filled with the hope of martyrdom, he perceived a couple of sheep browsing among the scanty tufts of herbage that straggled over the sandy wilderness. "My brother, trust in the LORD," he cried; "for in us He has fulfilled those words of His Gospel :—'Behold, I send you forth as sheep in the midst of wolves.'" The wolves appeared; a party of Arabs, who, however, instead of slaying the two Franks on the spot, conveyed them, "with many vile words and hard blows, and in cruel bonds" to the camp of the Sultan. Admitted to his presence, Francis, with his usual serene courage, announced that he had been sent by GOD to show him and his people the path of salvation. He preached (in what language we know not) the Holy Trinity and JESUS CHRIST the SON of the Most High. The Sultan listened with respect; impressed by the preacher's dignity of mien, and "admiring the courage and fervour which he saw in this man of GOD." He invited him to remain at his court. "For His love will I gladly remain with you, if you and your people will be converted to CHRIST; and if you are doubtful whether or not to abjure the creed of Mohammed for the gospel of CHRIST, let a

---

[1] That is, the Chapter of the Straw Huts; so called from the little cabins, or wigwams, of straw and rushes, in which the brethren lodged.

great fire be lighted, and I will enter into it with your priests, so that it may be known which faith should be esteemed holiest and most sure." The Sultan replied that none of his priests would willingly submit to so perilous a trial. "I will enter alone," said Francis, "if, should I be burned, you will impute it to my sins; but should I come forth alive, promise me you will embrace the religion of CHRIST."

The offer was not one which the Sultan could accept; but he was so moved by the fervour and sincerity of the enthusiast that he pressed upon him abundant gifts. To his surprise they were refused; and when after a sojourn of nearly a month Francis discovered that his mission was a failure, he returned, with the Sultan's permission, and surrounded by every circumstance of honour, to the Christian camp. Thence he passed through the Holy Land and the kingdom of Antioch, gaining numerous converts and warming many hearts. Rumours of innovations recalled him to Assisi. On the way there he paused at Bologna (August 15, 1220,) where he found that the community of Brothers Minor had had built for them a stately convent, rich in artistic decoration. The sight grieved him sorely, and it was with difficulty he could be induced to extend his forgiveness to the friars who had thus sinned against the great principle of his Rule. At Assisi also he discovered much to grieve him; Fra Elias, whom he had left behind him as vicar, having introduced many novelties, among others "a careful and elaborate dress," with wide sleeves and costly fringe, as unlike as possible to the plain brown frock of the true Franciscan. Francis prohibited and repealed the changes. More to his liking were the news that reached him from Africa of the glory of martyrdom attained by five of the brethren; who, crossing from Seville into Marocco had experienced many adventures; and at length were offered wealth and honours and beautiful wives if they would embrace the creed of the Crescent. They spat on the ground to signify their contempt of the bribe. Enraged, the king himself clave the head of one of them with a sword; the others endured terrible cruelties before death released them. Francis received the intelligence with thankfulness to GOD, and sent his gratulations to the convent of Alonquir, which had thus given birth to the first " purple flowers of martyrdom."

The continual accessions to the Rule rendered necessary, unless the brotherhood was to become unmanageable, the institution of a Third Order, or class, of Brothers Minor, in 1221—2. These were called the Brethren of Penitence. They were allowed to retain their social position; to live *in* the world, though not of the world; but none were admitted until they had discharged their debts, and made restitution of all unlawful gains. Women could not enter, if married, without the consent of their husbands; and the form and colour of their dress were prescribed, silk being forbidden. The Tertiaries took the following vow:—" I promise and vow to GOD, the Blessed Virgin, our father Francis, and all the saints of Paradise, to keep all the commandments of GOD, throughout my life, and to make satisfaction for the transgressions I may have committed against the Rule and manner of life of the Order of Penitents, instituted by Francis, according to the will of the visitor of that Order, when I am admitted into it." They were required to hold aloof from all public spectacles, dances, and stage performances; and not to bear arms, except for the defence of their country or the Church. They were to abstain from unnecessary oaths, to fast often, and eat no meat four days in the week; and several times daily to repeat the *Pater Noster*, followed by the *Gloria Patri*. Other regulations were enjoined, with the double object of teaching them to lead a pure and self-denying life, and of binding the Brothers and Sisters together by a bond of mutual sympathy and common obligation. The significance of this Third Order, which was at once a proof of the sagacity and " reasonable service" of S. Francis,—of his keen insight into the needs of humanity, and his success in supplying them,—is fully appreciated by a recent writer, who says:—" The Third Order rose into instant distinction and importance, and was joined by a crowd of noble and powerful persons. Saint Louis of France, his mother and wife, were all members of it. And so was S. Elizabeth of Hungary, and many other princesses, who, after lives of much Christian charity and fervent devotion in their natural sphere, transplanted their zeal and sanctity into the stricter enclosure of the professed sisterhood. Wherever the preaching friars penetrated in their absolute poverty, breaking upon the slumbering imagination and torpid faith of the world as with a sign from heaven, the laity crowded into this Religion, which was possible—which did not require the renunciation of other duties, and yet linked them to the holiest men on earth, and gave them the support of a definite Rule. It was the first reappearance in the Church, since its full hierarchical establishment, of the democratic element—the Christian people, as distinguished from the simple sheep to be fed, and souls to be ruled. The humblest Tertiary had a certain place in the Church, which the proudest prince had not possessed before."

In 1223 Francis made ready and revised his Rule for final confirmation by the Pope; and there would seem reason to believe that this was not done without some more or less open opposition on the part of Fra Elias and a few other brethren. When it was completed, Francis took the all-important document to Rome, where he preached with wonderful effect before the Pope and Cardinals, and obtained from Honorius a bull sanctioning the Order in due form, (November 29th.) Afterwards, with the Pope's permission, he celebrated Christmas with a novel ceremony, which commended itself at once to the sympathies of the people. It was no other than a representation of the conditions attending our LORD's Nativity. The manger was introduced, and the ox and the ass, the Holy Mother, and the cradle in which lay, sleeping, the Divine Child. The friars sang new canticles; a Mass was interpolated, and S. Francis preached with his accustomed fervour. Such was the origin of the Presepio of the church of Ara Cœli at Rome,[1] of the Christmas spectacle visible to this day in many a convent chapel and village church in Italy.

[1] "The simple meaning of the term *Presepio* is a manger, but it is also used in the Church to signify a representation of the Birth of CHRIST. In the Ara Cœli the whole of one of the side-chapels is devoted to this exhibition. In the foreground is a grotto in which is seated the Virgin Mary, with Joseph at her side, and the miraculous Bambino in her lap. Immediately behind are an ass and an ox. On one side kneel the shepherds and kings in adoration, and above, GOD the FATHER is seen, surrounded by clouds of cherubs and angels, playing on instruments, as in the early pictures of Raphael. In the back-

In the following year a mission was sent to Germany, and Francis, who had been reconciled to Fra Elias, yielding up to him the active and immediate supervision of the Order, retired for rest and repose to the solitude of Monte Alverno.[1] He was accompanied by the brethren, Fra Masseo, Fra Leo, and Fra Angelo, and they purposed to celebrate there the Lent of S. Michael. It is said that as he ascended the oak-clad slopes, the birds from all around flocked to bid him welcome, perching upon his head, and shoulders, and arms, and carolling their loudest merriest strains. "Dearest brethren," exclaimed S. Francis, "I think our LORD JESUS CHRIST must be pleased that we should dwell in this solitary place, since our brothers and sisters, the birds, rejoice so at our coming." One morning,—shortly after he had taken up his abode on the green height, and under the shade of leafy boughs, fast mellowing with the soft red colours of autumn,—he was praying in an ecstasy of devotion, his worn and stricken frame scarcely able to endure the beatings of its striving, vehement spirit, when suddenly he saw in a vision, or as his fevered imagination supposed, in real being, a great figure as of a Seraph. It had six wings, two of which were arched over the head, two stretched as for flight, while two veiled the body; the body, as he perceived with awe and trembling, of the Crucified CHRIST. "And when he saw this," says Bonaventura, "he was greatly amazed, and mingled joy and sorrow filled his heart. For while he rejoiced at the gracious look with which he was regarded by CHRIST under the form of the Seraph, the nailing to the cross pierced his soul with the sword of grief and pity. He marvelled hugely

ground is a scenic representation of a pastoral landscape, on which all the skill of the scene-painter is expended. Shepherds guard their flocks far away, reposing under palm-trees or standing on green slopes which glow in the sunshine. The distances and perspective are admirable. The miraculous Bambino is a painted doll, swaddled in a white dress, which is crusted over with magnificent diamonds, emeralds, and rubies."—W. W. Story, *Roba di Roma*, i. 72, 73.

[1] The Monte Alverno, or Monte della Vernia, is situated on the frontier of Tuscany, near the sources of the Arno and the Tiber. It was bestowed upon the Order by Sir Orlando of Chiusi, a Tuscan noble, who had become one of the great Preacher's most fervent disciples.

at the appearance of a vision so past finding out, knowing that the infirmity of the Passion could in no wise agree with the immortal nature of a Seraphic being.

" At length, he understood from it by the revelation of the LORD, that a vision of this kind had, by the foreknowledge of GOD, been so presented to his sight that the friend of CHRIST might know that he, not through martyrdom of the flesh, but by kindling of the spirit, was to be altogether transformed into the likeness of CHRIST Crucified.

" The vision, therefore, disappearing, left a wondrous fire in his heart, and a no less wondrous sign imprinted on his flesh. For immediately on his hands and feet began to appear the marks of nails, just as he had but shortly before seen them in the form of the Crucified One."

The biographers of Francis represent him as constantly working miracles; but none of them equal this miracle of the Stigmata wrought upon him, if the record may be trusted, under such awful circumstances. The record rests, however, as might be supposed, on no completely satisfactory testimony.

According to Bonaventura, Francis related the wonderful particulars to Fra Illuminato, but there is no proof that he related them to any other of the brethren, and even for this we have no other authority than Bonaventura. The "Tres Socii" profess to have received the account which they include in their life of their Master from their companions; while Thomas of Alano asserts that Fra Elias had seen, and Fra Ruffino touched the sacred wounds. But Ruffino himself makes no such assertion. Yet we have from Bonaventura so exact a description of the Stigmata that it is impossible to regard it as wholly imaginary :—" His hands and his feet appeared pierced through the midst with nails, the heads of the nails being seen in the insides of the hands and upper part of the feet, and the points on the reverse side. The heads of the nails in the hands and feet were round and black, and the points somewhat long and bent, as if they had been turned back. On the right side, as if it had been pierced by a lance, was the mark of a red wound, from which the sacred blood often flowed and stained his tunic." Francis endeavoured, in his great humility, to conceal these crowning proofs of his covenant

L

with GOD, and the wound in his side he hid with special care; but we are assured that the curiosity of his disciples penetrated every concealment. Pope Alexander IV. publicly declared that with his own eyes he had beheld the stigmata on the saint's dead body. It became an article of the Franciscan creed, and though the rival Dominicans hinted their doubts, it became the creed of nearly all Christendom.

What then, in this rationalistic age, which reduces everything to the test of scientific proof, what shall we say about it? Was it all a delusion? The evidence is cumulative, but not wholly satisfactory,—shall we pronounce the statements of Bonaventura, and the Tres Socii, and Alano to be fictitious? Were there *any* marks? We incline to believe that there *were;* and to readers indisposed to accept the miraculous, we would suggest that they may have been self-inflicted, either deliberately, as a penance, or in one of those uncontrollable mental and spiritual ecstasies to which, during the last ten years of his life, the saint was subject. His imagination spurned the bonds of reason; the mind, acted upon by a physical condition which could not have been healthy, a condition of exhaustion induced by immense labour, an ascetic life, and intense devotional exercise,—wandered into dreams and delirious visions, the true character of which it was no longer able to determine.[1]

After his seclusion at Monte Averno, Francis returned to Assisi, but though he continued to work and pray as

---

[1] "Were we to treat the story as proved and authentic, we should find ourselves plunged into a whole world of unexplored wonders, which we can neither ignore nor interpret. It is a truism to say that every great religious movement is attended by some demonstration of power, unknown and mysterious, which baffles all the explanations of philosophy. The age of miracles, we say, is past; but there are a hundred wonders, more surprising than absolute miracle, which spring up about us, whenever we endeavour to understand the history of religion in the world, and its action upon men. Signs and portents attend every crisis of that history. From Savonarola to Wesley, and from Wesley to our own day, every great spiritual awakening has been accompanied by phenomena which are quite incomprehensible, which none but the vulgar mind can attribute to trickery or imposture, and which we find it difficult enough to ascribe solely to the highly strained feeling and nervous excitement which might be supposed to be working in the hearts of its subjects. Every explanation that has ever been given of the Tongues,

before, it was evident that his energies were failing, and that the day of his departure was near at hand. He was still in the very prime of manhood, at that epoch when the body reaches its highest vigour, and the mind attains its greatest elasticity. It was not the weight of years that bowed and broke him, but the weight of the labour he had crowded into those years, and the constant spiritual excitement under which that labour had been accomplished. With some difficulty he was persuaded to take the medicine and nourishment which his condition required; Fra Elias, who attended upon him, being compelled to adjure him in the Name of JESUS CHRIST. His strength, however, continued to decline, and his eyesight giving way to such an extent as to threaten blindness, he journeyed to Rieti to consult a celebrated oculist, at the invitation of Cardinal Ugolino.

On the way he stopped at S. Damian's, to comfort and console S. Chiara. And while he was there, the night following his eyes grew worse, so that he could not even see the light; wherefore, since he was unable to depart, S. Chiara made him a little hut of rushes, that he might rest the better. But, between his physical pain, and the multitude of mice which disturbed him greatly, he was unable to gain the slightest repose, by night or day. And as his sufferings increased he began to think and to know that they were GOD'S punishment upon his sins, and so he thanked GOD with all his heart and mouth; and he cried with a loud voice, saying:—" O my LORD, worthy am I of this, and of far worse. O my LORD JESUS CHRIST, Who hast shown Thy mercy on us sinners in divers pains and torments of the body, grant grace and strength to me, Thy lamb, that through no weakness or torment or pain I may fall from

of the trances of the Exstatics, of the cries and struggles of those newly brought into the Church, of all the vague mysterious wonders which attend every spiritual crisis, has failed to make them comprehensible. It is difficult to attribute to the direct interposition of GOD incidents which are really not moral incidents at all, and which have no results important enough to justify such an agency. Yet we cannot assert, without a rare amount of disbelief in human nature, and cynical disdain of our fellow-creatures, that the volition of man has had to do with these extraordinary phenomena."—Mrs. Oliphant, *S. Francis of Assisi*, pp. 267, 268.

Thee." And at this prayer a voice came from heaven, saying:—"Francis, answer Me: were all the earth gold, and all the seas and springs and streams balm, and all the mountains and hills and rocks precious stones; and thou hadst found another treasure more precious than these things, as gold is more precious than earth, and balm than water, and precious stones than mountains and rocks—and with this weakness that far more precious treasure were given thee, oughtest thou not to be with it well content and very light of heart?" S. Francis replied:—"Lord, I am unworthy of so precious a treasure." And the voice Divine said to him:—"Be of good cheer, Francis, for this is the treasure of life eternal, which I have in store for thee; and now from henceforth I invest thee with it, and thy weakness and affliction are but an earnest of that blessed treasure."

At Rieti the saint was welcomed by admiring crowds. The oculist pronounced that the disease of the eyes was due to excessive weeping, Francis being persuaded that whoever would attain to a life of perfection must cleanse his conscience daily with abundant tears. He was solicited to refrain from the injurious practice:—"It is not meet, Brother Physician," he exclaimed, "that for love of that light which we share here below with the flies, we should shut out the least ray of the Eternal Light which visits us from above; for the soul receives not the light for the sake of the body, but the body for the sake of the soul. I would rather lose the light of the body, therefore, than repress those tears by which the inner eyes are purified, that so they may receive God." The exaggeration here will be at once detected by the reader, but it was natural enough to the fervid imagination that scorned and abhorred the body as interposing, like a curtain, between the soul and its God. The oculist pronounced an operation necessary, that of cautery; and the saint bore it with almost more than human courage. When he saw the iron on the fire, being heated, he exclaimed, with a touch of mingled pathos and humour—"O Brother Fire, before all other things the Most High hath created thee of exceeding comeliness, powerful and beauteous and useful; be thou to me, in this my hour, merciful and gentle. I beseech the Great Lord Who hath created thee, that He may temper for me thy heat, so that I may be able patiently to endure thy burning me." As the oculist withdrew the iron, glittering with white heat, he made the sign of the cross, and sat steadfast and unflinching. Into the tender flesh plunged the hissing instrument, until from ear to eyebrow the cautery was drawn! He was asked if the pain were not severe. " Praise ye the Most High," he answered; "for truly I tell you that I felt neither heat of fire nor pain of body." And, turning to the physician, he said :—" If it be not well burnt, thrust in again." Beholding in the weakness of the flesh such wonderful strength of spirit, the physician marvelled, and extolled the miracle of GOD, saying :—" I tell you, brethren, I have seen strange things to-day."

Little benefit was derived from this agonizing operation; and Francis grew so blind and feeble that four brethren, " men of fortitude and devout spirit," were ordered to attend him constantly, lest haply he should meet with some misadventure. His infirmities daily increased; his flesh was consumed; there remained "nothing more than the skin attached to the bones." Still he caused himself to be carried about in a litter that he might preach to the people who flocked lovingly around him. A certain simple brother grieved deeply to see him so cruelly tortured :—" Brother," he said, " pray to GOD to deal more gently with thee, for His hand is heavier upon thee than thou hast deserved." " If I did not know thy innocence and simpleness," retorted Francis, gravely, " I should from henceforth abhor thy company, because thou hast dared to blame the Divine judgments which are executed upon me." As the signs of coming dissolution multiplied, he grew anxious to return to Assisi ; nor were the people of Assisi less anxious for his return, inasmuch as they feared he might die elsewhere, and so deprive their town of the infinite glory that would attach to the possession of his relics. He reached his native town in safety ; and its familiar air, pure, bland, yet refreshing, temporarily rekindled the flickering lamp of life. We find that he paid a visit to Cortona, in the vicinity of the shining waters of the lake of Perugia. But again he experienced a desire to return to Assisi. The whole town came forth to meet him ; half in sorrow at his sufferings, half in joy that his bones would be laid in their midst. He rested awhile—dying slowly—at the Episcopal Palace; and then went on to the Portiuncula, "the holy house of GOD," which he charged the brethren never to abandon. Before he passed into the convent he turned towards Assisi, which shone brightly among the green foliage on the hill, and blessed it. He saw it never more.

He occupied his last days in dictating his testament or will, in which he bequeathed his solemn dying injunctions to the members of the Order, and urged upon them the duty of implicit obedience to the Rule, and the principles on which it was founded. Prostrate on the bare earth, clothed only in a hair-shirt, with ashes sprinkled upon him, he there awaited the coming of the awful Shadow. It would seem, however, that after having thus emblematically renounced the things of this life, he was re-conveyed to his humble pallet, when he called his disciples around him, and extending his hands and crossing his arms "in the form of that sign which he had ever loved," he blessed them, whether present or absent, in the name and in the power of the Crucified. "Farewell," he said; "farewell, my children in the fear of the LORD. Great tribulation and temptations will come upon you; but blessed are they who persevere in the work which they have begun. And now I go to GOD, to Whom I commend you all."

He then desired them to bring the Gospels and to read the beginning of the 13th chapter of S. John:—"Ante diem festum paschæ." When they had ended, with weak accents, faltering and gasping often, he began to sing the 142nd Psalm:—"Voce mea ad Dominum clamavi." They were his last words. As the voice failed and sank into silence, the soul of Francis of Assisi passed into the rest of GOD.

It was Saturday, the 4th of October, 1422. And all the brethren and children of the holy father who had been called to witness his departure, with a great multitude who had voluntarily come together, spent the night in praising GOD, so that it seemed not to be a requiem for the dead, but the rejoicing of angels. And the next day they reverently interred the body in the cathedral of Assisi.

The later years of the saint are thus sketched by Dante :—

S. FRANCIS OF ASSISI.

"When numerous flock'd
The tribe of lowly ones that traced *his* steps,
Whose marvellous life deservedly was sung
In heights empyreal; through Honorius' land
A second crown,[1] to deck their Guardian's virtues,
Was by the Eternal Spirit inwreathed; and when
He had, through thirst of martyrdom, stood up
In the proud Soldan's presence, and there preach'd
CHRIST and His followers; but found the race
Unripened for conversion; back once more
He hasted (not to intermit his toil),
And reaped Ausonian lands. On the hard rock,[2]
'Twixt Arno and the Tiber, he from CHRIST
Took the last signet,[3] which his limbs ten years
Did carry. Then, the season came that He
Who to such good had destined him, was pleased
To advance him to the meed which he had earned
By his self-humbling; to his brotherhood,
As their just heritage, he gave in charge
His dearest lady :[4] and enjoin'd their love
And faith to her; and, from her bosom, will'd
His goodly spirit should never part, returning
To its appointed kingdom; nor would have
His body laid upon another bier."

Paradiso, canto xi. 87—110.

[1] The bull of confirmation issued by Pope Honorius III.
[2] Monte Averno.   [3] The stigmata.   [4] Poverty.

S. CATHARINE OF SIENA:

"LA BEATA POPOLANA."

" A smile amid dark frowns—a gentle tone
Amid rude voices."
SHELLEY.

[*Authorities*:—"The Letters" of S. Catharine have been collected, in four vols., by Tommaseo, 1860; and there is a very careful biography (in German) by Hase, "Catarina von Siena." We may also name, as sympathetic and comprehensive, Mrs. Josephine Butler's "Catharine of Siena : a Biography" (1879); and Chavin de Malan's "Histoire de S. Catharine de Sienna" (1846). We have used the French translation of the "Letters" by Cartier, which also includes a version of her "Dialogues." Reference has been made to Dean Milman's "Latin Christianity," Canon Robertson's "Christian Church," and Mr. J. Addington Symonds' "Sienna and S. Catharine," in the Cornhill Magazine, vol. xiv., pp. 299—312.]

S. CATHARINE OF SIENA.

CHAPTER I.

IN the fertile folds of the Tuscan plain, between the pine-clad Apennines and the Mediterranean, stands the ancient city of Siena; now grievously fallen from its high estate, but, in the fourteenth century, the seat of a republic which rivalled Florence. Wooded valleys wind gently around it, the ridges between them crowned with castles; and all lead up to the hill on which cluster the towers and walls of the capital. Another and a lower eminence to the west bears on its summit the stately church of S. Dominic. In the hollow between them, the Contrada d'Oca, formerly dwelt the poor classes of the Sienese population; and there, to this day, may be seen the house in which was born the most famous of the daughters of Siena, Catharine Benincasa, or S. Catharine. There, too, stands the chapel erected to her memory, with the golden legend over its door of "Sposæ Christi Katharinæ Domus." It is a pleasant spot, for the hillsides are softly wooded, and adorned with olive-plantations, and a streamlet murmurs softly in the shade.

"Catharine of Siena," says her biographer, Raymond, "was to the fourteenth century what S. Bernard was to the twelfth, that is, the light and support of the Church. At the moment when the bark of S. Peter was most vehemently buffeted by the tempest, GOD gave it for pilot a poor young girl who was concealing herself in the little shop of a dyer. Catharine travelled to France to lead the Pontiff, Gregory XI., away from the delights of his native land; she brought back the Popes to Rome, the real centre of Christianity. She addressed herself to cardinals, princes, and kings. Her zeal, kindling at the sight of the disorders which prevailed in the Church, led her to exert her activity in order to overcome them; she negotiated between the nations and the Holy See; she brought back to GOD a multitude of souls, and communicated, by her teaching and example, a new vitality to those great religious orders which were the life and pulse of the Church."

Of the story of this noble and heroic woman, who was born into an age marked by the gross corruption of Society and the Church, and into a land scourged by war and pestilence, I shall essay to present a brief but accurate record.

To Giacomo Benincasa, of Siena, surnamed Il Fullone, or The Dyer,—a loyal GOD-fearing man, profoundly respected by his neighbours,—was born by his wife Lapa no fewer than five and twenty children. Of these Catharine was the survivor of a fragile pair of twins, who first saw the light in 1347. Her twin-sister Jane lived only a few days. Catharine lived to make for herself a name in history.

Of her husband Lapa was wont to say:—"He is so moderate and mild in his words that he never gives way to anger, though it would have been justifiable on many occasions. If he saw any of his household vexed or excited he would soothe them by saying:—'Now, now, do not say anything which is unjust or unkind, and GOD will give you His blessing.' On one occasion he was much injured by a fellow-citizen who had robbed him of money, and made use of falsehood and calumny in order to ruin his character and his business. He never would hear his enemy harshly spoken of, and when I, thinking there was no harm in it, would express my anger against my husband's detractor, he would say:—'Let him alone, dear, let him alone, and GOD will bless you. GOD will show him his error, and will be our defence.' This soon came true, for our adversary confessed that he was in the wrong."

It was good to be brought up under the eye of such a father, and at an early age Catharine developed many gracious gifts and qualities, which he did not fail to cultivate.

Hence she became so beloved that the neighbours constantly sought her,—finding in her society and childish innocent prattle such sweetness and consolation, that they gave her the name of Euphrosyne, meaning joy or satisfaction. There was an ineffable sweetness in her smile, in which her eyes as well as her lips partook. Everything seemed to ripen in the sunshine of her frank, happy nature, and she was not less fond of birds, and beasts, and flowers, than of her fellow-creatures. Tradition represents her as favoured, even in her young years, with celestial visions. By the side of that convent-church of S. Dominic to which I have already referred was placed a small chapel; and thither she frequently repaired to spend whole hours in silent communion with her LORD. One evening, when she was six years old, her mother sent her with her little brother Stephen, to take a message to the house of an elder sister. On their return, the sun was setting, and the excitable and imaginative Catharine, in the richly tinted clouds of evening above the gable end of S. Dominic's church, saw a vision of JESUS in glorious apparel, supreme in majesty and beauty. As she gazed, the SAVIOUR looked tenderly upon her, and stretched forth His hand in the act of benediction. While she was absorbed in silent ecstasy, her little brother descended the hill in the belief that she was following him. Turning round, he saw that she lingered on the summit, looking towards the gold and purple magnificence of the sunset. He called, but she answered not. Running back to her, he seized her hand :—" Come on," he said, " why do you tarry here?" With a start, as if awakened from a profound trance, she broke out sobbing :—" Oh, Stephen, could you but have seen what I saw, you would never have disturbed me thus." And as the vision had vanished, she turned her face homewards, weeping.

Frequently listening to stories of the lives of the saints, and of all they had done and suffered, and of their lifelong seclusion from the world in savage and remote places, she was induced, when about seven years old, to form the idea of going on a pilgrimage into the Desert. For this purpose she frequently betook herself to secluded nooks, to muse and dream away the hours, but, sooner or later, her privacy was always intruded upon. She must go further away; that was evident. So, one morning, she set out boldly to reach the Desert. It was natural to suppose that the ravens would provide her with food as they provided the prophet Elijah; but she prudently took with her a loaf of bread to supply her wants if the ravens failed her. Leaving the city behind her she boldly made her way towards a range of distant hills, where, as the houses were scattered far apart, she felt assured that she must be on the border of the wilderness. Creeping into a little cave over which a rock impended, she began to pray and meditate in happy mood, and there she remained until the evening when "GOD suddenly revealed to her that He designed her for another mode of life, and that she must not leave her father's house." Thereupon she hastened home; tradition asserting that she was carried by angels, or miraculously supported so that her foot did not touch the ground.

Her next amusement was to gather around her a congregation of children of her own age, and deliver to them extemporaneous sermons, which are said (no doubt with much exaggeration) to have been eloquent and powerful. When she was twelve years old, her parents began to talk of her marriage, though knowing no one among their acquaintances whom they regarded as worthy of her. As for Catharine herself, she had already resolved to adopt a celibate life, and to take a vow of perpetual virginity, that she might be the freer to act in GOD's service. There arose, consequently, a struggle between her parents and herself when a young man of good birth and high character presented himself as a suitor. Her parents subjected her to a stern discipline with the view of overcoming her opposition; but while gentle and affectionate she was resolved. Forbidden to have a room to herself, she elected to share the chamber of her little brother Stephen, because she could take advantage of his long hours of absence in the day, and his deep boyish slumber at night, to continue the prayers and vigils in which her soul delighted. Her quiet, unassuming steadfastness had a great effect on the minds of her parents; they could not but feel that she was animated by no weak caprice, but by some over-mastering purpose; and what that was, her father dimly perceived when, entering her room suddenly one evening, he found her engaged in prayer. Her attitude and expression were as a revelation to him; and it is easy to believe that they would move him greatly, without adding the legendary embellishment that he saw the light resting upon her head in the shape of a snow-white dove.

A quick imagination, an impressionable temperament, and a habit of fervent prayer and meditation,—given these, and what may we not expect as the result in a girl of tender years? Excited by her constant desire to assume the Dominican habit, and become a preacher, she saw S. Dominic in a dream, and she heard him say, as he smiled upon her: —" Daughter, be of good cheer. Fear no let or hindrance, for the day cometh in the which you shall be clothed with the mantle you so eagerly covet." Ah, with what a rapturous emotion she arose that day, and how her heart burned within her, as gathering around her all her family, she addressed them in most earnest words:[1]—" For a long time you have decided that I should marry, but my conduct must have proved to you that I could not accept of the decision. Yet have I refrained from explaining myself, out of the reverence I feel towards you, my parents. Now, however, my duty compels me to break my silence. I must speak candidly to you, and reveal the resolution I have adopted,—a resolution not of yesterday, but dating from my early years. Know, then, that I have made a vow, not lightly, but deliberately, and with full knowledge of what I was doing. Now that I am of maturer age, and have a better knowledge of the purport of my own actions, I persist, by the grace of GOD, in my resolution, and it would be easier to dissolve a rock than to induce me to change my mind. Give up, therefore, for me, dear friends, all these projects for an earthly union: it is impossible for me to satisfy you on this point, for I must obey GOD rather than man. If you wish me to remain as a servant in your house, I will cheerfully fulfil all your will to the best of my power; but if you should be so displeased with me as to make you desire me to leave you, know that I shall remain immovable in my resolve. He Who has united my soul to His, has all the riches of earth and heaven, and He can provide for and protect me."

[1] Mrs. J. E. Butler, pp. 32, 33.

Words so courageous and so firm as these affected Catharine's parents and family to tears; they felt that further pressure would be useless and unjustifiable. "GOD preserve us, dearest child," said her father, "from any longer opposing the resolution which He has inspired. We are satisfied that you have been actuated by no idle fancy, but by a movement of divine grace. Fulfil without hindrance the vow you have taken; do all that the HOLY SPIRIT commands you; henceforth your time shall be at your own disposal; only *pray for us*, that we may become worthy of Him Who has called you at so tender an age." Turning to his wife and children, he added:—"Let no one hereafter contradict my dear child, or seek to turn her from her holy resolution; let her serve her SAVIOUR in the way she desires, and may she seek His favour and pardoning mercy for us: we could never find for her a more beautiful or honourable alliance, for her soul is wedded to her LORD, and it is not a man, but the LORD Who dieth not, we now receive into our house."

Thenceforth she was allowed to retain as a cell or oratory that little private chamber, which became her favourite resort, and the scene of her wonderful communion with Heaven. Giving herself up to prayer and meditation, she remained there for three years; during which she prepared herself for her future work by vigilant self-examination and lofty intimate spiritual intercourse with her GOD. At the same time she taught herself the lessons of mortification and abstemiousness. Her diet was of the plainest; she gave but little time to sleep; she lay upon the bare boards without any covering; her garments were of the coarsest wool, but always scrupulously clean, for cleanliness and exterior neatness she cherished as a sign of inward purity. The night was consumed in prayer, in pouring into her SAVIOUR'S ear her love and anxiety; not till the first sound of the matin-bell did she retire to her wooden bed for a brief repose. She confessed to Raymond of Capua, in later life, that her victory over sleep had cost her more pain and trouble than any other of her struggles; and that she had undergone indescribable anguish in crushing out the natural desire for rest. "Such conquests over self and over the infirmities, even over many of the just and natural demands of the body, have never been absent in the lives of those whom, *par excellence*, we call 'the Saints,' those who have left behind them an influence which is of GOD, and imperishable; an influence which even the most sceptical must confess to have been benign, and charged with blessing for humanity. Catharine's health was delicate, yet she possessed an extraordinary nervous energy, and even a muscular strength which astonished those who saw her exert it in the performance of any generous or helpful act. She suffered all her life from a weakness of the stomach, which made it difficult for her to take any food without pain, succeeded often by violent sickness and vomiting. She was also subject to attacks of faintness and prostration, especially in the spring, which would last several weeks."

This excess of self-mortification, this abuse of religious discipline, will account for the visions and delusions to which such holy enthusiasts as S. Catharine were subject. With a nervous system wrought up to the highest tension by a constant violation of the natural laws, the imagination necessarily did what it would. In the silence and solitude of the recluse's cell, the brain, excited by intense efforts of religious meditation, and tyrannised over by the disordered physical organisation, was prepared to realise every passing fancy, to give shape and form to every fugitive idea. The air was peopled with angelic figures; it trembled with celestial voices; it brightened with the glory of the Divine Presence. Such a condition of prolonged excitement was fatal to the mental health of the sufferer, disordering his ideas and withdrawing his intellectual balance; it was fatal also to his physical health. The chord was drawn too tightly; and, before the piece was played out, it snapped. To a premature grave was hurried the incomplete life— if, indeed, that life can be called incomplete, which, so far as the bystanders can judge, has fulfilled its appointed work. Thus it came to pass that Catharine of Siena died at thirty-three, before she had accomplished half the span which the Psalmist allots to humanity; but what had she not done in the short interval between the beginning of her activity and that apparently too-early death? She had preached to infuriated mobs; she had borne the balm of consolation to plague-stricken men; she had exposed the

M

corruptions of the Church; she had replaced the Pontiff in his ancient chair; she had averted war, and consummated peace; and, above all, in a dark luxurious age, she had shone upon the world like a vision of purity and beauty, as a light shines in a dark place.

To the Order of S. Dominic belonged a lay fraternity of brothers who undertook to sacrifice, at need, their lives and their earthly goods; their wives also were pledged never to impede or discourage their husbands in their work. The associates were known as Brethren and Sisters of the Militia of JESUS CHRIST; they wore the black and white habit of S. Dominic. Catharine desired to become a preacher, and carry the lamp of Christian faith into the cities she visited; as a preliminary ceremony it was necessary that she should be enrolled as a *Mantellata* (the name borne by the wearers of this cloak or mantle of S. Dominic.) Her mother made an application to the Fraternity to receive her; but was informed that it was not the custom to give the mantle to young maidens; and that hitherto it had been confined to widows of mature age, or to wives consecrated to work with their husbands. It was added, that the Mantellatas had no cloister or separate building reserved for them, but each must be able to rule her life in her own home. The application was pressed upon the Sisters, and at length they consented to admit her, if she were not "too handsome;" for they were bound, they said, to avoid the inconveniences that might spring from malicious report. Catharine was not open to the objection urged. Her face was attractive from its expression of gentleness, candour, and thoughtfulness; but could not be called beautiful. It was remarkable for its openness and sunny cheerfulness; the forehead was broad and smooth, but too receding; the chin and jaw firmly defined and rather prominent; the hair and eyebrows of a dark brown; the eyes, a clear grey or hazel. There was an exceeding charm in her smile, and all her movements were full of a natural ease and elegance. Her address was very winning, and in her manners she set aside the conventionalities of the time, obeying the dictates only of her own heart. "Young men who would come with some feeling of awe to visit the far-famed saint, and not without fears concerning the interview, were taken by surprise, gladdened, and reassured by her frank approach, her two hands held out for greeting, her kind, sisterly smile, and the easy grace with which she invited them to open their hearts." Notwithstanding the influence she acquired, her extended reputation, and the deference shown her by the most illustrious personages of the age, she preserved to the last the simplicity and the unassuming demeanour of a "Daughter of the People." And the people in return bestowed upon her their abounding affection, which is shown to this day by the loving epithets attached to her name. She is called "The Daughter of the Republic," "the Child of the People," "the Mantellata," "the People's Catharine," "Our Lady of the Contrada d'Oca," "the Beloved Sienese," and the "Beata Popolana."

Immediately upon her reception as a Mantellata she did not plunge into an active life. She had first to undergo a bitter spiritual trial. "The great enemy of man advanced to the dread assault of her soul," so that she seemed to pass through the Valley of the Shadow of Death. The most humiliating temptations assailed her; she saw in her dreams impure orgies, in which the words and gestures of lewd men and women invited her to join. The conflicts she endured were of the most painful character; the result, probably, of physical reaction as well as of mental excitement; but she endured them bravely, praying all the more earnestly, and working all the more assiduously; and there are few attacks of the Devil which may not be successfully resisted by Work and Prayer! These two talismans won for Catharine a happy victory; but this danger past, she had to strive with one of a subtler nature; one which did not repel by its loathsomeness, but enticed by its natural sweetness. She was young; she was an Italian; her brain was glowing with fancy, her heart throbbed with tender feelings; and the temptation of human love appealed to her strongly. Thoughts of happy wedlock, of happy motherhood, broke in upon her daily meditations, and haunted her dreams by night. The sacred strains of the Church seemed to blend with the soft accents of the troubadours. A voice said to her:—"Why so rashly choose a life in which thou wilt be unable to persevere? Why resist the holy impulses of nature which come from GOD? It is possible to become a wife and a mother, and yet to serve GOD. Many among the saints were married. Think of Sarah and Rachel of old; of many of later years; think of S. Bridget, Queen of Sweden, who was wife, mother, and prophet."

But Catharine persevered. She had resolved to dedicate herself wholly and absolutely to Heaven, and to that resolution she adhered. It was well that she did so; she had her special work to do, which as wife and mother, with other claims, other duties, other responsibilities, she could never have done. For most women, the post of duty is to be found in the domestic life; and they can best serve GOD by bringing high and holy influences to bear upon their household circles; but ever and anon we meet with exceptions, with women whose intellectual powers or lofty sympathies would be wasted if confined to so limited a sphere; women who, like Miriam of old, are evidently set apart for a great vocation. And the part chosen by Catharine of Siena, as by other saintly women, has also this beneficial characteristic; that it points out a way of usefulness to unmarried women; that it teaches them how they may employ the single life to their own spiritual benefit, and to the advantage of the sick, the sorrowing, and the oppressed.

After this second conflict Catharine enjoyed a brief interval of peace. Then came a third temptation. She had been assailed through the passions and through the affections, and had defeated the assault; the third attack was the most insidious, for it sought to find an ally in her intellectual pride. She was beset by the demon of doubt, which haunted her mind with sceptical arguments and cynical suggestions. And in this last combat she lost the support of the Divine Helper Who had hitherto sustained her. Her faith was in danger, and CHRIST the Consoler seemed to recede further and further from her side. The darkness of night closed around her; there was no radiance of hope to cheer her spirit, and guide her hesitating steps. Oh, how great the agony when the foundations on which we have built seem suddenly to crumble away beneath our feet! when the Heaven to which our prayers have been sent up, seems to vanish into a bewildering mist! when even the cross on which we have leaned snaps like a reed, and we fall prostrate in a great dread! Then, indeed, if we yield—if for one moment we cease to wrestle—we are lost. But Catharine summoned all her energies; when prayer was the most distasteful, she prayed most earnestly; when divine things were most unreal, she clung to them most fervently. When the darkness was deepest she searched most eagerly for light. When doubts were most constant, she sought most determinedly to renew and revive her belief. Throwing herself at the feet of GOD, she besought Him not to leave her. Repairing to the church on the hill, she spent the greater part of three days in striving, anxious prayer; such prayer as seems almost to be wrung out of the soul with tears of blood. The evil one was still beside her:—" Poor wretched creature, thou canst never pass thy life in such wretchedness as this! Behold, we will torment thee to death unless thou dost promise to obey us." Catharine murmured in her heart:—" Be it so; I have chosen sorrow and suffering for CHRIST His sake, and I am willing, if need be, to endure until death." Straightway a glorious light descended from above, so that the church was filled with celestial brightness. The devils fled, and One brighter than the angels came and soothed her, and spoke to her of her agony and her triumph. "LORD," she exclaimed, "where wast Thou, when my heart was so tormented?" "I was even in its midst, My child." "Ah, LORD," she replied, "Thou art everlasting Truth, and humbly do I bow before Thy word; but how can I believe that Thou wert in my heart when it ached with wicked and rebellious thoughts?" "Did these thoughts," said the LORD," give thee pleasure or pain?" "Oh, a supreme pain, a terrible anguish!" Then spake the LORD:—"Thou wast in this pain and sadness, because I Myself was hidden in thy soul. My presence it was which rendered those thoughts insupportable to thee; thou didst strive to repel them, because they filled thee with horror; and thou wast bowed down with suffering, because thou didst not succeed. When the period which I had permitted for the duration of the struggle had elapsed, I sent forth the beams of My light, and the shades of hell were dispersed, because they cannot resist that light. Because thou hast accepted these trials with thy whole heart, thou art delivered from them for ever; it is not thy sufferings that please Me, but the *will* that has borne them so heroically."[1]

Shortly after this, Catharine's soul was wrought up to that height of ecstasy which has been symbolised by so many of the Italian painters, as by Fra Bartolommeo and Correggio, in their pictures of the "Marriage of S. Catharine;" pictures in which we see the Virgin Mary guiding the hand of the Child JESUS to place a ring on the finger of Catharine as a sign of her divine espousals. The dream or vision, as Catharine herself described it to her friends, was the evident result upon her imagination of the long mental conflict she had undergone. She saw her SAVIOUR approach, and put upon her finger a golden ring, set with a diamond of indescribable splendour. He said to her:—"I, thy Creator and Redeemer, espouse thee in faith and love. Keep thou this token in purity, until we celebrate in the presence of the FATHER, the eternal nuptials of the Lamb. Henceforth, daughter, be thou bold and true; perform with a courageous spirit the works My Providence shall assign to thee; and thou shalt prevail over all enemies."[2]

Here we may allude for a moment to that communion between Catharine's soul and GOD, of which the hagiologists make so much, relying upon the phrases she frequently employs in her letters, such as "My GOD told me to do this," and "the LORD said to me." Each individual soul, in its intercourse with GOD, stands by itself. To some ears the heavenly voices sound dimly and uncertainly; by others they are heard with a wonderful distinctness. They have so utterly severed themselves from the world, and so completely bent all their thoughts and feelings to the realisation of spiritual gifts, that they seem, as it were, to hold a close and intimate converse with their GOD and FATHER. To what extent GOD reveals Himself to those blessed souls, or how far in their ecstasy they are borne upwards, or whether the imagination sometimes beguiles the spirit, who shall decide?

---

[1] "Here you see," says S. Francis of Sales, "were the embers covered over with ashes, while temptation and delectation had entered the heart and surrounded the will, which, aided only by the SAVIOUR, resisted all evil inspirations with great disgust, and a persevering refusal to consent to sin." ("The Devout Life," pt. iv. c. 4.)

[2] Acta SS. *Vita Cath. &c.*, 114, 115.

For my own part, I am content to leave this subject to the reader's own feelings, in the belief that it is one which does not admit of scientific treatment:—"I will not attempt any explanation or apology for the manner in which one saint constantly speaks of that which the natural eye hath not seen, nor the ear heard, but which GOD has in all times revealed to them that persistently seek Him. Those who have any experience of real prayer, know full well that in the pause of the soul before GOD, after it has uttered its complaint, made known its desires, or sought guidance in perplexity, there comes the clearer vision of duty, and the still small voice of guidance is heard, rectifying the judgment, strengthening the resolve, and consoling the spirit; they know that this influence, external to us, and yet within us, gently and forcibly moves us, deals with us, speaks with us, in fine. Prayer cannot truly be called communion, if the only voice heard be the voice of the pleader. Be still, be silent, then, dear reader, if you are disposed to object. If *you* have not yet heard that voice of GOD speaking within you, it is because you have not yet pleaded enough with Him; it is because you have not yet persevered long enough in the difficult path of divine research."[1]

It was now that Catharine taught herself to read, in order that she might study for herself the Scriptures, and the lives and writings of holy men; and bringing to the task a devout enthusiasm, her progress was so rapid as to suggest to her friends the idea of miraculous interposition. Some years later she learned to write; and the strength and breadth of her natural powers are proved by the admirable beauty of her style, which has been compared to that of Dante.

CHAPTER II.

IN 1365 Catharine, by various influences, was led to abandon her seclusion, and mix in the affairs of active life. We may judge of the extent to which she had carried her solitary habits from the circumstance that her first step in

[1] Mrs. Butler, "Catharine of Siena," pp. 38, 39.

this direction was simply to join her parents, and brothers and sisters at the family repasts. This interruption of her self-communings and continual devotions appeared to her so grievous, that we are told she wept bitterly when it was imposed upon her by her divine guide. "Wherein have I offended Thee, my GOD?" she said; "why dost Thou send me from Thee? What should I do at table? It is not by bread alone that man lives: are not the words that proceed out of Thy mouth better adapted to impart strength and energy to the pilgrim's soul? Thou knowest better than I, that I fled from the society of men in order to find Thee, my LORD and my GOD; and must I again mingle in worldly affairs, to fall again into my former worldliness and folly, and perhaps offend against Thee?" Then the LORD answered her—not, she told her confessor, in the very words she herself employed, but so that she understood what things He desired of her:—"Be calm, My child, thou must accomplish all justice, that My grace may become fruitful in thee, and in others. I will not that thou shouldst be separated from Me; on the contrary, I will that thou shouldst be united to Me more closely by charity towards thy fellow-creatures. Thou knowest that there are two commandments of love; to love Me, and to love thy neighbour. I would have thee walk not on one foot, but on two feet, and fly to Heaven upon two wings. Call to mind that from thy infancy I have encouraged thee by My Spirit in zeal for the salvation of souls. Why then dost thou wonder and grieve if I now lead thee to what thou hast desired from thy childhood?" Catharine replied:—"LORD, not my will, but Thine be done: for I am only darkness, and Thou art all light. But I beseech Thee, O LORD, if I presume not too much, how shall that be done which Thou hast said, and how can I, who am so feeble and miserable, be of service to my fellow-creatures? My sex is an obstacle, as Thou, LORD, knowest, through many causes; as well because it is contemptible in men's eyes, as because modesty forbids us any freedom of converse with the other sex." To which the LORD answered:—"The word impossible belongeth not to GOD: am I not He Who created the human race, both man and woman? The gift of My Spirit I pour out on whom I will. With Me there is neither male nor female, neither plebeian nor noble, but all things are equal, and I can do all things equally well. It is as easy for Me to create an angel as the lowest insect, the whole host of heaven as one worm. It is written concerning Me, that I have done whatsoever I will; and nothing that is intelligible can be impossible to Me. Why, therefore, dost thou perplex thyself how this thing is to be done? Dost thou think I cannot accomplish that on which I have resolved? But because I know thou hast spoken out of humility, and not out of faithlessness, I will answer thee. Know then, that at the present time the pride of man has grown so great, especially in those who esteem themselves wise and learned, that My justice can no longer bear with them, and will visit them straightway with a heavy chastisement. But, because I love mercy, and because My pity is ever over all My works, I will send to them first a wholesome and profitable confusion, that they may acknowledge their error, and humble themselves; even as I did to the Jews and Gentiles when I sent to them simple persons inspired by Me with divine wisdom. Yea, I will send to them *women*, unlearned, and by nature feeble, but filled by My grace with strength and courage, for the confusion of their frowardness. If they acknowledge their error and humble themselves before Me, I will make My pity and mercy to increase towards them, that is, towards such as receive My messengers with reverence, and obey My teaching conveyed to them in these frail but chosen vessels. But if they despise the rebuke designed for their healing, I will visit them with so many humiliations that they will become a byword to the whole world; for herein is the most just and the most frequent punishment of the proud, that whereas they, carried away by the wind of their pride, seek to raise themselves above themselves, they are dejected and cast down even below themselves. Whereupon, my daughter, make thou haste to obey Me, without further hesitation, for I have a mission thou must fulfil, and it is My Will that thou go forth into the world:—Wheresoever thou mayest go in the future, I will be with thee: I will never leave thee, but will visit thee, and guide all thy actions." Then Catharine, prostrating herself at the SAVIOUR's feet, said humbly:—"Behold, I am the LORD's handmaiden; be it unto me even as Thou wilt."

This dialogue probably represents with much accuracy the conflicting views which agitated Catharine's mind before she entered upon an active career. Having once set her hand to the plough, it was not in her nature to turn back : and thenceforth her life was one of incessant labour. At first her energies were employed in what is pre-eminently woman's sphere; in ministering to the sick, feeding the hungry, and pouring balm and oil into the wounds of the suffering heart. She went to and fro doing good. Her delicate frame might often be seen in the streets of Siena, bowed beneath the weight of the gifts she carried to the poor. No hovel was so squalid that she refused to enter it; no disease so loathsome that she refused to wait upon it. And in her charity there was a loftiness, a generosity of spirit that rose to the height of heroism. The magistrates of Siena had ordered the expulsion from the hospital of an old leprous woman named Tocca. By promising that she would attend her, Catharine procured her re-admission; and in fulfilment of her promise, visited her twice a day, until her death. Persons of Tocca's class are often seriously ungrateful for services rendered to them; and Catharine's gentle attentions elicited from her only the most virulent abuse. Nor did the Mantellata meet with a better return from a woman whose cancer she dressed; the woman, in conjunction with a sister of the convent, inventing slanders against the reputation of her benefactress. Lapa, when this cruelty came to her ears, forbade her daughter to wait any longer on so miserable a creature; but Catharine threw herself at her mother's feet, and would not rise until the prohibition was retracted. It is pleasant to know that both this woman and old Tocca were conquered at last by Catharine's persistent goodness, and became her most devoted admirers.

The feeling which animated the Athenians against Aristides the Just is one that is often excited in mean and ungenerous natures by conspicuous excellence, moral or intellectual. To the vicious no reproof is so stern, and none so hard to be forgiven as that which is conveyed by a virtuous life. It is not difficult, therefore, to understand the malevolence with which many of the Sienese, and even of the Dominicans themselves, regarded this noble young girl, with her selfdenial, her patient forbearance, her burning zeal. They murmured against her, says Raymond of Capua, her friend and biographer, as envy always murmurs against the great and good. Some derided her asceticism, and shrugging their shoulders, said :—" I warrant you she feeds well enough in secret." Others found an excuse for their own more indulgent way of living in the assertion, that all the saints by word and example had denounced singularity. Others enlarged on the truth that all excess is vicious, even, said they, excess in self-denial, an excess of which, you may be sure, they themselves were never guilty ! Some with a fine affectation of candour, professed their respect for her intentions, but believed her to be the victim of dangerous delusions. Others again, less cautious in their jealousy, calumniated her publicly, protesting that she was influenced by mere vanity and a desire to attract applause. Her confessor, a certain Father Thomas della Fonte, was so moved by these incessant reports, that he advised her to moderate her fasts and restrict her prayers; advice which troubled her sorely, for she feared at first that she might have been misled by spiritual vanity. Yet how could she deny herself recourse to what was her sole consolation, hope, and guidance ? She entered into a full explanation of her motives and feelings to her confessor, with the result that he exclaimed :—" Henceforth act according to the inspiration of the HOLY GHOST : for I perceive that GOD will accomplish great things in you."

Palmerina was a Sienese lady, who had joined the sisterhood of which Catharine was the youngest member, and had dedicated all her wealth to GOD. Though not naturally of a mean or ignoble disposition, she conceived a violent jealousy of the young Mantellata, so that the mere mention of her name roused her worst passions, and she lost no opportunity of speaking of her injuriously. Her antipathy became notorious, and proved to Catharine a source of intense grief. As was her wont in all seasons of trial, she sought counsel of her GOD. " Wilt Thou suffer, O FATHER," she exclaimed, "that I should be the occasion of injury to a soul which Thou hast created so noble ? Is this the good that Thou hast promised to effect by me ? Well do I know that my sins have been the cause of it; but lo, I will not cease to claim Thy mercy for my sister, till Thou savest the soul of that beloved one from sin and death." Her prayers were heard, and her gentle forbearance wrought such a change in Palmerina's temper, that she sought out her injured sister, and with tears implored her forgiveness. Nor was she content until she had acknowledged her ill-doing in public, and spoken of Catharine as one "without guile."

It was specially distasteful to those religious professors in whom self-love still flourished unchecked, that so young a maiden should surpass all others by the severity of her morals, and the ardour of her devotion. If they allowed her to go to Communion, they insisted that she should finish her prayers immediately and leave the church. While engaged in prayer, Catharine often fell into a kind of trance or ecstasy, in which she became insensible to all outward conditions, and like S. Paul seemed caught up into the third heaven. Raymond relates that finding her, on one occasion, in this state of spiritual rapture, he heard her murmuring to herself:—*Vidi arcana Dei,* (" I have seen the secret mysteries of GOD;") and after she had returned to her home, she repeated,—*Vidi arcana Dei,* as if the awful sight had so impressed her that she could not bring back her thoughts to earth. "Why," said Raymond, "why do you say these words? Can you tell us nothing of the glories you have seen?" "Impossible!" said she; "so vast the distance between what my spirit contemplated when GOD drew it up to Himself, and what may be described in human speech, that I should feel I was falsifying what I saw in speaking of it,—this only can I say, that I saw ineffable things." Once when she was discovered in such an ecstatic mood by some of her enemies, they seized her roughly, carried her out of the church, and flung her down upon the stones outside, in a swoon, alleging that their rough treatment was the proper cure for her "illusions," just as the world seems to think that genius should be cured of its "extravagance" by persecution. Raymond, when he arrived on the spot, found three of her female friends bending over her where she lay in the scorching rays of the noontide sun, rubbing her hands, and tearfully awaiting her return to consciousness.

Great, however, is the blessedness of Patience. They who wait are they who conquer. Catharine not only lived down the small maliciousness and paltry jealousy of her adversaries, but won the love, the esteem, and the confidence of the Sienese. That restless population soon learned to welcome her as the Peacemaker, who did not fear to throw herself into the midst of their contentions, for the purpose of reconciling opposing factions, and removing the causes of strife. She frequently mediated between the artisans and their employers. Gifted with great natural eloquence, she addressed the surging crowds as they gathered in the streets on quarrel bent, and implored them for the love of JESUS to be at peace with one another. Her influence daily increased, strengthened as it was by the general belief that she was specially favoured with divine revelations. The proud nobles of Siena gladly accepted her mediation and solicited her advice; and happy was she if she could restore peace where enmity had prevailed; if she could compose the quarrels of families; if she could reclaim the sinner from his sin.

Young Francis Malavolti, a member of a Patrician house, was induced to visit the saintly daughter of the wool-dyer. The first visit was not the last; he learned to appreciate her holy conversation, and to delight in it, but as soon as he was left to himself, his evil habits regained the mastery, especially gambling, of which he was passionately fond. By these frequent lapses he greatly tried the forbearance of his counsellor, but she prayed earnestly for a divine benediction on her exertions, and after her death he forsook the paths of vice, and gave himself up to the service of GOD. Vanni, a Sienese painter, distinguished by his fierce and unrelenting temper, and suspected of having instigated several secret murders, was persuaded by one Friar William of England, to go and see the saint. Unwillingly he consented, but he took care to state his resolution of contemning any advice she might give him. What followed is narrated by Raymond of Capua, who was at the Fullonica, waiting for Catharine's return from some errand of mercy, when the painter arrived.

"I went to meet him," he says, "with a joyful heart, told him of her absence, and urged him to wait a little; to beguile the time, I introduced him into her little room. After ten minutes or so, Vanni grew weary, and said languidly :—'I promised Friar William that I would call upon this lady, but she is absent, and my work makes it impossible for me to stay longer; be so kind as to make my excuses to her.' I was much distressed at Catharine's absence, and in order to detain him I began to speak of reconciliation with one's enemies; but he interrupted me, saying : 'See now, you are a priest and a religious man, and this good lady has a great savour of sanctity. I must not deceive you, and therefore I tell you frankly that I do not mean to do anything of the kind which you advise; useless is it to preach to me on such a subject, you will gain nothing by it. It is already no small concession on my part that I have spoken to you with so much freedom of what I conceal from others. No more will you obtain; so I beg you to torment me no more upon this matter.'

"At that moment Catharine arrived, and I could perceive that her appearance was as unwelcome to him as it was grateful to me. As soon as she saw us seated in her room she smiled, and this man of the world she received with singular grace and kindness. Seating herself, she inquired the motive of his visit. Vanni repeated what he had just said to myself, protesting that he would make no concession. In reply, she represented with equal force and vividness how greatly he was his own enemy; but he steeled his heart against her arguments. She then retired, in order to pray alone, and I remained with Vanni so as to gain time. Not many minutes had expired before he looked up and said to me :—' For courtesy's sake, I will not refuse her utterly. I have four great enmities; I will give up the one which it will most please you I should give up.' Then he rose to go away; but before reaching the door he suddenly exclaimed :—' My God! what a consolation my heart feels at my having uttered that one word of peace.' And he added :—'O my Lord and my God! what power is it which retains and triumphs over me? Yes, I am vanquished,—I confess it! I cannot draw my breath.' The heart which had been long bound in the iron bonds of hatred and sullen revengefulness was stirred to its depths, and struggling to free itself from that cruel thraldom, it already experienced the sense of coming peace and freedom. Catharine again approached him. He fell on his knees, sobbing, and said :—' Dear lady, behold me ready to do whatever you desire of me relative to peace, and all else. I see now that Satan held me in chains. I submit myself to your guidance ; in pity, direct my soul.' Catharine regarded him with a joyous smile, and gave thanks to GOD. ' Dear brother,' she said, ' I spoke to *you*, and you refused to hear me : then, I turned to GOD, Who has not cast back my prayer.' For many years after this," adds Raymond, " I was Vanni's confessor, and can bear witness that he made constant progress in virtue, and that he bore with resignation some sore trials which befel him through the hostility of others."

The remarkable influence of Catharine was consolidated, so to speak, by her heroism during the plague of 1374. Siena then lay for months in the shadow of death. Men, women, and children died by hundreds ; the pestilence seized them, and in a few hours they were gone. All business stood still ; the corn rotted in the harvest fields, for there were none to reap and gather. Almost every house wore some sign of mourning. Through the silent, lonely streets resounded the terrible cry of the grave-diggers :— " Bring out your dead." But soon there were none to bring them out ; or if the ghastly procession started, you would see the priests suddenly cease from their chanting, or the coffin-bearers in their labour, to sit down by the wayside, and die. A panic of fear was upon the city. The judgment-seats were empty ; there were no prosecutors, and none accused ; the laws were suspended by the terror ; the magistrates no longer needed. It was in this awful emergency that Catharine, with her company of fellow-workers, shamed the population out of their cowardice by the sublimest devotion to duty. She penetrated into the most loathsome alleys ; she went where the infection was the strongest, and the sufferers the poorest ; she stood by the bedside of the stricken ; she wrapped the plague-spotted body in a decent shroud ; and all the while she cheered the living by the calmness of her bearing, and consoled them by the fervour of her prayers. Inspired by her lofty example, the Mantellatas rivalled one another in deeds of devotion and generous self-sacrifice. Not a few of them fell victims to their holy task ; but their companions, knowing well that they had passed into the presence of their Redeemer, bestowed the last kiss upon their foreheads, and then resumed their labour of love with increased zeal.

CHAPTER III.

CATHARINE'S repute for sanctity now spread far and wide; and in the eyes of the people she assumed a mystic character as one who enjoyed direct communication with Heaven. Less superstitious minds could not refuse their admiration to her devoted courage, to the purity of her enthusiasm, to the nobility of her motives. Such was the impression produced upon the inhabitants of Pisa that they sent a deputation to invite her to visit them; and when, after some consideration, she assented, and in company with her mother, several Dominican fathers, and three or four Mantellatas, arrived there, one evening in June, 1375, they sent forth their chief magistrate and principal citizens to welcome her, as they might have done to welcome some famous conqueror or powerful prince. Lodgings were provided for her in the house of the Buoncontis, where she received those who desired to consult her, and with her secretary's assistance conducted her vast and various correspondence. Many of her letters at this time related to public affairs; to the discussions between the Italian Republics; or to the project of a new Crusade, which greatly occupied her imagination. The same idea had occurred to the mind of the Queen of Cyprus, and her ambassador at Pisa rejoiced to obtain the powerful support of the Maid of Siena. With rare political sagacity Catharine perceived that while the Crusade might prove effectual in checking the aggressive progress of Mohammedanism, it would also promote the peace and prosperity of Italy by drawing off the bands of foreign mercenaries and "free-lances" who, living by the sword, pillaged Italy from north to south. As she afterwards said to Pope Gregory XI. :—" The undertaking of a Crusade would be the best security for the peace of Christendom. The turbulent soldiery who caused so much strife and vexation would gladly join in such an enterprise; few would refuse to serve GOD when the service gave them employment in their own professions. Thus, the fire in Italy would die out for want of fuel to feed it. Several excellent objects would be accomplished at once; Christendom would obtain tranquillity; many criminals would be removed from the scene and occasions of their criminal acts; and numbers of infidels might be converted and saved.

Her efforts to realize her scheme were vigorous and well directed. She wrote to the beautiful but licentious Joanna of Naples, informing her that the Pope had issued a bull recommending a Crusade, and urging her to set a noble example by taking up the Cross; to Bernabo Visconti of Milan, she enlarged on the glory, pure and unstained, he might acquire in such an adventure; to the Queen of Hungary she showed how it might roll back from her dominions the tide of Turkish invasion; to Sir John Hawkwood, the famous English Condottiere, she commended it as a higher object for his ambition to become the servant and warrior of CHRIST than the leader of ruthless soldiers, who sold their courage to the most liberal bidder. The fervour and persistency of her appeals seemed likely at one time to command a general response; and preparations were being made for an enterprise which would probably have exercised a great effect upon the later history of Europe, when a different direction was given to the thoughts of men by the rebellion of the Papal States against Rome. The Florentines also joined in determined resistance to the Papal authority, and in March, 1376, were formally put under ban and interdict. An atrocious intimation was given that they might be made slaves; and when both Genoa and Pisa, forgetting their old rivalry with Florence, refused to take advantage of the permission, they too were visited with an interdict. Catharine was then compelled to defer all hopes of a crusade until the breach between Rome and Italy could be closed up.

Exhausted by mental labour and physical effort, Catharine fell ill, and for some months suffered severely. In spite of all the care and skill of her friends, her weakness increased; she fainted frequently; and, on one occasion, lay for a whole day in such a condition of insensibility and rigid immobility, that all who waited beside her thought she was dead. At the hour of vespers she recovered, to tell her friends that, as she believed, her soul had actually been parted from her body, and permitted to enter the Golden Gates and look upon the glories reserved for the saints of CHRIST. On another occasion, when she had regained sufficient strength to resume her daily visits to the chapel attached to her residence, she spent there some hours of solitary meditation. As she remained longer than usual, her friends went to seek her. They found her prone upon the ground, with eyes closed, and unconscious of all that transpired around her. Silent, they watched and waited, while the shades of evening slowly gathered around the holy altar, and deepened in the nave and choir. All at once, while they looked on in awe and astonishment, she raised herself upon her knees; stretched forth her arms until to the spectators her figure resembled that of a cross; her countenance was "all on fire;" her eyes were fixed in a settled wistful gaze on something which could not be seen by others; a strange smile hovered about her lips; still and rigid, she remained in this posture for several minutes; when suddenly she fell to the ground, like one who has received a death-wound in heart or brain. Her friends conveyed her tenderly to the house of the Buonconti, and by her side, when she awoke to a sense of the outer world, sat her friend and confessor, Raymond of Capua. "Father," she whispered to him, "I bear in my body the marks (*stigmata*) of the LORD JESUS." Afterwards she spoke more fully:—"I saw my LORD extended on His cross; from each of His Five Wounds streamed towards me a ray of heavenly light. My love for Him, and my soul's yearning to throw itself out of the body towards Him, were so strong, that they raised me from the ground on which I was prostrated, and supported me while I gazed upon Him. The five bright rays streaming towards me pierced my hands, my feet, and my side with a pain so sharp that I fell, as if dead. Then I besought the LORD that His blessed wounds might not appear visibly in my body; so that none but myself may know my secret pain."[1]

Upon this delusion it seems unnecessary to make any

[1] *Acta Sanctorum, Vit. Cath.*, cc. 192—194.

comment. It need not affect our estimate of Catharine's character, for it is certain that she was herself deceived; that it was no ingenious invention, designed to impose on the minds of men, and enhance her reputation as a favoured instrument of Providence, but the half-delirious fancy of a heated imagination, acted upon by certain physical conditions. We can surely forgive her this weakness when there was so much in her that was pure, true, and noble. Generally, she well understood the limits of her powers, and great as was her enthusiasm, her humility was greater. She never sought, she rather shrank from and dreaded, the repute which clung about her, and the extravagant admiration of her friends. There was a gentle wisdom in her conduct not less worthy of note than her fervid piety. A striking illustration is supplied by her dealings with Pietro Albizi, the jurist, and Giovanni Gutalebracia, the physician, who in their disgust at the fame and influence enjoyed by a mere woman, sought an opportunity of exposing her to ridicule. Waiting upon her for this unworthy purpose, Gutalebracia began by saying :—" Messer Pietro Albizi and I have heard, madam, of your learning as well as of your virtues, and we are here in the hope of benefiting by your spiritual instruction. We are desirous of knowing how you understand the passage in which it is said that GOD spake in order to create the world. Has GOD a mouth and a tongue?" He propounded other questions of a similar nature, and then awaited her reply. It was given with modest dignity :—

" I am surprised that you, who are, as you inform me, teachers of others, should present yourselves before a poor woman whose ignorance it would be much more proper that you should enlighten. But as you wish me to answer you, I will do so as GOD will enable me. What advantage would it be to me or to you to know how GOD spake in order to create the world? GOD is a Spirit, and what is necessary for us all to remember is, that our LORD JESUS CHRIST, the SON of GOD, assumed our nature, and suffered and died for our salvation. Yea; the essential thing for me is to believe this, and to think upon this, so that my heart may be filled with love towards Him Who hath so abundantly loved me. This is the true science."

She continued in this strain with so much fervour, that Messer Pietro was moved to tears. Suddenly removing his bonnet of crimson velvet from his head, he fell on his knees, and asked her to forgive him for having come with the evil intention of putting her to shame. Catharine extended her hand, helped him to rise, seated him beside her, and entered into a long conversation with him upon " the things that are not of this world." Thenceforward he was enrolled among her sincerest and warmest admirers.

The influence of Catharine prevented Siena, Lucca, and Arezzo from joining the great league of the Italian States against Rome, of which Florence was both heart and head. She mourned bitterly over the troubled condition of the Holy City, then abandoned by its Popes, who lived in luxurious indolence at Avignon; and during the earlier and purer period of the stormy career of Rienzi, the last of the Roman Tribunes, she was his faithful friend and counsellor. Her political sagacity predicted the schism that broke up Christendom three years later; though she looked beyond that time of trouble and disunion to a distant future, when, as she hoped, Christendom would return to its primitive simplicity, and acknowledge the SAVIOUR Who had redeemed it by His own blood. Sorely disturbed by the miserable dissensions of the Church, she addressed an eloquent and animated letter to Pope Gregory XI., urging upon him an immediate return to Rome, which, in the absence of its proper head, was grievously oppressed by its patrician rulers. The vices of the clergy and the ignorance of the people she depicted with great power and frankness. She repeated her entreaties and remonstrances with a sublime courage. " You idly put your trust," she exclaimed, " in your soldiers, those devourers of human flesh; and so prevent the fulfilment of your desires for the reform of the Church. Place your hope rather in CHRIST Crucified, and in the good government of the Church by virtuous pastors. Let it please your Holiness to seek out true and humble servants of GOD as pastors in the Church, men who desire nothing but the glory of GOD and the salvation of souls. Alas, what corruption, what confusion, do we now behold! Those who should be examples of virtue and simplicity, who should be stewards of the wealth of the Church for the good of the poor and of erring souls, are a thousand times more deeply involved in the vanities and luxuries of the world than are the laity; for, indeed, many of the laity put their pastors to shame by their pure and holy lives. It seems, indeed, that Eternal justice now permits that to be done by force which is not done for love's sake. It seems that GOD permits the Church to be robbed of her power and wealth in order to learn that He wills her to return to her primitive state of poverty and humility, and of regard for spiritual rather than temporal things; for ever since she has sought temporal possessions she has fallen from bad to worse. It seems just, indeed, that He should permit her to suffer these tribulations. Open your eyes, Father, and see what those people are who are called apostles of the flock, and how they devour the poor; how their souls are filled with greed and hatred; how they have made their bodies vessels of every kind of abomination."

Her efforts were not confined to the Pope: she wrote with equal earnestness in the cause of peace to the governments of the Italian States. The Florentines had suffered considerably from the evils of warfare and the pressure of the Papal interdict, and at the suggestion of Nicolas Soderini, one of their most eminent citizens, resolved to invite Catharine to mediate between them and the Pope; a striking proof of the remarkable position this wool-dyer's daughter occupied. At their request she repaired to Florence, which she appears to have briefly visited two years before, on the occasion of some great Dominican festival. She was received with the profoundest respect; and during the fifteen days she remained in the bright city on the Arno, crowds daily assembled at the gateway of Soderini's palace, to see her as she passed out and in on her various errands to the different leaders of the republic. Having succeeded in composing the internal dissensions of Florence, she accepted the mission of pacification its inhabitants desired to impose upon her; and ill and feeble as she was, undertook the journey to Avignon, in the hope she might reconcile the Pope to his rebellious subjects, persuade him to resume his proper seat in Rome, and promote a new Crusade,—the last an object on which her hopes were still firmly set.

It was on the 18th of June, 1376, that she and her companions entered Avignon; where Pope Gregory placed at her disposal the palace of an absent Cardinal, with the chapel attached to it. After resting for a couple of days, she was admitted to an interview. In the gorgeously decorated hall of the Consistory, where the Pope was seated in a magnificent chair, with his Cardinals, in purple robes, on either side, stood the humble Sienese maiden, attired in a gown of white serge, over which fell her "carefully-patched Dominican cloak." She showed no sign of embarrassment or confusion, so that the dignity of her bearing and her calm self-possession astonished the spectators. Gregory felt at once that he was in the presence of a superior mind. She addressed him in Tuscan, Raymond acting as interpreter, and Gregory replying in Latin. After a long conversation, in which she gave signal proofs of keenness of observation, the Pope said to her:—"I commit the treaty of peace wholly to your decision. This is a token to you of my earnest desire for peace. I wish the negotiation to rest entirely in your hands; and I entrust to you the honour of the Church."

There was a war party in Florence as well as a peace party, and in Catharine's absence the former obtained predominance; so that when she notified the success of her mission, and desired that ambassadors might be sent to carry on the formal negotiations, a considerable delay ensued. To Catharine's mortification it soon became apparent that the ruling faction were determined to thwart her efforts; and when ambassadors arrived, she discovered that they came to draw the sword rather than to proffer the olive. For one whose whole soul was absorbed in an ecstasy of love and a thirst for peace, the disappointment was bitter; so bitter that, for a moment, the saint was forgotten in the woman, and she wept. Recovering herself, she continued her efforts; but they were fruitless. The negotiations failed, and the ambassadors returned to Florence.

She was more successful in her object of awakening in the Pope's breast a sense of his duties to his Italian subjects, and inducing him to return to Rome. She addressed herself to his conscience, and Gregory, a weak man but not a bad man, yielded. It is said that, in passing into the presence of the Pope, Catharine moved through a suite of state rooms, unparalleled in the whole world for magnificence. The windows looked out upon a landscape of great beauty, brightened by a winding river, and bounded by the white peaks of the remote Alps. The scene within was not less striking. At every step the visitor was arrested by some object of beauty; the breathing marble, wakened into life by the skilful chisel of the ancient sculptor; the glowing canvas, fresh from the easel of the greatest painters of the day; desks of carved oak or ebony, wonderful in their plastic forms; and gorgeously illuminated missals, the work of rapt monastic scribes, to whom time was nothing and labour a religion. One day Catharine remained for some time in silent study of one of these rich volumes. At length, Gregory, who had been standing by her side, exclaimed:—" It is here that I find rest for my soul,—here, in the study of books and the contemplation of nature." Catharine turned quickly upon him:—" In the name of GOD, and for the fulfilment of duty, you will close the gates of this sumptuous palace; you will turn your back upon yonder beautiful country; and you will depart for Rome, where you will live amidst ruin, tumult, and pestilence." Reluctantly Gregory accepted what he knew to be his proper work; but a fierce opposition was raised by the majority of his Cardinals, who were loth to leave the luxurious indolence of Avignon, and shrank from close contact with the stormy restlessness of the Italian life. At the Pope's request Catharine addressed the Consistory, and with fearless candour she inquired of its purple-clad members, why, in the councils and court of the Head of the Church, where every Christian grace ought to flourish, she found the development of the worst vices? Silence, the silence of shame and conviction, was the only answer. After a pause, Gregory made an effort to mitigate the sharp condemnation, and hinted that she had not been long enough at Avignon, nor had she seen enough of his court, to be able to form an accurate judgment. Hitherto she had sat deferentially before him; but at these words she rose to her feet, drew up her wasted figure to its full height, and stretching her hand towards heaven, exclaimed:—" I declare, in the name of Almighty GOD, that I perceived more distinctly the horrors of the sins which are committed in this court, while I was yet in my little room at Siena, than even do those who are in the midst of its vices." The Pope, we are told, made no answer; and the Cardinals were forced to own that "never man spake like this woman," while some protested, that "it was not a woman that spoke, but the HOLY GHOST Himself."

She held several conferences in the hall of the Consistory, in which she surprised "the learned doctors" of the Papal Court by her knowledge and clear interpretation of Holy Writ. Three prelates of high rank, who had been absent from Avignon at the time of Catharine's arrival, inquired of the Pope whether she was really as saintly as common report declared. Gregory replied:—"Truly I believe she is a saint." "Then, if it please your Holiness, we will pay her a visit." "I think," said the Pope drily, "you will be extremely edified." They went; and how they fared we learn from the narrative of one of Catharine's little household:—

"Coming to our house about nine o'clock, the prelates knocked at our door. I ran to open to them. 'Inform Catharine,' said they, 'that we wish to speak to her.' Immediately the Blessed Maid came down, with Friar John, and several other friends. The prelates bade her be seated, and she sat down beside them on the terrace. Then, in a haughty tone and with sharp words, they began to speak to her, endeavouring to wound or irritate her. 'We come from our lord the Pope,' they said, 'and we wish to know whether the Florentines did actually send you to him as is pretended. If they did, it shows that they have not among them a man of sufficient ability to treat of such important business with so great a prince. If they did not, we are surprised that a mean little woman (*vilis femella*) like you should presume to speak with our lord the Pope on so high a matter.' Catharine, always preserving her calmness, answered them humbly, but in a manner which plainly excited their surprise. After she had fully satisfied them on this point, they put to her some very delicate and subtle questions, especially on the subject of her close communion with heaven, asking her to explain the meaning of the Apostle's words where he declares that Satan changes himself into an angel of light, and desiring to know how she could prove that her own revelations were not the delusions of the devil. The conference lasted until late into the night, and I was witness of it. All Catharine's sayings were full of a marvellous wisdom and prudence. Friar John Tantucci, who was a doctor of theology of Cambridge, often desired to reply for Catharine; but, in spite of his learning, the prelates were so dexterous that they fairly worsted him in argument, and at last said to him :—'You should be ashamed to argue like that in our presence; let *her* reply; she satisfies us better than you do.' One of the prelates was an archbishop of the Minor Friars, a hard man, who disputed with a Pharisee-like pride; he would not accept in good faith what Catharine said, and wrested her words. The two others finally turned upon him, and said :—' Why question her any longer? She has answered all these things more clearly than any doctor among us could have done.' Then the dispute came to be between them and the archbishop. At last they retired, and they told the Pope that never before had they met with so lowly and enlightened a soul. But the Pope, when he learned next morning how the prelates had behaved to Catharine, was exceedingly mortified and hurt, and he sent an apology to her, assuring her that the prelates had acted wholly of their own will, that he had not in any wise commissioned them to do what they had done, and advising her to refuse to see them if they repeated their visit. In the evening, Master Francis, the Pope's physician, said to me :—' Do you know who those prelates are?' 'No,' I replied. 'Well,' said he, 'know, that if the learning of these three prelates were put in one scale of the balance, and that of the whole Roman Church in the other, the acquirements of these three would outweigh the other; and if they had not found Catharine so well-grounded in wisdom and knowledge it would have been the worse for her.'" It is unfortunate that the names of the prelates have not been recorded.

Catharine was opposed not only by the will of the Cardinals, but by the arts of the frail and fair ladies who were maintained by them in splendid shame, so that at times the task she had undertaken seemed to pass beyond the limits of the practicable. In sore discouragement she withdrew from the Papal presence, and sought her usual and only refuge, that of prayer. She wept and prayed; she prayed and wept; her tears as her prayers all springing from the same source of a pure and boundless love. At last the Pope came to notice and to feel her absence, and sent an urgent request that she would come to him. She obeyed; and then, as though he was starting a new subject, he asked what she thought of his return to Rome. As she remained silent, he pressed her more and more earnestly. After awhile she excused herself from answering: it was unfitting that she, a poor and ignorant woman, should aspire to advise the Sovereign Pontiff, who was surrounded by so many able counsellors. Gregory grew much concerned lest he should have disgusted by his irresolution his most trusted monitor. "Catharine," he said, "I do not ask you to give me *advice*; I ask you to reveal unto me the *will of God*." She remained silent. She had already made known to him what she believed to be the Divine will, and she cared not to speak further. Silence was always golden in Catharine's view; *acts* and not *words* were the principle of her religious system. Then said the Pope:—"By your obedience I command you to tell me the will of GOD in this matter." Bowing her head, she replied:—"Who knows more perfectly the will of GOD than your Holiness? Have you not pledged yourself by a secret vow?" It was true; but the Pope supposed that the fact was known only to himself, and now convinced that Catharine's appeal was prompted by Heaven, he threw aside all vacillation, and announced to the Cardinals his determination to quit Avignon.[1]

He entrusted to Catharine the necessary preparation, and by the 13th of September everything was ready. Early in the morning of that memorable day he left the palace, with his Cardinals, all mounted on white horses, richly caparisoned. Chariots followed, loaded with treasure; then came the chaplains and domestic servants of the Pope, and the carriages of the Cardinals and the Papal household. Armed

[1] Gregory was also influenced by the remonstrances of S. Catharine of Sweden, as well as by a regard for his interests in Italy, which were being ruined by his absence. It is said, moreover, that he took to heart the repartee of a bishop, who, on the Pope's asking him why he did not go to his diocese, sharply retorted the question on his questioner.

knights, with equerries, soldiers, and valets, headed and brought up the rear of the procession, which passed through the city amidst sullen and silent crowds. By way of Aix and Auriol, the Pope proceeded to Marseilles, where he took ship; but owing to a prevalence of winds and storms, he did not reach Genoa until the 13th of October. Catharine, who had travelled by a different route, awaited him there, and confirmed him in the resolution which the constant murmurs of the Cardinals and various untoward circumstances had already shaken. Shaken? I should rather say, overthrown; for shortly after landing he had held a consistory which almost unanimously voted in favour of returning to Avignon, and he had confirmed the decision. But Catharine's prayers and representations, aided by his own remorse, induced him to revert to his original determination; and on the 29th he again embarked, and set sail for Rome. Again the voyage was protracted by contrary winds, so that it was actually the 14th of January, 1377, before the Papal galleys entered the mouth of the Tiber. His entrance into Rome on the following day was welcomed by demonstrations of popular rejoicing at the termination of the so-called "Babylonian Captivity" of seventy years. But it did not bring about that peace which Catharine had hoped for; and the Pope groaned inly at the discomfort he experienced in his ruined capital from the turbulence of the nobles and the insolence of the citizens. The situation was one in which a clear brain and a strong will were needed; and, unfortunately for himself, Gregory had neither. He was one of those well-meaning men who, because of their weakness, are always doing wrong; who, through their timidity, throw away their own rights. He had not the courage to effect those reforms in the Church which could alone have secured its tranquillity and conciliated the people. They were urged upon him by Catharine in several impassioned letters. He acknowledged their necessity, but took no steps towards their accomplishment. For Catharine herself, however, he cherished the deepest respect, and, soon after his re-establishment in Rome, he availed himself of her assistance in negotiating with rebellious Florence.

Says Raymond of Capua, who had acted as Catharine's intermediary:—" During my sojourn in Rome, I was commanded by my Order to accept the charge of prior of a Roman convent, so that it was impossible for me to return to Siena. Before leaving Tuscany, I had had an interview with Nicolas Soderini. We had discussed the affairs of the Florentine Republic, and, in particular, the malevolence of the Eight of War (or military council), who, while professing to desire peace, continually fomented rebellion. Soderini said :—' I assure you that the people of Florence and all the honest citizens desire peace ; but some obstinate spirits that govern us are a hindrance.' I asked if for this evil no remedy could be found, and he replied :—' Yes ; if some reputable citizen, taking deeply to heart the cause of GOD, could come to an agreement with some of the leaders of the Guelph party, and bring about the removal from office of one or two of the worst of our present rulers, I think the public good might be secured.'

"For several months I had been busily discharging my duties as Prior, and preaching the word of GOD, when, one Sunday morning, an envoy from the Pope informed me that his Holiness desired my presence at dinner. I obeyed, and when the repast was over, the Holy Father said to me :— ' I am told that if Catharine of Siena went to Florence, peace would be concluded.' I replied :—' Not only Catharine, but all of us, Holy Father, are ready to serve you, and, if need be, to suffer martyrdom.' His Holiness continued :— ' I do not desire that *you*, Raymond, should go to Florence, for the people would ill-treat you ; but I wish that *she* should go, for, because she is a woman, and they hold her character in great veneration, they will be careful not to harm her, and will listen to her advice. Consider what powers it is advisable she should receive, and present them to-morrow evening for my signature, that this matter be not delayed.' I obeyed; and forwarded the bull of Gregory to Catharine, who immediately set out for Florence."

CHAPTER IV.

CATHARINE went to Florence, and strove very strenuously to put an end to the dissensions which raged between the two great factions of the Guelphs and Ghibellines, as well as to effect a reconciliation between the Florentines and the Church. In the frequent tumults which prevailed, she incurred great personal danger. The Eight of War were jealous of her friendship with Soderini, and provoked against her the hatred of the populace by pretending that she was an enemy to the democratic party. Once the angry mob burned down the house in which she resided, and when she escaped to another and yet another, followed her with incendiary torch, until the citizens feared to offer her an asylum. It was unsafe for her to be seen in the streets. Shouts were raised of "Where is that accursed woman? Bring her out, and we will burn her alive. Cut her in pieces!" But she who had preserved her courage when assailed by the powers of hell was not the woman to blench before an infuriated multitude. With her usual calm confidence she knelt down in a deserted garden, and offered up her fervent prayers to GOD. A band of zealots, armed with halberds, swords, and clubs, pursued her to her retreat:—"Where is the wicked woman? Where is Catharine?" Hearing their cries, she went forth and stood before them. The leader of the band rushed forward, brandishing his sword, and shouting furiously:—"Where is Catharine?" Kneeling, she said in a firm, unshaken voice:—"I am Catharine, do whatever GOD permits you to do to *me*, but, in His Name, I forbid you to approach or molest any who are with me." This wonderful serenity abashed the rioter; he dropped the point of his sword to the ground; he cast down his eyes; her gaze overpowered him. He bade her begone. "Nay," she answered, "I am very well here, where would you have me go? For CHRIST, and for His people I am ready to die; nor is there anything I more earnestly desire. If you are ordered to kill me, do so at once, and without fear; I am in your hands; and know this, no harm will come to you from any of my friends." Confused and ashamed, the man withdrew, carrying with him his followers, and Catharine's friends and disciples, pressing round her, saw that she was weeping; weeping for the poor wretches who had menaced her life. "FATHER, forgive them," she said, "for they know not what they do!"

Pursuing her object with unabated ardour and unflinching perseverance, she laid the basis of a better understanding between the Pope and the Florentine Republic; and both sides agreed to send ambassadors to a congress to be held at Sargana for the settlement of the affairs of Italy. The Venetians and the Genoese, Joanna of Naples, and the Duke of Milan were also represented at this congress, and a general pacification was agreed upon, when the death of Gregory, who had long been fighting against disease, occurred in March, 1378. Then, for awhile, the thoughts of men were turned from treaties of peace by the great schism which almost rent the Roman Church in twain. To the vacant chair of S. Peter was raised Urban VI., a man of great vigour of character, but of a haughty and self-reliant disposition. With a strenuous hand he immediately began to sweep away some of the abuses that were gravely weakening the Church, and to reform the lives of the clergy; but he pursued his object with an unwise zeal that stirred up against him a great mass of envy. Catharine, who had learned to know him at Avignon, appreciated his honest efforts for the Church's welfare, while she saw the evil that would result from his arrogance of will. And, therefore, she advised him to temper enthusiasm with charity, and to listen to the teaching of Christian counsellors, though never failing to commend, and encourage him in, his good works. The majority of the Cardinals, however, rebelled against a Pope who was so resolutely determined to abate their luxuriousness, and supported by the King of France and the Queen of Naples, declared the Holy See vacant, August 9, 1378, proceeding soon afterwards to the election of a new Pope, Robert of Genoa,[1] with the title of Clement VII. In the great ecclesiastical quarrel which followed, Catharine was on the side

[1] The character of this bold, unscrupulous man of genius, half-warrior, half-statesman, appears in his famous saying:—"Certe non servirem Deo, si non faceret mihi bonum." (Certes, I should not serve GOD, if it brought me no gain.)

of Urban; and from her home at Siena,—whither, her work at Florence being happily completed, she had retired,— she issued letter after letter to ecclesiastics and politicians, to strengthen them in the same cause. To Urban her advice and assistance seemed so valuable that he invited her to Rome in order the more easily and the more frequently to consult her; and with some hesitation she obeyed the summons, and attended by a train of more than forty nobles, priests, and women, she arrived in the Holy City on the 28th of October.

At the Pope's request she appeared in the Consistory, and addressed the assembled Cardinals[1] on the trials and troubles of the Church, with an eloquence which moved them to astonishment, and a fire that kindled in them a new energy. Her exposition concluded with an animated appeal:—" Be of good courage," she said, " most holy Father. Whom do the blows of your enemies injure? Whom but themselves? Their arrows return to wound their own breasts. And you, too, reverend pastors, who surround our supreme pastor, be of good heart, and enter fearlessly into the struggle forced upon you. If GOD be with you who can be against you? Fight, and fight earnestly; but with no other weapons than prayer, repentance, virtue, love." When she had concluded, Urban rapidly translated her speech to the Cardinals, adding:—" What a reproach it is to us, my brethren, to yield to hesitancy and fear! I stand ashamed before this poor humble woman. Poor, humble, do I call her? Yea, but not in contempt,— as referring only to the natural feebleness of her sex. That she should be afraid, while we were courageous and determined, would be no matter of surprise; whereas, it is we who are timid, while she, fearless and calm, inspires us with her noble words. Does she not put us all to the blush? What should CHRIST's Vicar fear, though the whole world were against him? CHRIST the All-Powerful, Who is stronger than the world, can never forsake His Church."

Now was witnessed the spectacle of Christendom divided into two Papal factions, the Urbanites and the Clementines;

[1] To counterbalance the defection to Clement, Pope Urban had created twenty-nine new Cardinals.

a division which lasted for forty years, and unquestionably helped to prepare the way for the Lutheran Reformation. France declared for Clement, England for Urban, who had also the support of Germany and Bohemia, Hungary, Poland, and Portugal, while Scotland out of opposition to England, sided with Clement. Urban carried with him almost all Italy except Naples. The chief European thrones were at this time occupied by youthful sovereigns, whose authority was insufficient to decide the contention; nor was there, as in the former schism, any one commanding mind, like S. Bernard, who, by throwing all his weight into the scale of one of the claimants could ensure that the other should be generally regarded as an anti-pope. On each side were saints and prophets whom their contemporaries regarded with reverence; and Catharine of Siena, Catharine of Sweden, and the royal friar-prophet, Peter of Aragon, who embraced the cause of Urban, were to some extent counterbalanced by Vincent Ferrer, the famous Spanish Dominican preacher, and the miracle-working Cardinal-Bishop of Metz. Still, the influence of the Maid of Siena was undoubtedly much greater than that of any of the others; and Urban solicited her to use it for detaching Joanna of Naples from the party of his rival. Catharine addressed the queen in a series of pathetically eloquent letters, endeavouring to win her, not only as an adherent to Urban, but as a penitent to the Cross of CHRIST. It is not known, however, that these appeals were successful. In her interposition with Florence, Siena, Bologna, and Venice, however, Catharine was more happy, and she confirmed them in their allegiance to the man who, in her belief, had been rightly and validly elected to the chair of S. Peter.

But the time was swiftly approaching when, on earth, Catharine could no longer serve the great cause she loved. She had long suffered from an incurable disease, against which she had striven nevertheless, with all her unbounded energy. We are told that she was reduced to the most pitiably emaciated condition, and that she was tormented with a continual thirst; but she still laboured and prayed without ceasing. Those who saw her believed her to be rather a phantom than a human being; her body was visibly consumed, but her soul rose serene and joyful above every trial. Wonderful power of Faith, which can thus elevate the spirit above the consciousness of pain and affliction, which renders tolerable the anguish of the present by revelations of a glorious future ! Every day Catharine received those who sought her advice and assistance in matters of public or private interest; every day she visited the sick at their bedside, and the prisoner in his cell; every day she corresponded with the leaders of the Church in all parts of distracted Christendom; every day she repaired to S. Peter's, to offer up prayers for the welfare of the people; every evening she retired to her room to pray and meditate during the greater part of the night. She was the right hand of the Pope, who did nothing without her counsel; the stay and support of the Roman people, who trusted solely to her guidance. The sword was wearing out the scabbard. A life of such activity would have tried to the utmost a robust frame; what then must have been its effect on the enfeebled and exhausted Catharine?

Feeling that her end was approaching, and longing to be gone; desiring to depart where beyond the world's clamorous voices prevails the Sabbath-rest of the children of GOD,—she addressed her final advice to Pope Urban, encouraging him to persevere in the reformation of the Church, and not less urgently beseeching him to guard against his infirmities of temper. Letters of farewell were also written to her dearest friends and disciples. And thus the end drew rapidly nearer. It was accelerated by an accident which befell her on Sexagesima Sunday, 1380, when she would seem to have fallen, perhaps from weakness or fatigue, upon the steps of S. Peter's, and injured her spine, or violently shaken the muscular system. Her sufferings were thenceforth cruelly increased. During Lent, every morning after communion, her companions were compelled to lift her from the floor, and carry her to bed as if she were dead. Yet in the evening of each day she would revive, and arise and march to S. Peter's, a mile distant; would remain there for Vespers, returning home completely exhausted. In this course she persevered until the third Sunday in Lent, when she bowed beneath the burden of her sufferings, and the weight of the anguish which tortured her soul in view of the sins daily committed against GOD, and of the

O

perils and evils of the Church. She could no longer leave her bed; her body was that of a skeleton covered with a transparent skin. On the morning of Sunday the 29th of April, the flickering flame of life seemed suddenly to die down in the socket. She lay motionless and insensible,—the weeping friends around her bed believed, indeed, that she had already departed. It was thought advisable to administer extreme unction, when a sudden change came over her. She revived; but only to undergo, as it appeared, a last terrible assault from Satan. What misgivings oppressed her; what sense of something left undone; what agonizing but unreal doubt, who shall tell? It is certain that for several hours she endured a painful spiritual conflict, in which she gesticulated wildly like some earnest pleader for forgiveness, and sometimes uttered wandering incoherent words, and sometimes frowned, and sometimes smiled. The cup put to her lips was bitter, and she drank it to the dregs. At length she was heard to say distinctly:—"No, never! never for vain-glory, but for the honour and glory of GOD!" Then she ejaculated fifty or sixty times,—raising her thin white hand, but forced to drop it again through excessive weakness:—"Peccavi, Domine, miserere mei" (LORD, I have sinned, have mercy on me). Or she would sigh, as she gazed around her:—"Saints of GOD, have pity on me!" All at once the struggle ended; a light broke over her countenance, like sunshine upon troubled waters; her eyes, previously wet with tears, gleamed with a heavenly radiance; the battle was fought, and the victory won. Repeating her SAVIOUR's words, she prayed earnestly for her disciples and companions:—"Holy FATHER, keep through Thine own Name those whom Thou hast given me, that they may be one. I pray not that Thou shouldest take them out of the world, but that Thou shouldest keep them from the evil. Sanctify them through Thy truth; Thy word is truth." Having bestowed her blessing on the watchers by her bedside, and feeling that the last moment was at hand, she exclaimed:— "Yea, LORD, Thou callest me, and to Thee I come; not in reliance on my own merits, but solely on account of Thy infinite mercy, which I implore in the name, O JESUS, of Thy precious Blood." Several times she uttered the words:—"O precious SAVIOUR! O precious Blood!"

With a countenance that shone like an angel's, she said:
—"FATHER, into Thy hands I commend my spirit!"—and so, without a groan, died.

It was on the festival of S. Peter Martyr, and at six o'clock on the evening of Sunday, the 29th of August, 1380, at the age of thirty-three years, that Catharine of Siena expired. She was buried in the Church of the Preaching Friars, known now as the Church of the Minerva; but a year later, at the solicitation of the republic of Siena, the head was severed from the decayed body, and removed to Catharine's native city, where, with great festal pomp, the sacred relic was interred in the old church of S. Dominic.[1] In 1461, during the Papacy of Pius II., (Æneas Silvius Piccolomini), himself a Sienese, the name of Catharine was enrolled in the Roman calendar of Saints.

"Some of the chief Italian painters," says Mr. Symonds,[2] "have represented the incidents of S. Catharine's life and of her mystical experience. All the pathos and beauty which we admire in Sodoma's 'S. Sebastian,' at Florence, are surpassed by his fresco of S. Catharine receiving the Stigmata. This is one of two subjects painted by him on the walls of the chapel in San Domenico. The tender devotion, the sweetness, the languor, and the grace which he commanded with such admirable skill, are all combined in the figure of the saint falling exhausted into the arms of her attendant nuns. Soft undulating lines rule the composition, yet dignity of attitude and feature prevails over mere loveliness. Another of Siena's greatest masters, Beccafumi, has treated the same subject with less pictorial skill and dramatic effect, but with an earnestness and simplicity that are very touching. Colourists always liked to introduce the sweeping lines of her white robes into their compositions. Fra Bartolommeo, who showed consummate art by tempering the masses of white drapery with mellow tones of brown or amber, painted one splendid picture of the marriage of S. Catharine, and another in which he represents her prostrate in adoration before the Mystery of the Trinity. His gentle and devout soul sympathised with the

[1] This relic is yearly exhibited, on the 8th of May, the Festa of S. Catharine, when Siena decorates itself *en fête*.
[2] Cornhill Magazine, Vol. for 1866, pp. 311, 312.

spirit of S. Catharine. The fervour of devotion belonged to him more truly than the leonine power which he unsuccessfully attempted to express in his great figure of S. Mark. Other artists have painted the two Catharines together,—the Princess of Alexandria, crowned and robed in purple, having her palm of martyrdom, beside the nun of Siena, holding in her hand the lantern with which she went about by night among the sick. Ambrogio Borgognone makes them stand one on each side of Madonna's throne, while the Infant CHRIST upon her lap extends His hands to both, in token of their marriage."

I have shown the reader, as fully as my limits will permit, the nature of the various gifts,—the sublime disinterestedness, the all-absorbing enthusiasm, the force of character and mental power, the intense devotion, and heroic courage,—which made Catharine of Siena what she was, and gave her the position she so worthily occupied. This daughter of a poor tradesman, imperfectly educated, without powerful friends, not even endowed with that personal beauty which is in itself so powerful an instrument, influenced the councils of sovereigns and statesmen, controlled popes and princes, rebuked ecclesiastics, and openly censured the greatest men in Europe for their vices. Her burning piety and her glowing eloquence swayed principalities and peoples. She made popular a doctrine which of all doctrines the world most bitterly dislikes,—the doctrine that we live for the sake of others.[1] But if men could have resisted her prayers or her appeal, was it possible for them to resist her example? Must not the meanest nature have felt a touch of exaltation when it saw her going forth into the most squalid districts on incessant errands of mercy and goodwill, when it heard of the chivalrous intrepidity with which she nursed the plague-stricken, and received their latest sighs? Even at this distance of time, her actions have

[1] The law of love was the law of S. Catharine's life. We read it in one of her prayers, which, to this day, is used by the people of Siena :—
"O Spirito Santo, o Deità eterna Cristo Amore! vieni nel mio cuore; per la tua potenza trailo a te, mio Dio, e concedemi carità con timore. Liberami, o Amore ineffabile, da ogni mal pensiero; riscaldami ed infiammami del tuo dolcissimo amore, sicchè ogni pena mi sembri leggiera. Santo mio Padre e dolce mio Signore, ora aiutami in ogni mio ministero. Cristo amore. Cristo amore."

a vitality which bids us recognise their generosity, their excess of sympathy and love. There may be some disposed to smile at the record of her visions and ecstasies; to sneer at her wild fancy of an espousal to her Redeemer; to shrug the shoulders when her biographers speak of her heart as taken from her side that the heart of CHRIST might be substituted for it; but calmer judgments will allow for the hallucinations of a morbid nervous system, and admire the moral dignity and the intellectual energy which triumphed over the most unfavourable conditions. And cold indeed must be the heart that does not kindle with emotion when it recalls the story of Nicola Tulda,—a story that will form a fit conclusion to this sketch.

Nicola Tulda, a young knight of Perugia, had been condemned to death on a charge of treason. The accusation was false, the sentence unjust, and the young knight rebelled against it, pacing up and down his prison desperately, and refusing to be comforted. Priests exhorted him in vain : he loved life, and shrank from a shameful death. It chanced that while at Siena he had often heard the name of Catharine, and the thought occurred to him that she might save him. She went to the prison, and though she could not deliver him from his doom, she reconciled him to it. From her conversation he received such comfort, that he willingly made confession ; but he exacted from the saintly woman a promise, by the love of GOD, to stand by the block beside him on the day of his execution. She kept her promise. In the morning, before the great bell of the Campanile tolled, she was in his cell, and went with him to the Holy Communion, which, till then, he had never received. Humbly bowing himself to the will of GOD, he feared only that his courage might fail him at the last moment. But the infinite mercy of the SAVIOUR so inspired him, that he continued to repeat :—" LORD, be near me ; LORD, do not leave me ; if Thou wilt be near me, all will be well, and I shall die content." These were the words he sighed out as he leaned his head upon the bosom of Catharine, who consoled him, saying :—" Be of good courage, dear brother, you are soon going to your heavenly marriage-feast ; you go there bathed in the precious Blood of the Lamb, and with the beloved Name of JESUS on your lips." At an early hour she repaired to the place of execution, where she waited for him, praying. Kneeling, she laid her own head on the block, as if endeavouring to realize the pain, the bliss of martyrdom. She longed for it herself, she says,[1] but the axe did not respond to her wish. In her ecstatic meditation, she lost all sense of time and place; she saw nothing of the vast crowd that surged around the scaffold. Then arrived Nicola, walking "like a gentle lamb," and laughing for joy when he saw her. She made on his breast the sign of the cross, and said :—" Go, gentle brother, to your eternal marriage, and enter upon the life which knows no end." Calmly he knelt, with Catharine by his side; she placed his head upon the block; she whispered to him of the Lamb. He replied with two words only :—" JESUS ! Catharine !" The axe fell, and she caught the bleeding head in her pious hands. She closed her eyes, and said :—" LORD, *I will*, and Thou hast promised me what I will,"—and lo, "as clear as the daylight," she saw the SON of GOD receive the penitent soul into His bosom. "A deep peace," she writes, "fell upon me. So dear was the blood upon my dress, that I could not bear they should ever wash it off. I envied him because he had gone on before, full of joy and love, like a bride, who, having reached the bridegroom's door, turns, and bowing her thanks and her farewells to the companions who have gone with her to the threshold, enters the home of her beloved."

[1] See her Letters, edited by Tommaseo, (to Raymond of Capua.)

GIROLAMO SAVONAROLA:

THE REFORMER OF FLORENCE.

"It was the habit of Savonarola's mind to conceive great things, and to feel that he was the man to do them. Iniquity should be brought low; the cause of justice, purity, and love should triumph; and it should triumph by his voice, by his work, by his blood."—GEORGE ELIOT.

"From his early youth to the day in which he was led forth to die on the gallows, he was always equal to himself, in the innocence of his life, in the love of truth, in his charity towards the human race."—PADRE MARCHESE.

[*Authorities*:—Guicciardini, "Storia Fiorentina;" Sismondi, "Italian Republics;" Villari, "La Storia di Savonarola;" Capponi, "Storia della Repubblica di Firenze;" Von Reumont, "Lorenzo de' Medici;" T. A. Trollope, "History of the Commonwealth of Florence;" Burlamacchi, "Vita del P. F. Girolamo Savonarola;" F. Myers, Lectures on Great Men; Dean Milman, Essays, &c., (ed. 1870).]

GIROLAMO SAVONAROLA.

CHAPTER I.

AT Ferrara, on the 21st of September, 1452, was born Girolamo Savonarola. His father, Niccolo, was the son of a distinguished physician of Padua, who had been invited to Ferrara by its prince, Niccolo d'Este; his mother, Elena, a woman of elevated mind and singular force of character, belonged to the illustrious house of Buonacorsi of Mantua. Biography proves that men of genius generally inherit their endowments from their mothers. Such was the case with Girolamo. He was conscious of his debt to her; and in the trials and sorrows of his later life it was always into his mother's ears that he poured his confidence.

Wonderful tales are told of his boyhood, but they are not supported by any authority which can be safely accepted. What is certain is, that he was of a grave and quiet disposition, with none of that vivacity which we are accustomed to regard as a grace and charm of childhood. His intellectual promise, however, was such that his parents looked to him to build up the fortunes of his family as a great physician, and his grandfather superintended his education with vigilant carefulness. On the death of the latter, in 1462, his father undertook to instruct him in logic and philosophy, while to acquire the other branches of learning he was sent to a public school. He amply repaid the labour of his teachers; manifesting not only an ardent love of knowledge, but a great capacity of acquiring it. The quick wit and skill he showed in debate, and his thorough mastery of the old scholastic philosophy, with all its subtleties, as expounded by S. Thomas Aquinas, "the Angelic Doctor," led his companions to regard him as one destined to a high renown and a brilliant career. Nor was this conviction lessened by his seriousness of mood and his love of retirement. He was prematurely old. Shunning the pastimes and occupations of those of his own age, he employed himself in building brick altars, and in musing on the social contrasts that met his eye. Italian society was then almost at its worst—vice, corruption, and luxury running riot in the higher classes, and the lower languishing in the bondage of poverty and depression. He could hear the groans of the unfortunates and the clashing of their chains in the loathsome subterranean prisons of Ferrara, while over their heads throbbed the sounds of viol and lute, and silver and majolica glittered on the festal board. So he went to and fro, sad and dejected; fasting frequently; praying oft in the deserted churches; murmuring to himself at every fresh example of wrong-doing and ill-living, "*Heu! fuge crudeles terras, fuge littus avarum!*" His chief recreations were playing some "mournful melody" on the lute, or giving expression to his melancholy thought in simple but energetic verse. Thus he grew up into manhood; and he stood just upon the threshold of active life when the sadness of his soul was deepened by a private sorrow.

Close to his father's house lived a Florentine exile, of the noble family of the Strozzi, between whom and the young Savonarola sprang up a lively intimacy. He was naturally attracted to a citizen of the famous republic which had won such honours in art and literature, in war and commerce; the republic glorified by the genius of Dante. He regarded him as suffering from the injustice of cruel foes, as suffering for the love of freedom and the cause of patriotism; and from what he saw in his refined home he began to understand that there might be a people differing greatly from the inhabitants of Ferrara. Strozzi had a natural daughter; and Savonarola loved her. Glowing with a new dream of happiness, he ventured to reveal his passion; but was met with the haughty reply that a Strozzi could not condescend to ally herself with a Savonarola. In his sudden indignation, the young man made a scornful answer, reminding her of the fault of her mother; and they parted. Thus were all his bright fresh hopes withered in a moment; thus was he once more thrown back on his own gloomy thoughts. This incident increased his despondency. Wherever he gazed, all was barren. The world's joys were Dead Sea apples, which crumbled into ashes on the lips of the fools who ate them. Again and again he exclaimed, in the words of Polydorus :—"*Heu! fuge crudeles terras, fuge littus avarum!*" and he felt a strong desire for some peaceful asylum, where his spirit might no longer be vexed by "the great misery of the world, the iniquities of men, the rapes, the adulteries, the robberies, the pride, the idolatry, and the cruel blasphemy." "I could not bear," he continues, "the great wickedness of the blinded peoples of Italy; and so much the more that I saw virtue everywhere disdained and vice held in honour. This was the greatest suffering that I could have had to endure in this world; on which account I prayed every day to the LORD JESUS CHRIST that He would deign to raise me up out of this mire. And I made continually short prayers to GOD with the most fervent devotion, saying :—'Show Thou me the way that I should walk in, for I lift up my soul unto Thee.'"

His profound depression is seen in his poem, "De Ruina Mundi," written in 1472,—a remarkable poem to have been the work of a youth of twenty,—as gloomy as Byron's most misanthropic utterances, but with a gloom that sprang from a higher and more spiritual source :—

" Videndo sotto sopra tutto il mondo,
    Ed esser spenta al fondo
Ogni virtute ed ogni bel costume,
    Non trovo un vivo lume,
Nì pur chi de' suoi vizi si vergogni . . .

" Felice omai chi vive di rapina,
E chi dell' altrui sangue più si pasce :
    Chi vede spolia e i suoi pupilli infasce,
E che di povre corre alla ruina.
    Quell' anima è gentile e peregrina
Che per fraude e per forza ha più acquisto ;
    Chi sprezza il ciel con Cristo,
E sempre pensa altrui cacciare al fondo . . .

"Se non che una speranza
Pur al tutto non lascia far partita,
Ch'io so che in l'altra vita
Ben si vedra qual alma fu gentile
E che alzò l'ale a più leggiadro stile."

[. . . Seeing the whole world in confusion; with every virtue and lofty habit dead; no light shining in the darkness; and none ashamed of their vices. He calls himself happy who lives by rapine, and feeds on the blood of others; who robs widows and his own wards; who drives the poor to ruin. That soul is considered gentle and refined which gains the most by force and fraud, scorns heaven and despises CHRIST, and constantly devotes its thoughts to the destruction of its fellows. But there is still one hope which does not abandon me. In the other life it shall be clearly seen whose spirit was tender and kind, who elevated his wings to reach a purer air.]

Daily his prayers increased in fervency, and daily he sent up the frequent aspiration :—" O LORD, make known to me the way in which I am to guide my soul!" The more he saw of life and the world, the deeper was his disgust; its religious and moral darkness drove him to any sanctuary where he might rest, alone with himself and with his GOD. Nor was this, as Dean Milman points out,[1] the act of a timid, over-scrupulous, superstitious mind. It was forced upon him by the pressure of external conditions on a sensitive conscience. Perhaps in no era of the civilized world since CHRIST, unless we except the worst days of the Lower Empire, was the moral state of mankind, in some respects, at a lower level, a greater depth of degradation. Never were the two potent enemies of human happiness, cruelty and sensuality, so dominant over all classes; and in those vices Italy, in one sense "the model and teacher of the world," enjoyed a fatal pre-eminence. The only asylum then open to a man of deep conviction was the Church; and the admiration which Savonarola felt for S. Thomas Aquinas inclined him to become a member of the order of S. Dominic. In 1474, while on a visit to Faenza, he heard a sermon from an Augustine monk that led him to carry his inclination into action. "I heard a word," he said, long

[1] Quarterly Review, xlix. 3.

afterwards, "which I will not tell you now, but to this hour I have it in my heart." What this mysterious word was, he never made known; but such was its potency, he returned to Ferrara resolved upon adopting the monastic life. And to this resolution, notwithstanding domestic trials, he steadfastly adhered. He felt the bitterness of parting from his parents, and especially from his mother; and for nearly a whole year he underwent a painful struggle, but his decision was irrevocable. The evening before the day which he had secretly fixed for his departure, he was sitting with his lute, and transmuting his sadness into melody. His mother seemed all at once to understand what was inly troubling him, and exclaimed :—" My son, that is a sign we are soon to part." He durst not raise his eyes from the ground, but he had resolution enough to continue, with trembling hand, to touch the strings of his instrument.

Next day, the 24th of April, was the Feast of S. George, and all Ferrara made holiday. Unobserved, Savonarola stole out of the city, and made his way to Bologna, where he applied at the Dominican convent for admission, offering to serve in the humblest capacity. He was at once received, and began to prepare for entering on his novitiate. This step taken, he wrote affectionately to his father, endeavouring to comfort him, and explaining the motives which had governed his conduct. "The cause," he said, "was this, that I could no longer endure the gross corruption of the age, could no longer bear to see vice triumphant throughout Italy, and virtue prostrate in the dust. It was no ill-considered resolve, but one adopted after much meditation and long-endured grief. I had not the heart to make it known to you, from the fear that I might not have courage enough to carry it into execution. Dearest father," he concluded, "do not allow your sorrow to be added to mine, already most severe. Take courage, comfort my mother, and send me your blessing together with hers." He added that, near the window at home, he had left some papers which would more clearly explain his views. His father, searching in the place indicated, found a small tractate, entitled, "On a Disregard of the World," and read in it an indignant denunciation of the vicious habits of the time :—
"'There is no one, not even one," exclaimed the writer,

"remaining who desires the good; we must learn from children and women of low estate, in whom alone survives a shadow of innocence. The righteous are oppressed, and the people of Italy are become like the Egyptians who held God's people in servitude. But already," continued the young seer, " already we discern famines, and inundations, and pestilences, and many other signs of coming evil announcing the wrath of the Almighty. Part, O Lord, part again the waters of the Red Sea, and drown the wicked in the waves of Thy indignation."[1]

At this crisis of his life we may describe the young man who, with so absolute a contempt of the ordinary pleasures of youth, had withdrawn himself from the world. He was neither tall nor short; of a dark complexion; with eyes that flashed from under thick black brows, a wide mouth, full and yet firmly compressed lips, an aquiline nose, and a furrowed forehead. He was not handsome, not even well-favoured; but the careful observer could not but detect in that dark melancholy countenance an expression of reserved power, and that air of stern endurance and decision which marks the hero, the saint, the future martyr. His temperament was what is called sanguine-bilious, grave and melancholy, with outbursts of passion; his nervous system was sensitive to an extreme. In short, his whole nature was that of a man born to do great things, and to suffer acutely in doing them; a man of strong will, yet susceptible to imaginative impulses. His manners, though unpolished, were simple and even pleasing. His discourse, though rude and unadorned, was effective and powerful, and well adapted to impress a popular audience by its rough and manly eloquence. Such was Girolamo Savonarola in the year 1475.

In his conventual life he gave himself up to meditation upon holy things. All his leisure was spent in thought and prayer. His vow of poverty he kept in the spirit and to the letter; eating barely enough to sustain life; wearing the roughest and coarsest garments, though always insisting on their cleanliness; and long shoes, turned up at the points, because, he said, they would be full of precious stones in Paradise. His fasts were so frequent and severe as to re-

[1] Villari, i. 19.

duce him to emaciation; and when walking in the cloister, he looked more like a spectre than a living man. His bed was of wicker-work, covered with a sack of straw and a woollen sheet. His obedience to the monastic discipline, his humility, his modesty challenged the admiration of his superiors and his brethren. He seemed to live a life apart altogether from the ordinary life of men; a life in which he held constant communion with his GOD. It was, at all events, a happy life; and the happiest that Savonarola ever knew. It gave him what his heart had craved for, liberty and peace.

I have spoken of his humility and his modesty; but these did not prevent him from bearing witness to the truth, where such a witness was needed, nor from sharply rebuking the follies of humanity when they were obtruded on his notice. It is said that, on one occasion,[1] he was visited by two monks of Vallombrosa, who were so impressed by the contrast between their comfortable garments and his coarse habit that they felt it necessary to apologise. "They wore such fine cloth," they said, "because it was so much more lasting!" "Ah," replied Savonarola, "what a pity it is that S. Benedict and S. Giovanni Gualberto did not know that; for then they might have worn the same!" Perceiving his rare gifts, his superiors utilised them for the benefit of the monastery by appointing him to teach the novices. This duty he discharged with scrupulous fidelity, though it occupied hours he would fain have devoted to prayer and solitary meditation. He found time, however, to commit to memory the whole of the Scriptures; and he carefully and copiously annotated every book he read, especially his Bible and his Breviary. These studies forced upon him a comparison between the Church of his own time and the Church of the Fathers, and led him to the conclusion that the vices he had deplored as existing in the World existed also in the Church. An earnest seeker after Truth,—possessed with a passionate hate of falsehood and wrong,—he could not and would not shut his eyes to the corruption that seethed around him. A lover of peace, he would not cry "Peace," where no peace was; a lover of liberty, he would not allow it to be confounded with licence. As, prior to entering his

[1] Burlamacchi.

novitiate, he had written on the "Ruin of the World," so he now wrote upon the "Ruin of the Church." "Where," he asks of her, "where are thy ancient doctors; thy ancient saints; the learning, the love, the purity of the Past? Where are the gems and sparkling diamonds that adorned thee? Where are thy burning lamps and thy beautiful sapphires? Where thy pure white stoles and melodious chants?" Then the Church, whom he pictures as a chaste virgin, leads him by the hand into a cavern, and says:—
"When I saw proud ambition enter Rome and sully the sacred places, I retired to shut myself up in this retreat, . . .

'Ove io conduco la mia vita in pianto,'

'Where I spend my life in tears.'"

And she shows him the wounds which disfigure her comely body, and her dishevelled tresses; so that Savonarola, overwhelmed with grief, implores the saints in heaven to have compassion on such misfortunes:—

"Prostrato è il templo e l'edifizio casto,"—

"The temple and the chaste abode all prostrate lie."

"Who has wrought this misery?" he inquires; and the Church, pointing to Rome, replies:—"Yonder proud and deceitful harlot." Then he lifts up the aspiration of his soul:—

"Deh, per Dio, donna,
Se romper si potria quelle grandi ale?"

"O God, lady, that I could but break those mighty wings!"

To which the Church answers:—

"Tu piangi e taci; e questo miglio parmi,"—

"Weep, and hold thy peace; for such to me seems best."[1]

But to hold his peace was impossible to a man of Savonarola's fervid disposition, and to break the mounting wings of Rome, the wings that carried only to perdition, became his fixed desire. It is difficult to understand how, in those

[1] "Poesie del Savonarola," canzone ii., quoted by Villari.

gration. Savonarola was then despatched to Florence, which had escaped the turmoil, and offered a secure and peaceful asylum. There he entered the Convent of S. Mark, little dreaming of the renown with which he was to invest it; of the unhappy, yet brilliant days he was to spend within its walls. Already the Convent had its associations of interest. It had been built from the designs of the celebrated architect, Michelozzo Michelozzi, at the expense of Cosmo de' Medici. It contained a valuable library of manuscripts, and was the resort of the most learned men of the time. Its walls had been enriched with beautiful frescoes by the famous Frà Angelico. And the father and religious founder of its

there. Enthusiast as he was, Savonarola was nothing if not practical; and the *shrewd* side (so to speak) of his character, which contrasted so strangely with the imaginative, but gave him much of his power over men, comes to the front in the following letter to his mother :—" No monks," he says, " or, at least, very few, gather the fruit of a holy life in their own country; and we are enjoined by the Holy Scriptures to go from our own homes; for no one finds so much trust reposed in him in his own country, as a stranger does, either in his sermons or in his counsels . . . If it has pleased GOD, unmindful of my sins, to elect me to so high a calling, for which I cannot be too grateful, be you contented that I am working in CHRIST's vineyard, away from my home, where I find, by full experience, that I benefit my own soul, as well as the souls of others, incomparably more than I could have done at Ferrara. Had I remained there, and there endeavoured to do what I do in other cities, I know that the same thing would have been said to me which was said to CHRIST by His countrymen, who, when He was preaching to them, said :—'Is not this man a carpenter, and the son of a carpenter, and the son of Mary!' and they would not listen to Him. So would they have said to me :—Is not this Girolamo the man who was guilty of such and such sins, and is like one of ourselves? We know well who he is. Many a time have people said to me in Ferrara, some of those who saw me moving about from city to city thus employed, that our friars must stand in great need of assistants; as much as to say,—' If they employ thee, who art so mean a person, on such important work, most assuredly they must greatly require assistants.' But away from my native town, such things have never been said to me. On the contrary, when I am about to leave a place, both men and women lament; and they deeply appreciate what I have told them. I do not write this for the praise of man, for I take no pleasure in praise, but solely to explain my object in absenting myself from my native country; and to show you that I do so voluntarily, conscious that it is pleasing to GOD, and healthful for my own soul and the souls of my neighbours; and this is more precious to me than all worldly treasures, which, in comparison with what I profess, are as dust."—Appendix to Villari, i. 349.

brotherhood was S. Antonino, a philanthropist of truly elevated character.

Savonarola's early days at San Marco's were days of tranquil happiness. He was delighted with all he saw around him; with the fair and fertile landscape, the softly-flowing Arno, the undulating outlines of the Tuscan hills, the gentle manners and speech of the Florentines. He appreciated the natural and artistic charms of that " flower of Italian cities," Firenze la bella : and its artistic splendours deeply impressed his imagination. The paintings with which Angelico had adorned the convent seemed to transport him to a world inhabited by saints and martyrs, and white with the wings of angels. He felt all the influence of the holy traditions of San Antonino and his works of love; and he rejoiced in the companionship of his brethren, who were far more refined and cultured than any he had previously known. He looked forward, therefore, with eager hope to a season of mental and spiritual calm. But this delusion did not last long. He soon discovered that if Art flourished at Florence, so did immorality; and the wonderful campanile, erected by the genius of Giotto, the still more wonderful dome raised high in the air by the daring of Brunelleschi, could not divert his earnest mind from the contemplation of the currents of vice and iniquity that raged around him. He saw that the ruler of Florence, the magnificent Lorenzo, with all his elegant learning and political craft, was steeped in profligacy and an adept in tyranny ; he saw that the people were given up to a refined but terrible sensuality and to the most cynical unbelief. He saw that his fellow-monks were immersed in worldly cares and pleasures, and shared in the prevailing scepticism. The gloom which had hung over him in Bologna returned : the times were out of joint ; and he felt that he was entrusted with the dangerous mission of setting them right. Once more he brooded sadly over the corruption of both the Church and the World. Once more he girded up his loins, that he might stand forward and deliver his testimony to the righteousness of GOD.

After serving for awhile as instructor of the novices, 1482—1486, he was appointed preacher. But, as at Ferrara, he was not successful in this capacity. He was too much in earnest, and too neglectful of rhetorical graces to please the

Florentines. His pronunciation was harsh, his gesticulations were vehement; his language was abrupt and ungraceful; so that his congregation of hearers seldom numbered more than five and twenty, while to the church of Santo Spirito, where a certain Mariano da Gennazzano preached, hundreds could not gain admission. One of his followers, Benivieni, said to the Monk of S. Mark's :—" My good father, it cannot be denied that your doctrine is useful here, and necessary; but your mode of conveying it is ungraceful, especially when contrasted, as it is every day, with Father Mariano's." Savonarola replied :—" Elegance of language must yield to simplicity in preaching the truth." There was nothing in the success of Gennazzano, who trusted wholly to elocutionary artifices, to humiliate Savonarola; yet, as Villari observes, he who knows with how many sorrows the first steps in life are haunted, and with what uncertainties the mind must struggle before it learns self-reliance, and how much an orator gains in force and fire if he enjoy the sympathy of his hearers, will readily believe that Savonarola could not feel indifferent to the coldness with which he was received. But he felt it more as a priest of GOD than as a man. He suffered because his hearers closed their ears to the Divine Word, and he attributed it to his own shortcomings that they would not listen to the truth. At first he thought of abandoning the pulpit, and confining himself to his duties as *Lettore;* but soon his natural energy prevailed over the temporary depression, and he resolved to do his utmost to wake a slumbering world from its deadly lethargy.

Who shall wonder that, in these circumstances, his quick and warm imagination daily grew more exalted? He felt like one of the prophets of old, when contending against the vices and ingratitude of the Hebrew people. He believed himself commissioned by Heaven to wage war against the corruptions of Rome. Fasting oft, praying constantly, brooding over the darkness of the age, his mind became susceptible to sudden phases of excitement. One day, the heavens seemed all at once to open before him; he saw a representation of the future calamities of the Church; he heard a voice commanding him to declare them to the people. If he had felt any doubts before respecting the authority and character of his mission, they vanished now;

he was charged with a solemn duty, and resolved to discharge it to the uttermost. The visions in the Old Testament and the Apocalypse were arrayed before his mind as realities; they prefigured the sufferings of Italy and the Church, and the regeneration which would be accomplished through his labours. Voices on all sides echoed in his ears, and called upon him not to falter in the path on which he had entered, not to bend beneath the burden of his work, not to shrink before the frigid indifference of the Florentines. Possessed with a holy enthusiasm, this Hero of the Cross cast away his shield, and drew his sword, and flung himself into the tumult of the battle.

In 1484 Pope Sixtus IV. died, and for a moment there was a hope that the evils of the Church might be remedied by the election of some worthy successor. In the interval Savonarola composed a "Song of Praise," in which, addressing our LORD, he exclaimed :—

> "Deh! mira con pietade in che procella
>   Si trova la tua sposa,
> E quanto sangue, oimè! tra noi s'aspetta,
>   Se la tua man pietosa,
> Che di perdonar sempre si diletta,
>   Non la riduce a quella
> Pace che fu quando era poverella."
>
> [. . . . Ah, look with pity on Thy Bride
>   Amidst the storms of life!
> What blood will flow unless Thy hand
>   Compose the impious strife.
> Thou who dost live but to forgive,
> Let not thy handmaid be made dumb once more,
> As in her poverty in days of yore.]

But all dreams of reform disappeared on the election of Innocent VIII., whose excess of vice was such that he actually taught men to regret the death of Sixtus! With a deep anguish in his heart, Savonarola repaired on a preaching mission to the town of San Geminiano, among the mountains of Siena (1485.) There he found a ready acceptance, and waxing strong in the sympathy of his hearers, he began to announce, as with prophetic inspiration, the words that for the rest of his life composed his ringing war-cry, the words which summed up all his anxious meditations and "sessions of thought,"—"La Chiesa sarà flagellata, e poi rinnovata, e ciò sarà presto;" The Church will be scourged, and then renovated, and that quickly! These three points he undoubtedly believed to have been divinely revealed to him, but at the outset, looking upon his hearers as not yet ready to receive the voice of GOD, he based them upon natural reason and the authority of Scripture. The Old Testament supplied him with a legion of arguments to prove that the sins of the Church would inevitably be visited by GOD with His awful chastisements. And these arguments he expounded all the more forcibly because they had originally suggested the ideas which his passionate imagination afterwards transformed into real existences, into revelations of the Divine Mind. And so it came to pass that whenever he denounced the moral corruption of the age and predicted its punishment, his courage rose, his genius shook off its fetters; his language flowed more freely, was more effective and eloquent; the attention of the people was arrested, and the rush of his burning invectives carried his hearers along with it. At San Geminiano he awoke to a full consciousness of his powers. Moreover he discovered that the forebodings which haunted his own heart, lurked in the hearts of his hearers, and that, in announcing a coming doom, he did but give expression to the fear which secretly oppressed the Italian people.

In 1486 we find him at Brescia, where he delivered an exposition of the Apocalypse, and in earnest language and with a voice of thunder, arraigned the people for their sins, and warned them that the wrath of GOD was at hand. He spoke to them of the four and twenty elders, whose seats were before the great white Throne, and he pictured one of them rising to declare the future wars of the Brescians; how that their city would fall into the hands of raging enemies, and rivers of blood flow through its streets; how that virgins would be outraged, and wives torn from their husbands; how that children would be done to death before the weeping, aching eyes of their mothers; how that all the country round would stand aghast at the sight of so much blood and misery. And he concluded with an impassioned exhortation to repentance, for the LORD would still have compassion on the good. The mystical images, the burning words of the preacher, produced a deep impression; he spoke like one who had authority from Heaven so to speak. And when, in 1512, the fierce soldiers of Gaston de Foix broke into Brescia, and slew six thousand persons in its streets, the Brescians remembered the Apocalyptic Elders and the predictions of the Monk of S. Marco.

These Lenten sermons at Brescia mark the crisis or turning-point in Savonarola's career. Thenceforward his name and repute spread throughout Italy; thenceforward his faith in his mission knew no wavering. But, in proportion as he realised to himself the nature of that mission, his modesty and humility increased. He was no Mohammed, arrogantly proclaiming a new creed, but a servant of JESUS CHRIST, delivering the message with which he was charged. In his prayers, and in his discourses on the faith, his enthusiasm so absorbed his whole nature, that his companion, Frà Sebastian of Brescia, told every one that Savonarola, while on his knees, was frequently in a trance; that he so burned with ardour as, after celebrating mass, to be frequently compelled to withdraw into solitude and silence; and that sometimes the head of Savonarola appeared to him crowned with a halo or mysterious light.

Attending a chapter of the Dominicans, held at Reggio, the enthusiast made the acquaintance of Giovanni Pico, Prince of Mirandola. He was then not above twenty-three years old, but his precocious abilities and extraordinary erudition had already procured him the name of "the Phœnix of Genius." Posterity has not confirmed the flattering judgment of his contemporaries; but there is no reason to doubt the facility of his genius, the charm of his conversation, and the easy grace of his manners. No more striking contrast can be imagined than that which this bright and handsome youth, with his fair hair falling loosely over his shoulders, presented to the austere Friar, who sat apart from the throng, his hood drawn over his head, his dark eyes glowing with unfathomable depths of thought, his brow lined and seamed with furrows, his face gaunt and pale. Yet on that very day they became friends, and friends they remained to the end of Pico's life. In Pico, says Villari, neither renown, nor praise, nor his high opinion of himself,[1]

---

[1] "A man so justly called the Phœnix of his age, and so extraordinarily gifted by nature, ought not to be slightly passed over, though he may have left nothing which could be read with advantage. If we talk of

had been able to corrupt the heart. His disposition, differing greatly from that of most scholars of the Renaissance, was essentially good, and ingenuously open to the inspirations of goodness and truth : this it was which sufficed to unite in a close and lasting friendship two men of natures so widely dissimilar.[1]

Into the discussions of the chapter Savonarola threw himself with all his soldier-like ardour, and he astonished the Dominicans by his nervous eloquence not less than by his bold denunciations of the profligacy of the clergy. The impression which he made on the mind of Pico was so great[2] that, from that day, he was never weary of eulogizing him. He spread his fame over all Italy; and on his return to Florence, never rested until he had induced Lorenzo de' Medici to urge Savonarola's recall to the Convent of S. Mark. Accordingly in the Lent of 1490 the monk reappeared in Florence. His friendship with Pico quickly assumed a confidential character; Pico's admiration of his teacher increased; and it may be conjectured that only his premature death prevented him from assuming, as Savonarola had done, the habit of the Dominicans.

In the quiet asylum of S. Mark's, surrounded by Fra Angelico's seraphic faces, Savonarola resumed his work as instructor of the novices. But he was not allowed to remain in the obscurity he sought. The renown of his eloquence had extended far and wide, and many who had once heard him with indifference were now eager to listen to his lectures. Some pressure having been put upon him by his friends, he reluctantly consented to the admission of a few strangers; and in the cloister of S. Mark's, near a damask rose-tree, which the loving reverence of the monks has renewed from time to time to the present day, he began to expound the Book of Revelation to a limited audience. This served only to whet the public curiosity, and he was constantly urged to return to the pulpit. Finally consenting, he

---

the admirable Crichton, who is little better than a shadow, and lives but in panegyric, so much superior and more wonderful a person as John Picus of Mirandola, should not be forgotten."—*Hallam*.

[1] Villari, i. 84.
[2] Burlamacchi says :—" From that time Pico felt as if he were unable to live without him."

besought his hearers, one Saturday, to pray to the LORD in his behalf, and added :—" To-morrow I shall speak in the church ; and after the lecture there will be a sermon." That morrow was Sunday, the 1st of August. S. Mark's was crowded ; and a great silence prevailed within its walls when Savonarola stepped forward and mounted the pulpit. He chose for his subject the prophetic images of the Apocalypse, and he applied them to the circumstances of the age with a terrible eloquence which appalled his hearers. " On the 1st of August," he has himself recorded, " I began to explain publicly the Apocalypse in our Church of S. Mark. During the whole course of that year I continued to set before the people these three propositions :—1. The Church of GOD must be renovated, and that in our time ; 2. Italy is to be scourged before this renovation ; 3. All these things will happen very quickly. I endeavoured to demonstrate these points to my hearers, and to persuade them by probable arguments, by allegories taken from Holy Scripture, or by other similitudes or parables drawn from what was taking place in the Church. I insisted upon reasons of this kind ; and I kept back the knowledge which GOD gave me by other means, because men's minds seemed to me not yet in a condition to understand such mysteries."

His success was so great that, in the following Lent, he was appointed to preach in the Cathedral, and thenceforth, for seven eventful years, he became a Power in Florence, its recognized spiritual teacher, its counsellor, and guide. It is true that, at first, his genius wavered for a little ; his enthusiasm seemed to sink beneath the burden of the responsibility he had assumed ; he temporarily lost faith, we may suppose, in his celestial visions and divine revelations ; and abandoning his exposition of the three points, his picture of a scourged and renovated Italy, he preached only on general moral precepts and religious subjects. But he quickly recovered his faith and courage. One day, at dawn, after a night spent in mental struggles, he heard a voice say to him :—" Fool that thou art, seest thou not that it is GOD's will thou shouldest keep to the same path ?" And his hesitation immediately vanished. He knew no more doubts, no more fears. He lashed the vices of the people with a merciless hand ; neither the rich nor the poor, neither the learned nor the ignorant, neither the rulers nor the ruled, escaped the scourge of his impetuous oratory. He had a work to do—CHRIST's Church to build up, Italy to regenerate—and he laboured to do it with all his powers of mind and body.

I have spoken of his eloquence. It is one thing to read, and another to hear; one thing to read the printed page at a time far removed from its original composition, and in the serene quiet of a nineteenth-century study; another to hear the sublime conceptions and pitiless invectives as they fall from the lips of the speaker, and are confirmed, as it were, by the shudder and the sympathies of excited thousands. But even to the modern reader Savonarola's sermons throb with a rare and genuine power. The arguments are frequently confused, the exposition is frequently incoherent; we are conscious of much that is imperfect and ill-digested, or fantastic and unsound; yet through all the life of a strong and passionate genius makes itself palpable. It is a great man who speaks to us, and a man terribly in earnest. And if such is the impression made upon us now, what must have been the emotions of those who heard the living voice,—who saw the inspired speaker as, upon the three outstretched fingers of his left hand, he marked off,[1] one by one, the three great, urgent, pregnant propositions that formed the basis of his teaching? What must have been their emotions as at one time he painted the miseries that awaited sinful Italy, the chastisements that she must receive from the Divine wrath; at another, exulted in anticipations of the glorious redemption that afterwards awaited her?

"Perhaps," says an eloquent living writer, "while no preacher ever had a more massive influence than Savonarola,

[1] To this characteristic habit George Eliot, in his "Romola," makes Monna Brigida allude :—"The three doctrines of their blessed Frà Girolamo—the three doctrines we are all to get by heart, and he kept marking them off on his fingers till he made my flesh creep : and the first is, Florence, or the Church—I don't know which, for first he said one and then the other—shall be scourged ; . . . but then after that, he says Florence is to be regenerated. . . . And then, the third thing, and what he said oftenest is, that it's all to be in our days : and he marked that off on his thumb, till he made me tremble like the very jelly before me." A powerful imitation of Savonarola's style of discourse occurs in chapter xxiv. (Book ii.) of this remarkable romance.

no preacher ever had more heterogeneous materials to work upon. And one secret of the massive influence lay in the highly mixed character of his preaching. There were strains in it that appealed to the very finest susceptibilities of men's natures, and there were elements that gratified low egoism, tickled gossiping curiosity, and fascinated timorous superstition. His greed of personal predominance, his labyrinthine allegorical interpretations of the Scriptures, his enigmatic visions, and his false certitude about the Divine intentions, never ceased, in his own large soul, to be ennobled by that fervid piety, that passionate sense of the infinite, that active sympathy, that clear-sighted demand for the subjection of selfish interests to the general good, which he had in common with the greatest of mankind. But for the mass of his audience all the pregnancy of his preaching lay in his strong assertion of supernatural claims, in his denunciatory visions, in the false certitude which gave his sermons the interest of a political bulletin; and having once held that audience in his mastery, it was necessary to his nature—it was necessary for their welfare—that he should keep the mastery. The effect was inevitable. No man ever struggled to retain power over a mixed multitude without suffering vitiation; his standard must be their low needs, and not his own best insight."

There was little theological teaching in Girolamo's sermons; there never *is* in sermons that really grasp the public mind; and what there was showed no special critical acumen. Savonarola was not a theologian, but a practical reformer; a reformer of life and conduct, not of doctrine. His sphere of action differed wholly from that of Luther. He had no fault to find with the Church's profession of faith, or with its government; it was against the abuses of the Papal court, and the moral corruption of the age, that he directed his vehement assaults. He wanted to make men lead better and purer lives; he had no call to correct their views of transubstantiation or justification by faith. In the ordinary sense of the word, therefore, he had no share in the Reformation; and yet there can be no doubt that his fervent denunciations of the prevailing abuses prepared the way for the great Lutheran movement. His sermons, in their directness of application and plainness of speaking, remind us of

Latimer, though they attain to a much higher order of eloquence. They are the sermons, not of a dogmatic theologian or exegetical commentator, but of a religious enthusiast, deeply concerned for the salvation of the souls of his fellowmen.

As, for example, take his denunciation of Gaming:— " If you see any in these days addicted to Gambling, believe not that they are Christians : no, they are worse than the infidels ; they are ministers of the Devil, and celebrate his festivals. They are misers, blasphemers, swearers, detractors of others' good repute, slanderers, robbers, murderers, full of all kinds of wickedness. During these holidays I do not allow you to gamble in any manner : you must be constant in prayer, continually rendering thanks to GOD in the name of the LORD JESUS CHRIST. He who games, and he who permits gaming will be accursed : cursed is the father who games in the presence of his son, cursed the mother who games in the presence of her daughter. Whoever thou art, if thou gamblest or sufferest gambling, I declare thee accursed : I tell thee that thou shalt be accursed in the city, in the fields, in thy harvests, in that which thou mayest leave when thou art gone, in the fruit of thy body and thy land, in thy herds of cattle, and thy flocks of sheep ; thou shalt be accursed in thy goings out and thy comings in."

With equal force and simplicity, he condemned usury and excessive gains :—" You then, through your avarice, lead an evil life, both body and soul. You have devised various methods of profiting by money, and by exchanges, which you call regular but are really most unjust. You have corrupted public functionaries and magistrates. No one can convince you that usury or unjust exchanges are sinful ; rather you defend yourselves to the perdition of your souls. No one is now ashamed to lend upon usury ; rather they who do not are judged to be fools ; and thus in you is fulfilled the saying of Isaiah :—' They declare their sin as Sodom, they hide it not,' and that of Jeremiah, ' Thou hadst a harlot's forehead and refusedst to be ashamed.' Thou sayest that gain is a good and happy thing ; but CHRIST says, ' Blessed are the poor in spirit, for theirs is the kingdom of heaven.' Thou sayest that happiness consists in worldly pleasures, but CHRIST says, ' Blessed are they that mourn, for they shall be comforted.' Thou sayest that a life of bliss consists in fame and renown; but CHRIST says, 'Blessed are ye when men shall revile you, and persecute you.' The Life hath manifested itself, yet no one learns it, no one longs for it, no one follows after it. CHRIST, therefore, laments over you, for He endured much to reveal this life in order that all might be saved; and He hath good ground of complaint against you; for by the mouth of the prophet He declares :—'We are weary with calling, my tongue cleaves to the roof of my mouth, for all day I have exhorted you with the voice of the preacher, and no one listens.'"

But Savonarola frequently rose to a loftier and nobler strain, as in his sermon upon the Epiphany :—

"' Now, when JESUS was born in Bethlehem of Judea, in the days of Herod the king, behold, there came wise men from the East, to Jerusalem, saying, Where is He that is born King of the Jews? for we have seen His star in the East, and are come to worship Him.' Mark the words, and observe the mysteries. Behold, then, that He by Whom all things were made, has this day a temporal birth. JESUS the Beginning of all things, after He had created the universe, was born, and had for His mother a young virgin. Yea, He who holds the world in the hollow of His Hand is conceived by a Virgin. He, Who is above all things, begins by having a native land. He begins by becoming of the same country with men, a companion of men, a brother of men, a son of man. Behold how GOD cometh near you. Seek the LORD, then, while He may be found; call upon Him while He is near. This is truly the bread that falls from Heaven, and refreshes the hearts of men and angels, so that it is the bread common to both.

"Listen, therefore, brethren, and be not as sinners are. Open your eyes and see who they are that come hither. I declare unto you, O men, and let my voice be heard by the sons of men. 'Behold the wise men:' Behold the Chaldeans, men who were not born among Christians : men who never received baptism; men who were never instructed in the laws of the Gospel; men who never partook of the Sacraments of the Church; men who never heard the voice of a preacher. *Behold the wise men of the East*,' coming from a wicked and perverse generation, from distant lands, regardless of pecuniary loss, or of toil, or of dangers. *They came.* When did they come? When the world was overwhelmed with idolatry, when men worshipped stocks and stones, when the whole earth lay concealed in darkness, when all men were filled with iniquity. When did they come? When JESUS was a little child, when He lay on straw, and was feeble, and had wrought no miracles. *We saw His star in the East*, the star which heralded His advent. Behold the men who saw the star before there were any miracles; when as yet the blind man had not been made to see, nor the deaf to hear, nor the dead been recalled to life; no other visible wonder had occurred. *And we are come to worship Him.* We have made a long journey, so that we may adore the footsteps of yonder infant. If we could but see Him, could but worship Him, if we could but lay our gifts at His Feet, we should be blessed. We have left our native land; we have left our parents; we have left our friends, we have left kingdoms, we have left great riches : we have come from a far off land, through many dangers, in this great haste, solely to worship Him. This sufficeth us; this we value more highly than our kingdoms; this we long for more than life itself. What, then, my brethren, shall we reply to all these things? What, through our faith shall we say? Oh, living faith! oh, boundless love! But behold the perfidy of the Jews! How great the hardness of their hearts; for neither by miracles, nor by prophecies, nor by such a voice were they moved.

" But why should we launch our reproaches at the Jews, and not rather at ourselves? Because we see the mote in our brother's eye, and perceive not the beam in our own! Behold, the LORD JESUS is not at this day a little child in the manger, but glorious in Heaven. He has preached, has worked miracles ; was crucified, and rose again ; sits on the right hand of the FATHER; has sent the HOLY SPIRIT upon earth; has sent forth the Apostles, has subdued the nations. Already the kingdom of heaven is opened unto all ; behold, its gates are opened, the LORD has led the way. The Apostles and the martyrs followed in His steps. But ye are lazy, all labour oppresses you ; ye have no desire to tread in the path that He has trod. Lo, how avarice increases daily,—how the whirlpool of misery widens! Luxury has contaminated all things; pride rises to the very clouds. Ye are the devil's children, and wish to fulfil your father's desires. Oh, do not the words of Holy Writ itself declare how little good is to be expected from you!—'Behold, I go to a people who did not know Me, and did not call upon My Name. I have stretched out My hand to an unbelieving generation which walks in the path of perdition, which provokes Me to anger.'"

The vast influence which Savonarola was rapidly acquiring soon began to give umbrage to Lorenzo de' Medici; and one day the great preacher was waited upon by five of the leading Florentine citizens, who blandly represented the probability that his plain speaking would endanger himself and his convent. "I well understand," said Savonarola, interrupting them, "that you have not come here of your own accord, but have been sent by Lorenzo. Tell him to prepare to repent of his sins, for the LORD spareth not persons, and feareth not the princes of the earth." Astonished at his tone of independence, they warned him that he ran the risk of banishment. "I have no fear of exile," he rejoined, "for this city is no more than a grain of lentils on the earth. But though I am a stranger, while Lorenzo is not only a citizen, but the first of citizens, it is I who will remain, and he who shall leave the city." And he added some remarks on the state of Florence which showed that he was a keen and an accurate observer, with a surprising knowledge of the political currents of the times. Not long after this curious interview, he uttered the first of his celebrated predictions, to the effect that a great change in the affairs of Italy was impending, and that the Pope, the King of Naples, and Lorenzo the Magnificent, were near the end of their days.

In July, 1491, he was elected Prior of S. Mark's, and his first step was an illustration of his views of ecclesiastical independence. He broke through the custom that had prevailed for a new prior on his election to pay homage to the Medici. "I regard my election," he said, "as coming from GOD alone, and to Him only shall I pay obeisance." Lorenzo was offended at Savonarola's boldness:—"See now," he said, "here is a stranger who has come into my house, and will not deign to visit me." But appreciating Savonarola's power over the people, he endeavoured to win him to his side, first, by frequent attendance at S. Mark's to hear Mass, and next by sending rich presents to the convent and large donations for the poor. When these stratagems availed not, he engaged Gennazzano as a rival preacher, in the hope he would draw off the Frate's congregations. In this, too, he was disappointed; the friar's cold rhetoric could not hold its own against the enthusiastic eloquence of the Prior of S. Mark's. To what measures he would next have had recourse, who shall determine? But Death stepped in to remove him from Savonarola's path, and fulfil the first part of Savonarola's prediction. He had for some time been suffering from a severe internal disease, and early in April, 1492, his physicians were compelled to own that their remedies were useless. Guicciardini tells us that the fatal termination of his illness was indicated by many omens.—A comet had appeared a short time previously. Wolves were heard to howl. A mad woman in Santa Maria Novella cried out that a bull with horns of fire was burning the whole city. The lions in a menagerie had fought together, and one specially fine lion had been killed by the others. Last of all, a few days before the prince's death, the lightning struck the dome of the cathedral, and caused several very heavy stones to fall,—and they fell towards the Medicean palace.

Lorenzo had lived a life of profligacy and open unbelief; but he desired to die the death of the righteous man. He took the sacraments, and he made confession, and he received absolution,—still he was not satisfied. He mistrusted the men who ministered to him in those last moments, and having no faith in their virtue or truthfulness, he could not feel content with their glib assurances of salvation. By his bedside sate his philosophic friends:— Pico della Mirandola was there, and Poliziano, but their elegant scholarship and airy Neo-Platonism could not soothe his fears. Suddenly he remembered that there was one man in Florence who spoke the truth,—the stern Prior of S. Mark's; and the thought came home to him that if Savonarola could tell him his sins were forgiven, he could believe, and be at rest. Frà Girolamo was summoned; and when apprised of Lorenzo's dangerous condition, he repaired to the palace. The interview that followed was one of the most remarkable recorded in history. On his deathbed lay Lorenzo the Magnificent, "the usurping destroyer of Florentine liberty, the philosophic sceptic, the licentious poet, the recklessly profligate man of pleasure, the fraudulent banker, the unscrupulous betrayer of the most sacred trusts;" by his side, still stern and unbending, stood the religious enthusiast, "whose only worldly thought or interest was a passionate love for that liberty of which the other was the sworn foe, to whose every sentiment, feeling, principle, habitude, the whole life and conduct of Lorenzo was inexpressibly hateful and revolting."[1]

When Savonarola arrived at Carraggi, the Medici's luxurious villa, Pico della Mirandola was with the dying prince, but as the Prior entered he left the apartment. Lorenzo, turning to the spiritual guide he had summoned, confessed that three things weighed heavily on his conscience, and that for the guilt of these he longed to be assured of pardon: first, the sack of Volterra, whose peaceful inhabitants he had mercilessly slaughtered; second, the appropriation to his own use of the funds destined for the dowries of the Florentine daughters; and, third, the shedding of so much innocent blood, and the destruction of so many innocent victims after the conspiracy of the Pazzi. Lorenzo, while he faltered out this confession, fell into a violent agitation; and Savonarola endeavoured to compose him by reminding him of the goodness and mercy of GOD.

"But three things are necessary," he said, when Lorenzo had ceased to speak; "three things are necessary before you can hope for the forgiveness of your sin."

"And what are they, Father?"

Drawing himself up to his full height, as he stood there in his white Dominican tunic and scapulary, Savonarola replied,—raising his right hand with three fingers extended,—[2]

"First, it is necessary that you should have a full and lively faith in the mercy of GOD."

"That I have most fully."

---

[1] Trollope, iii. 461. [2] Villari, ii. 141.

"Second, it is necessary that you restore, or enjoin upon your sons to restore, all that you have unjustly taken away from others."

This condition fell as a heavy burden on the dying prince; but after a severe inward struggle, he notified his consent by bowing his head.

"Lastly," and the Confessor seemed to rise above himself, as he spoke; "lastly, you must restore to the people of Florence the liberties of which you have deprived them."

His countenance was grave, his voice solemn, and with eyes intensely fixed on Lorenzo's face, he awaited the answer. But dearer to the dying Medici even than the salvation of his soul, was the greatness of his family; and collecting all his failing energies, he turned his back upon the Prior in contemptuous silence. Then, without giving him absolution, Savonarola departed; and a few hours afterwards, torn with remorse, the spirit of Lorenzo the Magnificent passed away, (April 8, 1492.)

Of this prince, whom Fortune favoured rather than any commanding genius, Villari has drawn a masterly character. " He was, in fact, thoroughly the man of his age. All the qualities of his soul were qualities of the intelligence only. His very manners [which are said to have been fascinating] were the product of intellectual culture, and not of amiability of heart. The patronage he accorded to men of learning was a mere matter of state policy, or arose simply from a desire for amusement. Singular, indeed, was the manner of life he led. After having laboured with all the force of his will and of his intellect at the destruction of the last shred of Florentine liberty by means of some new law; after having caused some citizen to be deprived of his property, or, perhaps, put to death, he would repair to his Platonic Academy, and dispute with warm interest about 'virtue' and 'the immortality of the soul.' Then, on quitting his 'Academy,' he would sally forth in company with a group of the most abandoned profligates of the city, singing through the streets his 'Carnival Songs' [*Canti Carnavaleschi*], and steeping himself to the lips in the most abominable debaucheries. Returning to his palace, and sitting down to supper with Poliziano and Pulci, they would write verses, and discourse critically of poetry. And he threw himself so completely into each of these various occupations in turn, that, for the time being, it seemed as if each were the sole employment of his life. But what is most remarkable of all is, that in this so varied course of life, there cannot be referred to him a single act or trait of virtue, or of truly generous sentiment, towards his subjects, his friends, or his family. And it may be considered as certain that if any such had been discoverable, his indefatigable eulogists would not have omitted to commemorate it."

Such was Lorenzo de' Medici. That he corrupted his age is, perhaps, too unlimited an assertion ; it will be more correct to say, that he did nothing to elevate or purify it: or that the age made him what he was, and he in his turn reacted on the age. Unquestionably, Florence, under his government, sank into a terrible slough of vice. Its artists and men of letters, its nobles, politicians, and populace, were all equally corrupted ; corrupted in mind and heart ; and as devoid of any public or private virtue as of all sentiment of morality. Religion was degraded into a mere instrument of government or a base hypocrisy. The people had no faith ; neither civil nor religious, neither moral nor philosophical. Even scepticism itself, continues Villari, did not exist in their minds as an active principle of energy. Their predominant characteristic was an apathetic indifference to all principle ; and in their features full of intellect, acumen, subtlety, a smile of cold superiority and scornful compassion was the prevailing expression, called forth by the slightest display of enthusiasm for a noble or a generous idea. They did not, as a sceptic philosopher would have done, meet any such with opposition or with doubts. They simply looked down on it with supreme pity ; and this inert force of theirs opposed a far greater obstacle to all virtue, than a debased and open war against it. Such a condition of morals necessarily had a very powerful effect upon intellectual culture.

Lorenzo, says Villari, seconded the age in all its tendencies. From being corrupt he made it enormously corrupt; impelling it down the deep decline of degradation by every possible means. Abandoning himself to pleasure, he caused his subjects to wallow yet deeper in the same mire, with the view of stupifying and brutalising them. So it came to pass that, in his day, the life of Florence was one long orgy of festivals and pleasure.

He was succeeded by his son Piero, who, in almost every respect, except in his love of despotic power, was the opposite of his father. Of a robust frame and handsome countenance, he abandoned himself to dissipation and bodily exercises. He improvised verses with an agreeable facility and had a graceful delivery; but all his ambition centred in excelling in horsemanship and the feats of the tourney, in games of foot-ball, boxing, and tennis; and in these he considered himself so consummate a master as constantly to challenge persons who had a reputation for skill in such pastimes. From his mother he inherited all the pride of the Orsinis; but he had none of his father's popularity of manner and easy courtesy, and offended by his violence and churlishness not only the more distinguished citizens of Florence but also the Italian princes. To the affairs of government he gave no heed, though jealously concentrating the power of the State in his own hands, and daily destroying some of those forms and shadows of liberty which Lorenzo had carefully preserved because he perceived that they were much affected by the people.

Savonarola's influence with the Florentines daily extended, and the multitude gathered round him as the leader of the opposition to the despotism of the Medici. His prestige was confirmed by the death of Pope Innocent VIII., on the 25th of April,—which fulfilled the second part of his prediction. And the minds of men were still more strongly drawn towards him when, under the new Pope, the infamous Alexander Borgia, all those evils seemed impending over the Church and over Italy which he had so persistently foretold. As for himself, he felt a deeper and more enthusiastic faith in his mission, blended, perhaps, with a certain pride in and love of the power which he was beginning to wield. His position was one that directly appealed to the imaginativeness which was at once his weakness and his strength. He preached with greater fervour; his denunciations assumed a more prophetic character; and to his mind excited and stimulated by a thousand causes, visions came more and more frequently.

Thus, in the Advent of 1492, he had a dream, which took to his disordered fancy the semblance of a vision, and was accepted by him as a divine revelation. He saw, or thought he saw, blazing against the dark blue sky, a hand with a drawn sword, bearing the legend, *Gladius Domini super terram cito et velociter* (The sword of the LORD upon earth, and that swiftly.) Clear and distinct, he heard mysterious voices which promised mercy to the good, threatened chastisement to the wicked, and proclaimed that the wrath of GOD was at hand. Suddenly, the sword was turned towards the earth; the air darkened; showers of swords and arrows and fires descended; terrific thunder rolled through the vault of Heaven; while the whole earth was scourged with wars, pestilences, famines. The vision disappeared with a command to Savonarola to threaten the world with these punishments, to inspire men with the fear of GOD, and to induce them to implore of GOD to provide the Church with just pastors, who would take loving care of the souls that had strayed from the right path. This vision was afterwards represented upon an infinite number of medals and in engravings; and was considered as generally symbolical of Savonarola and his teaching.

The Frate's superiors, at the instigation of Piero de' Medici, sent him, in the Lenten-tide of 1493, to preach at Bologna. There, however, he lacked the inspiration which he found in his well-loved Florence; and in a city ruled by the iron-handed Bentivoglio, he was compelled to limit the scope of his discourses. But though he produced no very great impression, his name attracted considerable audiences, among whom the wife of Bentivoglio was always included. She came late; and with her retinue of ladies, gentlemen, and pages, made so much noise as to disturb the preacher. On the first two or three occasions he attempted to reprove her quietly by pointedly stopping short in his discourse, until the stir had subsided. The reproof was taken amiss, and the noise increased. The Prior then alluded to the sin of disturbing the faithful in their religious duties. The haughty lady, resenting his boldness, came every day with a louder din and more ostentatious disrespect; until, one morning, checked and chilled in the flow and rush of his impetuous discourse by her conduct,

Savonarola could no longer control himself, but exclaimed, with a loud voice :—" Behold, behold the Devil, who comes to interrupt the word of GOD !" Beside herself with rage, she ordered two of her attendants to murder him in his pulpit ; but for so sacrilegious an enormity they could not muster the necessary audacity. Unable to endure the thought of having been humiliated by a friar, she then sent two other of her followers to do him some "grievous injury" in his cell. But the Prior received them with so intrepid a bearing, and addressed them with such an air of command, that their courage failed them, and they slunk from his presence, discomfited. On the day of his return to Florence, he said publicly from the pulpit :—"This evening I shall start for Florence, with my wooden flask and walking-stick, and shall sleep at Pianoro. If any one requires anything of me, let him come before the hour of my departure. But know that my death is not to take place at Bologna." He left the city unmolested, and none dared to dog his footsteps. While he was yet some miles from Florence, he was so spent with fatigue that he felt unable to continue his journey, nor could he take any food. But, behold, the vision of an unknown man, who restored his strength and vigour, came to him ; and after accompanying him to the S. Gallo gate, said :—" Remember to do the work for which thou hast been sent of GOD," and disappeared.

He found Florence in a state of great perturbation, for as the tyranny of Piero showed itself more openly, the discontent of the people grew more profound. They looked to him to lead them, and to redress their grievances ; and passionately devoted to liberty, a patriot as well as a religious enthusiast, with that delight in the exercise of power which is felt by most men who know that they are capable of wielding it, he was not unwilling to undertake the task. But as matters stood he was liable at any moment to be despatched by his superiors in Lombardy or Rome to some place far from Florence, and against this it was necessary to provide. He bethought him that the Dominicans in Tuscany, down to 1448, had been separated from the Congregation of Lombardy, and he resolved upon recovering their original independence. He set to work with his usual energy, and such was his address that he actually succeeded in obtaining the support of Piero to the petition which he addressed to the Pope and his consistory. He despatched this petition in charge of two of his most devoted followers, Frà Domenico da Pescia and Frà Alessandro Reinuccini; and after a warm opposition on the part of the Lombards, obtained the Papal assent.

Having thus secured the independence of S. Mark's, and confirmed his own position,[1] the Reformer next directed his energies to the task of restoring discipline in the convent. At one time he had had dreams of retiring with his brethren to a solitary mountain, and living as poor hermits; but this was the extravagance of his youthful fancy. He now saw that it was wiser and more courageous to live in the world, in order to reform it, and to train up good and religious men, who should be ready to die for the Truth, instead of anchorites immersed in a religion of selfishness. To correct evil habits, to rekindle faith, and to purge the Church of its corruptions, were the objects he set before him. These effected, he would depart from Italy; and accompanied by a small band of trusty followers, would go forth, a Hero of the Cross, to proclaim the religion of CHRIST in the lands of the East. Meantime, the practical side of his character asserted itself. The first reform on which he insisted, was the practice of poverty, in obedience to the rule of S. Dominic. On the wall of the dormitory Frà Angelico had painted the figure of the Founder, with an open book in his hand, on which that rule was inscribed:—" Be charitable, be humble, practise poverty with cheerfulness: may my curse, and the curse of GOD, fall upon him who shall bring possessions into this Order." These stern words, nevertheless, had been set aside; but Savonarola revived them, literally and in the spirit: he stripped the cells of their ornaments, he clothed the monks in garments of coarser texture, and he forbade the introduction of illuminated books, crucifixes of gold and silver, and similar luxuries. Acting upon S. Bernard's maxim, that Work is Prayer, he established schools in which the monks were taught painting, sculpture, architecture, and the art of copying and illuminating manuscripts. The priests and higher clergy (*prelati*) were charged with the care of the confessional and

[1] Burlamacchi, pp. 45—47.

the education of the novices; while those most skilled in theology were sent into different cities to preach the word of GOD. As essential to a right understanding of Holy Scripture, Savonarola promoted the study of Greek and Hebrew, and the Oriental languages.

Savonarola practised as he taught. His garments were always of the coarsest texture; his bed was the hardest in the convent, his cell the most poorly furnished; he worked the most laboriously; none equalled him in fervency of devotion. His intense ardour communicated itself to his monks; so that the convent became a centre of piety and earnestness and religious zeal. Applications for admission were received daily, and the regard and affection which S. Mark's excited rekindled the popularity of the Dominican Order. Encouraged by these signs of success, Savonarola resumed his sermons in the Advent of 1498, and to an audience constantly enlarging he spoke with constantly increasing boldness. Half the power of an orator depends on the sympathy of his hearers, and of this sympathy Savonarola was now assured. Was he not the head of the Tuscan Congregation? Did he not by his manner of living recall the memory of the Saints of old? Had not his predictions been marvellously fulfilled? These circumstances strengthened that hold upon the multitude which his daring eloquence had first given him; so that he became something more than a religious teacher,—he was also a popular leader. In his Advent Sermons he denounced, in the most uncompromising language,—language which necessarily found an echo in the hearts of the poor and oppressed,—the immoral lives and luxury of the Italian princes and higher clergy,— the depravity that festered in the very vitals of the State. "Those wicked princes," he exclaimed, "are sent as a punishment for the sins of their subjects; they are verily a great snare for souls; their halls and palaces are the refuge of all the beasts and monsters of the earth, and a shelter for caitiffs and every kind of wickedness. Such men repair to their courts because they find there the means of indulging and giving loose to all their evil passions. There we see the wicked councillors who are for ever devising new burdens, new imposts, new ways of sucking the blood of the people. There we find the cajoling philosophers and flattering poets, who, by a thousand lies and fables, trace the genealogy of these iniquitous princes from the Gods; and, what is still worse, there we find priests who adopt the same language." Directing his fiery shafts of invective against the clergy, he said:—"See ye not that they are bringing everything to ruin? They have no judgment; they cannot distinguish between good and evil, between truth and falsehood, between sweet and bitter: things good appear to them evil, things true as false, the sweets are bitter to them and the bitter sweet. Ye see prelates prostrating themselves before earthly affections and earthly pomps; they no longer lay to heart the salvation of souls; enough for them if they receive their fees and tithes; their sermons are written to please princes, and win their praise. But worse yet remains: not only have they pullèd down the true Church of GOD, but created one after their own fashion. This is the church of to-day; no longer built with 'living stones,' that is, by Christians established in an earnest faith and inspired with love. Go to Rome; traverse all Christendom; in the houses of the great prelates and the great lords nothing is thought of but poetry and the art of rhetoric. Go and see, and you will find them with books of the Humanities in their hands, giving themselves up to the delusion that they can lead the souls of men aright by their knowledge of Virgil and Horace and Cicero. Do ye wish to see the Church guided by the hand of the astrologer? Ye will not find great lord or great prelate, but he is in secret intercourse with some necromancer, who predicts to him the hour when he must ride or when he may safely enter on any business. These same great lords durst not move a step contrary to the directions of their astrologers."

In the same strain of fire-hot indignation he continued:— "Only in two things in GOD's temple do they delight, and these are the paintings and the gilding with which it is embellished. Thus it is that in our church there are so many beautiful external ceremonies in the solemnization of the holy offices, splendid vestments and draperies, with candlesticks of gold and silver, and numerous chalices, all of which have a superb effect. There you see great prelates with jewelled mitres of gold upon their heads, and silver croziers, standing before the altar in brocaded copes, slowly intoning vespers and other masses with much ceremony, accompanied by an organ and choristers, until you become confounded, and these men appear to you as men of great gravity and holiness, and ye believe them to be incapable of error, and they themselves believe that all they say and do is commanded in the Gospel. Men feed upon these vanities and rejoice in these ceremonies, and they affirm boastingly that never was the Church of CHRIST in so flourishing a state, or divine worship so well conducted as in this day; and that the early prelates were mere shams, *prelatuzzi*, in comparison with those of our own times. They certainly had not so many golden mitres, or so many chalices; and they parted with such as they had to relieve the necessities of the poor; but our prelates get their mitres and chalices by depriving the poor of their scanty sustenance. Do ye understand what I would say? In the primitive Church the prelates were golden and the chalices wooden; but now the Church has chalices of gold and prelates of wood. They have established amongst us the festivals of devils; they believe not in GOD; they make a mock of the mysteries of our religion. What doest Thou, O LORD? Why slumberest Thou? Arise, and take Thy Church out of the hands of the Devil, out of the hands of tyrants, out of the hands of wicked prelates. Hast Thou forgotten Thy Church? Dost Thou not love her? Hast Thou no care for her? We have become, O LORD, the opprobrium of the nations. Turks are masters of Constantinople; we have lost Asia, we have lost Greece; we have sunk into tributaries of infidels. O LORD GOD, Thou hast dealt with us as an angry Father; Thou hast banished us from before Thee. Hasten the punishment and the scourge, that there may be a return to Thee and Thy fear."[1]

This was language which everybody could understand, and it appealed to the democratic tendencies that always lurk in the breast of the populace. What wonder that thousands hung enchanted on his lips? What wonder that in the humble homes of Florence the Preacher's name became a household word? Not only the "plain-speaking" won the hearts of his hearers, but the heroic courage that ventured upon it, the daring intrepidity that thus openly

[1] Burlamacchi.

arraigned the wealthy and powerful, and lashed with firm hand their sins and their follies?

Having, in his Advent Sermons, made clear the necessity and the swift approach of the Divine judgments, Savonarola, in the following Lent, proceeded to construct a mystical Ark, wherein all who desired to escape the coming deluge might find salvation. This Ark, literally the Noachian one, was symbolical of the gathering together of the good; its length was Faith, its breadth was Charity, its depth was Hope. He continued the subject throughout his Lenten discourses; and, after putting before his hearers every day some new picture, he finally exhibited one which represented the virtues distinctive of all true Christians. And, in his Easter Day sermon, the Ark was completed. "Let every one hasten," he cried, "let every one hasten to enter into the Ark of the LORD. Noah invites you all; the door is open! But, remember, the time will come when it will be shut, and many will repent that they had not entered therein."

Such was the Ark; but what signified the Deluge? Savonarola did not forget to describe it, and the crowds that filled the vast aisles of the Duomo seemed to surge to and fro in the vehemence of their emotions, as the preacher, gaunt and wan, standing before them in his long white tunic, with hands upraised, and eyes glowing like red hot coals, poured out a torrent of graphic sentences. A politician, keenly observant, Savonarola had watched the action of the French Court, and had convinced himself that Charles VIII. meditated the invasion of Italy, and the conquest of Naples.[1] That monarch set his forces in motion in the early autumn of 1494; on the 5th of September they rolled down the rugged declivities of the Alps, and entered Turin. On the 21st, Savonarola stood up again before the excited masses in the Duomo. There was a pause of intense silence. Then, suddenly, with a terrible voice he exclaimed:—"Behold, I, even I, do bring a flood of waters over the earth!" That voice, we are told, was as a thunderclap bursting in the church; those menacing words struck a strange terror into the heart of every hearer. Pico della Mirandola, who was present, relates, that a shudder ran through all his frame, that his hair stood on end as he

[1] Sismondi, "Histoire des Français," xv. 140, et sqq.

listened; while Savonarola himself has recorded that, on that day, he was not less moved than his audience. The news had arrived of the French invasion; and the people saw in that coming of armed hosts the Flood which the Preacher had foretold. The sword of GOD's justice was about to fall. The Divine interposition in which he had so strenuously believed was to become a fact. The tread of the warriors and the clash of the weapons were in his ears so many voices from the Almighty, announcing that He would chastise the guilty, and sweep away the abominations of luxury and uncleanness. The sword of GOD upon the earth, swift and sudden !

Let me borrow from George Eliot a picture of the various classes composing the immense audience in the dimly-lighted Duomo. "There were men of high birth, accustomed to public charges at home and abroad, who had become newly conspicuous not only as enemies of the Medici and friends of popular government, but as thorough *Piagnoni*,[1] embracing the doctrines and practical teaching of the Frate, and looking up to him as to another Elijah. There were also men of family, brave simple lovers of a sober republican liberty, who preferred fighting to arguing, and had no reasons for thinking any ideas false that would keep out the Medici and allow scope for the exercise of public spirit. At their elbows stood doctors of law, whose legal studies had not so entirely absorbed their ardour as to prevent them from becoming enthusiastic *Piagnoni*. Among the dignitaries who carried their black lucco or furred mantle with an air of habitual authority, might be seen an abundant sprinkling of men with more contemplative and sensitive faces; scholars inheriting such illustrious names as Strozzi and Acciajoli, who were already disposed to assume the cowl, and join the community of S. Mark's; artists, inspired with a higher and purer ambition by the teaching of Savonarola, with its love of Purity and Justice, and its deep unquenchable hatred of Wrong, like that young painter who had lately surpassed himself in his fresco of the Divine

---

[1] "*Piagnoni*," "Mourners," or "Whimperers,"—the name given to Savonarola's party. They were also known as "Frateschi." His opponents, chiefly young men of loose life and looser principles, were called *Arrabbiati*, or "the furious."

Child on the bare wall of the Frate's bare cell,—unconscious yet that he himself would one day wear the tonsure and the cowl, and be called Frà Bartolommeo.[1] There was the mystic poet, Girolamo Benivieni, preparing to carry tidings of the beloved Frate's speedy coming to his friend Pico della Mirandola, then counting his last hours as they rapidly glided by. There were well-born women attired with such scrupulous plainness, that they were distinguished from their less aristocratic sisters chiefly by their air of refinement. There was a predominant proportion of the genuine *popolani*, or middle class, sensible of the great fact that their purses were threatened by war-taxes. And, more striking and various perhaps, than all the other classes of the Frate's disciples, there was " the long stream of poorer tradesmen and artisans, whose faith and hope in his Divine message varied from the rude and undiscriminating trust in him as the friend of the poor, and the enemy of the luxurious oppressive rich, to that eager trusting of all the subtleties of Biblical interpretation which takes a peculiarly strong hold on the sedentary artisan, illuminating the long dim spaces beyond the board where he stitches, with a pale flame that seems to him the light of Divine Science."

All these heterogeneous elements were fused together for the time by the influence of Savonarola's genius, which spell-bound into silence even such of his enemies or critics as mingled with the crowd.

The minds of all were so dominated by terror that they already saw in imagination the city deluged with blood. The masses hastened, in their panic, to demand protection from Savonarola. All his prophetic utterances had been fulfilled. The three princes whose death he had foretold had one by one descended to the tomb.[2] The *Flagellum Dei* which he had announced was at hand. Already the avenging sword was at their gate. Only he who had predicted these woes, only he who had seen them coming while yet afar off, could be supposed to know their remedy. In this way the Preacher's fame spread throughout Italy; every eye was turned towards him; and by force of circum-

[1] Frà Bartolommeo (Baccio della Porta) was born in 1469, died in 1517.
[2] Ferdinand, King of Naples, had died on the 25th of January, 1494, thus carrying out Savonarola's threefold prediction.

stances he became a democratic leader. The ablest citizens of Florence sought his counsel, and the party which supported him rose at once to supremacy. That the vast power thus placed in his hands had no injurious effect upon his character, we cannot pretend. It fed his thirst for personal predominance, but this personal predominance and this lust of rule were ennobled by his fervent devotion to the truth, his hatred of the wrong, his sympathy with the oppressed.

CHAPTER III.

WITH pomp of banner and spear, with the sheen of waving plumes and silken surcoats, with Scotch archers in their glittering uniform, Swiss halberdiers, and agile Gascon troopers, with a splendid array of nobles and knights, and youthful pages, with glitter of gold and jewels, Charles of France entered Florence (November 17.) Piero de' Medici had previously fled; and the Signory, or magistrates, were left to make what terms they could with the invader. With their independence however, the Florentines recovered their ancient heroism, and they assumed an attitude of such firm resolution that the Most Christian king found it advisable to be moderate in his demands. His first proposition had so provoked the ambassadors of the Republic that they contemptuously refused to accept it; whereupon, turning round in hot wrath, Charles exclaimed:—"We shall sound our trumpets!" Capponi, one of the Syndics, immediately replied:—"And we will ring our bells!" The menace frightened Charles into concessions. It was then agreed that a free intercourse and cordial friendship should subsist between the King and the Republic; that their subjects should receive mutual protection; that Charles should be entitled the Restorer and Protector of Florentine liberty; that a sum of 120,000 florins should be paid to him in three instalments; and that Pisa, which had profited by his invasion to rebel against Florence should be pardoned on its acknowledging obedience. It was also stipulated that Piero de' Medici should not approach nearer than 200, and his brother 100 miles, to the Tuscan territory.[1]

During these negotiations it was the influence of Savonarola that had preserved peace and order in the city. After the conclusion of the treaty, Charles VIII. showed no inclination to depart, and it was Savonarola whose influence delivered the Florentines from his unwelcome presence. At the request of the Signory he betook himself to Charles's palace, and was graciously received,—for Charles was almost as strongly persuaded of the divine commission of Savonarola as the most fervid *Piagnone*. Addressing him with his usual directness, he said :—"Most Christian Prince,[2] thy stay causes great danger to this city, and to thy enterprise. Thou losest time, forgetting the duty that Providence hath imposed upon thee, to the grave injury of thine own spiritual welfare, and the world's glory. Listen, then to the servant of GOD. Proceed on thy way, and tarry no longer. Forbear to bring ruin upon this city, and provoke not the wrath of the LORD." Charles immediately yielded; and about three in the afternoon of the 28th of November, the battalions of France defiled through the streets of Florence, and proceeded on their southward march.

Relieved of the presence of the French, the citizens prepared to establish a settled government, and resolved on the election of twenty Accoppiatori, with dictatorial power (*balia*,) and authority to choose a Signory[3] and all the magistrates for one year. They were also ordered to select from among themselves a Gonfaloniere di Giustizia. But a very brief experience demonstrated the futility of this project. The Accoppiatori had neither the will nor the capacity to govern, and were unable to agree among themselves. There was a war to be carried on for the reduction of Pisa; the whole Florentine country was in disorder, and needed pacification; and money must be found to pay the sums promised to the king of France. It was evident that a new and efficient

---

[1] Guicciardini, "Storia Fiorentina," iii. 115, et sqq.

[2] "Most Christian" (*Il Cristianissimo*) was the ordinary style and title of the Sovereign of France.

[3] The Signory, with the Gonfaloniere, constituted the supreme magistracy. It consisted of eight members, called *Priori*.

government was indispensable; but it is easier to detect a want than provide a fitting remedy for it. Two leading schemes attracted discussion; one proposed by Soderini, contemplated the establishment of a Great Council, with power to elect the magistrates and make the laws; another, recommended by Vespucci, provided for a smaller Council, with the view of keeping the government in the hands of the *ottimati*, or aristocracy. Men already in office naturally favoured the latter plan; but the great body of the citizens inclined towards the former.

The dispute was determined by Savonarola. Hitherto he had confined himself in his sermons to general exhortations, such as a Christian priest who was also a patriot, might properly deliver. But the pressure of events now carried him further. The people looked to him for guidance, and how could he refuse it? He was urged forward, moreover, by his professed love of liberty and his grandeur of purpose. To purify the government of Florence, to exalt the State, to rescue it from the hands of the wicked; these were his objects. They could be secured only by placing public interests above private, and the Great Council was the only plan by which public interests would obtain an adequate representation. On the 12th of December he preached a remarkable sermon. After insisting on the necessity of a thorough spiritual reform, he affirmed that the groundwork of a Christian government must be, that no individual should have any benefit but what was general, and that the people alone should have the power of choosing the magistrates and approving the laws. "A Great Council," he said, "is the best form of Government for this city, one similar to that of Venice. I recommend, therefore, that the people be assembled under their sixteen Gonfalonieri, and that each of the sixteen divisions should propose a form, that from these sixteen, the Gonfalonieri should select four, to be delivered to the Signory, who, after praying to GOD, should choose that which they conceive to be the best. And of this be assured, that a form of Government so chosen by the people must come from GOD. I am of opinion that that of Venice should be the one chosen; nor need you be ashamed to imitate it, for the Venetians received it from GOD, the giver of every good thing. And since this form of

Government existed in Venice, there has been no kind of strife or dissension; an irresistible proof that it is in accordance with the Will of GOD."[1]

He added some counsels of equal sagacity, in regard to a readjustment and diminution of taxation. He proposed also that while all important offices should be filled up by nomination or election, the minor ones should be filled by lot, as an encouragement that all citizens might have a share in the administration of the State; that public prayers should be offered for the Divine blessing; and a general reconciliation should be effected between the citizens of the old and of the new Government.

He repeated these ideas in later sermons, and with a moderation and prudence that surprised his auditors who had not expected from the enthusiast so much practical wisdom. He was frequently consulted by the Signory; and eventually agreed to preach in the Duomo before all the magistrates and people in final explanation of his views. On this occasion he laid down four principal propositions:—

"First. That in all things they should have the fear of GOD before them, and that there should be a reform of manners.

"Second. That the formation of a popular Government for the benefit of the whole community, should precede all considerations of private interest.

"Third. That there should be a general peace (or amnesty,) absolving the friends of the late Government from blame; remitting also, in their case, all penalties; and allowing a certain indulgence to those indebted to the State.

"Fourth. That a general Government should be established, which should include all citizens who, according to the ancient statutes, formed a part of the State; and he recommended the Grand Council of Venice as the best model they could adopt, modifying it to suit the particular character of the Florentine people."[2]

These propositions show that it is possible to be an enthusiast and yet to be a statesman; that a passionate hatred of wrong and injustice is not incompatible with shrewd

[1] Guicciardini, "Storia d'Italia," lib. ii., *passim*.
[2] Villari, i. 253.

blood having been shed, in Florence, 'the city of tumults.'" The greatest marvel is, however, that it was the result of the power of a single man, of a simple friar, who suggested, directed, and completed it from the pulpit, by the mere force of his will and magic of his eloquence. He had no powerful allies, no recommendations of birth or rank or wealth; he was not supported, like Cromwell, by a victorious army; he could not even share in the government which he established. He was compelled to stand apart from the machinery which he called into existence. Yet, by the persistence of his genius, and the moral magnificence of his character, he accomplished a revolution. May we not believe that he had, as he himself declared, though not in the sense in which he understood it, a direct inspiration from GOD, a divine mission? And surely the loftiness of his aims, and the moral grandeur of his achievements may induce us to judge him leniently when we find him bewildered by the fervour of his imagination, and falling into delusions as to his prophetic powers and his celestial visions. On this point he himself was not always well assured. If at times he openly proclaimed his revelations and asserted his prophetical character, at others he withdrew his pretensions, and ascribed his predictions of future events to a process of simple reasoning. "I am neither a prophet," he said, "nor the son of a prophet. I do not dare to assume that awful name; but I am certain that the things I foretell will come to pass, because they spring from Christian doctrine, from the spirit of evangelical charity. In truth, the sins of Italy are your sins, by virtue of which I am a prophet; and they ought to make each one of you a prophet. Heaven and earth prophesy against you, but you neither see nor hear them. You are struck by mental blindness; you shut your ears to the voice of the LORD Who calls you." What is certain is, he was no impostor. If he deceived others, it was because he was himself deceived. Inspired by great thoughts, cherishing noble conceptions of a renovated Church and a purified community, filled with the ardour of a genuine enthusiasm, he could not always distinguish between the visions that rose out of his own imagination and the visions which came, as he supposed, from the throne of GOD. Nor did he see the danger which his occasional convictions of his supernatural power necessarily involved. The multi-

administrative capacity; and that if Savonarola loved power it was in order that he might direct it to great ends. His eloquence, fervid and clear, poured a flood of light into the minds of the people, and as they passed in crowds through the busy streets, they cried aloud for "the Great Council after the manner of the Venetians." The party who would have thrown the State into the hands of the patricians, were swept aside by the popular vehemence, and on the 23rd of December, a law was passed which constituted the *Consiglio Maggiore* on the lines submitted by Savonarola. It also established a smaller Council of eighty citizens, not under forty years of age, to be called the *Consiglio degli Ottanti*, and renewable every six months, who would act as the assessors of the Signory. Further organization followed, a consolidation of the laws was also ordered, and an inquiry instituted into the system of taxation. In these measures, all based upon popular principles, and evidencing unusual statesman-like forethought, Savonarola's recommendations were almost literally adopted. It was through his influence too, that an amnesty was passed. It may be added that if any provision contrary to his views was adopted, it was always of an extreme character; a proof of his admirable moderation. But it was seldom that any opposition was offered to his recommendations, and in the settlement of Florence he was the moving spirit, at once heart and brain; labouring earnestly to perfect its Government, so that a regenerated Florence might become the centre of a grand reform of the Church and the World. For, as he afterwards said to his judges, his purposes were few but great (*le mie cose erano poche e grandi;*) so great that his age was not ripe for them; he was before his time.

Summing up the work in which he bore the chief part, his biographer says:—" In a single year the freedom of a whole people was established; liberty was granted to them to carry arms; the system of taxation was reformed; usury was abolished; a law for a general amnesty passed; the administration of justice amended; and the Consiglio Maggiore founded, to which the affection of the Florentines continued more steadfastly attached than it had ever been to any other of their political institutions. And all this, without a sword having been drawn, without a civic riot, without a drop of

tude, credulous in his days of triumph, were sure, on the first reverse, to fall into a profound scepticism, and to demand some proof of a gift so exceptional. They would repeat the cry of the old unbelievers :—" If Thou art King of the Jews, save Thyself!" " If thou art a prophet work for us a miracle !" It is a painful thing, as Villari says, for a man to be called upon to give a reason for being superior to reason ; to prove that he is raised above humanity by arguments which humanity can understand. When this demand is made upon him, the beginning of the end has come.

Meanwhile, his teaching and example produced a remarkable effect in the moral condition of Florence. Men and women felt themselves exalted and purified; they lived a purer life; they were animated by higher motives; they meditated nobler aims. The women gave up their costly ornaments, dressed with simplicity, and walked modestly; licentious young men, as if by magic, became devout and chaste; instead of the lewd carnival songs introduced by Lorenzo de' Medici, religious hymns were chanted. The change was similar to that which in our seventeenth-century England was wrought by the spirit of Puritanism. During the hours of mid-day rest, tradesmen might be seen in their shops reading the Bible or some one of Savonarola's treatises ; habits of prayer were resumed ; the services of the Church drew eager worshippers ; alms were freely given. Most wonderful of all was it when, touched by scruples of conscience, bankers and merchants refunded sums of money unjustly acquired, amounting, not infrequently, to thousands of florins. The reform was so complete and so general that the world looked upon it as miraculous ; it seemed as if that millennial era of peace and purity, to which the Church had always looked forward with wistful eyes, had at last begun. Savonarola, exhausted by his vast mental labours and spiritual excitement, was broken down and suffering from sickness ; but a new vigour poured into his veins as he contemplated this great work of GOD. Happy for himself, perchance, if in this hour of promise, he had been called away ; but he was reserved for a higher if a sadder destiny, for a death which was gloriously to seal and confirm the lessons taught by his life.

His personal influence finds a remarkable illustration in

the story of Bertuccio, the painter. A handsome and accomplished youth, he had plunged into every kind of dissipation, and was treading the paths of vice with reckless step, when the fame of Savonarola first began to spread. Bertuccio did not join in the general admiration, but, on the contrary, attached himself to the Arrabbiati, and lost no opportunity of levelling his sarcasms at the Piagnoni. One day, however, a noble matron, whom he was visiting, spoke to him earnestly of the Friar's sermons, and, after much persuasion, induced him to accompany her to the Duomo. His confusion on finding himself in such a multitude of devout worshippers was extreme, and his first thought was that of escaping from their glances of surprise; but he remained, though reluctantly. When Savonarola mounted the pulpit, he no longer wished to retire. Having once fixed his eyes upon the great Preacher, he could not again withdraw them; and the words he heard sank deep into his heart. The sermon ended, he took a solitary walk, and for the first time his mind was directed to his inmost self. After much communing, he returned home, a changed man. He cast away his perfumed dresses, his cards and musical instruments, and abandoned his gay companions. He became a constant attendant on Savonarola's sermons, and thus derived encouragement to persevere in the bitter struggle he had to wage against his rebellious passions. As soon as he thought the victory complete, he repaired to S. Mark's, and threw himself at the feet of the Frate. With faltering lips he expressed his desire to assume the monastic habit. Savonarola impressed upon him the danger of a hasty resolution, described the difficulties and hardships of the monastic life, and ended by advising him to submit himself to a longer probation, by leading a Christian life out of the convent, before he ventured to cross the threshold. The advice was profitable; for Bertuccio had again a fierce contention with his unruly passions, and sometimes lapsed. But eventually the work of repentance and reform was finished, and Bertuccio, calm and assured, returned to Savonarola. Even yet, the Frate, who had watched him closely, would not allow him to assume the cowl, but appointed him for a time to visit the sick and attend the burials of the dead. Occasionally he called him to his cell, that he might advise and teach and direct him; nor was it until the 13th of December, 1495, that he allowed him to take the vows by the name of Fra Benedetto.

While Savonarola was thus the leading mind, the virtual ruler, of Florence, he was not insensible to the dangers of his position. I have already dwelt on the remarkable combination of the imaginative and the practical in his character; and history shows us that with however ecstatic a spirit he approached the contemplation of the things not of this life, he regarded worldly affairs with the cool sagacity of a veteran politician. He rightly estimated the force of the tendencies which threatened the permanence of the moral and civil reform accomplished by his teaching. He knew the fickleness and weakness of the multitude, and the insincerity of the upper class. In one of his later sermons he exclaimed:—" But what, O LORD, shall be the reward granted in the other life to him who is victorious in battle? A thing which the eye cannot see, which the ear cannot hear; everlasting bliss. And what the reward granted in this life? 'The servant shall not be greater than his master,' answers the LORD. 'Thou knowest that after preaching I was crucified; so martyrdom will befall thee also.' O LORD, LORD, grant me, I pray Thee, this martyrdom; and make me ready to die for Thee, as Thou hast died for me. Already the knife is sharpened for me. But the LORD tells me:—' Wait yet for a little while, so that the things may come which have to follow; and then thou wilt use that strength of soul which shall be granted thee.'"

By this time the success which had attended the French expedition against Naples had excited a very general feeling of alarm amongst the Italian princes, and a league was formed between the republic of Venice, the Duke of Milan, the Pope, the Emperor, and the King of Spain, ostensibly to defend Italy against the Turks, but really in order to arrest the progress of King Charles. The day that this confederacy was privately settled Philip de Commines wrote to inform his sovereign of its existence; and the latter immediately despatched a messenger (probably De Commines himself) to Savonarola, to inquire if there would be danger in his return to France. "Tell *Il Cristianissimo*," replied the Frate, "that GOD has bestowed upon him many benefits, and has permitted him to gain so great a kingdom without difficulty; and although since then he has committed many sins, GOD will not fail him, nor need he have any fears as to his enemies, for he will return with victory into his own realm of France."

A curious account of Savonarola is given by De Commines:—"He always affirmed," says the chronicler,[1] "that our King would come into Italy, saying that he was sent by GOD to chastise the tyranny of the princes, and that none would be able to oppose him. He likewise foretold that Charles would come to Pisa and enter it, and that on that day the State of Florence would be dissolved; which came to pass, for Piero de' Medici was driven out that day. Many other things he predicted long before they occurred; as, for example, the death of Lorenzo de' Medici. And he openly declared that he knew it by revelation; as likewise he predicted that the reformation of the Church should be wrought out by the sword. . . . Many persons censured him for pretending to receive divine revelations, but others believed him: for my part, I think him to be a good man. I asked him whether our King would return safe into France, considering the vast preparations made against him by the Venetians; of which he gave a better account than I could give, though I had recently returned from Venice. He told me that he would encounter some difficulties on the way, but would overcome them all with honour, though he had not a hundred men in his company; for GOD, Who had conducted him thither, would guard him back again. But, because he had not applied himself as he ought to have done to the reformation of the Church, and because he had permitted his soldiers to rob and plunder the poor people (as well those who had freely opened their gates to him as the many which had opposed him), therefore GOD had pronounced judgment against him, and before long it would fall upon him.

"However," adds the historian, "he bade me inform him that, if he would have compassion upon the people, and would command his soldiers to do them no wrong, and punish them when they disobeyed, as was his office, GOD would then mitigate if He did not revoke His sentence; but that it would not suffice for him to plead that he did

[1] Philip de Commines, livre viii., chap. 3.

them no wrong himself. And he said that he would meet the King when he came, and tell him so with his own mouth ; and this he did, and earnestly solicited the restitution of the Florentine towns. When he spoke of the sentence of GOD against him, the death of the Dauphin came into my mind, for I know nought else that would touch the King so sensibly. These things I have thought it well to record, to make it the more manifest that the whole expedition was a mystery conducted by GOD Himself."

Towards the end of 1495, Piero de' Medici made an attempt to recover the sovereignty of Florence, but failed for want of sufficient military force, and in consequence of the resolute attitude maintained by Savonarola and his Frateschi, who, on this occasion, were supported by the Arrabbiati. The Frate met with a more powerful enemy in Pope Alexander Borgia, who resented his stern denunciations of the profligacy of the clergy and the corruption of the Church, and had been bribed to favour and support the Medicean party. In the summer of 1495 he invited Savonarola to Rome, employing language of the warmest flattery; but plots against his life had already begun, and it was well known that the Frate would either be murdered by the way or left to perish in the dungeons of S. Angelo. His friends, therefore, entreated him not to move from Florence. He himself was unwilling to disobey the Pope, though he saw the danger that lay in obedience. Fortunately, a legitimate excuse occurred for refusing the insidious invitation. He had scarcely been cured of a severe internal complaint, of which, in the opinion of his physicians, he might have a relapse. They prohibited him from undertaking any long journey, and even added that, if he would save his life, he must suspend his preaching and his studies. On the 28th July, therefore, he took his leave of the people, and appointed his friend and follower, Frà Domenico Buonvicini (Domenico da Pescia) to take his place. He also addressed a letter to Pope Borgia, explaining the state of his health, and defending himself from the charges brought against him. A private intimation appears to have been given him that the Pope was satisfied, but, urged on by the Mediceans, Alexander soon afterwards issued a brief, peremptorily commanding him to appear in Rome. In reply, the Frate reappeared in his pulpit, and preached the sermons which encouraged Florence to resist the attempts of Piero de' Medici. The Pope then issued an order, prohibiting him from preaching, and the Frate again retired from the pulpit.

Unable to cease from good works, Savonarola, since he might not preach, resolved on effecting a reform of the disgraceful customs and excesses attending the Carnival festivities, during which all Florence had been wont to abandon itself to unbridled orgies. Even the children partook of the excitement of their elders, importuning people for money, lighting bonfires, singing indecent songs, and finishing with a game of stone-throwing by which lives were always lost. To abolish these ancient practices would not have been possible; Savonarola wisely contented himself with giving them a new direction. He had small altars erected, before which children were placed to ask for alms, not for themselves, but for distribution among the poor. He taught them to sing hymns and sacred carols, some of which he himself composed for their use, while others were written by the poet Benivieni. He organised them under a number of leaders, and caused them to pass through the streets in procession and visit the several churches. In short, he substituted a wholesome and profitable amusement for the licentious pastimes that had demoralised those engaged in them, and disturbed the peace and order of the city.

At the close of 1495 or the beginning of 1496 occurred a remarkable incident, which it would be difficult to accept as probable, if it were not authenticated by numerous historians. The Pope had remitted the power of granting permission to Savonarola to resume his preaching, to a learned Dominican bishop, with instructions to ascertain if his sermons embodied any doctrines worthy of condemnation. The Bishop, in reply, informed the Borgia that Savonarola had said many things both wise and true; that he had certainly denounced the simony and corruption of the clergy, but not without justification; that he showed the greatest respect for the dogmas and authority of the Church; and that, in his opinion, the Pope's best plan was to make him his friend, and, on a fit occasion, invest him with the purple of a Cardinal. So to the man whom his enemies accused of heresy, of perversion of the Scriptures, of designs against all established authority, his Holiness hastened to offer a Cardinal's hat, on condition only that he changed the style of language he had been accustomed to employ in his sermons. Need we add that the offer was rejected with indignant contempt?

He received, however, a new licence to preach, and proceeded to exercise his recovered freedom in the Lent season of 1496. His first sermon was delivered on the 17th of February. Great precautions were taken by the Signory to prevent any disturbance of the public peace. They knew that the Duke of Milan had hired assassins to murder the Frate, and that the Arrabbiati were equally ready with the secret dagger. Guards were therefore stationed along the streets, and Savonarola was accompanied and surrounded by a large body of his friends and disciples, fully armed. The people received him with tumultuous joy, so that his enemies durst not attempt any hostile manifestation, and he passed into the Duomo, with shouts and blessings ringing in his ears. In the pulpit he stood erect, with a stern grave face, and his deep-set eyes flashing from beneath the heavy brows. The church was so densely crowded that no one could stir; yet so profound was the silence, that "the very breathing of the preacher might be heard." Subduing his emotion he began his discourse, which he threw into the form of a dialogue :—

"Tell us, Friar, why you have rested so long and have not come forth to aid your soldiers? My sons, I have not been at rest, I have been in the field, and engaged in defending a rock, which would have involved you, too, in destruction, if it had been overthrown; but now, through the grace of GOD, and your prayers, we have been saved. But, Friar, have you not been afraid of being killed? Assuredly not, my sons; had I been afraid, I should not stand here now, for my present danger is far greater than any that threatened me in the past. Have you then had some scruples of conscience about preaching? Not I. Why, then, did you desist? We have heard that a sentence of excommunication has been received, and that you have been commanded not to preach : have you read that sentence? Who sent it? But let it be as you say, do not you remember my telling you that if it came it would have no effect, and would not assist those wicked ones who are full of lies?" Then he proceeded to explain the reasons for his silence, and the position he assumed with respect to the Head of the Church. He declared the entire Catholicity of his teaching; he believed, he said, all that the Holy Roman Church believed. But though the Church was infallible in her dogmas, no such infallibility attached to the Pope, who could not command him to do anything contrary to the Gospel or to Charity. When it was evident that the orders of our superiors were contrary to those of GOD, and especially to the principles of Charity, no obedience ought to be vouchsafed to them; for it was written:—*Oportet obedire magis Deo quam hominibus* [We ought rather to obey GOD than man.]

After some further exposition he concluded with an animated apostrophe:—

"In you, young men, I place my hope, and in you are the hopes of the LORD. You will govern the city of Florence rightly, for you have not inclined to the evil example of your fathers, who will not detach themselves from tyrannical rulers, who will not see how great a gift the LORD has bestowed upon the people in the gift of liberty. But ye, old men, ye stand all day collected in groups, and in your shops, talking wickedly, and ye sent out from Florence letters teeming with lies, leading many to the belief that I am a disturber of Italy, as, indeed, hath also been alleged against me in papers of authority. O fools! Who hath bewitched you that ye should not obey the truth (*Quis vos fascinavit non obedire veritati?*) Where are the troops, where the funds, that I should compass the disturbance of Italy? It is not I who disturb Italy; but I do most solemnly warn her that she *will* be disturbed. I proclaim that your sins hasten the coming of the scourge. A great war, ye unbelievers, will force you to lay aside your pomp and haughtiness. And as for you, ye women, a fearful pestilence will compel you to dismiss your vanities, and the evil tongues will be silenced by a terrible famine. Fellow-citizens, if ye walk not in the fear of GOD, and be not loyal to your free Government, the LORD will cause evil to come upon you, and all the happiness promised to Florence will be reserved for your children."

The sermons which Savonarola delivered in the Lent of 1496 were his finest efforts. It was then, as Dean Milman says, that his eloquence swelled to its full diapason. His triumphal course began with the Advent of 1494, on Haggai and the Psalms. But it was in the Carême of 1496, on Amos and Zechariah, that the preacher girded himself to his full strength. He had attained the very height of his authority; yet he could not but be conscious that there was a deep and dangerous rebellion brooding in the hearts of the hostile factions at Florence, and that already ominous rumours began to be heard from Rome. He that would know the power, the daring, the oratory of Savonarola, must study these "sermons." And in studying them, he must remember they were preached to Italian audiences, whose emotions were easily stirred, in a time of great events and great passions; he may then form some idea of their tremendous effect, of the power which was wielded by their preacher.

The year 1496 was one to test that power to the utmost, for it loaded the Florentine Republic with calamities. Florence was beset by dangers and menaced by a host of enemies. Its commerce and industry had suffered greatly during the revolutionary changes of the past two years; the sum paid to France and the expenses of the war against Pisa pressed heavily on its resources; while famine stalked through its streets, and was followed, as usual, by pestilence. Venice, Milan, and the German Emperor were assisting Pisa, and while the Florentine coast was harassed by the Venetian and Genoese ships, Leghorn, its only seaport, was invested by an army of Pisans and Imperialists. Its Government, nevertheless, maintained a bold heart, raised money and troops with untiring energy, and seemed to gain fresh courage from each new defeat. They despatched ambassadors to France, and obtained aid both in soldiery and corn; but the supplies and promised reinforcements, when most urgently needed, were prevented from entering the harbour of Leghorn by a succession of violent gales. To increase the trials of the Government the Pope once more silenced the voice which alone could stimulate the people to exertion or nerve them to endurance. But when the relief fleet was driven back, the need of Savonarola's eloquence grew so imperative that the Signory urged him to defy the Papal mandate. He consented. Once more he mounted the pulpit of the Duomo (October 28th); and addressed the thousands who, with haggard faces and restless eyes, crowded passionately around him. He spoke to them in words of uncompromising faith and courage. Let them but repent, he said, and succour would be given to them. Let them return to GOD; let them lay aside all thoughts of overthrowing their free government and surrendering to the enemy; let them resort to all human means for aid, and lend to the State, without interest, whatever moneys they had at their command; let them be united and cease from their dissensions; and he would consent to have his frock stripped from him if GOD did not come to their help. "I tell you," he exclaimed, and the deep tones of his voice seemed to infuse new strength into the hearts of his hearers; "I tell you that if ye do as I bid you, I will be the first to go forth against your enemies with the crucifix in my hand, and we will drive them as far as Pisa, ay, and further still."

On the following day, the miraculous image of the Madonna dell' Impruneta, which for a century and a half had been brought into Florence on any occasion of famine, flood, pestilence, or war, and never without bringing deliverance with it, was fetched from its sanctuary at l'Impruneta, six miles from the gate of San Piero, and borne in solemn procession through the crowded streets towards the Duomo. First went the Florentine youth, carrying high in their midst the white image of the Holy Child; next, the Companies of Discipline, all wearing a garb which concealed the whole head and face, except the eyes, like a shroud, but each Company distinguished by its own badge and colour; then followed the Benedictine monks, in robes of white,— the Franciscans, in gray, with knotted girdles round their waists,—the Augustinians, in black,—the Carmelites, in white over dark,—the Servites, in unrelieved black,—and, after them, the Dominicans, with black mantles over scapularies, including in their ranks the great Preacher, in whom most Florentines placed their hope and trust. Next might be seen the Frati Umiliati or Humbled Brethren, and a long train of tonsured heads; the twenty-one incorporated Arts of Florence, each with its proud distinctive banner; and the secondary Officers of State in every variety of habit. The interest deepened as the Canons of the Duomo appeared, carrying in silver casket the head of San Zenobio, Bishop of Florence, who had saved the city a thousand years before; for they preceded the Archbishop in his gorgeous pontificals, and the sacred twofold Tabernacle, or Shrine, containing the blessed image of the Virgin, found long, long ago in the soil of l'Impruneta, "uttering a cry as the spade struck it." Behind it marched a train of priests and chaplains, and the procession closed with the Priori and the Gonfaloniere, attended by their guards and pages.

The long array had reached the Porta Santa Maria, when a horseman, breathless with haste and soiled with dust, crossing the bridge La Carraia, galloped full speed by the Lung' Arno, with olive-branch in hand, making for the Palazzo of the Signory. Immediately the crowd beset him, and eager-eyed men, seizing his bridle, gasped out the inquiry then on every lip:—"What news from Leghorn?" What news? why, glad tidings of great joy! The galleys from France, laden with corn and wine, with soldiers and arms, had arrived in the harbour, driven in by a strong south-westerly gale which at the same time had forced the enemy's fleet to keep their distance! The words of the messenger passed from mouth to mouth until all Florence was in a state of frantic excitement. The bells were set a-ringing; thanksgivings were offered up in the churches; while the populace cried aloud that Savonarola was a true prophet, and that his sermon had wrought their salvation.

The hostility of the Pope was influenced by this latest action of the Preacher, and he endeavoured to fetter him by including the convent of S. Mark's in a new congregation, the Tusco-Romano, which would necessarily destroy its independence. But Savonarola detected his object, and boldly refused to join the proposed combination. On the 26th of November he returned to the pulpit, and during Advent preached a course of eight sermons on Ezekiel, in which he gave his hearers and the magistracy much sound political advice. Thus the close of 1496 showed his name and authority at the highest pitch, and the party which embraced his teaching and principles in possession of the field. But, at the same time, the contention with Rome had increased in bitterness, and the Pope seemed filled with

S

an ungovernable hatred of the Frate and the government he had created. Nor were internal troubles wanting. The spirit of faction had free course in the city, and the plots of the Arrabbiati and the Bigi (or Mediceans) were so numerous and so insolent, that Savonarola was forced to advise an increased severity of administration and some restriction of the course of proceeding in the Consiglio Maggiore, in order to prevent the government from being usurped by those whose secret object was its destruction.

The moral influence at this time exercised by Savonarola received a remarkable illustration in the absence of the excesses which used previously to disgrace the Carnival season. The Arrabbiati contemplated a revival of the old scandalous orgies, and of the stone-throwing by the children, which had previously given great delight to the populace; but the reforms instituted by Savonarola were strictly maintained. His fervid follower, Frà Domenico of Pescia, collected the children in their several bands or companies, and sent them through the city—to demand from rich and poor alike the surrender of all their gauds and gewgaws, books with indelicate pictures, playing-cards, dice, carnival dresses and masks, rouge-pots, powders, perfumes, and other "vanities" which were called "the anathema." On receiving them, they repeated a prayer which had been composed by Savonarola, and proceeded on their moral inquisition. On the last day of the Carnival, February 7th, an imposing religious spectacle was organised. Early in the morning, men, women, and children were present at a Solemn Mass celebrated by the Frate, who, with his own hand, dispensed the Sacrament to the kneeling multitude. After returning home, and partaking of a frugal meal, they marched in grand procession through the city, with Donatello's Holy Child[1] before them; a long line of lads and striplings, clothed in white, and carrying red crosses and olive wreaths. Others went to and fro with silver trays to receive contributions for the hungry and needy, to be placed in the hands of the Buonuomini di San Martino. On reaching

---

[1] The Holy Child, supported by four angels, was represented as pointing with His left hand to a crown of thorns, while with His right He blessed the people. This sculpture is now preserved in the Church of San Lorenzo.

the Piazza del Signoria, they formed there an octangular structure, 60 feet high, with a circumference of 240 feet at the base. It was arranged in fifteen tiers or stages, on which were piled all "the vanities" collected during the festival, surmounted by the effigy of a Venetian merchant who was said to have offered 22,000 florins for the collection, and a grotesque image symbolic of the old Carnival. Singing religious hymns, the children set fire to this Pyramid of Vanities, which quickly sent up a great flame and smoke to Heaven; the trumpets of the guard of the Signory rang out an exultant peal; the great bell of the Palazzo was tolled; and the multitude raised a loud shout of triumphal joy, as if, in that blazing pile, they saw the sign and token of a victory over Hell itself.[1]

But if this strange ceremony were a striking proof of Savonarola's influence, it also marked the climax of that influence. Thenceforward it began to decline.

CHAPTER IV.

IN his Lent sermons the Frate showed himself prepared for excommunication, and boldly defied it. Never had he more strenuously assailed the abominations practised at Rome, never had he more bitterly deplored the corruptions of the Church. "Come hither," he exclaimed, "thou profligate Church! I gave thee, saith the LORD, beautiful vestments, and ye have made idols of them. Ye have applied the sacred vessels to purposes of pride, and the Sacraments to simony; by your luxuries, ye have made yourselves shameless harlots; ye are worse than the beasts that perish; ye are monsters of abomination." Addressing his audience, he said :—" I have been sent to whisper something into your ears, and I have obeyed. Do ye keep at rest, until ye hear the summons, 'Lazarus, come forth!' I stand in this place because the LORD hath sent me, and I wait until I am called. Then shall I

---

[1] A minute account of the "Bonfire of Vanities" is given by Burlamacchi.

speak with a loud voice that will be heard throughout Christendom, and will cause the body of the Church to tremble, as the voice of GOD made that of Lazarus tremble." "I know full well," he continued, "that there is one at Rome who daily sets to work to do me injury. But he is not actuated by zeal for religion; he plots because he is sunk in slavery to great and mighty lords. Some pretend that the Frate has yielded, and sent one of his followers to Rome. I can tell you that the party at Rome do not do my bidding; and had flattery been my habit, I should not this day have been in Florence [an allusion to the offer of the Cardinal's hat], nor should I wear a tattered gown, and I should have known how to escape from danger. But, O LORD, this is no part of my desire; Thy Cross is all I wish for: oh, cause me to be persecuted: I ask this favour of Thee, that Thou wilt not allow me to die in my bed, but that I may shed my blood for Thee, as Thou didst shed Thine for me. Meanwhile, my sons, be not afraid, for the LORD will support us."

The opposition to Savonarola and his party, however, was rapidly extending and deepening. The Mediceans, or Bigis, were ceaseless in their activity; the Arrabbiati maintained their old attitude of hostility; the emissaries of Rome secretly poisoned the minds of the weak and credulous against the Frate; while the poor were wrought up into a condition of restlessness and discontent by the severity of their sufferings. Famine had again laid its harsh clutch upon the city, and in its train came a ghastly cohort of diseases, with the dreaded Plague closing up their rear. The opportunity seemed so favourable to Piero de' Medici, who had watched with satisfaction the struggle between the Piagnoni and the Arrabbiati, that, with 1,300 men, he advanced upon Florence (April 18th). But intelligence of his movements reached the city; the people rose in arms; the gates were closed; and when Piero arrived in front of the gate that looks towards Rome, he found his friends unprepared to receive him, and was compelled to fall back.[1] This attempt gave temporary prominence to the Arrabbiati, who succeeded in electing one of their leaders as Gonfaloniere, and immediately directed their whole strength, supported by the Duke of Milan and the Pope, against Savonarola and

---

[1] Guicciardini, "Storia Fiorentina," iii. pp. 147—150.

his followers. After his sermon on Ascension Day their more violent members made a desperate attempt upon his life, but he was surrounded and defended by his people, who escorted him in safety to the Convent. The Signory, siding with the Arrabbiati, allowed his assailants to escape unpunished, issued a proclamation forbidding any friar, in whatever order he might be enrolled, to preach; and even meditated the great Preacher's banishment. The moment seemed favourable for a fresh demonstration on the part of Rome against the audacious monk who ventured to attack its corruptions, and the Pope hurled at him a sentence of excommunication. In reply, the Frate boldly declared the sentence invalid, because founded upon false reasons and unsupported accusations. His party steadfastly adhered to him; but the Arrabbiati gained fresh insolence from the patronage of Rome, and drew around them all the wild and disorderly spirits of the city. That Florence which Savonarola had laboured to reform and dedicate to CHRIST fell back into its old and evil ways. A miserable reaction set in; the churches were empty, the taverns full; "women came forth in indelicate attire, and their hitherto concealed jewels and new ornaments of luxury were everywhere displayed; perfumed youths roamed through the streets singing coarse carnival songs beneath the windows of their mistresses, who no longer blushed to hear them." Anonymous ballads and songs and sonnets, ridiculing Savonarola and his doctrines, were published, and at night, when the friars were chanting the services in S. Mark's, they were disturbed by shouting and singing, and even by stone-throwing.

The end was not yet come, however. Another political change took place, and the Piagnoni recovered the administration of affairs, which they retained for several months. Meanwhile, the struggle between Savonarola and the Pope daily increased in bitterness; and proved (as Villari says) a constant source of grief both to Government and people. Both were distressed by seeing a man who had done so much for his country and for religion pursued with an unjust hatred; and, by espousing the Friar's cause, they placed themselves and the Republic in a continual and increasing state of discord with Rome. The most vehement letters were repeatedly addressed to the ambassador, Alessandro Braccio, urging him to use every exertion to obtain the absolution of Savonarola. "We desire you," wrote the Signory, "to knock incessantly at the door, and never cease to call out and employ all possible means; that you do not desist nor spare any amount of trouble, until you gain your object." But the Pope was not to be persuaded. On the contrary, he was watching and waiting for a more favourable opportunity of carrying out his designs. Savonarola lived in retirement in his convent, occupying himself in writing new tracts, and in publishing some which he had already written; such as his "Exposition of the Ten Commandments," "Ten Rules for Prayer in Times of Great Tribulation," "On the Mystery of the Cross," "Lament of the Spouse of CHRIST," "Exposition of Habakkuk," and "Triumph of the Cross."

Openly defying the Papal excommunication, Savonarola broke his enforced silence on Christmas Day, celebrating the three Solemn Masses, and administering the Sacrament to all the friars in the convent, and to a multitude of the people who had assembled there. At the earnest request of his friends, and with the consent of the Signory, he resumed his preaching, and mounted the pulpit in the Duomo on the first Sunday in Lent, 1498. He continued to preach throughout the spring of 1498 with all his old faithfulness and courage, and reasserted his extraordinary influence over the people. On the last day of the Carnival another "Bonfire of Vanities" attested to the re-awakened enthusiasm. From Florence the stir and fever spread throughout Italy and over Europe, raising a general antagonism against the shameless excesses of the Court of Rome, and preparing men's minds for that doctrinal revolution of which Luther was to be the chief author. The efforts of the Pope and his councillors to silence their formidable adversary were redoubled. They threatened Florence with an interdict, and by means of this threat succeeded in obtaining from the Signory a decree prohibiting him again from preaching. On the day that it was passed Savonarola delivered what proved to be his last sermon, in which he spoke of the difficulties he had encountered in putting forward his doctrines, the long and violent struggle he had been forced to sustain, and the resistless impulse which had governed his actions.

He concluded by predicting that new disasters were threatening Florence, new misfortunes awaiting her. "You are in fear of the interdict," he said; "but the LORD will send one who will deprive the wicked both of life and property. We shall accomplish by prayer what we cannot effect by preaching; and we recommend that course to all good men. O LORD, I commend them to Thee, and I pray Thee to defer no longer the fulfilment of Thy promises."[1]

Though silenced he was not inactive. He entered into correspondence with the principal sovereigns of Europe, urging them to summon a General Council for the reform of the Church; and it is not improbable that if his advice had been taken the Lutheran movement would never have taken place, or it would have been carried out by the Church herself. France was inclined to move, England seemed favourable, Germany was enthusiastic, and Savonarola had much reason to hope for the issue he so anxiously desired, when an event occurred, which not only baffled his purpose, but compassed his destruction.

A Franciscan friar of Puglia, from the pulpit of Santa Croce, made a vehement attack upon the Frate and his teaching; denouncing him as a heretic, a schismatic, an impostor, and challenging him to prove the truth of his doctrines by submitting to the Ordeal of Fire. Similar challenges had often been given, and Savonarola had wisely passed them by in silent contempt; but on this occasion the gage thrown down was rashly taken up by Frà Domenico, one of the most enthusiastic, but at the same time, one of the most unwise and imprudent of the Frate's disciples. Publishing his master's celebrated Three Conclusions, he declared himself prepared to support them by the Ordeal of Fire. Thus, the question had assumed a certain gravity before Savonarola could interfere; and it was eagerly taken up by the Arrabbiati, who saw in it a certain and sure means of injuring the man they hated. The Franciscan contended that the challenge was addressed to him, and him alone; and the Arrabbiati perceived that if he refused it, his reputation with the people would be injured, and an opportunity would probably arise of instigating a riot in which he might easily be put to death. On the other hand, if he accepted it, they

[1] Villari, ii. 261.

believed that he would be burned. They obtained the assent of the Signory to their murderous design. And a copy of the disputed Conclusions being publicly issued, a formal invitation was given to those who wished to maintain and defend them by the ordeal of fire to come forward and sign it.

Spurning all advice, the impetuous Frà Domenico presented himself and affixed his signature. The plotters, however, found it not so easy to induce the Franciscan to sign. He informed the Signory that he could not put himself in competition with Frà Girolamo either in sanctity or knowledge of doctrine; yet he was ready to pass with him through the fire (apparently from a secret persuasion that the Frate's sanctity would save both of them). But as for Frà Domenico, he had nothing to do with him. The Signory, however, assured him that he would not be required to enter the fire; all they wanted of him was to say that he *would* do so; and at last obtained from him a declaration that he would submit to the ordeal if Frà Girolamo consented, but that as to the trial with Frà Domenico, he would substitute for himself his conventual brother, Giuliano Rondinelli.

The plot worked as the Frate's enemies expected. A belief in his supernatural powers had always prevailed among the Frateschi, and had been fed by his own declarations of the visions with which he had been favoured, the revelations that GOD had vouchsafed to him. They had always been as eagerly denied by the Frate's opponents: and it seemed to his friends that now a great opportunity had presented itself for him to prove beyond question the supernatural character of his gifts, and pour shame and confusion on the heads of his accusers. If he passed through the fiery ordeal unhurt, which none of them doubted, who would afterwards dare to dispute his mission? Would not all the world recognise him as a messenger specially sent from GOD? Others besides Frà Domenico offered themselves for the ordeal; two more brothers of S. Mark's, Frà Malatesta Sacramoro, and Frà Roberto Salviati, subscribed the challenge. The great body of the Piagnoni, however, while acknowledging that if they walked through the fire unhurt, it would be a miracle, felt that the miracle would be grander and more complete if performed in the person of Savonarola himself.

At first the Frate exerted himself strenuously against the projected Ordeal. For he temporarily lost confidence in his own visions; he could not convince himself that a living creature could pass through the fire and yet live: and he saw in the failure of the ordeal the ruin of all his grand schemes for the regeneration of the Church. But when it had become inevitable, he strove to gain courage from the eagerness and zeal of his follower. If he had so much faith, must it not be inspired by Heaven? For himself, if the Pope's legate would attend, if the ambassadors of all the Christian Powers would be present, and would promise that a General Council should be called on his performance of the miracle, he would enter the flames, and trust to GOD to protect His servant. Until then, he would continue to discharge the duties laid upon him. Frà Salvestro, a man whose influence over Savonarola was in undue excess of his real value, declared that, in a vision, he had seen the angels of Frà Girolamo and Frà Domenico, who had assured him that these brethren would pass through the fire as triumphantly as the Three Children passed through the fiery furnace. And so the Frate was persuaded to withdraw his opposition. The Ordeal was finally fixed for the 7th of April; and it was agreed that, on the part of S. Mark's, Frà Domenico should appear as champion, on the part of the Franciscans, Giuliano Rondinelli. The place chosen was a platform in the Piazza della Signoria, measuring eight feet in breadth by sixty feet in length, on which was heaped up a pile of fuel, with tan and rags and other combustible material, leaving a central passage, about three feet wide, for the two champions to walk in. It was agreed that the mass should be lighted at one end; that they should enter at the other; and then that it should be lighted behind them.

To prevent a tumult, or any interference with the ordeal, three large bodies of armed men were stationed in the Piazza: in front of the Palazzo of the Signory, five hundred of their hired soldiery; on the opposite side, at some distance, five hundred *compagnacci*, under Dolfo Spini, one of the leaders of the Arrabbiati; and in front of Orcagna's Loggia, three hundred armed citizens, under Savonarola's true and trusty adherent, Marcuccio Salviati. On the morning of the 7th, Savonarola celebrated a solemn mass in S. Mark's, after which he addressed the people in brief and earnest words.[1] It is evident that he detected the design of the Signory and the intentions of his enemies, that he perceived the snares which had been so skilfully woven round him :—" I cannot assure you," he said, "that the Ordeal will take place, for it does not depend upon us; but this I can tell you, that if it does, the victory will assuredly be ours. O LORD, we have no need of these miraculous proofs for our belief in the truth; but since we have been challenged we cannot shrink from maintaining Thy honour. We are certain that Satan could not promote this matter to the injury of Thy honour, or contrary to Thy Will, and therefore we go forth to combat for Thee; but those our enemies worship another god, and their works are far different from ours. O GOD, this people wishes for no other thing than to serve Thee! My people, is it your desire to serve GOD?"

Whereupon all cried with a loud shout, " We do! we do!"

The mace-bearers of the Signory arriving to announce that all the preparations were complete, the friars of S. Mark's immediately formed in procession, led by Frà Domenico, who, wearing a flame-coloured velvet cope, and carrying a tall cross, advanced between his brethren, Francesco Salviati and Malatesta Sacramoro, his head erect, his countenance serene, his eyes bright with exalted faith. Behind him, in a priest's white robe, marched Savonarola, holding in his hands a vessel containing the consecrated Host; and then followed upwards of two hundred monks, clothed in the Dominican habit, and chanting in deep grave tones the exultant psalm, " Let GOD arise, and let His enemies be scattered." They reached the Piazza about half an hour after noon, and passing through the barricaded entrance two by two, took up their stations in that half of the loggia which had been allotted to them—the other half being occupied by the Franciscans—while all the Piagnoni joined in the psalm, filling the air with a roar of voices. The multitude was immense :—since early morning there had been

[1] Burlamacchi.

a gradual swarming of the people at every coign of vantage or disadvantage offered by the façades and roofs of the houses, and such spaces of the pavement as were free of access. Men were seated on iron rods that made a sharp angle with the rising wall, were clutching thin pillars with arms and legs, were astride on the necks of the rough statuary that here and there surmounted the entrances of the grander houses, were finding a palm's breadth of seat on a bit of architrave, and a footing on the rough projections of the rustic stonework, while they clutched the strong iron rings or staples driven into the walls beside them.

Hitherto Savonarola had been inly tortured by his doubts as to the lawfulness of the trial, as well as by his sense of the artifice of his enemies in contriving it. But when he saw the excitement of the multitude, and the eager vehemence, the uncontrollable zeal of Frà Domenico, all prudential considerations and scruples of conscience were set aside. His ardent nature responded to the fervour around him, and he was not less anxious than Domenico himself that the trial should begin. But where was the Franciscan champion? Both he and Francesco di Puglia were in conference with the Signory, who, now that the crisis had come, would fain have shrunk from action. What was to be done? The Franciscans had no intention of allowing their champion to enter the fire; at the same time they were resolved that the refusal should come from Savonarola, in order to destroy his credit with the multitude. To gain time, they pretended that Frà Domenico's cope was enchanted, and therefore insisted that it should be taken off. While declaring his disbelief in incantations, Savonarola consented to their demand. They next refused to allow the Dominican to carry into the fire his crucifix, alleging that it would be profaned. To this objection Savonarola also yielded, but Domenico then said that he would hold the consecrated Host. The Franciscans immediately raised a fresh clamour. It was impious to carry the Sacrament into the fire; did he wish to burn it? He contended, supported by Savonarola, that even if it were burned, only the accidents would be consumed; that the Substance would not be touched. Here was a nice theological subtlety, on which any amount of discussion might arise; and at once both parties plunged into a maze of casuistical argument. Meanwhile, the crowd, cold, exhausted, and hungry, grew impatient of the long delay, and angry murmurs arose on every side. Reports were circulated attributing the interruption of the spectacle to Savonarola, and many demanded why he himself did not enter the fire, and place beyond cavil his miraculous power. The afternoon drew on apace; the clouds increased in density, the air turned colder; and still the debate in the loggia dragged its slow length along. Neither side would give way; and profiting by the circumstance, which had probably been foreseen and anticipated, the Signory finally issued an order that the proposed fiery trial should not take place. At the same time a storm of rain broke over the city, and the people saw that all was over. Their anger at being disappointed of a sensation became almost ungovernable; and it was with extreme difficulty that the Dominicans contrived to effect their return to their Convent, escorted, sword in hand, by the brave soldiers of Salviati. There Savonarola shut himself up in his cell, his mind oppressed with a great gloom. The jeers and taunts of the crowd had wounded him sorely; they were a foretaste of bitterness to come. And moreover, the thought *would* obtrude itself upon him that he had been faithless to his work; that he ought himself to have entered the blazing fire, relying upon GOD's miraculous interposition, and have silenced the injurious voices of his enemies. But then another thought succeeded: would this miraculous interposition have been vouchsafed? Was he justified in demanding or expecting it? Would it not have been tempting GOD? And finally, the dreadful question, which he had never been able to answer with complete satisfaction, presented itself: was his mission really from Heaven? Those visions, those revelations of his, were they really divine? He passed a sad and anxious night; but before morning he was strengthened by prayer, and when on the following day, Palm Sunday, he once more mounted his pulpit in San Marco, it was with unaffected composure and serene patience that he contemplated his doom, and declared himself ready to suffer death in the cause of CHRIST and His Church.

That afternoon the Convent was assailed by furious bands of Arrabbiati, whose numbers were swollen by hundreds of the disappointed populace. They were met with a sturdy resistance. For the monks, suspecting that a crisis was at hand, had arms within their walls, and some of them fought with the vigour of veteran soldiers. There were laymen, too, who, in order to be of service, had lingered in the church, and who could wield their weapons with indomitable zeal. There was firing from the high altar close by the great crucifix; there were volleys of stones and hot embers from the convent roof; there was hand-to-hand fighting in the cloisters. Savonarola was grieved at this resort to force. Putting on his cope, and taking a crucifix in his hands, he said :—" Let me go, for this storm has risen on my account:" and he prepared to yield himself to the enemy. A cry of lamentation went up from the bystanders; friars and laymen crowded round him, and with tears exclaimed : —" Do not, do not forsake us : you will be torn in pieces, and what shall we do without you?" Yielding to their entreaties, he called upon all to follow him; and, with the Host in his hand, led a procession round the cloisters and into the choir, where he told his brethren that prayer was their only lawful weapon. Throwing aside their arms, all knelt down before the Sacrament, chanting :—" Salvum fac populum Tuum, Domine" (Save Thy people, O LORD).

It was about this time that the Signory sent their mace-bearers to make proclamation that sentence of exile had been passed against Savonarola, and that he was required to leave the Florentine territory within twenty-four hours. Most of those who heard regarded the proclamation as a stratagem of the enemy's, it seemed so improbable that the Signory would take the part of the rioters against a man who had rendered such signal services to Florence. The attack continued, and the assailants were actually reinforced by the soldiers of the Signory. Some set fire to the doors; others scaled the walls, and broke into the cloister; and, after sacking the infirmary and some of the cells, forced their way into the Sacristy, and thence into the choir. The friars who were kneeling there in prayer, sprang to their feet by a natural impulse of self-defence, and with lighted tapers, or wooden and brazen crucifixes struck at the faces of their foes; who, believing themselves attacked by a company of angels, fled in the utmost disorder. Then those who, at Savonarola's bidding, had laid down their arms, again resumed them, and a fierce struggle took place in the cloisters, while the great bell (*la Piagnona*) of the Convent rolled its deep tones of alarm over the city. The conflict deepened. Here Baldo Inghirlamo and Francesco Davanzati led on their followers; there Andrea di Luca della Robbia, sword in hand, pursued the retreating foe; while Frà Benedetto and others of the brethren poured showers of stones and tiles from the roof upon the besieging forces. In the church more than one of the monks handled his arquebus with skill and determination; especially a certain Enrico il Tedesco, who, from the pulpit, shot down several rioters, exclaiming each time he fired:—" Salvum fac populum Tuum, Domine, et benedic hereditati Tuæ." So vigorous was the defence that, if it had been possible to rouse the Piagnoni in the city, and bring them up to the relief of the Convent, Savonarola might have been saved. Francesco Valori, one of the leaders of the Frateschi, had made an attempt, letting himself down from a back wall of the Convent; but on his way to the Palazzo, he fell in with some members of the powerful Medicean families, and was attacked and killed.[1]

At this crisis of the fight, the Signory, active in their hostility to Savonarola, issued a new proclamation, denouncing as rebels all who did not leave the Convent within one hour. Some of the defenders then asked for a safe-conduct and departed, thus weakening the already too feeble body of the garrison. And as it was clear that the Signory had determined on crushing S. Mark's, the defence necessarily lost tenacity, and many were heard to speak of the advisability of surrender. No help came from without; and they were too few in themselves to make a much longer resistance. Savonarola and some of the brethren had remained engaged in prayers or attending to the wounded. Among the dying was a young man of the family of the Panicatiri, who had been laid upon the steps of the high altar, and while the din of conflict rolled into the holy place, received the Sacrament from the hands of Frà Domenico. His last words were words of rejoicing, for as his glazing eyes fell upon the figure of the beloved Master, he murmured :—

[1] Burlamacchi.

"Quanto è dolce ai fratelli ritrovarsi insieme" (Behold how sweet it is for brethren to dwell together.)[1]

It was now night; and the friars, worn with fasting and spent with effort, gladly ate some dried figs which their companions brought them. But the attack was renewed with fresh energy as the defence slackened; and great clouds of smoke and flame from the burning doors and woodwork rolled through the cloisters and into the church, compelling the monks to retreat into the choir, where Enrico il Tedesco and another, climbing behind the high altar, stationed themselves on either side of the great crucifix, and plied their fire-arms lustily.

Savonarola, lamenting the useless bloodshed, again took the Sacrament into his hands, and imploring his people to follow him, proceeded towards the Libreria Greca, a monument of the architectural genius of Michelozzi. On the way he encountered Frà Benedetto, who had just descended from the roof, eager to plunge into the stress of the fight below. Savonarola fixed his eyes upon him:—"Frà Benedetto, lay down your arms, and take up the cross. It has never been my wish that the brethren should shed blood." Benedetto immediately threw himself at the Frate's feet, laid down his weapons, and with the rest followed him into the library.[2]

"My sons," said Savonarola, "in the presence of GOD and before the sacred Host, with the enemy already in the convent, I confirm to you my doctrine. What I have spoken I have received from GOD; He is my witness in Heaven that I do not lie. I little thought that the whole city would turn against me; but the will of GOD be done. My last counsel to you is this: let your only weapons be faith and patience and prayer. I leave you with pain and sorrow, to place myself in the hands of my enemies. I know not whether they will take my life; but of this I am certain that, if I die, I shall be able to aid you in heaven far more than I have been able to do on earth. Be comforted; embrace the Cross; and with that you will find the haven of Salvation."

---

[1] Burlamacchi, who gives a graphic and minute account of the attack and defence of the Convent.

[2] Benedetto, *Cedrus Libani*, c. 9.

The commander of the guard of the Signory now threatened to turn his cannon against the Convent if the command of the Signory were not immediately obeyed. This was, that on a promise of safety to their persons, Frà Girolamo, Frà Domenico, and Frà Salvestro should be given up. Frà Malatesta Sacramoro, who had volunteered to undergo the Ordeal, held a private conference with the fierce soldier,— according to Villari, he had already resolved on betraying his Master—suggesting that, to ensure Savonarola's obedience he should obtain a written order. A delay occurred while this was waited for, which the Frate occupied in confessing to Frà Domenico, and receiving the Sacrament from him. It was then, too, that a memorable incident occurred. A young follower of Savonarola's, Girolamo Gini, who had long yearned to assume the Dominican dress, was at vespers when the clash of arms began. He immediately seized his weapon, to lay it down again at the Master's command. But resolute to prove his zeal in the good cause, he ran into the midst of the enemy, carrying his crucifix, and thirsting for death. Seriously wounded, he entered the Library, and throwing himself on his knees before Savonarola, prayed that after his baptism of blood he might be received into the brotherhood. His request was granted; it was the Frate's last act of authority.

A proposition was made by some of the brethren that Savonarola should be lowered down from the wall to seek safety in flight, and for a moment he hesitated, as if inclined to act upon it. But the Judas of the community, Frà Malatesta, decided him against it by the cruelly artful question:— " Ought not the shepherd to lay down his life for his flock?" The words sank deep, as an implied reproach, into Savonarola's heart. He turned in silence to the brethren, and embraced them, beginning with Malatesta himself: then, with his faithful Domenico by his side,[1] he surrendered to the mace-bearer of the Signory, on his return with their formal mandate. His last words to his community were worthy of his life among them:—" My dear brethren, remember never to doubt. The work of the LORD will not cease to progress, and my death will only hasten it."

---

[1] Frà Salvestro's courage had failed him, and in the confusion he had contrived to hide himself.—Burlamacchi, p. 143.

"Loud was the roar of triumphant hate, when the light of lanterns showed the Frate issuing from the door of the convent with a guard who promised him no other safety than that of the prison. The struggle now was, who should get first in the stream that rushed up the narrow street to see the Prophet carried back in ignominy to the Piazza, where he had braved it yesterday—who should be in the best place for reaching his ear with insult, nay, if possible, for smiting him and kicking him. This was not difficult for some of the armed Compagnacci, who were not prevented from mixing themselves with the guards.

"When Savonarola felt himself dragged and pushed along in the midst of that hooting multitude; when lanterns were lighted to show him deriding faces; when he felt himself spit upon, smitten and kicked with grossest words of insult, it seemed to him that the worst bitterness of life was past. If men judged him guilty, and were bent on having his blood, it was only death that awaited him." More terrible to live, with the remembrance ever upon him of the ingratitude of that Florentine people for whom he had laboured so ungrudgingly, whom he had hoped to put in the fore-front of that glorious revolution he had meditated so long! More terrible to live with the knowledge of the insolent cruelty of that Florence he had sought to convert into "a city of GOD," a centre whence the light of a reformed State and purified Church should go forth to illumine the civilised world. To the Reformer who sees his work misunderstood and overthrown by those for whose profit it was designed, whose motives are misrepresented, whose claims are denied,—to whom the cup which he has filled with the wine of his best efforts is returned brimming over with vinegar,—to him, I say, death means happiness and life sorrow!

Savonarola and his companion were brought before the Gonfaloniere, who asked them if they still maintained that they spoke by divine revelation, and when they replied affirmatively committed them to their separate cells. Next day, Frà Salvestro ventured from his hiding-place, but was immediately detected and betrayed by Malatesta Sacramoro. The three Frati were then kept in custody to await their formal trial.[1]

[1] Burlamacchi, p. 144; Nardi, p. 156; Villari, ii. 304.

Great was the joy of Pope Borgia when he was apprised of the failure of the Ordeal, the singular change in the feeling of the populace, and the arrest of Savonarola. He showered his blessings on everybody concerned, on the Franciscans, and Frà Francesco, and the Compagnacci, and the Signory, who were addressed as "true sons of Holy Church." He was bountiful in his promises of good things, material as well as spiritual; but he was careful to suggest that, as soon as the trials of the three Brethren were over, they should be immediately given up to him to receive the punishment they deserved. Great was the joy of the Duke of Milan when he learned that this troublesome Friar, with his new views of princes and rights of the people, and his eloquent praises of liberty, was in the hands of his enemies. And still greater was the joy of both Pope and Prince when they found that Savonarola's powerful supporter, who, not improbably, would have interfered to rescue him, Charles VIII. of France, had died at Amboise on the very day of the failure of the Fiery Ordeal.[1]

CHAPTER V.

THE object of Savonarola's enemies was to secure his condemnation. As it was known that the ordinary courts of magistracy, "the Ten of Liberty" and "the Eight," were favourably disposed towards him and the Frateschi, the Signory resolved to set them aside; and, on the 11th of April, illegally appointed an extraordinary commission of seventeen members, most of whom were notorious as the Frate's bitterest and most unscrupulous enemies. To these the Pope added two canons. The unjust constitution of this tribunal, and the purpose for which it was called into existence, were so obvious, that one of the commissioners indignantly refused to serve, declaring that "he would have no part in the homicide." Savonarola, how-

---

[1] He died under peculiarly wretched circumstances, as Savonarola had often predicted would be the case if he abandoned "the work of the LORD."

ever, was immediately brought before it, and the question first put to him by the Signory was repeated. The answer, as before, was, that his doctrine came from GOD. He was supplied with writing materials; but the responses which he gave to the inquiries of his judges were so little calculated to justify the sentence on which they had already resolved, that they were at once destroyed; and consequently we possess no authentic record of his defence. It is impossible to put any trust in the official reports, from their grossly garbled and mutilated character.

On the 10th of April the interrogation was resumed, and to extort such a confession as their aim required, his judges ordered him to be tortured. A rope being attached to a pulley on a high pole, his hands were fastened behind his back, the end of the rope was wound round his wrists, and the executioner then hoisted him up and let him down suddenly, with a force which lacerated the muscles and sent a quiver of agony through every limb. This torture was repeated on Savonarola's sensitive frame, weakened by abstinence, long vigils, and incessant labours, until his mind began to wander, and his answers became incoherent. At last, in his pain, he cried out, in heartrending tones,—" O LORD ! take, O take my life !" He was then released from the executioners, and sent back to prison, praying, as he went, for those who had so despitefully used him :—" Forgive them, LORD, for they know not what they do !" How often he was subjected to the torture cannot be determined, but as the so-called " trial" lasted upwards of a month, it is certain that his sufferings were " long, continuous, and cruel."[1] It is stated by an eye-witness that in a single day he was hoisted by the rope fourteen times. Burlamacchi adds that live coals were applied to the soles of his feet, and that in the delirious condition to which he was thus reduced his wild and wayward words were carefully taken down as " spontaneously given," and recorded as his deliberate and conscious utterances. But Savonarola was ill fitted to endure protracted suffering, owing to his morbid sensitiveness of temperament; and to regard as genuine expressions of belief the incoherencies which dropped from his white lips in moments of physical anguish and nervous prostration, would be as

[1] Villari, ii. 312.

just as to fasten upon a madman the responsibility of words spoken in the gloomiest accesses of insanity. It is not necessary, therefore, to deny that he admitted the falsity of his visions and the uncertainty of his prophetic character. These were points on which his mind wavered in its healthiest and happiest seasons; how should he treat them firmly or clearly when broken down by torture? It seems to us that at no time of his life was he fully satisfied on his prophetic claims or the character of the supposed revelations. Now he was confident and well assured, only, a little later, to be racked with doubt and hesitation. We cannot reasonably expect that, in the agony of his long imprisonment, or while he was in the hands of the executioners, his doubt and hesitation would disappear. But it was only with respect to this always vague and mysterious subject that, even under torture, Savonarola showed any indecision. When pressed upon questions of doctrine or political conviction, he could be clear and definite enough. He held firmly by the great aim and purpose of his life, to redress wrong and injustice, and to promote a free and enlightened government. He still maintained that the Church must first be scourged and then renovated; and that if a General Council had been called, this result would have followed.

It is beyond dispute, as Villari remarks,[1] that throughout his trial, Savonarola proved himself to be the same man as we have hitherto known him. He exhibited a remarkable combination of genius with credulity; of profound reasoning with trivial sophistry; of lofty heroism with occasional lapses of distressing weakness; but in all and through all, on the whole, a sublime, a generous, and a powerful nature. First he affirmed and then he denied his prophetic power; but on all those points on which his mind and heart were clear, he proved invulnerable. We need not be surprised, therefore, that the Signory was greatly disappointed by the examination. They discovered to their intense mortification and regret, that notwithstanding tortures and falsifications, no charge could be established against Savonarola. The sole advantage they had gained was, that they had discredited the Frate in the opinion of his followers. Once deprived of the support he had received from the populace,

[1] Villari, ii. 321.

they felt that they could venture to condemn him, without being punished for a violation of law and justice.

It is not known, though we may conjecture, what means were employed to wring from him his signature to the deposition which affected to record his answers; but on the 19th of April, and in the presence of eight witnesses, he reluctantly attached it. When the witnesses in their turn had signed, he turned to them and said :[1]—" My doctrine is known to you, and is known to all. In this state of tribulation I ask of you only two things : take care of the novices, and see that they are preserved in that Christian doctrine in which we have hitherto maintained them; and pray for me to GOD, who has taken from me His spirit of prophecy." Whereupon the Judas-brother, Sacramoro, said :—" But are the things which you have subscribed true or false?" Savonarola, looking at him with an eye of scorn, turned his back upon the traitor, and vouchsafing no reply, returned to his prison.

The deposition, however, even after revision and mutilation by the Notary,[2] was not sufficient for the purpose of the Signory; and Savonarola, on the 21st of April, was subjected to a second examination. Again the result was disappointing. Nor did they make any profit from the examination of his followers, Frà Domenico and Frà Salvestro. The former exhibited a noble courage; was as serenely intrepid, as one of the martyrs of the primitive Church. The latter, on the contrary, abjured the doctrine of his master, and played as treacherous a part as Malatesta ; but his very confessions served only to demonstrate Savonarola's innocence. And the friars of S. Mark, though they, too, followed the stream, and deserted their superior, did but exalt his character, incidentally and involuntarily, in the letter which they addressed to the Pope, offering submission and imploring absolution. It was intended to incriminate, and yet it really exculpated him :—" Not only we," they

---

[1] Burlamacchi, p. 146.
[2] The work of garbling Savonarola's answers, so as to make out a case sufficient to legalize his condemnation, was undertaken by one Messer Ceccone, a notary of the Medicean party, for 400 ducats. He received, however, only 30; the Signory not being satisfied with his adroitness.

said, "but men of far greater genius, were deceived by the astuteness of Frà Girolamo. The subtlety of his doctrine; the rectitude of his life; the sanctity of his habits; his fervid devotion; his successful efforts to reclaim the city from vicious courses and from usury and crimes of all kinds; the many events by which, beyond all human conception, his prophecies were fulfilled; were altogether of such and so great a nature that, had he not himself retracted, saying, that his words did not come from GOD, we never could have withheld our belief in them. So entire was our faith, that we were all ready to offer up our bodies at the stake in support of his doctrine."

The Pope was desirous that Savonarola should be handed over to the ecclesiastical power, and sent to Rome, but the Signory replied that such a demand could not be granted without compromising the dignity of the Republic. They invited the Holy Father to send commissioners to examine the three friars anew: and to this proposal he assented. He named Giovacchino Tarriano, General of the Dominicans, and Francesco Romolino, Auditore of the Governor of Rome; who on the 19th of May arrived in Florence, bringing with them the sentence they were instructed to pronounce. In the interval between his last examination and their arrival, Savonarola had recovered his strength and energy, and with his strength and energy his old convictions; and he employed his time in composing Meditations on the 31st and the 51st Psalms, which are full of life and spirit. "I fervently pray," he wrote, "that all men may be saved, for the works of the just would greatly comfort me. I pray Thee, therefore, to turn Thine eyes towards Thy Church, where Thou wilt see how greatly unbelievers outnumber the Christians, and how every one has made a god of his belly. Send forth Thy Spirit, and renovate the face of the earth. Hell is becoming full and Thy Church empty. Arise, therefore, O LORD! Why sleepest Thou? Our sacrifices are not acceptable to Thee, for they are those of ceremony and not of justice. Where now is the glory of the Apostles, the strength of the martyrs, the simplicity of the monks?" His gaoler, who had conceived an affectionate reverence for him, besought him for some slight memorial, which might inspire him always to tread in the path of virtue. Savonarola complied with his request, and on the blank leaf of a book wrote the following *Rule for leading a virtuous life* :—

"A virtuous life depends upon grace; therefore, it is necessary to strengthen oneself to obtain it, and, when obtained, to exercise it. To inquire into our sins, and to meditate on the vanity of the things of this world, lead us to grace; confession and communion dispose us for receiving it. It is certainly a gratuitous gift of GOD. But when we are deeply impressed with a disregard of the world, and are forcibly drawn towards spiritual things, we may then say that if grace is not in us it is certainly near to us. Persevere, then, in a good life; in good works, in confession, and in all that brings us nearer to grace. That is the true and secure way for its exercise."

On the 20th of May the Frate was examined for the third time, and again most cruelly tortured. Vague and incoherent answers were drawn from him in the depths of his physical anguish; but not a word which could justify an accusation of heresy. "Hear me, O GOD!" he cried, in faltering accents, "Thou hast detected me in sin.—I confess that I have denied CHRIST. . . I have told lies. . . Florentine Signory, I denied through fear of torments. Be ye my witnesses. If I have to suffer I suffer for the cause of truth . . . that which I said, I received from GOD . . . O GOD, forgive that I have denied Thee. . . I ask forgiveness, I have denied Thee. . . I have denied Thee through fear of torments." The examination came to an end without having afforded to the Papal Commissioners the triumph they sought. They had but made their victim's innocence clearer. On the 22nd, however, they decided that the three Frati should die. One person only, a certain Agnolo Pandolfini, ventured a word on behalf of the Florentine Reformer. It seemed to him, he said, a most serious crime to put to death a man endowed with such excellent qualities; a man such as did not appear in the world more than once in a century. "He is a man," he said, "calculated not alone to rekindle decayed faith in mankind, but to spread abroad that knowledge with which he is so richly gifted. I advise you, therefore, to detain him in prison, if such be your desire, but to spare his life and furnish him with the means of writing, that the world may not lose the fruit of his genius." His appeal was set aside with the characteristically Italian maxim :—"A dead enemy makes no more wars." And that same evening the sentence of death was communicated to the three Frati.

At Savonarola's request they were allowed to meet together for one hour, which Savonarola employed in re-awaking Salvestro's dormant faith and moderating Domenico's too eager courage. After retiring to their separate cells they spent the night in prayer. Next morning (May 23rd) they again met, and Savonarola with his own hands administered the Sacrament, uttering a brief but earnest prayer :—" LORD, I know that Thou art that perfect Trinity, invisible, distinct, in FATHER, SON, and HOLY GHOST. I know that Thou art the Eternal Word; that Thou didst descend into the bosom of Mary; that Thou didst ascend upon the Cross to shed blood for our sins. I pray Thee that by that blood I may have remission of my sins, for which I implore Thy forgiveness. Pardon every offence or injury done to this city, and every other sin of which I may unconsciously have been guilty."

In the Piazza three tribunals had been erected on the marble terrace of the Palazzo; the one next the door was assigned to the Bishop of Vasona, a friend and disciple of Savonarola, on whom, with ingenious cruelty, the Pope had imposed the task of degrading the Frate, and consigning him to the secular power. To his right were seated the Papal Commissioners; and the third, near the Marzocco, was occupied by the Gonfaloniere and the magistrates. The scaffold was erected on the site of the ill-omened Ordeal of Fire. At its western extremity was raised a thick upright beam, with another beam across the top at right angles, the arms of which had been several times shortened in order to lessen its resemblance to a cross. Thence dangled three halters and three chains; for the three friars were first to be hung, and then their bodies were to be burnt. A large pile of combustible materials was accumulated at the foot of the gallows; from which the soldiers with difficulty drove back the multitude, rolling hither and thither in their emotion like the waves of the sea. It was a dumb emotion, however: over the scene brooded a sad and solemn silence, for even those who had most wished to see that day were conscious of a certain feeling of apprehension and awe. They were putting Savonarola to death, not because he had been deceived or had deceived others by his visions, but because he was good and great, too good and great for the age in which he lived and the people for whom he had laboured. Therefore they stood hushed and oppressed; and if there were any who exulted in the fall of the Preacher who had so unsparingly denounced their sins, they did not dare to give their exultation a voice. Many were present, too, who still retained their faith in their Master, and were silent with their sorrow, and wept, and prayed inly. Only close about the heap of fuel were heard occasional cries and yells ; the coarse insults of the desperate criminals whom the Signory had let loose from their prisons in order to disturb the last moments of the condemned.

A gloom seemed to overspread the Piazza like a cloud of darkness when Savonarola was led forth. At the foot of the stairs he was met by one of the Dominican friars of Santa Maria Novella, who had orders to despoil him and his companions of their habits, leaving them only their woollen under-tunics, with their feet bare, and their hands tied. Savonarola was deeply affected by this new insult, but he quickly recovered himself, and as the monk's frock was removed, exclaimed :—" O sacred dress, how much I longed to wear thee ! By the grace of GOD thou wast granted to me; and I have preserved thee unstained to this day. Nor do I now abandon thee, thou art taken from me."[1]

The three Frati then passed on to the first Tribunal, where they were re-vested in the religious habits ; and the Bishop, in deep distress, proceeded with the ceremony of degradation, stripping his former master of the black mantle, the white scapulary, and the long white tunic. In his agitation, stammering out the accustomed formula :— "Separo te ab ecclesia militante," (I separate thee from the Church Militant), he added—"atque triumphante." "Militante," replied Savonarola, calmly, "yes; but not *triumphante!* That does not belong to you."[2] These words were uttered in tones which thrilled the hearts of all who heard, so that they were ever afterwards remembered.

[1] Burlamacchi, p. 160.
[2] "Della militante si, ma della trionfante no, questo a voi non appartiene."—*Burlamacchi.*

Being thus degraded and unfrocked, the victims of hatred and injustice were formally handed over to the secular arm, after they had been declared schismatics and heretics by the Papal Commissioners. Romolino then absolved them from all their sins (bitterest of all the ironies of that terrible tragical scene !) and asked them if they accepted his absolution: they intimated their assent by a simple inclination of the head. Finally, they reached the tribunal of the Eight, who, according to custom, put their sentence to the vote. It was passed unanimously, and then read aloud. These wearisome mockeries at an end, Savonarola and his companions mounted the scaffold, and with firm slow step proceeded to the death-place at the further extremity, while the most abandoned of the furious rabble around were allowed to approach and hurl at them the foulest insults. Expressions of admiration and sympathy, however, were not wholly wanting. To a person who spoke a few words of comfort, Savonarola gently replied : —" In the last hour GOD alone can comfort His creatures !" To a priest named Nerotto, who asked him :—" With what mind do you endure this martyrdom?" he answered :— " Should I not die willingly when the LORD has suffered as much for me?"

His constancy, his unshaken courage, his faith sustained and inspired his two disciples. In this awful moment Frà Salvestro recovered his composure, and showed himself worthy of his master, worthy of the cause in which he died. Frà Domenico was so inspired with a serene exultation that it was recorded of him how he seemed like one going to a dance and not to death (*Ch'a danza e non a morte andasso*). He would fain have raised the triumphal chant of the *Te Deum*, as with bare feet and pinioned hands he passed on to the gibbet ; but at Savonarola's request he desisted, saying, " Accompany me then, in an undertone," and so they recited the entire hymn. He afterwards said :—" Remember that the prophecies of Savonarola must all be fulfilled, and that we die innocent."

Frà Salvestro was the first to suffer. As the fatal rope was fastened, he exclaimed :—" Into Thy hands, O LORD, I commend my spirit !" Domenico ascended the ladder with a radiant countenance, and a look of ecstasy in his eyes. Last came the turn of Savonarola, who was so absorbed in his anticipations of the Life Beatific that fast dawned upon his soul, that he seemed insensible to the things of earth. But on gaining the upper part of the ladder, he paused a moment, to survey with a piercing glance the crowd below and around,—that people of Florence who had once hung on his lips with such breathless adoration. Silently he submitted his neck to the hangman.

A shudder of horror shot, like an electric stroke, through all the multitude. Only one voice was heard to say :—" Prophet, now is the time to work a miracle !"

To ingratiate himself with the multitude, the executioner was guilty of ribald outrage on the Martyr's body even before it ceased to move, so that the magistrates judged it needful to send him a severe reprimand. He then displayed an unusual activity in the hope that the flames would reach Savonarola before life was quite extinct ; the chain, however, slipped from his hand, and before he could recover it, his victim had breathed his last breath. A gust of wind for some time diverted the blaze from the three bodies ; and those of the Piagnoni who were present raised the cry of " A miracle ! a miracle !" But ultimately the fire did its work. When it caught the rope that pinioned the arms of Savonarola, the heat caused a movement of the wrists ; so that, to the eyes of the faithful, he seemed to raise his right hand in the act of blessing the misguided creatures who had hunted him to his death.

The Signory ordered that the ashes should be collected, and thrown from the Ponto Vecchio into the Arno. But all their care could not prevent enthusiastic disciples from possessing themselves of relics of the great man who had so nobly and self-denyingly striven to promote the cause of light and love and freedom, and to recall the Church to the pure faith of its Divine Founder.

It was at ten o'clock in the morning of the 23rd of May, 1498, that Savonarola consummated his martyrdom. He was then in the 45th year of his age.[1]

---

[1] Nardi, " Istorie di Firenze," bk. ii. ; Guicciardini, " Storia Fiorentina," c. xvii. ; Villari, " Vita di Savonarola," lib. iv. c. 11.

S. FRANCIS XAVIER:

THE APOSTLE OF THE INDIES.

"There are who roam,
To scatter seeds of life on barbarous shores."
WORDSWORTH.

[*Authorities*:—The life and character of Xavier are best traced in his letters, which exist chiefly in a Latin translation, and have formed the foundation of the principal biographies. Of these I may name the copious memoir by the Père Bouhours, rendered into English by Dryden, and the "Vita Francisci Xavieri," by Horace Turselline, or Tursellinus, of which a quaint English version exists. Reference may also be made to Lucena and Faria, but for the English reader the most accessible and most comprehensive is the "Life and Letters of S. Francis Xavier," by Henry James Coleridge. (2 vols., 1876).]

S. FRANCIS XAVIER.

CHAPTER I.

WHAT are the qualities which make a man great? Are they not earnestness, breadth of sympathy, fortitude in adversity, temperance in prosperity, unshaken intrepidity, fertility of resource, and steadfastness of aim? Do we not find them exhibited by a Columbus, and a Bacon, a Newton, and a Gustavus Adolphus, a Luther, and a Milton,—by all those men who either in Thought or Action have largely influenced the world and helped forward the work of intellectual and moral progress? But then, these men have also been gifted with the divine power which we call genius, and there seems to remain yet another order or class of great men, who, without that rare endowment, have possessed and manifested all the moral elements of greatness: men who have sacrificed everything in life for the promotion of a noble cause or in the discharge of a solemn Duty, men who have devoted themselves to the defence of right and justice against triumphant Wrong and Tyranny, men who have laboured for the Faith they have believed, or the Country they have loved. To this order of Great Men belongs, if I mistake not, Francis Xavier. Protestant prejudice may set him aside because he was a servant of the Roman Church and a member of that powerful ecclesiastical organization which, under the name of the Jesuits, has attained an evil repute by no means undeserved. But we must learn, and we should rejoice, to recognise true greatness wherever it presents itself; and no one who traces Xavier's career with an impartial judgment will deny that, whatever the defects of his creed, he was pre-eminently a Great Man. He was, in the truest sense of the term, a Christian Apostle. Like S. Paul, in labours most abundant; in perils oft; counting nothing as gain which did not assist in bringing souls to CHRIST. A Hero of the Cross, gentle yet resolute, filled with a boundless love of his fellow-men, of an energy which never wearied, of a daring which never faltered,—he was one of the greatest Missionaries which the Christian Church has ever produced. In the cause of the Gospel he travelled some twenty thousand miles in heathen lands, and founded Christian communities which at his death numbered two or three hundred thousand members. A man of ordinary mental capacity, he had the amiability of a Heber, the passionate enthusiasm of a Martyn, the patriarchal simplicity of a Schwartz, the linguistic gifts of a Morrison, the faculty of winning native confidence of a Patteson. He preached and he printed; he contended publicly with the sages of heathendom; he reformed the lives of his own countrymen (the hardest work, alas! of a Christian missionary); he founded churches and presided over colleges; he catechised, and baptised; he visited the sick; he ministered to the poor; he travelled and translated; and all this, single-handed, and poor even to poverty. Was he not, then, a Great Man?

Francis Xavier was born in 1506, the year in which Columbus died. The name which he bore came from his mother, the heiress of the noble houses of Azpilqueta and Xavier. His father, Juan de Jasso, was also of noble birth, and for his learning and prudence was appointed Privy Councillor to King John of Navarre. The youngest of many children, he was carefully brought up in those traditions of Christian chivalry and religious enthusiasm which flowed from Spain's eight centuries of warfare against the Saracens. According to his biographer, Turselline, he was of an excellent constitution and comely person, of a quick wit, and more inclined to his book than children usually are. None more innocent, none more pleasant, none more affable than he: hence he was beloved by all, both at home and abroad. His purity in deed and thought was unsullied, and as is the nature thereof, it sharpened his intelligence, and prepared his mind as a fertile soil to receive the seeds of wisdom. Therefore, says Turselline, making no account of his brothers' speeches, who sought by warlike words to draw him to the profession of arms (the ancient ornament of their ancestors), he adhered to his resolution, and whether incited by the example of his father, or by the delight of knowledge, or nerved by a Divine impulse, he preferred the glory of learning before knightly praises. But he was not the less sensible to the desire of honour. Of a high and lofty spirit, he was fond of all athletic exercises, and no adventure was too bold for him to engage in. Above the middle size, well-proportioned, with robust limbs, blue eyes, and dark auburn hair, he seemed so well fitted to win renown with lance and sword, that all wondered when, carrying out his original purpose, and in his eighteenth year, he went up to the University of Paris. There he took his degree of Master of Arts at twenty; after which he lectured for some time on the philosophy of Aristotle at the College Beauvais. But he still retained his lodgings at the College of S. Barbara, and thus was thrown into contact with a remarkable man—fifteen years older than himself—who, about 1528, entered as a pensioner of that college. A remarkable man, though lame and unpretending in appearance, of whom a romantic story was told; how that he came of a noble Biscayan family, had served gallantly as an officer in the army, and in the late war had distinguished himself by an heroic defence of Pampeluna. How that he was severely wounded in that siege, his leg being broken; and how that, after it had been badly set but had got well, he, a dashing cavalier, fond of the smiles of beautiful ladies, had had it broken again and re-set, in order to preserve his straightness of limb. How that, while lying on his sick bed, he had beguiled his leisure by reading the " Lives of the Saints," and Ludolph of Saxony's " Life of CHRIST," and how this reading had been so blessed to the gay reckless soldier, that he had thrown off his burden of worldliness, taken up the cross, and devoted himself to his Master's service. When Francis Xavier became intimate with Ignatius Loyola, for such was the new student's name, he learned

U

further details of his strange career. He learned that, on recovering his health, he set to work to prove his zeal and faith by ministering to the sick in the hospital at Manresa, and afterwards by secluding himself for months in a lonely cave, and living upon roots and water. Thence he went on a pilgrimage to the Holy Land, where all he saw made a deep impression upon his mind and heart. About the same time he composed his book of the "Spiritual Exercises," and formed the conception of a new religious and missionary Order, whose members were to work only for the glory of GOD, by the salvation and sanctification of their own souls, by the education of youth, and by missions to the heathen. Carrying into it that spirit of discipline which he had imbibed as a soldier, he designed that the new Order should be bound to its Superior and to the Pope by a vow of implicit obedience. Moreover, its members were never to labour for money, never to acquire property, nor accept any ecclesiastical dignity. With the reputation of a saint, he had lived a saintly life at Barcelona, at Alcala, and at Salamanca; he had toiled, and sorrowed, and suffered, as is the lot of reformers in all ages and all countries. At Barcelona, some bravoes hired by cavaliers who resented the rigid rules he had introduced into a convent of nuns with whom they were acquainted, waylaid him, and so barbarously maltreated him, that he was left for dead. At Alcala and at Salamanca he had been imprisoned. Worst of all, he had made no progress in the development of his idea; his Order was still unformed; his mission unfulfilled. His early companions, those he had gathered at Barcelona, had undergone this same ordeal as himself at Alcala, and then abandoned the Cause! At Paris he was alone. Though Xavier could not but be interested in this recital, he was not, at first, strongly attracted towards Ignatius. He admired his spiritual energy, his all-absorbing zeal; but he was repelled by his coldness of demeanour, his unkempt person, his slovenliness of dress. To the brilliant young scholar there seemed, as indeed there was, a narrowness in his new friend's views of things; he was too much absorbed by one work—by one side of life. He cared little for letters; for pleasure, nothing. Probably Xavier would have dropped the acquaintance, but for Loyola's persistency. The enthusiast liked his young fellow-countryman, saw of what admirable stuff he was made, and determined to gain him as a recruit for CHRIST.

So the intercourse ripened. As they walked together, and read together, Ignatius would constantly ask him, what it would profit him to gain the whole world and lose his own soul. Xavier had dreams of becoming a renowned doctor, a great teacher of philosophy; but when he confided these dreams to his friend, he received no other response than, What shall a man receive in exchange for his soul? He was fond of amusements, but if he proposed to Ignatius that he should join in them, straight to his heart went that solemn question, What shall a man receive in exchange for his soul? By degrees the friendship grew more thorough. Xavier frequently experienced the need of money, and Ignatius was always ready to help him. Xavier could not but see how truly Ignatius lived up to what he professed; how sublime was his self-denial, how earnest his desire to convert men to CHRIST, how strict he was in all the observances of the Church. He could not but see that though his inferior in scholarship, intellectual readiness, theological learning, he was largely superior in all the higher qualities that ennoble humanity. It was impossible to ridicule or despise him. Xavier began to listen; and he who listens is half persuaded. There was certainly something lofty after all, in this man's purpose as in his conduct and character: might not his view of life be the right one? For five years Xavier had a hard struggle with himself, a hard struggle against the influence of Loyola; and then he bowed unreservedly at the feet of the man, at first his acquaintance and pupil, afterwards his friend, and thenceforth his master. Whatever he willed that he should do, or wherever he willed that he should go, he was ready to obey.

Loyola had gained the hearts and minds of five other disciples—one of whom, Peter Favre, the son of a Savoyard shepherd, was scarcely below Xavier himself in entirety of self-devotion,—and with these and Xavier he took the Sacrament in the Church of the Virgin at Montmartre, on the Feast of the Assumption, 1534. In that subterranean sanctuary, at dead of night, they bound themselves by a solemn vow to become Missionaries of the Cross, and to preach the Gospel of CHRIST to every man they met. But it was characteristic of the enthusiasm of Loyola that profound sagacity and prudence steadily controlled it. He did not immediately act on the offerings of the highly-wrought minds that had submitted to his rule; he resolved still further to test and prepare them for their great work by months of spiritual exercise and theological study. He did not fetter them by many obligations; his system was laid down on a few broad and simple lines. The little Society, while at the University, could not live in common; but they met on Sundays and Holy Days, were as much in one another's company as possible, and, for the purpose of fostering good-will and for the spiritual profit which results from the close intercourse of congenial souls, invited one another to their simple meals, and thus revived the ἀγάπαι or "love-feasts" of the primitive Church. In March, 1535, Ignatius left them, and went on a journey to Spain : partly for his health, and partly to settle the private affairs of the three Spanish members of the brotherhood, Xavier, Laynez, and Salmeron, who were unwilling to expose themselves to the temptation of home and the remonstrances of friends. One more associate was added to the little band before Ignatius left, Claude Le Jay, of Geneva. Two more were gained after his departure, when Peter Favre acted as his substitute or lieutenant, namely, John Codurius and Paschase Brouet. Their time was pleasantly and profitably spent in daily meditation and examination, in spiritual reading, in weekly confession and communion; in teaching in the schools, ministering in the churches, and relieving the poor and distressed.

On the 15th of November, 1536, they finally left Paris and set out for Venice, with the ultimate object of passing on into the Holy Land, to attempt its conversion to the faith of CHRIST. The journey before them was not without its difficulties and dangers; for most of them were Spaniards, and war was then raging between France and Spain. They resolved, therefore, on a circuitous route, which would avoid the provinces occupied by the hostile armies, and they assumed the dress least likely to provoke suspicion, the long frock and hat of the Parisian students. Each one, moreover, carried his pilgrim's staff, his rosary round his neck, and on his shoulders a leathern satchel, containing a Bible, a Breviary, and a manuscript volume of theological notes. While within French territory, the Frenchmen among them were to answer, in the name of all, any questions that were asked; while the Spaniards, if they should be interrogated, would reply, that they were students of Paris, on a pilgrimage. There was a celebrated shrine of S. Nicholas, near Metz, and this would be the first great stage of their journey. Afterwards, they would pass into German territory, where the Spaniards would answer in the name of all, and the Frenchmen, if separately questioned, would reply, as the Spaniards had done before, that they were on a pilgrimage,—the second shrine they had in view being that of the Virgin at Loretto. Each day, before starting, they spent a considerable time in united prayer, and again every evening, when the day's march was over. Those who were priests said mass every morning when possible, and the others received Holy Communion. The whole day was so arranged that the journey was relieved and occupied by meditation, prayer, and spiritual conversation.

In this way our strange band of enthusiasts proceeded to Venice, where they arrived on the 1st day of January, 1537, and were joyfully received by Ignatius. As a year was to pass before they sailed for Jerusalem, they determined to spend a part of it among the poor in the Venetian hospitals, and the rest in a journey to Rome to obtain the blessing of the Pope. Xavier was appointed to serve in the Hospital of the Incurables, to wait upon the sick, dress their wounds or sores or ulcers, make their beds, sweep their rooms, and prepare their food, while carefully watching over the welfare of their souls, teaching and consoling them, preparing them for the last Sacraments, and after their death carrying them forth for burial. It was here in Venice, says a recent writer,[1] that he won the grace, never to find any wound or ulcer, however loathsome in itself, a cause of horror or disgust.

At the end of nine or ten weeks, leaving Ignatius in Venice, the Society set out on foot for Rome. It had been determined that they should practise the strictest poverty, though so rigid a rule was surely unnecessary, and might have seriously compromised the success of their great projects; wherefore they took with them neither money nor pro-

[1] H. J. Coleridge, "Life and Times of S. Francis Xavier," i. 43.

visions. It was Lent; and they forbore to seek any dispensation from the rule of fasting. For nine persons to obtain food and lodging by begging was no light task; and frequently they underwent the greatest sufferings. Often they obtained no shelter at all for the night; for days they had no other food than the cones of pine-trees. At Ancona, we are told, Xavier, the brilliant Parisian scholar, and the son of one of the noblest families in Spain, went to and fro in the market-place, bare-footed, with his robe tucked up to his knees, begging among the market-women, from one an apple, from another a radish, from a third some other vegetable. It is impossible not to admire so complete a devotion; it is impossible not to regret that it was developed in an unwise direction.

After visiting Loretto, they went to Rome, where each found an asylum in the Hospital of his own nation. Pedro Ortiz, the Spanish minister, presented them to the Pope, who gave them the desired permission to go to Jerusalem, while doubting whether they would have the opportunity, and placed at their disposal a considerable "alms." Returning to Venice, they renewed their vows of poverty and chastity, and on the 24th of June, 1537, were admitted to priests' orders. War breaking out between Venice and Turkey, the Pope's doubts became a certainty, and the Society, finding that their hopes of reaching Palestine were baffled, resolved to disperse into some of the chief cities of Italy, to carry on their labours for the good of souls. Xavier repaired to Bologna, and exerted himself with a charity that knew no pause in preaching in the public places, catechising children, hearing confessions, and visiting the prisons and hospitals. He was called to Rome, towards the end of the winter, by Ignatius, who had chosen the Sacred City as the scene of his ministrations; and at Easter they were joined by the rest of the brethren. Ignatius then unfolded to them his design of erecting the Society into a religious order, adding the vow of obedience to the vows of poverty and chastity which they already professed. They would thus perpetuate, beyond the term of their own lives, the golden bond of brotherhood which united them; and their Order, multiplying itself in all countries, might endure until the end of time. He met with a ready acquiescence from his companions, but his plans for the organisation of the Society were not matured until the summer of 1539; and the Pope's assent was not obtained until the autumn. Another year elapsed, owing to the opposition raised by some of the Cardinals, before his formal sanction was given in the Bull *Regimini militantis Ecclesiæ* (September 27, 1540).

But before this final seal had been set upon the new Order, Xavier had left Rome. On the 15th of March, Ignatius called him into his cabinet, and informed him that he had chosen him, along with Simon Rodriguez, for the first missionary expedition of the Society to the East Indies. His companion had already sailed; he was to depart on the following day in the train of the Portuguese ambassador. Pedro de Mascarenas. To hear was to obey. Xavier betook himself to the Pope's presence, and received his parting blessing; embraced Ignatius for the last time; and then, without luggage, purse or scrip, with only his Bible and his Breviary, a small sacramental vessel of silver, and a crucifix suspended from his neck, this self-denying and self-sacrificing man set out on that long and memorable journey which, twelve years and a half later, was to terminate on the rugged island of San Chan, within sight of the ancient shores of China.

CHAPTER II.

FROM Rome, Xavier proceeded by way of Loretto, to Bologna, where the recollection of his former Apostolic labours ensured him an enthusiastic welcome. Thence he travelled through France and Spain into Portugal, the journey occupying three months. His route through Spain carried him within sight of the castle of Xavier, but he denied himself an interview with his widowed mother and saintly sister, lest it should turn him aside from the high purpose to which he had devoted his life. To the Ambassador who urged him to take the opportunity, he replied, that they would all meet with the greater joy in Heaven for not having taken leave of one another on earth. This incident is often quoted as an illustration of Xavier's Apostolic zeal, but we do not understand that the Christian's faith compels him to crush the sweet domestic affections when their indulgence cannot hinder the work he has to do. And to a man who has taken upon himself the whole armour of CHRIST, the tears of mother and sister would never prove a discouragement or a hindrance. On his arrival at Lisbon he found that the departure of Simon Rodriguez had been countermanded, and that he was to go forth on his holy enterprise unaccompanied by any member of the Society. He remained some months at Lisbon, combating the King's earnest desire that he should stay and work in Portugal, and he was able to record his vote, by letter, for the election of Ignatius as the first General of the Order of Jesus. On the 7th of April, his thirty-fifth birthday, he sailed from Lisbon, attended by Father Paul of Camerino, a Portuguese priest, and Francis Mancias, an unlettered novice.

"The king," he writes, "sends us away fully laden with favours of every kind from himself, and has also recommended us very particularly to the Governor whom he is sending this year to India. We are to sail with the latter in his own flag-ship. He has shown us much kindness, even to taking upon himself the care of everything for our passage, and forbidding us or any one else to trouble himself about the preparations or equipment necessary for us while we were at sea. He has already settled that we are to be his guests at table every day. This I mention, not to show off whatever honour or convenience for us this implies, as if we took pleasure in the advantage to ourselves,—for we would certainly rather dispense with it,—but that you may understand, and in your zeal for GOD's glory may rejoice in, the good ground which we have in this great affection for us on the part of the Supreme Governor of the Indies, for expecting great assistance from him towards that on which our whole heart is set,—the conversion of the heathen there,—and that you may congratulate us on the favourable opportunity offered to us, of carrying the name of JESUS CHRIST before the native kings of India, with whom, as every one knows, the authority and influence of the Portuguese Governor is supreme."

The voyage to the Cape of Good Hope is now accomplished in less than five weeks; it occupied for Xavier and the "Governor of India" five months. But the time did not hang heavy on the hands of the great missionary. The ship was his parish, and he employed himself every day in incessant pastoral duties. There were nearly a thousand soldiers and seamen on board, and the spiritual care of so large a company absorbed all his energies. He mingled with them freely, saying to each a word in season; exhorting all to a religious life; hearing confessions, and administering Holy Communion. It was observed that the men soon abandoned their foul oaths and jests, and that many enmities were converted into friendships. Scurvy broke out,—as was common enough in those days, on board crowded and ill-provided ships, tossed week after week upon unknown seas,— scurvy broke out like a pestilence, and created such a panic by its ravages, that friends coldly neglected friends, and the sick were left without attendants. In this extremity Francis and his companions waited upon them untiringly; and the missionary dressed their food with his own hands, washed them and their linen with his own hands, and with his own hands prepared and administered their medicines. He gave up his cabin to the sick, and his allowance from the Governor's table he shared with those most in need of it. He prayed with the whole crew every Sunday, and, as it has been well put, there was not a day in which he did not pray *for* them. He was consumed by an unquenchable fire of Apostolic charity; all his care was to save souls.

The ship put in at the island of Mozambique, on the eastern coast of Africa, to winter there. His labours increased, and with them his exertions; and his frame being exhausted by his works of love, he fell ill of a local fever, which brought him to the verge of the grave. But of his own illness he makes no mention in the letter descriptive of his voyage which he addressed to the Society at Rome :—

"We sailed," he writes, "in the same vessel with the Governor, who treated us the whole time with great consideration; and we had all of us fair enough health. All the time there was no lack of confessions to hear, either of the sick, or others, and we never missed preaching on the Sundays. I count it a great favour from GOD that, while I was passing over the realm of fishes, I found men to whom to announce the Divine mysteries and administer the sacrament of penance, quite as necessary on sea as on land.

"In the course of the voyage we touched at an island called Mozambique, where we wintered for six months, together with the whole multitude of persons belonging to five large vessels. There are two cities in the island; one garrisoned by the Portuguese, the other occupied by friendly Mussulmans. While we were wintering there, a great number of persons fell ill, and as many as eighty died. We quartered ourselves in the hospital all the time, employing ourselves in the service of the sick. Father Paul and Mancias waited on their bodily necessities; I attended to their souls also, hearing confessions continually and giving communion, but, alone as I was, I could not do all that was wanted for them. On Sundays I preached to a very large audience, as the Governor himself attended, and I was also often called away to hear confessions elsewhere. So that all the time we were at Mozambique we were busy. The Governor, his suite, and all the soldiers showed us great courtesy, and by the favour of GOD we spent these six months greatly to the satisfaction of all, and with much spiritual profit."

From Mozambique Xavier sailed for the Portuguese settlement of Goa. He touched, on the way, at Socotra, which he describes as an island about a hundred miles in circumference. A wild country, with no produce, no corn, no rice, no millet, no fruit-trees, no wine; in short, wholly sterile and arid, except that it had a wealth of dates, out of which its inhabitants made bread, and that it also abounded in cattle. "The people," writes Xavier, "are Christian in name rather than in reality; wonderfully ignorant and rude, unable to read or write. Still they pride themselves on being Christians. They have churches, crosses, lamps. Each village has its caciz, who answers to the parish priest, but knows no more of reading or writing than the people; they have no books, and know only a few prayers by heart."

Goa, the capital of Portuguese India, was an opulent and busy city, with many stately public buildings and some handsome churches. It was the seat of a bishopric, and it boasted of a college of recent foundation. Spiritually, however, it was dead. The Europeans had become infected with the corruptions of Mohammedanism and the poison of Asiatic profligacy. There was plenty of work for S. Francis, and first, among the European population. He went about, we are told, with great gentleness, making no violent attempt to effect a sudden reformation ; but accosting the Portuguese as he met them in the streets, he would request them to invite a poor priest to their ordinary fare. And this invitation being readily given, he, while sitting at table, would entreat the host to call in his children, and the children coming presently at their father's call, he would take them up in his arms, and clasp them to his bosom, thanking GOD Who had given the father such children for the hope of his family, and praying GOD to grant them a good and holy life. Then would he desire to see their mother,—generally, an Indian woman, and not married. When she appeared, he would speak sweetly unto her, and commend her heartily to his host, thereby to induce him to take her to be his wife ; saying that doubtless she was of an excellent disposition and lovely countenance, so that she might well be accounted a Portuguese, and that the children which he had by her were certainly worthy of a Portuguese to their father. Why therefore did he not marry her? What better wife would he desire? And he would do well to provide with all speed for his children's credit and the woman's honesty.

In his great zeal for the welfare of souls, he would go up and down the streets and highways with a little bell in his hand—Apostolic Legate though he was—and call upon all masters and heads of families for the love of GOD to send their children and servants to "the Christian Doctrine." And gathering together a great procession of children, slaves, and others, he would place himself at their head, singing aloud the Catechism to them, and lead them to church, where he would teach them the broad truths of CHRIST's religion in all simplicity. He made great use of singing in his teaching, as the early Methodists in their services made great use of hymns ; knowing that there is no surer way of winning the attention and impressing the memories of children and the ignorant. To the "ruder sort and to slaves" he was careful to speak in the homeliest and most direct language. Hence, says Turselline, arose that worthy custom of teaching and learning the Christian Doctrine which is at this day—about a century later than Xavier's time—practised in India. And because men reaped more fruit by it than was expected, the Bishop ordained that it should be adopted in other churches, so that, as he advanced himself in this "new piety," and those of the Society followed Xavier's rule, others were stirred up thereunto partly by the Bishop's command, and partly by the Society's example, and it came at last to be a custom throughout all India, to the great advancement of the Christian cause. This practice so spread abroad both in Goa and in other places, that everywhere in the schools, highways, streets, houses, fields, and ships, might be heard sung, instead of vain and idle songs, the principles of the Christian faith with great delight. Wherefore it grew to be a custom that children who could scarce speak should strive with one another to sing most of those verses by heart. And in this exercise, adds Turselline, Xavier gave a not less noble proof of his temperance and moderation than of his industrious labours. For of all that was given to him under the title of alms, he received nothing to himself, but gave all to the sick and poor as privately as he could, to the end that human praise might not deprive him of any reward in the sight of GOD.

For a year Xavier continued to preach, and catechize, and visit the sick; and, no doubt, the daily beauty of his life won as many souls to CHRIST as the fervour of his eloquence and the simplicity of his teaching. He was all things to all men, and in the work of reformation employed as much ingenuity and stratagem as a politician in carrying out some favourite scheme. And such was the success attending his efforts that, at all events, an *external* moral reformation was accomplished in Goa. It was swept and cleansed so as no longer to be offensive to the passer-by. There was a vast mass of wickedness which not even a Xavier in one year or in a life-time would have perceptibly reduced; yet much was done, and happily done,—the fire was kindled upon the altar,—the light revived that had almost flickered down into darkness. But great as this work was, it did not satisfy Xavier; his missionary enthusiasm could not be confined within the bounds of civilized life. Six hundred miles from Goa, in the extreme south of the Indian peninsula, dwelt a tribe of native Indians, the Paravas, engaged in the laborious and ill-paid calling of the pearl fishery. They had been nominally converted to Christianity some years before, but had forgotten everything except that they were supposed to be Christians. Poor in the extreme, living on rice and water, crowded together in wretched huts, few men could be more miserable, few in greater need of consolation. Xavier, on hearing of their condition, lost no time in proceeding to their succour. He dwelt among them as one of themselves; lived on the same meagre food; acquired a knowledge of their rude language. He baptized the children, and instructed them in the LORD'S Prayer and the Apostles' Creed. The Catechism, with great difficulty, he translated into their tongue. Every Sunday he collected them, men and women, boys and girls, in the church, where he began by calling on the name of the Most Holy Trinity, FATHER, SON, and HOLY GHOST; after which he recited the LORD's Prayer, the *Ave Maria*, and the Creed, in the native language; all repeating it after him, with infinite pleasure. Next he said the Creed, dwelling upon each article singly, and asking them whether they accepted it unhesitatingly; whereupon, with a loud voice and hands folded across their breasts, they would declare that they truly believed it. Their simple faith was not concerned about any theological subtleties! After explaining the Creed, Xavier went on to the Commandments, teaching that in those ten precepts was embodied the Christian law; and that every one who loyally observed them was a good and true Christian, to whom eternal salvation was assured. After this he recited the principal prayers, the congregation duly repeating them, and then went back to the Creed, adding the LORD'S Prayer and *Ave Maria* after each article, with a short hymn.

"The fruit," he writes, "that is reaped by the baptism of infants, as well as by the instruction of children and others, is quite incredible. These children, I trust heartily, by the grace of GOD, will be much better than their fathers. They show an ardent love for the Divine law, and an extraordinary zeal for learning our holy religion and imparting it to others. Their hatred of idolatry is marvellous. They get into feuds with the heathen about it, and whenever their own parents practise it, they reproach them, and come off to tell me at once. Whenever I hear of any act of idolatrous worship, I go to the place with a large band of these children, who very soon load the devil with a greater amount of insult and abuse than he has lately received of honour and worship from their parents, relations, and acquaintances. The children run at the idols, upset them, dash them down, break them to pieces, spit on them, trample on them, kick them about, and, in short, heap on them every possible outrage."

For fifteen months Xavier toiled in CHRIST's name among the Paravas. He then returned to Goa to seek assistance. For awhile he was detained at Goa by pressing duties; the reorganisation of the College established for the education of "pagan youths of different nations," and its cession, under the name of the College of S. Paul, to his Society of Jesus. (1544.) In June he returned, with some assistants, to the Fishery Coast, to find that its poor population had been attacked and plundered by a neighbouring tribe; so that many were homeless, and destitute of food and clothing, and famine was threatening them with its horrors. Xavier's piety was eminently practical; good works were the natural result of his absolute faith; and he at once applied his energies to the task of procuring twenty boat-loads of provisions from the nearest Portuguese station, which he distributed among the sufferers. Having thus relieved their immediate necessities, he resumed his pastoral duties with his usual ardour. He allowed himself only three hours and a half for sleep. The rest of the night was occupied in solitary meditation and prayer. As soon as the waters shone with the first beams of day, Xavier summoned his disciples to public worship; while, during the day, he taught the children and the new converts, visited the sick, administered baptism, heard confessions, and striking inland to other villages, preached there the gospel of CHRIST. At twilight the bell again rang for public worship. Having seen the Paravas peacefully resettled, he placed some of his missionary assistants among them, and proceeded into the kingdom of Travancore on the same evangelistic errand. There his energy was as persistent as his success was complete; in one month he baptized (it is said) ten thousand persons. The people demolished their temples and destroyed their idols, and thirty Christian chapels were built. No wonder that he provoked the deep hostility of the Brahmins, or that frequent attempts were made upon his life. The huts in which he rested were burnt down one after another, sometimes three or four in one day. Once, like Charles II., he saved himself among the leafy branches of a tree, at the foot of which raged his would-be murderers. He was compelled at times to sleep in the woods; and at others he went to and fro, guarded by a body of his loving disciples. He won the gratitude of the Rajah of Travancore by employing his influence and that of his followers to stay an invasion which threatened his territories. Thus he obtained the name of the "Great Father." The rajah did not embrace Christianity, as Xavier earnestly desired; but he gave him and his assistants permission to preach it freely throughout his dominions, a permission of which Xavier was not slow to take advantage. No thought of self-indulgence ever occurred to him; he passed hither and thither, preaching and baptizing and catechizing; day and night he was engaged in this holy warfare. What was the spell by which he worked such wonders? How did he contrive to impress himself upon the minds of all with whom he came in contact? John Williams and David Livingstone possessed something of this power of gaining the confidence of uncivilized peoples, but, as compared with Xavier, in a very trivial degree. With Xavier it was a kind of "spiritual magnetism;" so that he justly merited the title which his contemporaries gave him of the Thaumaturgos, or "Wonderworker" of the Church. Was it not owing to the deep and passionate love which he bore towards his fellow-men; a love so genuine, so boundless, so absorbing, that it shone in his eyes and illuminated his countenance?

That his sagacity was not obscured by his enthusiasm, and that his missionary system was based upon just and rational principles, we may see in the advice he gave to his assistant, Francis Mancias. Consider the wisdom and moderation displayed in the following instructions:—

" I beg and entreat you most earnestly, my dearest brother, to show the people you are with, and especially the adults and the aged, very great kindness and charity, and to aim at making yourself beloved by them in return. Rest assured that if you are beloved by them, you will be able to turn their hearts whatever way you wish. So bear, with moderation and wisdom, all their weaknesses and infirmities, and say to yourself, that if they are not yet all you desire, in time at least they will become so. If you cannot get out of them all the good you ask, take what you can get. You know this is my method. You should make up your mind to be to them what a good father is to bad children, and never to give up caring for them, providing for them, though all the time you perceive with how many vices they are covered. GOD Himself, though often offended by them and by us, does not cease to heap His benefits upon us. He might most justly destroy us, but in His mercy He very often seems blind to our sins, and helps us in our difficulties, that He may overcome evil with good. And so you, if you cannot do all you wish, be glad to do what you can, since it is not your fault that all the progress you desire has not been made. If at times you find yourself so distracted by a number of duties that you cannot manage them all, do as much as you can and be content with that, and even give thanks to GOD for the particular blessing that He has led you to work in a place where there are so many sacred duties to be performed that you cannot be idle, however much you might wish it, for this is in truth one of the greatest blessings that GOD bestows."

I might easily multiply my extracts; but this will show that Xavier was no unreasoning zealot, pressing forward impetuously and recklessly, and thinking nothing of the means as long as the end was secured; that he was, on the contrary, very gentle to and considerate of the feelings and feebleness of those among whom he laboured, and that he laboured, if with abundant fervour yet also with a calm, clear judgment.

It has often been to me a matter of wonder that the Missionary's life should command so little of the world's attention; that to the great body of readers the record of missionary enterprise should present so little attraction. They who turn with eagerness to the story that tells of the achievements of conquerors who slay their thousands and tens of thousands, cannot be induced to peruse the page that traces the labours of the hero of the Cross who saves thousands and tens of thousands of souls. Is the conversion of a heathen people to the religion of CHRIST so small a thing? Let it not be said that the missionary's career is wanting in romantic and picturesque elements. Unarmed and alone, he wanders among savage nations, carrying his life in his hand, braving danger in its most terrible aspects, patiently enduring privation and fatigue; and all this, without any such prospect of immediate reward and external glory as that which stimulates the ardour of the warrior. If the world had a better knowledge of what constitutes true greatness, if it had eyes to see the lofty beauty of self-sacrifice, if it could sympathize with that pure enthusiasm which dares all and braves all for the happiness of humanity, it would reserve its crowns and garlands for the Missionary.

In September, 1545, after travelling in Cochin, Xavier repaired to Malacca, accompanied by Joam d'Eyro, of whom the following quaint story is told :—

There was a certain young man, a merchant, called Joam d'Eyro, who came to S. Francis to confession, and hearing him discourse of divine matters, found there was certain other merchandise, far richer than that he trafficked in, of which he had never heard before. Wherefore, giving over his former trading, and desiring to become a vendor of more precious wares, he entreated Francis to receive him into the Society : who, at first, refused him absolutely,—possibly, because his keen insight detected in him a secret inconstancy and intractability of disposition,—yet at last, after much entreaty, he granted his prayer, and the young man, settling his affairs, began to distribute his goods among the poor. In executing this good purpose, however, he was more forward than constant. For while he was busy in disposing of his wares, he was strongly tempted by the common enemy of mankind, who did so work upon him, that though he had set his hand to the plough, on a sudden he began to look back, and sought again most greedily after those things which a little before he had contemned. Being thus wholly changed in mind, he packed up his wares in the most private way possible, and conveyed them into a ship, intending to be gone. But though he deceived others, he could not deceive Xavier, the one whom most of all he sought to deceive. Having collected everything which he thought requisite, he was about to depart, when Xavier sent after him a messenger. At first the young merchant proposed to himself to brave it out. " You are wrong, my lad," said he, " I am not the man you seek." " What," said the boy, "are you not called Joam d'Eyro?" "Yes," he replied. "Well, sir, Father Francis bade me run quickly, and call to him Joam d'Eyro." There was a fierce contention in the man's heart; but at last he determined to go, in the belief that, owing to the secrecy he had preserved, Francis would not know what had happened. He was undeceived as soon as he came into the Master's presence. Said the latter, simply: "You have sinned, Joam d'Eyro, you have sinned." Simply, but so forcibly, that Joam threw himself at his feet, saying, "Yes, father, it is true, it is true. I have sinned." "Confession! confession! my child," said Xavier. That same day the young man confessed and repented; that same day he sold the ship which he had bought; that same day he gave the price of it, and all that he had, to the poor; that same day he ended with more grace, and rose to a better life by penance than he had lost by his fault, having gained besides, by the experience of his own weakness, a great advance in self-knowledge and self-distrust.

Malacca, in the sixteenth century, was a city of great opulence, the centre of the commerce of Arabia, Persia, and India, on the one hand; of China, Japan, and the prolific Spice Islands, on the other. It enjoyed a bland luxurious climate, which was saved from becoming enervating by the fresh cool breezes which came across the seas, while the warm mists clothed its hills and valleys in the bright verdure of perpetual spring. Its population, gay and licentious in their manners, were famed throughout the Eastern world for their courtesy and refinement; their taste and wealth were shown by the handsome buildings which they had erected. On the day that the "holy Father," whose fame had preceded him, landed at Malacca, the shore was crowded with men and women, the old and the young, eager to welcome him. The largest mansions were thrown open for his reception; but, as usual, he preferred to take up his abode in the hospital; though, after awhile, he removed to the house of some poor friends, which crowned an eminence looking far across the purple ocean. He very quickly discerned the depth of corruption and degradation into which the city had fallen; how greatly it needed the work of an Apostle. The extent of the wickedness overpowered him, and at night he would kneel for hours before a crucifix, his eyes wet with tears, his face burning like fire, praying that upon this new Sodom and Gomorrah the thunderbolts of the Divine vengeance might not fall. All day long he toiled and struggled against the evil influences around him. He visited the sick in the hospital; said words of counsel to the criminals in prison; gathered the children together for the Catechism, and taught them holy songs, with which, after a time, the streets and houses began to sound very pleasantly; and at nightfall went through the crowded street, ringing his bell, and summoning the people to devotional exercises. He preached to the multitude on Sundays; but he gave instruction to the children daily, and frequently found leisure for sacred converse with the slaves.

Against the flood-tide of iniquity that rolled through the licentious city, even the energy and spiritual earnestness of a Xavier could not prevail. He shook the dust off from his feet against it as a testimony: foretold the calamities that its vices would bring upon it; and withdrawing the priests of the Society, left it to its doom. On New Year's Day, 1546, he sailed for the fair islands of the Eastern Archipelago. And first he visited Amboyna, where the nutmeg groves filled the air with perfume. He describes it as about ninety miles in circumference, and well-peopled with natives and foreigners. "It contains," he says, "six Christian towns or villages, which I visited one after another as soon as I landed, and where I baptized a great number of infants and children." Soon after Xavier's arrival, a Spanish fleet came into port, and remained for three months. "All that time," writes the saintly man, "how I was distracted with occupations I can hardly tell you. I stirred up all the crews to a regular and virtuous life by sermons; I heard their confessions, I visited their sick, and encouraged them at the hour of death to leave this world with resignation and confidence in GOD; a very difficult thing for those who have been by no means obedient to His divine laws." From Amboyna he sailed to the Moluccas. The voyage was beset with perils,—perils from pirates, and perils from tempests,—and in a storm the vessel which carried Xavier narrowly escaped shipwreck. At Ternate, the romantic island, with its perfumes of clove, which Magellan and Francis Drake afterwards brought to the fuller knowledge of the West, Xavier spent three months in his usual labours, and not without good result. "The converts," he writes, "took up the practice of singing hymns of the praises of GOD with so much ardour, that the native boys in the streets, the young girls and the women in the houses, the labourers in the fields, the fishermen on the sea, instead of singing licentious and blasphemous songs, were always singing the elements of the Christian doctrine. And as all the songs had been translated into the language of the country, they were understood equally well by the newly-made Christians and the heathen. And, by the mercy of GOD, the Portuguese in the country and the rest of the inhabitants, both Christian and heathen, conceived such an affection for me that I found favour in their eyes." The saintliness of the man, his self-devotion, his spiritual excellence, drew all hearts towards him, and filled them unconsciously with love and reverence. And it is just these qualities which make him so dear to us: as a Teacher he was defective; his theological learning was scanty, and he accepted a doctrinal system which we who are out of the Roman communion regard as marked by many and grave errors. He lacked the commanding intellect of a Bernard, the fire and vigour of a Savonarola; but as a Soldier of the Cross he was unsurpassed. When his friends would have dissuaded him from visiting those islands which he calls "Del Moro,"— either Gilolo or Celebes—because of the cannibal propensities of the inhabitants, he replied to them in words of the noblest courage:—

"You tell me they will certainly kill me: well, I trust if they do, it will be gain for me to die. But whatever death or torments they may prepare for me, I am willing to suffer, multiplied a thousand times, for the salvation of a single soul. I remember the words of JESUS CHRIST, Whosoever shall lose his life for My sake, shall find it; I believe them, and on these terms I am content to hazard my life for the name of the LORD JESUS." They urged other ills, and he answered:—"Though the evils you speak of are great, the evil of being afraid of them is greater." And after he had sojourned for three months among this barbarous population, he exclaimed, in a tone of rapture :—" You must know, my beloved brethren, how much these islands overflow with celestial joys. All these dangers and discomforts, when borne for the love of our LORD JESUS CHRIST, are treasuries filled full with heavenly consolations; so much so, that one might think these islands were just the places where, in a few years, one might lose one's eyesight from weeping so abundantly the sweetest tears of joy. Nowhere do I remember either to have been so flooded with so much of limpid and perpetual spiritual delight, or to have borne so lightly all fatigue and bodily trouble; though I was travelling about islands begirt with enemies, inhabited by not the most trustworthy friends, and entirely destitute of aught that would help in sickness, or preserve life when endangered. In short, it seems as if these isles should be called the islands of Divine Hope rather than of the Moor."

Ceram and Ulate were visited by S. Francis as well as Ternate and Gilolo, and wherever he went he founded and organised Christian communities, which he provided with regular teachers. He was back at Ternate in the Lent of 1547, and at Malacca in July, after an absence of a year and a half. There he found three members of the Society, who brought him glad tidings of further assistance from Europe; several others of the Society, four of them were priests, had arrived at Goa in the autumn of 1546, and had been already distributed along the Fishery Coast and in Travancore. At the time of his return, Xavier found the city in immediate danger of an attack from the Acheenese, that warlike race of Sumatra, who, some few years ago, gave the Dutch so much trouble. To Xavier, who seems to have inherited the old Spanish feeling of hostility against the Mohammedans, and who saw how intimately the success of Christian missions was then bound up with the maintenance of the Portuguese power, it was intolerable that the Acheenese should assume an aggressive and threatening attitude. He preached a holy war, and with so much fervour that a fleet of eight ships was equipped, and manned with 180 stout Portuguese soldiers. Before these gallant men sailed, Francis encouraged them with burning words, heard their confessions, gave them holy communion, and promised them a certain victory. He would fain have accompanied them, but the people would not suffer it. Reinforced by the opportune arrival of a couple of Spanish galleys, the "armament of Jesus" sailed against the infidels, and fell in with them off the mouth of the river Parles.

Then "the enemy's navy," says Turselline,[1] "being set in battle array, came down the river with the stream, and the banks and shores on both sides sounded forth with horrible shoutings and confused noise of drums. The first squadron was led by the admiral of the barbarian fleet, guarded on each side by four Turkish galleys. Then followed six other galleys, with nine ranks (or rows) of ships, and all abundantly appointed, not only with great ordnance, but also with plenty of small shot. The admiral, therefore, of the Portuguese, as soon as the first rank of the enemy was discovered, maketh towards them presently at unawares with three ships, commanding the rest to follow as they were ordered for the battle. Whereupon the barbarians, whether for want of skill, or rather of GOD's ordinance, sailing on headlong with fury, discharged all their great shot against the Portuguese before they could so much as reach them, so as the bullets fell all into the water without doing any harm. But a Portuguese gunner, shooting a very great bullet out of the greatest ordnance, struck the admiral of the Acheenese so flat, that presently he sunk and drowned her, which was not only a presage of a future victory, but rather the conclusion of the combat itself. For the Turkish galleys, staying their course, left off the fight, and began to help the captain and other principal men swimming to save themselves, which caused both their own and the fleet's whole overthrow. For the Turks had placed their galleys over thwart the river, and so had taken up a good part of the same, to receive in those that could swim unto them, not once thinking of the danger themselves were in, GOD had so besotted them. The six other galleys which followed the first squadron, coming down with the stream, ran upon the former which lay athwart, and all the rest of the nine ranks which came after fell against those which went before, and became so entangled with one another, and so dashed together, each one striving to get free from his fellow by force, that one would have thought there had been a battle among themselves.

[1] Turselline, bk. iii. §§ 10 and 11.

The Portuguese, perceiving manifestly that GOD's hand was in the business, failed not to follow the victory which was thus offered them from heaven. Wherefore presently calling out aloud upon the sovereign name of JESUS, they began to grapple with their enemies, and on every side to play upon them with their ordnance, lying there so entangled and burdened one by another that they were not able to stir. Thrice did they send out with all the violence they could the shot of all their great ordnance upon their ships, and no one shot was made in vain; nor was the enemy able to resist or make any use of their own artillery, being so thrust up together, and this without any loss to the Portuguese that assailed them. The victory was complete, and Malacca was delivered from all fear of an Acheenese attack."

To this period of Xavier's sojourn at Malacca an interesting incident belongs. A Japanese, of the name of Han-Gir, or Anger, came to him as a penitent, having been induced to travel a thousand miles by his Apostolic fame. He was a person of high rank in his own country, who had been compelled to seek refuge in a monastery of bonzes from the relatives of a man whom he had slain in a sudden quarrel. There his remorseful conscience would not suffer him to rest, and so he hastened to throw himself at Xavier's feet. The great missionary spoke to him earnestly but gently; not disguising the greatness of his sin, but dwelling upon the Divine mercy which was open to all who repented and believed. Anger became a convert; and to prove his sincerity, for Xavier never trusted to hasty resolutions, he sent him as a student to the college at Goa, with directions to await his arrival, which would not be long delayed. Anger accordingly set out for Goa, while Xavier paid a visit to his old and first converts, the Paravas. Thence he travelled along the coast, preaching and baptizing as he went, to the splendid Portuguese city. No sooner had he taken up his old quarters at the Hospital, than he bethought himself of his Japanese convert. He carefully instructed him, found him firm in the faith, and baptized him by the name of Paul. To Xavier he afterwards filled much the same position as Timothy filled towards the great Apostle of the Gentiles. He was his disciple, his son in the LORD, his constant and unwearied attendant. It was natural for Paul to desire that his countrymen should partake of the blessing which had fallen upon himself, and at his solicitations Xavier determined to undertake a voyage to Japan, then almost unknown to Europeans, and separated from Goa by a distance of three thousand miles. But, first, he had work to do at Goa; organizing work; he had also to wait for the coming of more assistants from Europe; and further he desired to renew his spiritual life by participation in the full ordinances of the Church, by intercourse with his brethren, and by spiritual meditation. And it would seem that at this period, in the college gardens of Goa, he enjoyed such devotional revelations as are sometimes granted to souls filled with an all-absorbing love of CHRIST; revelations which cannot be described in words; of which the recipient himself probably can form no definite idea; but revelations which have a wonderful power of strengthening, encouraging, and comforting.

Five more members of the Society having arrived, and been placed at their posts, Xavier set out on his Japanese expedition. On the 25th of April, 1549, he embarked at Cochin for Malacca, where he made a short stay, busying himself in his accustomed occupations. About sunset, on Midsummer day, he went on board a small junk belonging to a Chinese corsair called Nicoda, and next morning set sail and departed. The voyage occupied no fewer than seven weeks. On the Feast of the Assumption he landed in the Japanese port of Caxogima; and having learned something of Japanese from his convert Paul during the voyage, he proceeded at once to open his campaign, by translating the Apostles' Creed, and a brief plain explanation of it, and distributing copies among the people. Through the influence of Paul he obtained an audience of the Prince of Satsuma, who at first received him kindly, and gave him permission to teach and preach. But as he made many converts, the bonzes, or native priests, soon rose in opposition to him, and their opposition was all the more universal, because the Christian Missionary boldly denounced the terrible iniquities of which they were guilty. They induced the Prince to withdraw his patronage; and this he was the readier to do, because he had been disappointed in certain expectations he had formed of advantages of trade with Portugal.[1] No active

[1] Coleridge, ii. 283.

measures of persecution followed; but the attitude of the people underwent an immediate change. For some months Xavier confined his labours to the instruction of the converts already gained, to studying the language of Japan, and to translating into that language a summary of the Christian doctrine and of the life of CHRIST, which he had compiled for the purpose. The rest of his time was spent in prayer,— for prayer was Xavier's sword and shield and staff,—and in exercises of penance. " This," it has been said, "was the laying of the foundation of that famous Church of Japan which was to give an almost unexampled instance of heroic fortitude and constancy under persecution. The converts became more and more firm in the faith, and seem from the first to have been possessed with the spirit which afterwards animated so many Japanese martyrs."

Early in September, 1550, Xavier determined to repair to Firando, a place about sixty miles to the north of the modern town of Nagasaki. He travelled afoot, carrying all that belonged to him in a wallet, on his back, and attended only (for Paul was left at Caxogima) by a couple of Europeans and two Japanese servants. " Had you seen him," says Myers, " pacing wearily yet footsore, solitary yet singing, across the dreary and dangerous wastes of Japan, you could not but have called to mind, in spite of some strange differences, the noble prototype of all missionaries, minding himself to go afoot from Troas unto Assos. He had long been accustomed to endure hardness as a good Soldier of the Cross. Forty hours had he once been drifting on a plank; rivers he had forded, and unbroken forests he had forced his way through; he had been nigh unto death through sickness and the sword : but nowhere had he suffered so much as here : from perils and privations, from cold and nakedness, from hunger and from homelessness. But though his sufferings were great he loved the service—nay, I believe I may say he loved the suffering : for he seems never to have thanked GOD more heartily than when he was called upon to undergo all hardships for the name of CHRIST." Truest of heroes ! loftiest of enthusiasts ! Shall not we, who bend groaningly beneath our small daily troubles, and complain grievously of the pin-pricks of social inconveniences, take courage from thy example, and learn to bear the Cross in a spirit of cheerful hope?

From Firando Xavier led his companions to Facata, whence he sailed to Simonoseki, the port of Amanguchi, the capital of a considerable state on the larger island of Niphon. It was a town of great abominations, and Xavier began to preach in the streets and public places with his characteristic assiduity, and to confront the proud Japanese nobles with his usual courage. But the soil was unfavourable: the seed of Christian truth fell on the rock, and brought forth but a scanty harvest. Leaving Amanguchi early in December, 1550, Xavier set out on a long and weary journey to Meaco, with one of his European assistants and his Japanese disciples. "Neither the jests, nor the sneers, nor the fear of the unknown race, could hinder him from undertaking it. When they had to go by water, over certain parts of the sea, there were many pirates, and on account of these they had to hide themselves below the decks of the boats in order not to be recognized; and when they travelled by land, they went as servants of certain gentlemen on horseback, and had to run at a gallop to keep up and not lose their way. When they came by night to the inns, dead with cold and hunger and wet through, they found no sort of comfort there." Not infrequently their lives were in danger; the crowds to whom Xavier spoke of the Gospel assailing them with stones and arrows. But still he preached and catechized, and baptisms and conversions followed. At Meaco, as at Amanguchi, the labour was great and the harvest small; yet at least a beginning was made,—the Cross was planted,—the Church's foundations were measured out.

From Meaco Xavier returned to Amanguchi, and his second visit was more blessed than his first. The King, propitiated by letter and presents from the Governor of India and the Bishop of Goa, received him favourably, and gave him permission not only to preach, but to make converts. Xavier toiled with increased energy; he preached, he prayed, he disputed; and a glow of delight thrilled his soul when at length the result of his labour became apparent. In the space of two months, he records, as many as five hundred converts were received; and day by day he rejoiced over fresh accessions.

After he had spent about two years in Japan, ordaining elders, erecting churches, preaching and disputing, he began to think of returning to Goa, partly to look after the organization of the Society, and partly to seek men qualified by learning and intellectual vigour to carry on the work he had commenced. After paying a visit to the Prince of Boungo, and holding successfully a public disputation with the bonzes, he sailed for India on the 20th of November, 1551. In January, 1552, he arrived safely at Cochin. Thence he addressed to the Society in Europe a detailed account of his work in Japan, concluding with a notification of the grand resolution he had formed, the grandest of his life, of carrying the Cross into China. The latter paragraphs of his letter are so characteristic of the man, and admit us to so close a view of his high and holy temper, that I cannot forbear from quoting them :—

"Opposite to Japan," he says, "lies China, an immense empire, enjoying profound peace, and, as the Portuguese merchants tell us, superior to all Christian states in the practice of justice and equity. The Chinese whom I have seen in Japan and elsewhere, and whom I got to know, are white in colour, like the Japanese, are acute, and eager to learn. In intellect they are superior even to the Japanese. Their country abounds in all things, and very many cities of great extent cover its surface. The cities are very populous; the houses ornamented with stone roofings, and very elegant. All reports say that the empire is rich in every kind of produce, but especially in silk. I find, from the Chinese themselves, that amongst them may be found many people of many different nations and religions, and, as far as I could gather from what they said, I suspect that among them are Jews and Mohammedans.

"Nothing leads me to suppose that any Christians are to be found there. I hope to go there during this year, 1552, and penetrate even to the Emperor himself. China is that sort of kingdom, that if the seed of the Gospel is once sown, it may be propagated far and wide. And moreover, if the Chinese accept the Christian faith, the Japanese would give up the doctrines which the Chinese have taught them. Japan is separated from Liampou (which is a principal town in China) by a distance of about three hundred miles of sea. I am beginning to have great hopes that GOD will soon provide free entrance to China, not only to our Society, but to religious of all Orders, that a large field may be laid open to pious and holy men of all sorts, in which there may be great room for devotion and zeal in recalling men who are now lost to the way of truth and salvation. I again and again beg all who have a zeal for the spreading of the Christian faith to help by their holy sacrifices and prayers these poor efforts of mine, that I may throw open an ample field to their pious labours.

"I have nothing to say concerning India: the brethren there are charged to render you an account of what is going on. I have just returned hither from Japan, bringing back a sufficient amount of bodily strength, but hardly any strength in virtue and spirit; but I place all my confidence in the goodness of GOD and the infinite merits of our LORD JESUS CHRIST, that I may bring to its accomplishment, as I have designed it, this most irksome voyage to China. My hair has become quite white; but I am as active and robust as ever I was in my life. The labours which are undergone for the conversion of a people so rational, so desirous to know the truth and be saved, result in very sweet fruit to the soul. Even at Amanguchi, where the King allowed us to preach the faith, and a vast concourse of people gathered round us, I had an amount of joy and vigour and delight of heart such as I never experienced in my life before. I saw how by means of our ministry the spirit of the bonzes was broken down by GOD, and the most glorious victory over formidable enemies was gained. I delighted also to see the joy of our neophytes at the defeat of the bonzes, and their evident zeal to attack the Pagans and draw them to baptism, as well as their exultation when the battle was won, as they talked over their victories among themselves, when the superstitions of the heathen were put to flight. Those things made me so overflow with joy, that I lost all sense of suffering.

"Would to GOD that these divine consolations, which GOD so graciously gives us in the midst of our labours, might not only be related by me, but also some experience of them be brought home to our European Universities, to be tasted as well as heard of! Then many of those young men given up to study would turn all their cares and desires to the conversion of infidels, if they could once taste the delight of the heavenly sweetness which comes from such labours. And if the world knew and was aware how well the souls of the Japanese are prepared to receive the Gospel, I am sure that many learned men would finish their studies, and canons, priests, and prelates even, would abandon their rich livings to change an existence full of bitterness and anxiety for so sweet and pleasant a life. And to gain this happiness they would not hesitate to set sail even to Japan."

CHAPTER III.

FORESEEING the possibility that the great enterprise he meditated might be his last, that the mission on which he was bent might be a mission to death, he resolved to visit some of the churches he had planted, and, more particularly, to examine into the work and prospects of his College. He returned, therefore, to Goa, where, to his intense joy and gratitude, he found everything connected with the Missions prosperous beyond expectation. He was free, therefore, to devote himself to labours of supervision and organization; and his correspondence at this period is illustrative not only of his zeal, but of his practical sagacity and prudence, and close attention to details. All the surrounding churches came under his careful inspection, and to their priests he addressed much moral and always appropriate advice. For example, writing to Melchior Nuñez of Bazain, he cautioned him to expend the annual income of his college in the building up of spiritual temples rather than of material. He was to lay out no money on edifices, either of wood or stone, except such as were absolutely necessary, such as could not be left unbuilt without the gravest public inconvenience. If any plans of building were set before him with no other recommendation than their decorative character or stateliness of effect, they were to be declined on the ground that there were more urgent calls, matters of higher and more immediate importance. Any surplus of income over expenditure was to be devoted to the educating of native boys in wholesome knowledge and good manners. To Gonzalez Rodriguez of Ormuz, he wrote, that he was to be careful in preaching never to attack or wound any individual, directly or by allusion; nor to put forth opinions and doctrines of too speculative or refined a character, or for a mere ostentation of learning. All quibbles and affectations were to be sternly repressed; he was to speak of the vices most commonly committed in the town; to attack them with an ardent zeal for the divine glory, but with a modesty equal to his zeal. In his sermons he was not to reprove even public and notorious sinners who made a boast of their sins; he was to seek them in private, and give them brotherly advice. Golden words, like these, occur in all Xavier's pastoral letters; but in none, with greater solemnity, than in the farewell instructions which, just before his departure from Goa, he addressed to Father Gaspar Baertz, whom he had appointed to the Rectorship of the College of Santa Fè.

It is said that, in taking leave of his friends, he did not hide from them his conviction that they would see his face no more. It was an affecting farewell. He charged his brethren, with his last words, shedding many tears, to be constant in their vocation, and to cultivate that profound humility which springs from a true knowledge of self, and, above all things, a spirit of holy obedience and prompt submission. He made Gaspar "Provincial of the parts of Asia Minor," devolving upon him all his power, and he appointed him Rector of the College of Goa, to provide from thence for all other parts. And then he knelt on his knees before him, and offered him obedience on his own part and on the part of all who were absent, thus giving an example of that obedience which he had commanded; and all the fathers and brothers did the same with great consolation and joy, because such a pastor had been given them. After which took place the usual Maundy Thursday function. "There is none," says Mr. Coleridge, "in all the range of the Offices of the [Roman] Church more tender and loving than that of Maundy Thursday, when the altar puts on again its white festive dress for a short time; when the *Gloria in Excelsis* rings through the sanctuary still haunted by the mournful strains of the *Tenebræ* of the evening before; when but one Mass is sung, and so all the faithful, priests as well as laymen, crowd to the altar to receive the Blessed Sacrament on the day of its first institution from the hands of the Superior of the Church. Francis himself would probably say the Mass and give communion to all his brethren, to the students of the college, to the throngs of the faithful to whom he was so dear. Then he would bear in solemn procession, while the *Pange lingua* was being sung, the consecrated host, which was to be consumed on the following morning of Good Friday, to the altar of the Sepulchre, there amid lights and flowers to be adored without ceasing until the time came for the ceremony of the next day. . . . . He would then depart, with his heart full of love and thankfulness, never to return alive."

On arriving at Malacca, towards the close of the spring of 1552, Xavier found it afflicted with a plague, and immediately undertook the charge of the stricken, in which capacity his knowledge of medicine proved of signal service. His courage, his faith, and his skill carried him uninjured through this trial; and as soon as the pestilence had somewhat subsided, he began to prepare for his Chinese expedition. It had been arranged that he should accompany a commercial embassy, under Diego Pereira, but the jealousy of the Governor of Malacca thwarted the design, though Xavier pressed it with his utmost energy. No obstacles or difficulties could induce him to forego his labour of love, and after a tedious delay, he obtained permission to go alone. On the 25th of June he set sail for the island of San Chan, which lay over against Macao, the Portuguese port for commercial intercourse with China. There he endeavoured to obtain the means of passage to the Chinese shore; but the hostility of the Chinese to European priests was so well known, that no trader would incur the risk of taking him on board his vessel. It was feared, moreover, that the Chinese authorities, in their indignation, would prohibit any further trading. As soon as he had recovered from an attack of fever, Xavier, with indefatigable energy, went from one to the other, until at last, for the heavy price of 200 gold pieces, he engaged a Chinese merchant, with a small crew, to land him on some desolate part of the Chinese coast, and there leave him, while they returned in safety to San Chan. But the Portuguese traders obtained information also of this design, and again interfered. The Chinese merchant did not keep his engagement; his interpreter abandoned him; what was to be done? He resolved to go to Siam, and to endeavour to enter China that way. While he was preparing for this last desperate adventure, he was seized a second time by the fever. This was on Sunday, the 20th of November, after he had said mass. A presentiment of death was upon him, and he went on board the ship used as a hospital that he might fare in all respects like the meanest; but finding it difficult there to engage his thoughts wholly in devotions, he begged to be taken ashore. Untended and helpless, he was lying on the bare ground, exposed to the wind and weather, when a sailor named Jorge Alvarez, shocked at his condition, took him into his own hut—a shed made with poles and tarpauling—and gave him shelter.

Through the week he suffered greatly; lying in that miserable cabin, gazing up to heaven through a small window in the side, and praying tenderly and devoutly to a little crucifix which he held constantly in his hand. On the eighth day he was delirious for a time, and in his wanderings talked about his mission to China. After this he lost his speech; but he recovered it on the Wednesday, and thenceforward his mind was perfectly clear. He expressed a wish that the vestments and sacred vessels which he had used for Mass, as well as a manuscript of the Christian Doctrine which had been transcribed in Chinese characters, might be taken on board the ship. He spoke a good deal in ejaculations, but the lad who waited upon him could remember only those which were familiar to him, such as, "O sanctissima Trinitas!" "Jesu, Fili David, miserere mei!" and "Monstra te esse matrem!" Without physician or medicine, he lay a victim to the fever, which ran its course rapidly. On Friday, the 2nd of December, about two in the afternoon, he fixed a last rapturous gaze upon his crucifix; his face kindled with joy; sweet tears streamed from his eyes; and he passed away into his rest, repeating with his last breath the concluding words of that glorious

Te Deum which, for generations, has been the triumphant expression of Christian joy :—" In te, Domine, speravi; non confundar in æternum !" (In Thee, O LORD, have I trusted ; let me not be confounded for ever).

His remains were removed to Malacca, and interred in the church of Santa Maria del Monte. A twelvemonth afterwards they were translated to Goa, where, on the 17th of March, they were solemnly deposited in the sanctuary of the College Church.

The estimate which I have been led to form of "the Apostle of the Indies" has been so sufficiently set forth in the preceding pages, that I need not here attempt a formal analysis of his character. But lest the reader should consider me unwisely partial, and look upon my judgment as that of a panegyrist, I propose to give the words of the late Frederick Myers, whom no one will suspect of an excess of sympathy with the enthusiasts of the mediæval Church.

" We have before us," he says,[1] " the idea of a Missionary of the Gospel realised in a greater degree than I know of anywhere but in the Inspired Records of our Faith. We have an instance of a young man and a noble, renouncing pleasure and preferment, to take up the Cross : of a Sadducee becoming a Saint : of a Collegiate Professor converted to do the work of an Evangelist. We have a remarkable instance of sanctity and self-sacrifice united with charity and zeal ; and this alone is an approximation to the distinctive character of a Christian Apostle. Power of endurance and meekness beyond ordinary men were also conspicuous in Xavier : and these again are noble and Apostolic qualities. The most marvellous self-control was his—ever enabling him to calm a fiery nature into acquiescence in insult, and to submit to open shame with no other change of countenance than a smile, with no other utterance of the lips than a prayer. An uniformly cheerful man was he, always courteous, gentle, and genial—of the Pauline school. He had sold himself, or rather had surrendered himself, once for all, to work good in the sight of the LORD all his days : and so he never felt himself his own, but CHRIST's and his brethren's : and thus toil and affliction of all kinds

[1] Frederick Myers, "Lectures on Great Men," p. 102.

he counted his ordinary state; absence of suffering was his highest pleasure, and repose his only indulgence. And joined to these singular passive virtues was a peculiar continuous zeal, inspiring without inflaming him—manifesting itself rather by a fuller and more living development of the ordinary graces of the Christian character than by any partial or irregular outbreaks: so that you could not say that he was extravagant in any way, at the same time that you could not deny that he was altogether extraordinary. For a model of severe piety unrelieved by unceasing charity; of asceticism without gloom, and yielding gentleness never spoiled by insincerity—I know not where to point you in these later ages better than to FRANCIS XAVIER."

ANNE ASKEW:

AN ENGLISH MARTYR.

"The martyrs' noble army still is ours,
  For in the North our fallen days have seen
  How in her woe the tenderest spirit towers
  For JESUS' sake in agony serene."

KEBLE.

[*Authorities*:—Anne Askew's manuscript notes of her examinations and sufferings, written at the instance of her friends, are preserved by Bishop Bale (of Ossory),—see his "Select Works," published by the Parker Society, 1849,—and by Foxe, in his well-known "Acts and Monuments," of which we have used the 1641 edition (vol. ii. pp. 572—580, fol.). See also Strype's "Ecclesiastical Memorials," vol. i., pt. i. (Oxford, 1822), and Thomas Fuller, "Church History of Britain" (ed. 1845). An eloquent sketch occurs in Mr. J. A. Froude's "History of England from the Fall of Wolsey;" and Southey's "Book of the Church," may be consulted.]

ANNE ASKEW.

CHAPTER I.

ANNE, the second daughter of Sir William Askew, of Kelsey, in Lincolnshire, a gentleman of ancient and honourable lineage, was born in 1520. Of her early life and education few particulars have been recorded; but it is said that, as she grew up, she displayed not only very considerable personal attractions, but a refined taste, some poetical fancy, and a warm imagination. Her manners were gentle and attractive; for a naturally quick temper was restrained by strength of will and firmness of judgment. She gave many indications of more than ordinary force of intellect, and could not be prevailed upon to accept an opinion until she had carefully examined it. On the other hand, once convinced of its truth, she would never abandon it. Such a woman, in her right sphere, might have enjoyed a happy and useful life. Unfortunately, her father marred her career by committing her to an unsuitable marriage. A close neighbour of his was a Mr. Kyme, a man of great wealth and local influence, and it occurred to him and Sir William Askew that they could not do better than confirm their friendship and unite their estates by marrying the son and heir of Mr. Kyme to Sir William's eldest daughter. The lady dying before the scheme could be carried out, Anne Askew was substituted, in spite of her urgent protestations against a match in which her affections were not engaged. She reminded her father that scandal had been busy with the name of her proposed husband; but Sir William ignored her representations, and she was compelled to obey.

An union concluded under such conditions could not be crowned with happiness; but Mistress Anne Kyme earnestly strove to do her duty with her uncongenial husband, to whom she bore two children. While enduring her burden with as little repining as was possible, she met with a copy of Tyndale's newly published translation of the New Testament. It let in a flood of light upon her dark and dreary existence; she read it eagerly, and, as she read, her keen intelligence detected the errors of doctrine in which she had been educated. In the enthusiasm of a mind suddenly awakened from the lethargy of ignorance, she resolved to renounce a Church which, as it seemed to her, was founded upon falsehood and misrepresentation. She knew the bitterness of the hostility such a step would provoke, and the extent of the obloquy in which it would involve her; but she was incapable of hesitation or concealment where it was a question of right. She embraced, therefore, the "new heresy," the creed of the Reformers, which, in England, had been handed down from Wyclif; and to this creed she adhered with the characteristic tenacity of her temperament.

Her backsliding, as it was considered, brought down upon her head the coarse anger of her husband and the thunderbolts of sacerdotal wrath. To menaces, however, she was as indifferent as to cajolery; and her husband then expelled her from his house. Harsh treatment, however, did but rouse her courage; and, proceeding to London, she took the necessary measures to obtain a divorce, justifying herself by the teaching of S. Paul:—"If a faithful woman have an unbelieving husband, which will not tarry with her, she may leave him, for a brother or sister is not in subjection to such." (1 Cor. vii. 15.) In the metropolis she speedily made the acquaintance of several distinguished Lollard ladies; and it is said that Queen Katharine appointed her one of her maids of honour. Probably she was advised to drop her intended divorce suit; at all events she did not carry it into the courts; nor, if she had done so, could she have hoped to be successful. But she refused to bear her husband's name, and signed herself, as in her maidenhood, Anne Askew.

Before we proceed any further, a brief historical retrospect is necessary.

In 1539, Parliament instructed a committee to draw up a bill against diversities of opinion in matters of religion. But as this committee delayed reporting to the Houses, the Duke of Norfolk, in the Upper Chamber, submitted six articles of faith to free discourse. Long theological debates ensued, interrupted on the 23rd of May by the prorogation of Parliament for a week. On the 30th the King sent a message to the Peers to the effect that, with the aid of the Bench of Bishops, he had come to a conclusion on the Six Articles which would be acceptable to the Two Houses; but that to enforce them a penal statute would be required. Hence resulted "the bloody Act of the Six Articles;"[1] or, as the Protestants expressively termed it, "the whip with six strings," by which death by burning was adjudged to any person denying the first article, and confiscation of property for the first time, with a felon's death for the second offence, to any person denying either or all of the other five articles. These articles were thus set forth:—[2]

1. That in the Sacrament is present really, under the form of bread and wine, the natural body and blood of our SAVIOUR JESUS CHRIST, conceived of the Virgin Mary; and that after the consecration there remaineth no substance of bread or wine, or any other substance but the substance of CHRIST, GOD and Man.

2. That CHRIST was entirely in each kind, and therefore communion in both was not necessary.

3. That priests by the law of GOD may not marry.

4. That vows of chastity or widowhood, taken after the age of twenty-one, ought to be observed by the law of GOD.

5. That private masses might be lawfully used in the English Church, as by them good Christian people receive godly consolation and benefit.

6. That auricular confession was expedient, and ought to be retained, used, and frequented in the Church of GOD.

To ensure the effectual working of this Act, commissioners

---

[1] Act for Abolishing Diversity of Opinions, 31 Hen. VIII., c. 14.
[2] Fuller, Church History, ii. 98. Cf. Froude, iii. 210.

were appointed in every county, of whom three were to form a quorum, to sit at least four times in the year, with full power to receive information, accusations, and evidence, before a jury of twelve men, upon oath, and to declare sentence. In the commission was included the archbishop, or bishop, or his chancellor, or a commissioner named by him. Similar powers were bestowed upon justices of peace in their sessions, and upon every steward, under-steward, or deputy in his "law-days," so that a religious "reign of terror" was inaugurated in England.

The Act of the Six Articles was afterwards modified so far as to allow the offender an opportunity of recanting; but if he broke the law a third time, no mercy was to be extended to him. This was in 1544. In the following year its rigour was further abated. Parliament then provided that no indictment should lie unless brought within a year of the committal of the offence; that no person accused should be attached, or committed to prison before indictment, except by special warrant from the King; and that any preacher or reader not accused within forty days of his speaking against the Six Articles, should be acquitted. Other alterations were introduced with the view of rendering the Act a less intolerable burden; but it still remained a terrible engine of oppression.

Suspicions of heresy soon began to attach to Mistress Anne Askew; and one Wadloo, a cursitor of the Court of Chancery, and an adherent of the old faith, took lodgings next to her residence in the Temple, that he might gather evidence to justify her imprisonment. But, by the mercy of GOD, Balaams who go down to curse are often compelled to bless; and Wadloo was forced to own to Sir Lionel Throgmorton that she was the devoutest woman he had ever known; "for," said he, "at midnight she begins to pray, and ceases not for many hours, when I and others are addressing ourselves to sleep or to work."[1] But no sanctity of life, no excellence of character, could avert the bitter hostility of her husband and the Romish priests; and some incautious expressions eventually furnished them with the means of compassing her ruin. On one occasion, she had denied that the character or belief of the priest in any

[1] Strype, Ecclesiastical Memorials, vol. i. pt. i. p. 597.

wise diminished the efficacy of the Sacrament of the LORD's Supper, contending that, whether administered by Wycliffite or Papist, it was still the emblem of CHRIST's Blood and Body. On another, she had scornfully affirmed that she would rather read five lines of the Bible than hear five masses. On these grounds she was accused of heresy, and straightway arrested.

Her first examination took place in March, 1545, before a jury or inquest assembled at Saddlers' Hall, under the presidency of Christopher Dare. His questions pressed her closely as to the exact nature of her opinions on the dogmas of the Mass, Transubstantiation, Auricular Confession, and the connection of the priest's office with the administration of the Eucharist. Her replies were marked by singular readiness, discretion, and an almost epigrammatic force of expression. During her imprisonment she wrote a full account of her examination, which cannot but impress the reader with a conviction of her considerable intellectual powers.[1]

Christopher Dare asked her if she did not believe that the Sacrament hanging over the altar was the very Body and Blood of CHRIST. She replied, *more Socratico*, requesting to be informed why Stephen was stoned to death.

Christopher Dare. I cannot tell.

Anne Askew. No more can I answer thy vain question.

Christopher Dare. A woman testifies that you have read how GOD was not in temples made with hands.

"Then I showed him," she says, "the 7th and 17th chapters of the Acts of the Apostles, what Stephen and Paul had said therein. Whereupon he asked me, how I took those sentences? I answered, I would not throw pearls among swine, for acorns were good enough. Thirdly, he asked me, wherefore I said that I had rather to read five lines in the Bible than to hear five masses in the temple? I confessed I had said no less; not for the dispraise of either the Epistle or the Gospel, but because the one did greatly edify me, the other nothing at all. As S. Paul doth witness in the

---

[1] This narrative was published by Bishop Bale, with an introduction, in 1547, under the title of "First Examinacyon of Anne Askew, lately martyred in Smythfelde by the Romish Pope's Vpholders, with the Elucydacyon of John Bale," reprinted by the Parker Society.

14th chapter of his first Epistle to the Corinthians, wherein he said :—' If the trumpet give an uncertain sound, who will prepare himself to the battle?'

"Fourthly, he laid unto my charge, that I should say, if an ill priest ministered, it was the devil and not God. My answer was, that I never spoke any such thing. But this was my saying, that whosoever he were that ministered unto me, his ill conditions could not hurt my faith, but in spirit I received nevertheless the body and blood of Christ.

"Fifthly, he asked me what I said concerning confession. I answered him my meaning, which was as S. James said, that every man ought to acknowledge his faults to others, and the one to pray for the other.

"Sixthly, he asked me what I said to the King's book?[1] And I answered him, that I could say nothing to it because I never saw it.

"Seventhly, he asked me if I had the Spirit of God in me. I answered, I had not: I was but a reprobate or castaway. Then he said he had sent for a priest to examine me, who was there at hand.

"The priest asked me what I said to the Sacrament of the Altar, and required much to know my meaning therein. But I desired him again to hold me excused concerning the matter: none other answer would I give him, because I perceived him to be a Papist.

"Eighthly, he asked me, If I did not think that private masses did help the souls departed? I said, It was great idolatry to believe more in them than in the death which Christ died for us."

From Saddlers' Hall she was conveyed to the Lord Mayor's Court, where she was examined in much the same fashion, retorting with similarly prompt and pithy answers. She incurred a rebuke from the Bishop of London's Chancellor "for uttering the Scriptures." S. Paul, he said, forbade women to speak or talk of the Word of God. She replied, that she knew the Apostle's meaning as well as he, which was, that a woman ought not to speak in the congregation by way of teaching: and then she asked him, how many women had he seen go into the pulpit and

[1] "The Erudition of a Christian Man," written by various bishops and divines, and published by order of Henry VIII.

preach? He replied, None. Then, retorted she, you ought to find no fault with poor women, unless they have offended against the law.

Foiled by her woman's wit, the Lord Mayor committed her to prison, refusing to take the security of her friends. In the Compter she lay for eleven days, and a priest was sent by Bonner, Bishop of London, to examine her and give her good counsel, which, she characteristically adds, he did not. He first asked her, for what cause she was put in the Compter, and when she told him she did not know, he said "it was great pity she should lie in so loathsome a place without cause, and he was very sorry for her." But the next moment he remembered the instructions of his employers. It was told him, he said, that she denied the Sacrament of the Altar. She contented herself with replying :—"That that I have said, I have said." Would she be shriven (i.e., would she make confession)? Yes, she answered, if she might confess to Dr. Crome, Sir William Whitehead, or Huntington, each of whom she knew to be a man of wisdom. "As for you, or any other," she added, "I will not dispraise, because I know you not." Apparently with a feeling of mortification, the priest replied :—"I would not have you think but that I, or any other who may be brought you, shall be as honest as they : for if we were not, you may be sure the king would not suffer us to preach." To this she returned the saying of Solomon's :—"By communing with the wise I may learn wisdom, but by talking with a fool I shall take scathe." The priest seeing that he had met his match, changed the direction of his questions : —"If the Host should fall, and a beast did eat it, would the beast receive GOD or no? And did she intend to receive the Sacrament at Easter?" To the first she replied : —"Seeing that you have taken the pains to ask the question, I desire you also to assail it yourself, for I will not do it, because I perceive you are come to tempt me." And to the second :—"That else I were no Christian woman ; and thereat I did rejoice that the time was so near at hand."

On the 23rd of March she was visited in prison by her cousin Britaine (or Brittayne), who immediately afterwards went to the Lord Mayor, for the purpose, if possible, of obtaining her liberation on bail. The Lord Mayor was willing to do all that lay in his power; but could not move without the sanction of a spiritual officer, and requested him to wait on the Bishop of London's chancellor. This he did; but lo, the Chancellor could not act without the permission of the Bishop. He undertook, however, to bring the subject before Bishop Bonner, and requested Brittayne to see him the next morning, when he would let him know his lordship's pleasure. Accordingly on the morrow Brittayne returned, and found Bonner with the Chancellor. The Bishop expressed his willingness that " she should come forth to communication ;" and appointed her to appear before him for examination on the following day, March 25th, at three o'clock. At the examination, he said, some learned men would be present, " such as she was affectioned to," that they might see and report that she was not handled with rigour. Brittayne replied, that he knew no man his cousin had " more affection to" than any other. Yes, said the Bishop, she was partial, as he understood, to Doctor Crome, Sir William Whitehead, and Huntington. And he urged Brittayne to persuade his cousin to utter " even the very bottom of her heart;" and he sware by his fidelity, that no man should take any advantage of her words, neither would he himself lay to her charge anything she might confess, but, if she said aught amiss, he with others would be glad to reform her therein, with most godly counsel.

Accordingly, on the 25th she appeared before Bonner, and underwent a similar cross-examination to that which had befallen her at the hands of Christopher Dare. With professions of kindly feeling, which may not have been wholly insincere, he solicited her to unburden her mind, for that she did not need to stand in fear or doubt. Neither he, nor any man for him, should take advantage of her words. Therefore he bade her speak fearlessly. She replied that she had nought to say, for her conscience did not trouble her. " Then," exclaimed the Bishop, " I can give you no good counsel." " My conscience," she replied, " is clear in all things." " You drive me," continued the Bishop, "to lay to your charge your own report, which is this: You did say, he that doth receive the Sacrament by the hands of an ill priest, or a sinner, receiveth the devil and not GOD."

"I never spoke such words," was her indignant answer; "but, as I said before, that the wickedness of the priest did not hurt me, but in spirit and faith I received no less than the Body and Blood of CHRIST." "What saying is this, *in spirit?*" demanded he; "I will not take you at the advantage." She answered:—"My lord, without faith and spirit, I cannot receive Him worthily."

She had alleged (continued the Bishop) a certain text of the Scripture. Yes, she replied, none other but S. Paul's own saying to the Athenians, in the 17th chapter of the Acts of the Apostles, that GOD dwelleth not in temples made with hands. What then was her faith and belief in that matter?

"I believe as the Scripture doth teach me."

"But what if the Scripture doth say, that it is the Body of CHRIST?"

"I believe as the Scripture doth teach."

Again: "What if the Scripture doth say, that it is the Body of CHRIST?"

"I believe as the Scripture informeth me."

In various forms the Bishop pressed his question, but could obtain no other admission from Anne Askew than that in this and in all other things she accepted what CHRIST and His Apostles taught. Baffled by her reticence, he asked her why she had so few words? "GOD hath given me," she said, "the gift of knowledge, but not of utterance; and Solomon saith, That a woman of few words is the gift of GOD." He next accused her of having stated that the Mass was superstitious, wicked, and no better than idolatry. No; she had made no such assertion; but when she was asked whether private masses relieved the souls of the departed, she exclaimed, "O LORD, what idolatry is this, that we should rather believe in private masses than in the healthsome death of the dear SON of GOD." Then said Bonner: "What an answer is that!" "Though it be but mean," she rejoined, "yet is it good enough for the question."

Another of the Bishop's complaints was that she had reported herself to have been assailed at Lincoln by the questions of threescore priests. "Indeed," she answered, "I did say so. For my friends told me that if I came to Lincoln, the priests would assault me and put me to great trouble, as thereof they had made their boast; and when I heard it, I went thither indeed, not being afraid, because I knew my matter to be good. Moreover, I remained there nine days to see what would be said unto me. And as I was in the Minster, reading the Bible, they resorted unto me by two and by two, by five and by six, minding to have spoken unto me, yet went they their ways again without words speaking."

What a curious picture is here presented of the grave young woman, seated alone in the grand nave of Lincoln Cathedral, with the robed priests passing by her closely, or occasionally going up to her, but saying nothing, half contemptuous probably of a woman's wit when exercised with high questions of faith and doctrine! We must make some allowance for the anger of priest and prelate at what, no doubt appeared to them, the abominable pride and arrogance of Dame Anne Askew in throwing any doubt upon dogmas accepted by the Church for centuries, and pronounced sufficient unto salvation by "wise and learned doctors." Such an outbreak against all authority and tradition must have seemed almost incomprehensible to men never exercised by any scruples of conscience, and profoundly satisfied with the system in which they had been nurtured. That they should attempt to put down what, from their view-point, was necessarily an unjustifiable rebellion, we cannot wonder; though we may well condemn and regret the terrible cruelty to which in their panic of alarm and terror they resorted. I have sometimes thought that more to be pitied than the martyrs, with all their sufferings,—for these became as nothing in their hope of a crown of glory,—were the men who sent them to the stake or the gibbet.

Perplexed, and, perhaps, not a little angry, the Bishop ordained:—"There are many that read and know the Scripture, and yet follow it not, nor live thereafter." Accepting these words as conveying a personal insinuation, Anne Askew replied, with the simple dignity of innocence: —" My lord, I would wish that all men knew my conversation and living in all points; for I am sure myself this hour, that there are none able to prove any dishonesty against me. If you know any that can do it, I pray you bring them forth." The Bishop then retired, and anxious (I think) to save this serious and saintly woman from further molestation, he drew up a confession of faith on the old orthodox lines. Returning with the document in his hand, he proceeded to read it to her. According to Foxe,[1] it ran as follows :—

"Be it known of all faithful people, that as touching the blessed Sacrament of the Altar, I do firmly and undoubtedly believe that, after the words of consecration be spoken by the priest, according to the common usage of this Church of England, there is present really the Body and Blood of our SAVIOUR JESUS CHRIST, whether the minister that doth consecrate be a good man or a bad man, he doth receive it really and corporally. And, moreover, I do believe, that whether the said Sacrament be then received of the minister, or else reserved to be put into the pyx, or to be brought to any person that is impotent or sick, there is the very Body and Blood of our said SAVIOUR. So that, whether the minister or the receiver be good or bad; yea, whether the Sacrament be received or reserved, always there is the blessed Body of CHRIST really. And this thing, with all other things touching this Sacrament, and other Sacraments of the Church, and all things also touching the Christian belief, which are taught and declared in the King's Majesty's book, lately set forth for the erudition of the Christian people, I, Anne Askew, otherwise called Anne Kyme, do truly and perfectly believe, and so do here personally confess and acknowledge. And here I do promise, that henceforth I shall never say or do anything against the premises, or against any of them. In witness whereof, I, the said Anne, have subscribed my name unto these presents."

Having read this confession, the Bishop asked Anne Askew if she agreed with it. "I believe so much thereof," was her reply, "as the Holy Scripture doth agree unto," and she desired him to add this saving clause. Bonner answered, angrily, that she should not teach him what to write. And going forth into his great chamber, he read the paper to all assembled there, who immediately pressed

[1] Foxe, Acts and Monuments, ii. 575 (edit. 1641).

her to sign it, and acknowledge the indulgence with which she had been treated. She yielded to their importunity so far as to attach her signature thus:—" I, Anne Askew, do believe all manner of things contained in the faith of the Catholic Church." Bonner, irritated by the implied reservation, and weary of so long and fruitless a contest with a woman, passed hastily into his chamber, followed by Brittayne, who besought him for GOD's sake " to be a good lord" unto his cousin. The Bishop answered with scorn in his voice, that she was a woman, and that he was nothing deceived in her. "Then," said Brittayne, "take her as a woman, and do not set her weak woman's wit against your lordship's great wisdom."

Bishop Bonner, who was not wanting in good nature, and evidently had no desire to make a victim of Mistress Anne, was finally persuaded to release her, on the sureties agreeing to give bail for her forth-coming if called upon. Her cousin Brittayne, and one Master Spilman, of Gray's Inn, entered into the necessary recognizances, and she was set at liberty. The Bishop, with, perhaps, as Froude suggests, a kindly purpose, entered in his register that Anne Askew had appeared before him, and made an adequate profession of her belief.

CHAPTER II.

"BUT her name was written among those who were to serve Heaven in their deaths rather than their lives."[1]

In the summer of 1546, she was again apprehended, apparently from an anxiety on Bishop Gardiner's part to strike through her at Queen Katharine Parr, and Archbishop Cranmer, and other favourers of the new heresy. She was unfortunate in falling into the hands of the truculent prelate of Winchester, who had none of those scruples of a compassionate conscience which frequently moved Bishop Bonner to acts of mercy. At first she was brought before the King's Council at Greenwich, and examined in

[1] In her MS. notes of her Examinations, printed by Foxe.

reference to her relations to her husband. She replied that the Lord Chancellor (Wriothesley) already knew her mind in that matter. The Council were not satisfied, and said it was the King's pleasure she should give them full information. " I answered them plainly," she says, "I would not do so, but if it were the King's pleasure to hear me, I would show him the truth. Then they said it was not meet for the King to be troubled with me. I answered, that Solomon was reckoned the wisest king that ever lived, yet misliked he not to hear two poor common women, much more his Grace a simple woman and his faithful subject. So, in conclusion, I made them none other answer in that matter. Then my Lord Chancellor asked me my opinion on the Sacrament. My answer was this : I believe that so oft as I in a Christian congregation do receive the bread in remembrance of CHRIST'S death, and with thanksgiving, according to His holy institution, I receive therewith the fruits of His most glorious Passion."

Gardiner angrily demanded a more direct answer.

"I cannot sing a new song of the LORD in a strange land," said Anne Askew.

"You speak in parables."

"That is best for you; since if I were to show the open truth you would not accept it."

"You are a very parrot," exclaimed Gardiner, fiercely.

"I am ready to suffer all things at your hands; not only your rebukes, but all that shall follow besides; yea, and all that gladly."

After undergoing an examination of five hours, she was conveyed, in charge of the Clerk of the Council, to Lady Gamish's, where she passed the night. The next morning she was again brought before the Council, and closely questioned respecting her views of the Sacrament both by Gardiner and Wriothesley. She was cajoled with promises,[1] and tried with threats; but she remained steadfast to what she believed to be the truth. The day following, Sunday, she was "sore sick, thinking no less than to die," and

[1] The brilliant worldly Paget, to whom confessions of faith were "no things to die for," essayed the eloquence which had foiled the diplomatists of Europe. His arguments fell off like arrows from enchanted armour. Lord Lisle and Lord Parr, who believed as she be-

desired to speak with Bishop Latimer. This, however, was refused, and ill as she was, she was committed to Newgate.

While in prison she wrote down her belief in simple words, and in so doing wrote her condemnation :—

"I find in the Scripture that CHRIST took the bread, and gave it to His disciples, saying : 'Take, eat, this is My Body which shall be broken for you,' meaning in substance His own very body, the bread being thereof an only sign or sacrament. For, after like manner of speaking, He said He would break down the temple, and in three days build it up again, signifying His own Body by the temple, as S. John declareth it (S. John ii.), and not the stony temple itself. So that the bread is but a remembrance of His death, or a Sacrament of thanksgiving for it, whereby we are knit unto Him by a communion of Christian love, although there be many that cannot perceive the true meaning thereof, for the veil that Moses put over his face before the children of Israel, that they should not see the clearness thereof (Exod. xxiv. and 2 Cor. iii.). I perceive the same veil remaineth to this day; but when GOD shall take it away, then shall those blind men see. For it is plainly expounded in the history of Bel in the Bible, that GOD dwelleth in no thing material. 'O king,' saith Daniel, 'be not deceived, for GOD will be in nothing that is made with hands of man' (Dan. xiv.). Oh, what stiff-necked people are those that will always resist the HOLY GHOST! But as their fathers have done, so do they, because they have stony hearts."

The formal trial followed at the Guildhall, where she showed the same high courage in adhering to her belief. Her judges told her that she was a heretic, and condemned by the law, if she persisted in her opinions. She answered, simply, that she was no heretic, nor had she deserved death by any law of GOD. But as to her views of the faith, those she could not and would not deny, because she

lieved, tried to prevail on her to say as they said. "It was shame for them," she replied, "to counsel contrary to their knowledge." Gardiner told her she would be burnt. "GOD," she answered, "laughed his threatenings to scorn." Froude, iv. 206. Cf. with Foxe, ii. 576 (ed. 1641).

knew them to be true. They asked her if she denied the Sacrament to be CHRIST'S Body and Blood? Yea, she replied, for the same SON of GOD, Who was born of the Virgin Mary, was now glorious in Heaven, and would come again from thence at the latter day. And as for what they called their God, it was but a piece of bread. For greater proof thereof, they might note that if it lay in the pyx three months it would grow mouldy, and so turn to nothing that was good. Wherefore she was persuaded that it could not be GOD.

In her reaction against the Romish dogma of Transubstantiation she had fallen, you perceive, into the lowest depth of Zwinglianism, and it is clear that her belief respecting the Sacrament would not harmonise with the doctrine which the Church of England lays down in her present formularies. She maintained the truth, however, as she saw it, with a heroism that we cannot but admire, and that should encourage us, in our happier time, to a livelier faith and a more steadfast witness to it.

Her judges advised her to take counsel with a priest. She only smiled. They asked her, if it would not be for her good? She said she would confess her faults unto GOD, for she was sure that He would hear her with favour. Then, sentence of death was passed upon her, and she was taken back to prison.

In her narrative she adds:—" My belief which I wrote to the Council was this : That the Sacramental bread was left us to bê received with thanksgiving in remembrance of CHRIST'S death, the only memory of our soul's recovery; and that thereby we also receive the whole benefits and fruits of His most glorious Passion. Then would they needs know whether the bread in the box were GOD or no. I said, GOD is a spirit, and will be worshipped in spirit and truth (S. John iv.). Then they demanded, Will you plainly deny CHRIST to be in the Sacrament? I answered, That I believe faithfully the eternal SON of GOD not to dwell there; in witness whereof I recited again the history of Bel, and the 14th chapter of Daniel,[1] the 7th and 17th of the Acts, and the 24th of S. Matthew, concluding thus: I neither

[1] This is the Apocryphal portion; the History of Susannah and that of Bel and the Dragon.

wish Death, nor yet fear his might; GOD have the praise thereof with thanks."

After this examination Anne Askew addressed a letter to the King, then lying ill of the malady that soon afterwards terminated in his death, not imploring mercy, but only declaring that she was innocent of crime. She enclosed it under cover to the Lord Chancellor Wriothesley, and we may conjecture that it never reached the royal hands. It ran as follows :—

"The LORD GOD, by Whom all creatures have their being, bless you with the light of His knowledge. Amen.

" My duty to your Lordship remembered, &c.

" It might please you to accept this my bold suit, as the suit of one which upon due consideration is moved to the same, and hopeth to obtain. My request to your Lordship is only, that it may please the same to be a mean for me to the King's Majesty, that his Grace may be certified of these few lines which I have written concerning my belief; which when it shall be truly compared with the hard judgment given me for the same, I think his Grace shall perceive me to be weighed in an uneven pair of balances. But I remit my matter and cause to Almighty GOD, which rightly judgeth all secrets. And thus I commend your Lordship unto the governance of Him, and fellowship of all saints. Amen. By your handmaid,

"ANNE ASKEW."

The enclosure for the King's Grace ("my Faith," she calls it) was as follows :—[1]

"I, Anne Askew, of good memory, although GOD has given me the bread of adversity and the water of trouble, yet not so much as my sins have deserved, desire this to be known to your Grace. That, forasmuch as I am by the law condemned for an evil doer, here I take heaven and earth to record that I shall die in my innocence. And, according to that I have said first, and will say last, I utterly abhor and detest all heresies. And, as concerning the Supper of the LORD, I believe so much as CHRIST hath said therein, which He confirmed with His most blessed Blood. I believe also so much as He willed me to follow

[1] Select Works of John Bale, Bp. of Ossory (Parker Society), p. 217.

and believe, and as much as the Catholic Church of Him doth teach; for I will not forsake the commandment of His holy lips. But look what GOD hath charged me with His mouth, that have I shut up in my heart. And thus briefly I end, for lack of learning.

"ANNE ASKEW."

In this, remarks quaint Bishop Bale, she dischargeth herself to the world, against all wrongful accusations and judgments of heresy. Heresy, he continues, is not to dissent from the Church of Rome in the doctrine of faith : but a voluntary dissenting from the Scriptures of GOD ; and Anne Askew, and the Reformers generally, spurned the accusation of being heretics, pleading that they sought only to deliver the faith from the corruptions that encrusted it, and to restore it to its original purity as professed and maintained by the Church Catholic in the days of its primitive innocence.

During her confinement in Newgate Anne Askew gave expression to her feelings of constancy and courage in an exultant strain of song :—[1]

> " Like as the armèd knight,
>   Appointed to the field,
>   With this world will I fight,
>   And CHRIST shall be my shield.
>
> " Faith is that weapon strong,
>   Which will not fail at need :
>   Thy foes, therefore, among
>   Therewith will I proceed.
>
> " As it is had in strength
>   And force of CHRISTE'S way,
>   It will prevail at length,
>   Though all the devils say nay.
>
> " Faith in the fathers old
>   Obtainèd righteousness ;
>   Which makes one very bold
>   To fear no world's distress.
>
> " I now rejoice in heart,
>   And hope bid me do so ;
>   For CHRIST will take my part,
>   And ease me of my woe.

[1] Ibid. pp. 239, 240.

" Thou say'st, LORD, whoso knock,
    To them wilt Thou attend :
Undo therefore the lock,
    And Thy strong power send.

" More enemies now I have
    Than hairs upon my head :
Let them not me deprave,
    But fight Thou in my stead.

" On Thee my care I cast,
    For all their cruel spite :
I set not by their haste ;
    For Thou art my delight.

" I am not she that list
    My anchor to let fall
For every dazzling mist,
    My ship substantial.

" Not oft use I to write
    In prose, nor yet in rhyme ;
Yet will I show one sight
    That I saw in my time.

" I saw a royal throne,
    Where justice should have sit,
But in her stead was one
    Of moody, cruel wit.

" Absorbed was righteousness,
    As of the raging flood :
Satan, in his excess,
    Sucked up the guiltless blood.

" Then thought I, JESUS LORD,
    When Thou shalt judge us all,
Hard is it to record
    On these men what will fall.

" Yet, LORD, I Thee desire,
    For that they do to me,
Let them not taste the hire
    Of their iniquity."

After a few days' detention in Newgate, Anne Askew was removed to the sign of the Crown, where Rich and the Bishop of London endeavoured to persuade her into a recantation. They were as unsuccessful as Nicholas Shaxton, though the latter pointed to his own example as one she might follow, and thereby save her life. She dismissed him with the pregnant words :—"It would have been good for you never to have been born." Rich then sent her to the Tower, where he and one of the King's Council strove earnestly to draw from her admissions which might implicate Lady Suffolk, Lady Sussex, Lady Hertford, Lady Denny, and Lady Fitzwilliam. "No," she replied; "if she should pronounce anything against them, yet would she not be able to prove it." They pretended the King had been informed that if she would, she could name a number of "her sect." The King, she replied, was as well deceived in that behalf as he was dissembled with by them in other matters. How then was she maintained in the prison, and who willed her to adhere to her religious errors? She derived support and consolation, she answered, from no human source. All the help she had received was through the means of her maid; who, as she went abroad, described her mistress's sad condition to the London prentices, and they assisted her with money, though who they were she never knew. Her persecutors insisted that she had received money from several ladies. Yes: it was true that a man had placed ten shillings in her hand, with the information that they were sent by Lady Hertford; while another had given her eight shillings as a contribution from Lady Denny. Whether this was true or no, she was unable to say, as she spoke only from what her maid had said. "There are some of the Council," they furiously exclaimed, "who maintain you." She answered firmly, No.

But her questioners were dissatisfied. They suspected Lord Hertford and Archbishop Cranmer, and if they could justify their suspicion, it would greatly facilitate their intrigues to gain the ear of the King. The unfortunate lady, therefore, was taken from Newgate to the Tower, where the Chancellor and Rich, the Solicitor-General, were waiting to put her to the torture. They kept her on the rack "for a long time;" and because she suffered and did not cry, the Lord Chancellor and Rich actually racked her with their own hands until she was "nigh dead." Sir Anthony Knyvet, the Lieutenant of the Tower, then ordered her to be removed from the rack, when she immediately swooned. On her recovery, she was kept sitting for two hours on the bare stone floor—this poor, weak, exhausted woman "reasoning" with the Chancellor, who, despite his brutality, professed the utmost good will, and with flattering words urged her to give up her opinions. "But," she says, "my LORD GOD, I thank His everlasting goodness, gave me grace to persevere, and will do so, I hope, to the very end."

After enduring hours of anguish, she was brought to a house and laid on a bed, "with as weary and painful bones as ever had patient Job," but still praising and blessing GOD. Word came from Wriothesley that if she would abandon her errors she should want for nothing; if she would not, she should forthwith be committed to Newgate and burned. She replied, like a true hero of the Cross, that she would rather die than desert her faith; praying that GOD would open his eyes, so that the truth might have free course and be glorified.[1]

I suppose it was immediately after her removal to Newgate that she wrote the following letter to John Lascelles, or Lasselles, a gentleman of the bedchamber, persecuted, like herself, on account of his adoption of the Reformed doctrines :—

"O friend, most dearly beloved in GOD, I marvel not a little what should move you to judge in me so slender a faith, as to fear death, which is the end of all misery. In the LORD I desire of you not to believe of me such wickedness; for I doubt it not but GOD will perform His work in me, like as He hath begun.

"I understand the Council is not a little displeased that it should be reported abroad that I was racked in the Tower. They say now that they did there was but to fear me : whereby I perceive they are ashamed of their own uncomely doings, and fear much lest the King's Majesty should have information thereof: wherefore they would no man to noise it.[2]

---

[1] Foxe adds that Knyvet, when that torture was over, hastened to the Court, obtained admission to the royal presence, and informed King Henry of all that had taken place. The King, he says, "seemed not very well to like of their so extreme handling of the woman."—*Acts and Monuments*, ii. 578.

[2] "The abominable cruelty of Wriothesley and Rich is perhaps the darkest page in the history of any English statesman. Yet, as Wriothesley was a man who had shown at other times high and noble qualities, it is hard to believe that bigotry had entirely blinded him to all feelings of humanity." So says Mr. Froude (iv. 208); but it was

Well, their cruelty GOD forgive them. Your heart in CHRIST JESUS. Farewell, and pray."

She also wrote in the interval before her execution what Foxe calls her purgation or answer :—

" I have read the process which is reported, of them that know not the truth, to be my recantation. But as sure as the LORD liveth, I never meant anything less than to recant. Notwithstanding this, I confess that in my first troubles I was examined by the Bishop of London about the Sacrament. Yet had they no grant of my mouth but this, that I believed therein as the word of GOD did bind me to believe. More had they never of me. Then he made a copy, which is now in print, and required me to set thereunto my hand. But I refused it. Then my two sureties did will me in no wise to stick thereat, for it was no great matter, they said.

"Then with much ado, at the last I wrote thus: I, Anne Askew, do believe this, if GOD'S word do agree to the same, and the true Catholic Church. Then the Bishop being in great displeasure with me, because I made doubts in my writing, commanded me to prison, where I was awhile, but afterwards by the means of friends I came out again. Here is the truth of that matter. And as concerning that thing that ye covet most to know, resort to the 6th of John, and be ruled always thereby. Thus fare ye well."

On the 16th of July[1] the sentence of death was carried out. She was taken to Smithfield, "the scene of so many horrors," in a chair; accompanied by three more unfortunates, accused like herself of heresy,—Nicholas Belemian, a Shropshire priest; John Adams, a tailor; and John Lascelles. The four victims were chained to three separate stakes; Anne to one, John Adams to another, Belemian and Lascelles to the third. Upon a raised platform, under S. Bartholomew's Hospital, sat four members of the Council, namely, Wriothesley, the Duke of Norfolk, the aged

political jealousy, and not bigotry that animated Wriothesley. Mr. Froude thinks it possible that the rack was used rather to terrify than to torture, and endeavours to minimize Anne Askew's sufferings ; but it is on record that, at her execution, some days afterwards, she was still in so weak a condition ("so racked," says an eye-witness), that she had to sit in a chair, supported by two sergeants, during the sermon. Bale says she was racked "till the veins and sinews burst."

[1] Foxe says, but undoubtedly by mistake, in the month of June.

Earl of Bedford, and Sir Richard Southwell, along with the Lord Mayor of London, and other eminent personages. Before the fire was made ready, one of them hearing that the martyrs had bags of gunpowder about their bodies, a humane precaution to shorten their sufferings, and fearing that its explosion might drive the faggots about his ears, hastened to express his alarm; but was assured by the Earl of Bedford that there was no danger.

The dreadful preparations completed, Dr. Shaxton, an apostate, then in high favour with the authorities, began his sermon. Anne Askew listened with great attention, approving him when he spoke well; but when he said something amiss, contrary to true Scriptural teaching, interrupting him with the comment, "He speaketh without the Book." At its conclusion, the four victims said their prayers,—Anne Askew "with an angel's countenance and a smiling face,"[1] —while the multitude and concourse of the people was so exceeding great, that the barricades erected round the place of execution could hardly resist the pressure. Wriothesley then sent to Anne Askew letters offering her the King's pardon if she recanted. She refused even to look upon them, exclaiming:—"I came not hither to deny my LORD and Master." Similar letters were conveyed to the other sufferers,—but they joyfully emulated the constancy of their sister, and all encouraging and strengthening one another with words of hope and faith and love,—were rapt into an ecstasy of enthusiasm as if they already saw themselves, like Elijah, borne heavenward in a chariot of fire.

No further cause for delay existing, the Lord Mayor ordered the faggots to be lighted, crying with a loud voice, *Fiat justitia.* "And thus the good Anne Askew, with these blessed Martyrs, being troubled so many manner of ways, and having passed through so many torments, having now ended the last course of her agonies, being compassed in with flames of fire as a blessed sacrifice unto GOD, she slept in the LORD, leaving behind her a singular example of Christian constancy for all men to follow."

As the fire kindled, the sky was all at once overclouded; a peal of thunder broke above the heads of the multitude ("GOD knows," says John Lond, "whether I may truly

[1] See John Lond's narrative in Strype, *Eccles. Mem.*, i. pt. i. 599.

term it a thunder-crack, as the people did in the Gospel, or an angel, or rather GOD's own voice"); and the rain descended. "The sky," says Bale, quaintly, "abhorring so wicked an act, suddenly altered colour, and the clouds from above gave a thunderclap, not at all unlike to what is written in Psalm lxxvi. 8 :—'Thou didst cause judgment to be heard from heaven; the earth feared, and was still.' The elements both declared therein the high displeasure of GOD for so tyrannous a murder of innocents, and also expressly signified His mighty Hand present to the comfort of them which trusted in Him." The Papists necessarily placed a different construction on this sign from above; but in the present day there are few of any creed who will not feel that the sympathy of Heaven rather than its wrath will ever be vouchsafed to those who, for truth and freedom, silently, and "in fearless faith," bow like Anne Askew, their noble souls to death, and win the Martyr's crown!

S. FRANCIS DE SALES:

BISHOP OF GENEVA.

" His faith, perhaps, in some nice tenets might
Be wrong; his life, I'm sure, was in the right,
And I myself, a Catholic will be,
So far, at least, great saint, to pray to thee."
COWLEY.

[*Authorities:*—The following sketch is founded on H. C. Sidney Lear's "S. Francis de Sales," and "The Spirit of S. Francis de Sales," by Jean Pierre Camus, Bishop of Belley. Camus was consecrated Bishop of Belley (a see on the south-west side of that of Geneva), by Francis, at the exceptionally early age of 26. To his long and close intimacy with Francis de Sales we owe much of our knowledge of his character, and many of his wisest sayings, which are collected in "L'Esprit du bien-heureux François de Sales, Evesque de Genève, de M. Jean Pierre Camus, Evesque de Belley." The complete works of Francis de Sales were published in a neat edition at Lyons in 1819. Of the "Introduction to the Devout Life" there are several English translations; and it forms the subject of a lecture by the Dean of Norwich (Dr. Goulburn) in Kempe's "Companions for the Devout Life" (edit. 1877).]

S. FRANCIS DE SALES.

CHAPTER I.

IN religious literature few works more deservedly hold a foremost place than the "Introduction to the Devout Life" of S. Francis de Sales. It belongs to that small and precious category in which we find the "Holy Living and Dying" of Jeremy Taylor, the "Imitatio Christi" of Gerson, the "Spiritual Combat" of Scupoli, the "Devotions" of Bishop Andrewes, and the "Pensées" of Blaise Pascal. With the very best of these it is worthy to be ranked. Unlike most foreign devotional books, its sobriety of tone and freedom from excess of sentiment commend it to English readers. While almost equalling Jeremy Taylor's guide to Holy Living in the opulence and beauty of its imagery, it advantageously differs from it in the brevity and pithiness of its maxims. Another of its special merits is its *practical* character. It is meant and it is suitable for men and women who have to live in the world, and cannot shut themselves out from external temptation in the seclusion of the monastic cell. Its counsel is adapted to their daily wants. "My intention," says S. Francis in his Preface, "is to advise those who live in towns, in families, in the Court, and are by their condition obliged to a public life; who very often, under the colour of a pretended impossibility, will not so much as think of undertaking to live devoutly, imagining that just as no animal presumes to eat of the plant commonly called

Palma Christi, so no person involved in the current of temporal affairs should presume to seek the palm of Christian piety. And so I have shown them as the mother-of-pearl lives in the sea without ever absorbing a single drop of salt water; as near the Chelidonian Isles springs of sweet water rise in the midst of the ocean; and as the fire-fly hovers in the flame without burning her wings; even so a vigorous and steadfast soul may live in the world untainted by worldly breath, finding a well-spring of holy piety amid the brackish waters of secular affairs; and hovering among the flames of earthy concupiscence without singeing the wings of its devout life." Thus, then, it teaches us how we may sanctify " the trivial round, the common task," and make our daily work a road to bring us "nearer GOD." It sets before us a high standard, and it teaches us how to attain to it. It stimulates a yearning after the Devout life, and shows how that yearning may be gratified. It is the guide, philosopher, and friend who is always ready to direct us when we are in doubt, to support us when our feet stumble, to encourage us when we fall into despondency. If it occasionally verge too near the doctrine of Quietism, and do not sufficiently make clear the difference between a devout submission to the Divine Will and that acquiescence in it which annihilates the soul's moral force, even this tendency is not without its attraction to a soul weary of constant struggle and wrestle, and anxious for the refreshment of repose. On the whole, we feel that Marie de Medicis did not place too great a value on the book when she bound up in gold and gems the copy which she sent to James I. of England.

The "Introduction to a Devout Life" is divided into five parts. The first consists of "Counsels and Practices" designed to lead the soul forward to a formal dedication of all its powers and faculties upon GOD's holy altar. It begins with a definition of Devotion as the real spiritual sweetness which takes away its bitterness from every sorrow, and prevents consolations from disagreeing with the soul; which cures the poor of their sadness and the rich of their arrogance, keeps the oppressed from a feeling of desolation and the prosperous from insolence, averts grief and gloom from the lowly, and dissipation from social life, is as warmth in winter and refreshing dew in summer. It is the love of GOD intensified, and the love of our fellow-creatures as a corollary from it. Jacob's ladder is set before us as a type of the Devout Life : the two poles which support the steps are types of Prayer which seeks the Divine love, and the Sacraments which bestow that love; while the steps themselves are simply the grades or degrees of love by which we pass from virtue to virtue, either descending by good deeds on behalf of our neighbour, or ascending by contemplation to a loving union with GOD. In this sense Devotion is the perfection of Charity. If Charity or love be the milk of life, Devotion is the cream ; if it be a fruitful plant, Devotion is the flower ; if it be a precious stone, Devotion is its lustre; if it be a precious balm, Devotion is its perfume, even that sweet odour which comforts men and rejoices angels.

After demonstrating the suitableness of Devotion for every Vocation and Profession, S. Francis enlarges on the need of a Guide for those who would enter upon and make progress in the Devout Life. The pious Princess S. Elizabeth obeyed the direction of the venerable Conrad ; and Holy Scripture tells us that "a faithful friend is a strong defence." But the first step for all of us must be the cleansing of the soul, and the first purification must be from mortal sin. After this, we may aim at the conquest of all sinful affections by keeping ever before us a sense of the great evils which sin brings with it. This fear and this contrition we may acquire by careful and constant use of the Meditations prepared by S. Francis for the purpose :—Meditations, brief, but instructive, on Creation, the End for which we were created, the Gifts of GOD, Sin, Death, Judgment ; Hell, Paradise, the Choice between Heaven and Hell, and the Determination in favour of a Devout life. This Part closes with a general Protest, made with the view of confirming the Soul's resolution to serve GOD, and intended to be read over before the priest after a general confession, and previously to receiving absolution from him.

The second Part treats of the Means of Grace by which the soul is assisted in its cultivation of the Christian Graces. These may be summarised under the heads of Prayer, Meditation, Study of the Scriptures, the Public Services of the Church, Communion, and Confession. The weakest portion is that which refers to the hearing and reading of GOD's

A A

Word, for it says too little of the Bible and too much of the writings of holy men, excellent in themselves, but no sufficient substitute for the living oracles of GOD. In other respects, this second part of the treatise is, as Dean Goulburn remarks, not the least masterly, nor the least characteristic of the author's mind, nor the least edifying. Thus, he says of Prayer, that it opens the understanding to the splendour of the Divine Light, and the will to the warmth of the Heavenly Love. Nothing can so effectually relieve the mind of its many ignorances, or free the will from its perverse affections. It is as a healing water which causes the roots of our good desires to send forth fresh shoots, which washes away the soul's imperfections, which allays the thirst of passion.

Then, as to Spiritual Retirement, he says, very beautifully :—" The birds have their nests upon the lofty trees, and the stag retreats to the dense coverts to obtain protection from the sun's burning heat; even so should our hearts daily choose some resting-place, either Mount Calvary or the Sacred Wounds, or some other spot close to CHRIST, whither they can retire at will to seek rest and refreshment amid toil, and to be as in a fortress, guarded against temptation. Blessed, indeed, is the soul which can truly say :—' Thou, LORD, art my Refuge, my Stronghold, my Stay, my Shelter in the storm and in the noontide heat.'" He adds :—" There are few social duties of importance enough to prevent an occasional retirement of the heart into this sacred solitude. When S. Catharine of Siena was deprived by her parents of any place or time for prayer and meditation, our LORD inspired her with the thought of making a little interior oratory in her mind, into which she could withdraw her thoughts, and so enjoy a holy solitude amid her outward duties. And thenceforward, when assailed by the world, she was able to be indifferent, because, so she said, she could retire within her private oratory, and find comfort with her Heavenly Bridegroom. So she advised her spiritual daughters to make a retirement within their heart, in which they might at times abide. Do you in like manner let your heart withdraw to such a privacy, where, apart from all men, you can lay it bare, and treat face to face with GOD, even as David says that he watched like 'a pelican in the wilderness, or an owl in the desert, or a sparrow sitting alone upon the housetop.' .... When the blessed Elzear, Count of Arian-en-Provence, had been long separated from his pious and beloved wife Delphine, she sent a messenger to inquire after him, and he returned this answer :—' I am well, dear wife, and if you would see me, seek me in the Wounded Side of our Dear LORD JESUS ; that is my sure dwelling-place, and elsewhere you will seek in vain.' Surely he who spoke these words was a true Christian Knight."

The illustrations which S. Francis employs and the anecdotes which he introduces are always felicitous. Thus :— " When S. Fulgentius, Bishop of Ruspe, heard Theodoric, King of the Goths, harangue a general assembly of Roman nobles, and beheld their splendour, he exclaimed :—' O GOD, how glorious must Thy Heavenly Jerusalem be, if even earthly Rome be such as this !' And if this world can afford so much gratification to mere earthly lovers of vanity, what must there not be reserved hereafter for those who love the truth ?" Again :—" A great man of our own day, Francis Borgia, then Duke of Candia, was wont while hunting to indulge in many devout imaginations. ' I used to consider,' he said, ' how that the falcon returns to his master's wrist, and suffers him to hood his eyes or chain him to his perch, and yet men are so perverse as to refuse to turn at GOD's call.' S. Basil the Great observes, that the rose with its thorns preaches a lesson to men. ' All that is pleasant in this life,'—it seems to say,—' is mingled with sadness ; no joy is altogether pure ; all enjoyment is liable to be marred by regrets ; marriage is saddened by widowhood, children bring anxiety, glory often turns to shame, neglect follows upon honour, weariness on pleasure, sickness on health.' Truly the rose is a lovely flower," the Saint continues, " but it moves me to sadness, reminding me as it does that for my sin the earth was condemned to bring forth thorns." Yet again :—" It is said that Mithridates, King of Pontus, who invented the poison called after him *Mithridate,* so thoroughly impregnated his system with it, that when eventually he sought to poison himself that he might not be led into slavery by the Romans, he never could succeed. The SAVIOUR instituted the most holy Sacrament of the Eucharist, truly containing His Body and His Blood, in order that they who eat it may live for ever. And, therefore, whosoever receives it frequently and devoutly, so strengthens and confirms the life and health of the soul, that it is hardly possible for him to be poisoned by any evil desires."

Specially valuable in this second Part is the method of Meditation recommended to the reader. It is neither too curt and concise, nor too full of details; the disciple is not fettered by a crowd of harassing regulations, and yet the rules laid down are amply sufficient for his guidance. He who would deepen and strengthen the spiritual life should carefully study, and no less carefully follow, the directions here given by S. Francis. After the preparation, made by calling to mind the immediate Presence of GOD, and invoking His assistance, certain considerations follow, which constitute the body of the exercise. These suggest "the affections and resolutions;" and then come three concluding acts,—thanksgiving, oblation, and petition, with, last of all, " a little nosegay or bouquet of devotion :"—" When walking in a beautiful garden," he says, " most of us are wont to cull a few blossoms as we pass along, which we preserve, and the scent of which delights us during the day. So, when the mind explores some mystery in meditation, it is well to select one or more points that have specially arrested the attention, and are most likely to be helpful through the day, and this should be done at once before you quit the subject of your meditation, walking alone and in the same place."

The third Part embodies counsels concerning the practice of Virtue. I think, with Dean Goulburn,[1] that it is inferior to the chapters in Jeremy Taylor's "Holy Living" which take up this subject, but then the objects of the two writers are different, and so are their theological systems. The virtue on which Francis, as might be expected, lays the greatest stress, is that of Humility, and no doubt it is the virtue which forms the groundwork of the Christian economy, and lends its highest grace to the Christian life. Gentleness, patience, obedience, purity, upon these he also insists very strongly, and he has much to say that is worth being listened to upon Poverty of spirit, true and false Friendship, the practice of Bodily Mortification, Modesty in Dress, propriety

[1] "Companions of the Devout Life," p. 61.

of Conversation, hasty judgments, evil-speaking, and amusements and recreation. A treasury of wise counsel might be compiled from this part of S. Francis's treatise; and it is important to note that the counsel is eminently *practical*, the counsel of a large mind and larger heart, which have studied the outer world observantly, and analysed the mysteries of humanity. I select a few specimens :—

"Fasting and labour both exhaust and subdue the body. If your work be necessary or profitable to GOD's glory, I would rather see you enduring the exhaustion which comes from work than the exhaustion which comes from fasting. As a general rule, it is better to store up more physical strength than is absolutely needful, than to damage it more than is necessary. It seems to me that we ought to have in great reverence that which our SAVIOUR and Redeemer JESUS CHRIST said to His disciples :—' Eat such things as are set before you.' To my mind the virtue is greater in eating whatever is offered you just as it comes, whether you like it or not, than in always choosing the worst; for though the latter course may seem more ascetic, the former involves the greater submission of will, because it requires you to give up not merely your taste but your choice; and it is no slight austerity to hold up one's likings in one's hand, and place them at the mercy of all kinds of accidents."

"A quiet cheerfulness should be your aim in society. S. Romuald and S. Anthony are greatly lauded because, notwithstanding their asceticism, their countenances and words were always lively and courteous."

"Physicians are greatly influenced in their judgment of a man's condition by the state of his tongue; and our words are a true test of the state of our soul. 'By thy words thou shalt be justified, and by thy words thou shalt be condemned,' says the SAVIOUR. We are apt to apply the hand quickly to the place where we feel pain; and too, the tongue is quick in pointing out what we love. Even as the bee touches nought but honey with his tongue, so should your lips be ever sweetened with your GOD, knowing nothing more pleasant than to praise and bless His Holy Name. As we are told that when S. Francis uttered the Name of the LORD, he seemed to feel the sweetness lingering on his lips, and could not let it go."

"There is a light-hearted talk, full of modest life and gaiety, the Eutrapelia of the Greeks,—which we should call good conversation,—wherein we may obtain an innocent and kindly amusement out of the trivial occurrences which human imperfections afford. Only take care that this seemly mirth goes not to an extreme, and becomes ridicule. Ridicule excites mirth at the cost of one's neighbour; seemly vivacity and playful fun never lose sight of a trustful, kindly courtesy which can inflict wounds upon none. When the religious around him would fain have discussed serious matters with S. Louis at meal-time, he would reply :— 'This is not the time for grave discourse, but for general converse and cheerful recreation,'—out of consideration for his courtiers. Let our hours of recreation always be so spent, that we may win all eternity through our devotion."

"If one can remove from the object of an unworthy attachment, it is most desirable that one should do so. He who has been bitten by a viper cannot heal his wound in the presence of another suffering from the like injury; and so, too, one bitten with an injurious fancy will be unable to shake it off while he is near his fellow-victim. Change of scene is exceedingly helpful in subduing the excitement and restlessness of sorrow or love. S. Ambrose tells a story in his Second Book on Penitence, of a young man who, returning home after a long journey completely cured of a foolish affection, met the object of his former inclinations, who stopped him, saying :—'Do you not know me? I am still myself.' 'That may be,' was the answer, 'but I am not :'—so thoroughly and so happily had absence changed him. And S. Augustine tells us how, after the death of his dear friend, he soothed his grief by leaving Tagaste and going to Carthage."

"It is well for everybody to select some special virtue at which to aim, not as neglecting the rest, but as an object to the mind and a pursuit. S. John, Bishop of Alexandria, saw in a vision a lovely maiden, brighter than the sun, clothed in shining garments, and wearing a crown of olive-leaves. She said to him :—'I am the King's eldest daughter, and if thou wilt have me for thy friend, I will bring thee to behold His Face.' Then he understood that it was pity for the poor which GOD thus commended to him, and thenceforth applied himself so strenuously to practise it, that he is known to all men as S. John the Almoner. Eulogius Alexandrinus desired to devote himself wholly to GOD; but he had not courage either to adopt the solitary life, or to put himself under obedience, and therefore he took a wretched beggar, seething in dirt and leprosy, to live with him, vowing to honour and tend him as a servant does his lord and master. After a while, both desiring hugely to separate, they took counsel of the great S. Anthony, who said :—' Beware of parting company, my sons, for both of you are near your end; and if the Angel find you not together, you will be in danger of losing your crowns.' S. Louis esteemed it a privilege to visit the hospitals, where he was wont to minister to the sick with his own royal hands. S. Francis cherished Poverty above all things, and called her his Bride. S. Dominic preached the Gospel, and his Order thence take the name of the Preaching Friars. S. Gregory the Great especially rejoiced to receive pilgrims after the manner of faithful Abraham, and like him entertained the King of Glory unawares. Tobit gave himself up to the pious work of burying the dead. S. Elizabeth, although she was a mighty princess, loved pre-eminently to humble herself. When S. Catharine of Genoa became a widow, she devoted herself to work in a hospital. Cassian tells us how a certain devout maiden once besought S. Athanasius to assist her in cultivating the grace of patience; and he gave her as companion a poor widow, who was ill-humoured, irritable, and altogether hard to bear with; her incessant fretfulness gave the pious lady continual occasion to practise patient gentleness. And so some of GOD'S servants give themselves up to nursing the sick, helping the poor, instructing little children in the faith, reclaiming the fallen, building churches, adorning the altar, making peace among men. Therein may they be likened unto embroideresses who weave all manner of golden and silver silks on various grounds so as to produce beautiful flowers. Just so the devout souls who undertake some special act of devotion use it as the ground of their spiritual embroidery, and frame the other graces upon it, ordering their doings and affections better by means of this principal thread which runs through all."

The fourth Part contains some needful Counsels concerning Temptations, or, more correctly speaking, concerning the Hindrances to a Devout Life, for it deals not only with the larger temptations and greater occasions for sin, but with those "trials and crosses" to which even the most faithful soul is subject; such as anxiety and despondency, spiritual dryness and barrenness; and it assists us and encourages us to prevail against them. It shows how they arise, how they may be fostered, and how they should be resisted. The thought and the suggestion of evil are described, and the ways by which they may be expelled from the mind before they gain possession of it. Thus we are led on to the fifth and last Part, which instructs us in the necessity and the means of renewing and confirming those holy purposes to which we have already dedicated ourselves. "There is no clock," says Francis, "be it never so good, but must be wound up twice a day, morning and evening, and at least once a year taken to pieces, so that the rust it has gathered may be removed, what is burst or broken duly mended, and what is worn repaired. In like manner, he that has a true care of his heart will wind it up to GOD morning and evening, and many times examine into its condition, redressing and rectifying it; and at least once a year will take the works to pieces, to examine them carefully,—that is, all its affections and passions,—so as to repair whatever may be amiss. And as the clockmaker with some delicate oil anoints the wheels, the springs, and all the moving parts of his clock, so that its motions may be nimbler and the works less liable to rust; so the devout soul, after this process of self-examination, must be anointed with the Sacraments of Confession and the Eucharist. This exercise will repair the forces decayed by time, will kindle the heart, make freshly green again your good resolutions, and cause the graces of your mind to blossom anew."

A certain time every year is to be set apart for a retreat, during which you must, so to speak, "take stock" of your inner life. The original dedication of yourself to GOD's service must be reconsidered, and the circumstances under which it was made; this review will lead to acts of thanksgiving and prayer. After which you will examine how far ou have advanced; taking first, your relations towards

GOD; next, your relations towards your own soul; third, your relations to your neighbour; and lastly, your affections and desires. Then will follow certain meditations calculated to assist us in the renewal of our good purposes; on the excellency of the soul, the comeliness of virtue, the examples of the saints, the love of CHRIST, the love of GOD. They bring us to one grand conclusion, that the whole world is not worth one soul, and that the soul is worth but little without its good resolutions—the good resolutions, which, prayerfully carried out, fulfil and complete the Devout Life. And thus, as Dean Goulburn says, this most methodical, as well as most beautiful, winning, and persuasive work returns to its point of departure through a large circle of elevating and purifying sentiment, which, copious indeed, is never diffuse; like to some noble river, which, rising from the fountains of the great deep, winds through the various scenery of pasture and cornfield, glade and forest, until it pours itself into the ocean, and mingles again with its native waters.

I quote the concluding paragraph :—

"Finally, I beseech you by all that is sacred in heaven and earth, by your own Baptism, by the breast which JESUS sucked, by the tender heart which He bears towards you, by the bowels of compassion in which you place your hope, be steadfast and persistent in this most blessed undertaking to live a Devout Life. Our days glide away; death draws near. Says S. Gregory Nazianzen :—'The trumpet sounds a recall, in order that every one may make ready, for judgment is at hand!' When S. Symphorian was led to his martyrdom, his mother cried out to him :—'My son, my son, remember Life Eternal; look to Heaven, and behold Him Who reigneth there; for the short span of this life will soon be ended.' Even so would I say to you: Look to Heaven, and lose it not for earth; look at Hell, and plunge not into it for the sake of this passing existence; look at JESUS CHRIST, and deny Him not for the pleasures of this world; and if the Devout Life seem sometimes dull and onerous, join in the sweet strain of S. Francis of Assisi—

> 'Tanto è il bene ch' io aspetto
> Ch' ogni pena m'è diletto. . .'

'So great the bliss that I shall gain
I give no heed to earthly pain. . .'

Glory be to JESUS, to Whom, with the FATHER and the HOLY GHOST, be all praise and honour, now and ever, and to all eternity. Amen."

I proceed to sketch the life of the author of this immortal book, who, if we consider the character of the warfare he stoutly maintained against "the wiles of the Devil," may justly be classed among the Heroes of the Cross.

CHAPTER II.

AT the Château de Sales, near Annecy, on the 21st of August, 1567, was born, of a noble family, Francis Bonaventure de Sales. He was a seven months' child, his birth taking place prematurely after his mother's presenting herself at the church of Annecy in order to dedicate the unborn to GOD's service. How thoroughly he accepted and fulfilled this dedication, the story of his life will show.

It is said that the first connected words he uttered were :—" GOD and Mamma love me." Nurtured and led up in the ways of an earnest piety, he was happy in the home atmosphere which he breathed in his early years. When old enough to learn, he was taught the Catechism and the rudiments of the Faith by the Abbé Déage, and after receiving his lesson, he delighted to gather round him the children of his father's tenants by the ringing of a little bell, and to retail to them the knowledge he had thus acquired. He was a sweet-tempered, dutiful, and pure-minded child; but he was not that "perfect monster which the world never saw," except in children's story-books. The good in his nature, however, largely predominated over the evil, and it was encouraged and developed by wise governance. At six years of age he was sent to school. There he did not astonish his tutors by the brilliancy of a precocious genius; but it was observed that whatever he did, he strove to do as well as it could be done. It has been well said that this continued a characteristic throughout life. His favourite sayings were, " Peu et bon" and " Assez tôt, si assez bien ;" and the Bishop of Belley, his devoted friend, remarks that "Hurry he was wont to call the greatest enemy of true devotion," and that "he always urged people to do a little well, rather than a great deal imperfectly."

When ten years old he was Confirmed and made his first Communion; and in the following year, at his urgent request, he was formally consecrated to the priesthood by receiving the tonsure (Sept. 20, 1578). From his quiet school life at Annecy, his father, in 1580, determined to remove him to the College de Navarre in Paris, where it was customary for the young nobles of Savoy to complete their education. But its worldly tone and gaieties revolted him, and he obtained permission to transfer himself to the College de Clermont. He was accompanied by the Abbé Déage as his tutor, and his education was conducted in the most liberal spirit. Not only did he pursue those studies specially appropriate to the vocation he had chosen, but he acquired the accomplishments proper to his social position. He learned to ride and fence and dance, and this training greatly enhanced the physical gifts he had received from nature. Of a fine person, tall and singularly well-made, with regular features, large blue eyes, a delicate complexion, and a radiant smile, he seemed born to shine in courtly circles, where his grace of manner alone would have won distinction; but his heart never swerved from the choice it had voluntarily made. His thoughts were always on lofty subjects, the mysteries of life and death, the infinite wisdom of the Creator, the infinite love of CHRIST; and he refreshed and strengthened them by frequent perusal of spiritual books, one of which he always carried about him. Among these, at a later date, his favourite was Scupoli's "Spiritual Combat." He made considerable progress in rhetoric and philosophy, but applied himself with more zeal and satisfaction to the study of theology, while he learned Hebrew and Exegesis under Génébrard, the Benedictine. It may have been some questions suggested to his active intellect during this course of inquiry that led him, when he was seventeen, into the trial of a great fear. His faith wavered, and he became possessed with a dread that he should fall a victim to the first mortal sin that assailed him. For some time he endured exceeding anguish; but, rallying all his energies, he manfully strove against the temptation, and by redoubling his work and his prayers successfully overcame it. Thereafter he entered upon a life of so much asceticism that the Abbé Déage, fearing he would disappoint the hopes his father had conceived of a brilliant future by assuming the monk's cowl, recommended his pupil's removal to the University of Padua.

Thither, in 1587, he accordingly repaired, and began the study of jurisprudence. But to no other calling than that of the priesthood did the young man's aspirations point; and, not without some reluctance on the part of his father, it was at length decided that for this only should he be trained. Under the direction of the Jesuit Father, Possevin, he applied himself with grave resolution to the study of Holy Scripture, and the writings of the Fathers, S. Bonaventura and S. Thomas Aquinas. His mode of life was ordered by certain rules which he had prescribed for himself. His first thought on waking was to be one of praise; he would call to mind the shepherds at Bethlehem, and the holy women at the sepulchre, dedicating like them the dawn of day to his risen LORD, the *Lux Mundi*. Daily would he hear mass with all earnestness of soul; and a certain time was to be devoted to meditation. If he woke during the night he would kindle his heart with the words:—"At midnight there was a cry made, 'Behold the Bridegroom cometh, go ye out to meet Him!'" Remembering that CHRIST was born in the hours of darkness, he would ask of Him to be born anew in his heart; while the nightshadows should remind him of the darkness of indifference and sin, he would pray the LORD to dispel them with His own life-giving light. Yea, he would recollect the words of the Psalmist:—"Lift up your heads, and praise the LORD," and "I water my couch with my tears." Should any nocturnal terrors afflict him, he would remember that his Guardian Angel was by his side, and say:—"'He that keepeth Israel shall neither slumber nor sleep. He shall defend thee under His wings, and thou shalt be safe under His feathers. Thou shalt not be afraid for any terror by night. The LORD is my light and my salvation, of whom then shall I be afraid?"[1]

After laying down rules for his meditation, he proceeded to regulate his relations with the world. "I must neither despise," he says, "nor seem to shun any one in a proud critical spirit; but at the same time I must avoid too great freedom even with my best friends. I must neither do nor say anything wanting in decorum, and must specially avoid whatever may wound or annoy others, giving due honour to all. I will strive to be modest in speech, saying little, so as rather to be thought too silent than too talkative, affecting neither austerity nor melancholy.

"To all I will be friendly, but intimate with few; for it is hard to turn general intercourse to good account, and not to suffer from contact with impure minds. I will seek to attain unaffected gentleness, simple modesty, ease devoid of all traces of pride, kindness which absolutely refrains from contradiction, save when it is a duty, honest cordiality and frankness according to the person I am with.

"I will strive to adapt my intercourse to the position and character of those I meet, giving honour where honour is due."

In 1591 Francis took his Doctor's degree; after which he made a short tour in Italy, and in 1592, after a twelve years' course of study, rejoined his family at their then residence, the Château de Thuilles. As eldest son and heir he assumed the title of Seigneur de Villeroget; and in obedience to the wish of his father, who had not wholly renounced the hope of a distinguished secular career for his brilliant son, passed a legal examination at Chambery prior to his admission as advocate of the senate of Savoy. He himself, however, was firm in his adhesion to the dedication which his mother had made of her son; and his resolution was strengthened by an incident which he accepted as a warning from Heaven. His horse stumbled, one day, as he rode through the forest of Sonaz: and his sword, dropping from its belt, fell to the ground, where it lay, forming with the scabbard a perfect cross. At first

[1] "Life of S. Francis de Sales," by H. C. Sidney Lear, p. 25.

Francis thought nothing of the occurrence, except to fasten both sword and belt more securely; but the same thing occurring a second and a third time, he could not but see in it a sign that he was called to be a warrior of the Cross. A last struggle took place between the young man's religious convictions and his father's ambitious desires; the former prevailed, and on the 8th of June, 1593, Francis de Sales received minor orders. He preached his first sermon on the Octave of the Feast of Corpus Christi. " It is remarkable," says his English biographer, "that in spite of all his gifts of facility and composure, Francis underwent the most painful nervousness and timidity on this occasion, to such an extent, that when the bell began to sound announcing the sermon, he was seized with such a fit of trembling as to be unable to stand. There was but one remedy. Falling on his knees before GOD, the future Saint and Apostle implored GOD to be with him, to use the weak, human instrument to His own glory, and to speak through his lips, and so, rising up calm and strong in the power of the LORD, and losing all self-consciousness and timidity, he went to the Cathedral, where an expectant crowd eagerly awaited one so well known, and so personally interesting to most of them; and, realising to the full his responsibility before GOD, in preaching His word to CHRIST's flock, mounted the pulpit with even, unhurried steps, and in that sonorous, exquisitely modulated voice, which was one of his special gifts, fulfilled his appointed office." His sermon was instinct with a glowing eloquence which moved his hearers even to tears; and made such an impression on Bishop Granier, who had ordained him, that, after it was over, he went from one to the other, saying:—" Well, what think you of my son? Are not his words wondrous, and is not his utterance yet more so? Truly he is an Apostle, marvellous in word and deed, and GOD hath sent him to bring salvation to our people."

Thus did he enter upon his career of active evangelism, winning golden opinions from all men by the simplicity of his habits, the modesty of his demeanour, the beautiful purity of his life. He founded at this time a Confraternity called the " Penitents of the Holy Cross," of which he became the first Prior and his father a member. In the same year, 1593, he was ordained Deacon and Priest. Thenceforward his reverence for the sacerdotal office, and his gratitude to the Eternal Goodness Which had placed him in it, inspired him with such a spirit of self-watchfulness, that he seemed wholly transformed, as you might see in his face, his eyes, his bearing, his words, his actions, which were all stamped with a something well-nigh angelic, almost divine, which constrained men to love and venerate him. He made three solemn resolutions for his guidance, from which it may safely be said, he never departed. First, that the holy atmosphere of the Altar should be carried into every action, so that each moment of the day should be a preparation for the morrow's sacrifice : and if he were asked why he did anything, he might always be able to answer :—" I am making ready to celebrate." Second, that he would always approach the Altar in such a spirit as he would desire to have on his death-bed, and before the Judgment Seat of GOD. And, third, that he would aim at a perpetual union with JESUS CHRIST, through loving imitation and recollection, so as in very deed to be "one with Him."

Of his early labours as a preacher we obtain a glimpse from a remark he once made to his " Boswell," the Bishop of Belley :—" When I became Provost, I preached perpetually everywhere, in the cathedral, the parish churches, and for every small confraternity. I never refused to preach, acting on the principle of 'Give to them that ask you.' My dear father, who had spent most of his life in the camp or at Court, used to hear the bells ringing, and would ask who preached? 'Who but your son?' was often the answer. One day he took me aside, and said :—' Provost, you preach too often. Even on week days the bells go, and it is always the same story, the Provost, the Provost ! It was not so in my day, for sermons were much fewer. But then, to be sure, GOD knows they were something like sermons ! full of learning, carefully prepared ; more Latin and Greek in one than you put into a dozen ! Everybody admired them, and ran after them as if they were seeking manna ! But now you make preaching so common that nobody cares for it or for you !' You see my dear old father spoke to the best of his judgment. He meant no harm, but he looked at the matter from the world's viewpoint. Of this you may be sure; there is no fear of our preaching too much; 'nunquam satis dicitur quod nunquam satis discitur,' especially surrounded as we are by heresy, which is mainly spread by means of preaching, and must be counteracted by its own weapon."

As a preacher, S. Francis had a style distinctively peculiar to him. He had all the pithiness, directness, and lucid force of a Latimer, with much of the opulence of imagery and illustration of a Jeremy Taylor. There was nothing controversial in his sermons, and very little of dogmatic theology; he preferred to deal with the practical side of religion, to treat it as a matter of everyday duty, to enlarge on the gifts and graces that make up the Christian life. He loved his hearers to go away, not commenting on the eloquence of the preacher or the complexity of the doctrine, but resolving that they would in the future do something in the name and for the sake of CHRIST. "A man," he would say, "may show forth his erudition and power of utterance in a fine sermon, but the true sign that GOD speaks through his mouth is when his words convert sinners, and induce people to renounce their bad habits. The only real fruit of preaching is the overthrow of sin and the increase of righteousness. GOD sends forth His preachers now as CHRIST His Apostles, 'that they should go and bring forth fruit, and that their fruit should remain!'" He studied the extremest simplicity, and was careful to put what he had to say into brief strong sentences, which could be easily remembered. "The more you overcharge your hearer's memory," he would say, "the weaker you make it; just as you extinguish a lamp by overfilling it with oil, or kill a plant by overwatering." And again :—"When a sermon is too long, the end makes one forget the middle, and the middle the beginning."

But while he set so high a value on sermons, he was far from underrating the other offices of a priest. It will readily be understood that to serve at the Altar was for Francis de Sales not less a duty than a privilege, and it was seldom that he failed to celebrate the Eucharistic Sacrament daily. To the labours of the Confessional he gave himself up with assiduity, and was eminently fitted for their successful discharge by his knowledge of the human heart, his tender wisdom, and his broad vivid sympathies. At the age of twenty-seven, he was appointed Grand Penitentiary of the diocese, and persons of all ranks and ages flocked to him as their spiritual adviser. To visit the sick and relieve the poor was a work dear to one whose love towards his neighbour was inferior only—or rather was part of—his love towards his LORD and SAVIOUR. Yet, many and weighty as were these duties, there was yet another which he did not neglect. He knew that bricks cannot be made without straw, that an empty hand cannot sow; and he would say that priests ought not merely to cultivate their minds in preparation for their office, but that, as they were called upon to teach others, they should be continually teaching themselves. To build up others (*ædificare*) one must first build up oneself (*ædificari*). Unlike too many modern clergymen, who seem to lose the key of their libraries when they enter upon a pastoral charge, he set apart a portion of every day for reading; and the manuscript volumes which he left behind him attest his industry in analysing and criticising the books he read.

Chablais, a district of the Pays de Vaud, had alternately been in the possession of the Bernese and the Duke of Savoy, and, according as the one or the other prevailed, its inhabitants were dragooned into Calvinism or Catholicism. Passing into the hands of the Duke of Savoy in 1593, with some prospect of staying there, the Church once more desired to regain her children. For this purpose a special mission was considered necessary, and to lead such a mission Bishop Granier could find no one better fitted than the Provost. His father, by this time far advanced in years, was unwilling that he should be involved in an enterprise which must be laborious, and might be dangerous. Francis, however, was filled with a holy zeal which overcame the parental opposition, and accompanied by his cousin, Louis de Sales, he set out on the 14th of September, 1594. Day after day, in the bitter winter weather, he went to and fro, preaching and teaching, regardless of the opposition of the Genevan ministers. His faith and fervour were tested by many trials. On one occasion, losing his way in a wood, he was forced to climb a tree to escape the pursuit of a hungry pack of wolves; and overcome with hunger and fatigue, he tied himself with his girdle to a branch, lest he should fall. Next morning some peasants discovered him in a state of insensibility; but moved with compassion, they conveyed him to their hut, and tended him until he recovered consciousness. Yet again: a certain Genevan, who had taken an oath to kill him, concealed himself in a place where the Provost was sure to pass. The would-be murderer fired thrice: but though a skilful marksman, his gun missed fire each time, and Francis went on his way in safety, unconscious of the peril he had incurred. It was reported that he had sold himself to the devil, whose marks of ownership might be seen upon his body; and one day a furious crowd surrounded him, flinging this calumny in his teeth, and maltreating him sorely. With a serene smile he turned upon his persecutors:—"This, good friends," he exclaimed, as he made the sign of the Cross, "is the only mark which I bear on my body, and the only charm I use; but it is all-powerful; and protected by it I fear no storm that man can raise, am daunted by no opposing hosts." Arriving in a Calvinist village at nightfall, no peasant would receive him beneath his roof; and he and his cousin passed the night in the village bakehouse, which they found open, and still warm.

With a diligence that never relaxed and an enthusiasm that never failed, Francis continued his missionary work; and so great was the combined influence of his teaching and his daily life, that hundreds abandoned the Calvinistic heresy. It became necessary to furnish him with a staff of clergy, whom he animated with his own loving spirit, and led on from victory to victory. It must indeed have been difficult to resist the precepts of one who enforced and illustrated them by an example so powerful. On leaving his church, after preaching a vigorous sermon on the text,—"If any smite you on one cheek, turn to him the other also," a Calvinist, with an air of insolence, asked him whether he would be ready to act on his own teaching, if he received a blow that moment; adding, in a tone of contempt:—"I trow you be one of those who say and do not!" "Friend," answered the Missionary, calmly: "I know what I ought to do, but I know not what I might do, for I am feeble and frail; nevertheless, I trust in GOD, Who can make of the weakest reed a pillar of strength. But were I not to endure such an insult with a Christian spirit, you should remember that the Gospel which you quote, also bids you 'observe and do' what the preacher teaches, while it deprives you of excuse for evil doing by warning you not to take pattern by his works." The man rejoined :—" Our SAVIOUR did not offer His other cheek to the soldiers who struck Him." "Do you count Him, then, among those who say and do not? Say, rather, that He gave His whole body to them that smote Him." At this gentle answer the Calvinist turned away, softened if not convinced.

Gentleness and the tenderest sympathy, and a spirit of love and charity were weapons which Francis always used. He was unable to have recourse to two-handed swords and heavy battle-axes; he did not know how to wield them. The Bishop of Belley tells us that his serene mildness was almost inconceivable. One might say that he was meekness personified, rather than a man simply gifted with that grace; and thus he obtained such an ascendancy that every one yielded to him as a matter of course, while he, on his part, sought to give up everything to others, desiring nothing, except to see them serving GOD, and saving their souls. "It is so much easier," he would remark, "to adapt ourselves to others, than to seek to bend *them* to our opinions and will. The human mind is like a mirror that easily reflects the images cast upon it. In all things we ought to 'bring our gifts before the Altar,' not beyond that, inasmuch as we must not offend GOD; nor do I mean that we must not rebuke the sinner; only charity requires us to wait for the season when he will be best prepared to receive the remedy we would apply to him. Loud and immoderate zeal does more harm than good. Some people spoil everything by attempting too much : remember the old proverb, 'Chi va piano, va sano.'"[1]

The Provost's success in the Chablais mission pointed him out to Bishop Granier, who was gray with years and spent with the burden of duties to which he felt he was daily growing more and more inadequate, as the man who could best assist and support him in the post of Coadjutor.

[1] Who goes softly, goes safely.

He obtained the Duke of Savoy's consent to the appointment without difficulty; but it was not so easy to overcome the Provost's reluctance. Again and again he refused. The Bishop obtained the interposition of his parents; brought to bear on him the influence of the Chapter; plied him with incessant petitions, but could obtain no other answer than a negative. Finally, he betook himself to Cardinal de Medicis, who wrote to Francis and urged him to consent. Francis was at a loss for a reply; but after a few minutes of silent thought, he invited the Cardinal's messenger, the Abbé Critain, to accompany him to church, where each might say a Mass, and invite the guidance of the HOLY SPIRIT. The Abbé Critain first said Mass, Francis serving him; then Francis said Mass, and the Abbé served; after which for a long time Francis knelt before the Altar, laying bare his heart to GOD, and communing with Him in silent ecstasy. On rising, he said to the Abbé:—"Tell the Bishop that I have always dreaded the Episcopate, but since he persists in thrusting it upon me, I am ready to obey; and that if ever I do any good in it, it will be by virtue of his prayers. Say nothing, I beseech you, of what has passed." Bishop Granier, on receiving this welcome intelligence, exclaimed:—"Hitherto I have done little enough for my diocese, but now indeed I have accomplished a great work, having secured my dear son, Francis de Sales, as my coadjutor and successor."

The mental stress through which he had passed resulted in a dangerous illness; but, recovering, he went on a mission to Rome from the Duke of Savoy. The Pope received him with special distinction, and he drew all hearts towards him by the fascination of his personal gifts and the charm of his sanctity of life. Having satisfactorily discharged his errand, and received the Papal confirmation of his appointment, Francis returned to his diocese, and entered with fervour on his episcopal work. One of his earliest measures was to establish at Thonon the Sainte Maison as a kind of university and clergy-house, to serve as a diocesan centre and rallying-point. "It was to be ruled by a prefect and seven secular priests, who were to supply the parochial needs of Thonon, and educate the seven choir boys, who, it was hoped, were the beginning of a Seminary. To these priests were added a certain number of Capucin Fathers, whose mission was to preach in the surrounding country, as well as masters for an intended college for public instruction; while a fourth department was provided for the reception of persons desirous of religious instruction, who might also be taught ordinary handicrafts, whereby to maintain themselves." He had scarcely completed the organisation of the Sainte Maison when he was called away to take a last farewell of his aged father, who had been seized with a mortal sickness, and died on the 4th of April, 1601. He was not able, however, to receive his last sigh, having been ordered to preach the Lent Sermons at Annecy.

In 1602, Francis was sent by Bishop Granier to represent the condition of the diocese to Henry IV., and seek his assistance. The necessary arrangements were so slowly matured that he was detained at Paris until the following autumn. He preached constantly, and with his usual success, winning over many souls from their worldly entanglements. The persuasiveness of his eloquence and the attraction that lay in his earnest and gentle manner were well described by Cardinal du Perron, who on one occasion said:—"GOD has certainly given M. de Genève the key of hearts. If you want only to convince men, bring them to me and I will undertake the task; but if you seek to convert them, send them to M. de Genève!" One of Henry IV.'s ministers remarked that the Bishop had done him a great deal of good; "but," he added, "he has also done me an evil turn which will not easily be remedied; he has disgusted me with all other preachers!" And the King himself, no incompetent judge, pronounced him "the phœnix of prelates." Henry would fain have kept him at court, and he tempted him with successive offers of lucrative posts. Francis invariably answered that he had married a poor bride, and could not forsake her for a wealthier. The popularity which attended him, and the eulogiums showered upon him from all quarters, did not affect his simplicity of spirit; he went on his way with his usual modesty and sobriety; losing no opportunity of working in CHRIST's cause, and speaking the truth with plainness and in love. The Cardinal du Perron once observed to Henry that he was disposed to fling aside all his theological treatises and controversial folios, and apply himself to the imitation of the Coadjutor's sanctity and gentleness. "What I admire in M. de Genève," said the King, "is, that he does not know how to flatter!"

Francis had reached Lyons on his way home when the tidings arrived of Bishop Granier's death. He was deeply impressed by the responsibility which this event threw upon him; and before assuming the full duties of the episcopate, went into retreat for twenty days. During this period of retirement he drew up stringent rules for his own guidance, and that of his household, and the government of his diocese, to which he steadfastly adhered. On the 8th of December, 1602, he was consecrated in the parish church of Thorens by Archbishop Gribaldi, and Bishops Pobel and Maistret. On the 14th he was installed at Annecy; and from that day all his thoughts, affections, and faculties were devoted to the welfare of the flock GOD had committed to his charge. He lived and laboured like a Bishop of the primitive Church. All his private fortune he made over to his brothers: so that he had nothing to depend upon but the revenue of his see, which did not exceed £200 a year. He refused the state of an episcopal palace, and resided in a hired house of modest pretensions. Only two of the rooms were carpeted; in one he transacted business, in the other received strangers. His table was frugally kept, but every comer was welcome to it. His attire lacked the usual episcopal splendour; nothing of it was silk but the girdle. He kept neither carriage nor horses, and he had no retinue of servants. Small as was his income, he gave away a considerable portion in charity. No necessitous or deserving applicant knocked at his door in vain. One day his chaplain informed him that there was no money left. "So much the better," he exclaimed; "we approach but the nearer to our Great Example,"—which Example, indeed, was always before him. "But, as a practical matter," rejoined the perplexed chaplain, "on what are we to live?" "My son, we must fall back on our home resources." "Home resources! But those are all exhausted!" "I mean," said the Bishop, mildly, "that we must sell some of the furniture to buy food. Surely that will be using our home resources!" The furniture, however, was so homely and scanty, that it would not have long supplied the Bishop's purse.

There was an admirable good sense in the Bishop's practice; his religion was a rational and moderate-minded religion, with no excess but in love. Though duly observing fast days and seasons of abstinence, he laid no undue stress upon them; and had no sympathy with the rigorous asceticism that, by weakening the body, enfeebles and incapacitates the mind. Observing that his friend, the Bishop of Belley, fasted very frequently, he asked him, one day, whether it did not try him a good deal. The Bishop answered that he had seldom any appetite, and generally sat down to table without any desire to eat. "Then," said Francis, "you should fast but little." "Why, *mon père?*" said Belley; "does not Holy Scripture strongly inculcate the duty of fasting?" "Yes; but for those who have a better appetite than you have. You should practise some other good work; mortify your body in some other way." In the same spirit he would condemn any ostentation of humility. "A truly humble man," he would say, "does not *seek* to seem humble, but to be really so. Humility is so sensitive that it fears its own shadow, and can scarcely bear to be mentioned without risk of loss." And with one of his apt illustrations, he added:—" He who blames himself is often angling after praise; like an oarsman, who turns his back to the place he is making for, he does not mean you to believe the ill he says of himself, and it is out of very pride that he wishes to be thought humble." With shams of every kind he made quick work. M. de Belley took it into his head, admiration for his spiritual father prevailing over his judgment, to imitate him in every particular, copying his gestures, his mode of speaking, even his pronunciation, with a result that was far from satisfactory. One day Francis suddenly turned upon him :—" By the way, I hear strange news; I am told that you have recently amused yourself by mimicking the Bishop of Geneva in preaching?" "Well; and if it be true? is he an undesirable example? Does he not preach better than I do?" "Oh, yes, of course," said Francis, smiling; "but the worst of it is that I am told you imitate him so badly, that while you spoil the Bishop of Belley, you are not a whit like the Bishop of Geneva. You should do like bad painters, and write the name of the person you mean to represent below the effigy!" So, too, he condemned the habit of indulging in excessively prolonged private prayers before and after celebrating mass, to the great inconvenience of those who assisted.

His singular sagacity was always exhibiting itself, and he had an almost unequalled power of concentrating a world of truth in brief epigrammatic phrases like proverbs, which cling to the memory—and often to the heart—of those who heard them. Thus, to enforce the maxim that a rebuke administered ungraciously loses its power, he said :—" You will catch more flies with a spoonful of honey than with a whole barrel of vinegar !" And again :—" No sauce was ever spoilt by sugar." The Bishop of Chalcedon once displayed an unreasonable amount of irritability and impatience. " Do you know, brother," said Francis, "that I think you have really done a great kindness to at least one woman ? Guess whom I mean." The Bishop guessed in vain. " Well," continued Francis, " I mean the woman who would have been your wife if you had ever married !" M. de Belley once went to him to complain of some persons who had done him wrong. Francis listened to the tirade patiently, and acknowledged that the offenders were much to blame. " In the matter," he added, " I see only one thing really to your disadvantage." " And that— !" " That you should not know how to be wiser than they, and hold your tongue." That was a fine saying of his :—" Truth which is not charitable proceeds from a charity which is not true"—words that might well be written in letters of gold. Again :—" It is better to make penitents by gentleness, than to make hypocrites by severity." There was wisdom in the rule he laid down for a Bishop's guidance ; the wisdom of a large heart as well as of a clear intellect :—" All love and no fear." Employing one of his picturesque images, he said :—" There are no slaves in the royal galley of Divine Love ; every oar is worked by a volunteer." He was a great worker, but he did all his work well, because he would never do it in a hurry. " Soon enough," he would say, " if well enough." " People who try to do two things at once will fail in both ; you can't thread two needles at the same time." " No one is really poor," said this economist, " who has enough to live upon." His insight into the faults and follies of humanity comes out in the remark that—" If we really knew ourselves, instead of being astonished that we fall, we should rather wonder that we ever stood upright. We require to learn patience with everybody, but most of all with ourselves; being, as we are, more troublesome to ourselves than any one else is to us." In accordance with his own practice, he earnestly insisted that the clergy should study regularly, and not only theology, but general literature. "Those who fill up their time without allowing any portion of it for study resemble people who reject solid food, and endeavour to maintain life on innutritious and unsubstantial viands. Ignorance is almost worse than faultiness in a priest, since it disgraces not the priest only, but the priesthood."

I have no space to deal with the Bishop's diocesan work, or to dwell on the rare tact and tenderness which he exhibited in his relations with penitents, or the zeal and felicity he showed in catechizing children, or the combined firmness and consideration that marked his intercourse with his clergy. In every aspect of his life and character he was so loveable, that we may well call him the Model Bishop. That he should institute a Diocesan Synod, meeting annually, was what might have been expected from the thoroughness with which he did all his work; and he fully understood that a diocese could not be efficiently administered unless the closest intercourse and most entire confidence subsisted between the Bishop and his clergy. If the overseer hold himself aloof from his shepherds, what will become of the flock? His fame, however, with the Church at large, does not rest upon his episcopal labours, but upon the immortal devotional treatise, a summary of which I have already attempted. The "Introduction à la Vie Dévote" had its origin in some letters which he wrote for the instruction and guidance of one of his converts, a Madame de Charmoisy. These were copied by the Père Ferrier, for the benefit of the students under his charge; and their value being proved by experience, Père Ferrier begged the Bishop to publish them. About the same time Henry IV., through his secretary, entreated Francis to write a book which should show that religion was not incompatible with the pursuits of an active career; and for this purpose the notes addressed to Madame de Charmoisy were rewritten by the Bishop, and published in 1608 in the form now so familiar to the Christian world. The success of the "Devout Life" was immediate, and has been permanent. How many souls has it comforted! To how many has it been as a lamp shining in the darkness, and making clear the way they should go! How many has it strengthened in their resolution to live "a life worth living, a life sanctified by the love of GOD!" No one could have written it but Francis de Sales: and had he done nothing else, the Church must ever have held his name in grateful remembrance. His "Traité de l'Amour de Dieu," published in 1616, though less known, is a book of very great merit; but it lacks the universal applicability of the "Vie Dévote."

The long and intimate friendship which the Bishop maintained with Madame de Chantal, though characteristic of the man in its fervour and faithfulness, would have little interest for the general reader; but it must be noticed here in connection with the Bishop's foundation of the Order of the Visitation. This Order was instituted for the benefit of women, desirous of serving GOD, whose delicate health or age or other circumstances, such as widowhood, prevented them from joining existing Orders. Asceticism was not to be its principle: the Bishop cared little for the mortification of the body, but he cared a good deal for the discipline of the heart and mind. His order was to be governed by charity and the love of JESUS CHRIST, and devoted to the care of the sick and poor. The idea of it was conceived as early as 1605, but the Bishop was unable to realise it until five years later, when a house was taken at Annecy, and placed under the supervision of Madame de Chantal. It was occupied for the first time on Trinity Sunday, the earliest associates being Mademoiselle de Buchard and Jacqueline Favre, both of noble birth, and a pious servant, named Anne Jacqueline Coste. The new congregation had its sympathisers, but it had also its detractors, who said that the rules were too indulgent, and that the Bishop had founded a hospital rather than a monastery. To all which Francis calmly replied:—"When GOD's will is clear to us, we must go forward in spite of all that men may say. We must not take umbrage at unkind sayings when souls are to be saved, and if our congregation did but avert one mortal sin, I should be satisfied. People profess to think that it will go to pieces at my death, but I think our Mother in Heaven will do as much for it there as I can do here." GOD's blessing was given to the work, and in half a century the Order numbered a hundred and twenty houses. In one respect it differed from the Bishop's intention. He had designed its members to be uncloistered, and to go about freely among the sick and poor, combining the vocations of Martha and Mary; "a life to which he leaned, as more generally profitable and edifying for women, than one of greater restraint and less activity." But he was overruled by the Archbishop of Lyons, and consented that the Sisters should take the usual vows. The spirit in which he framed the Rule, however, was free from austerity and made no heavy demand on the consciences of the sisters. Writing to Madame de Chantal, he says :[1]—" I would have you to be extremely small and lowly in your own eyes: gentle and tender as a dove. Accept willingly all opportunities of humbling yourself; do not be quick to speak, rather let your answers be slow, humble, meek, and let your modest silence use an eloquence of its own. Bear with or make allowance for your neighbour; do not dwell upon the contradictions which you must encounter; turn from them to see GOD in all things, and acquiesce simply in all His decrees. Do everything for GOD, uniting yourself, or maintaining union by means of a simple glance or turning of your heart to Him. Never be hurried; do everything tranquilly and with a restful spirit; do not lose your inward peace for anything whatsoever, not even when all seems going wrong, for what do all earthly things matter, as compared with your heart's peace? Commend all to GOD, and keep yourself calm and still in the Bosom of His Fatherly Providence. When you find that your spirit has wandered thence, draw it back gently and with perfect simplicity; and never under any excuse entangle yourself in cares, desires, and affections. Our LORD loves you, and would have you wholly His. Seek no other arms save His to bear you up; no breast whereon to lean save that of His Divine Providence; seek not to see beyond Him and His Will. Let your will ever be so bound up with His as to be wholly one, and leave all else unheeded. Be of good courage, and

"Life of S. Francis de Sales," by H. S. Lear, pp. 203, 204.

abide humbly, waiting upon His Sacred Majesty. Desire nought save the pure love of our LORD; refuse nought, however trying, but put on JESUS CHRIST crucified, and love suffering in Him."

In the autumn of 1618, Francis went on a visit to Paris, where he was immediately called upon to preach, in all churches, and on all occasions, invariably attracting multitudes to hear him, and producing an impression for which his modesty was wholly unable to account. It is computed that during a year's sojourn in the capital he preached no fewer than three hundred and sixty-five sermons; as he often preached twice, and sometimes thrice, in a day. His repute for holiness of life was so great, that people pressed upon him in the streets to touch his garments as if a virtue lay in them; and his time was occupied in giving counsel to the numerous applicants who came to him with their sins and sorrows. The King, deeply moved by his many graces, offered him the Abbey of Sainte Geneviève, and Cardinal de Retz would fain have persuaded him to become his coadjutor and successor as Archbishop of Paris; but Francis wisely declined both positions, which were indeed unfitted for a man so closely resembling the early Fathers of the Church in his intense spirituality and simplicity. Though still in the prime of manhood, his excessive labours had impaired his strength, and he was glad in 1621 to seek a coadjutor for his own diocese, and to find one in his brother, Jean François, Bishop of Chalcedon. A conviction of approaching death took possession of his mind, and he hastened to make his brother acquainted with all the details of the diocesan organisation and the views he had formed for the welfare of the people. In thus setting his house in order, he acted with his usual calmness and deliberation. Day by day, however, the burden of the flesh grew heavier to bear; day by day, the end drew nearer. Swellings of the legs, with painful sores, and such an oppression on the chest that to breathe was pain, were warnings which he accepted with thankfulness and submission. Foreseeing that the night was at hand when he could no longer work, he gave himself up to the duties of his office with even an increase of his characteristic diligence. In November, 1622, he was summoned by the

Duke of Savoy to attend him on a visit to Louis XIII., at Avignon, and though his friends would have had him excuse himself on the ground of his ill-health, no such excuse was possible to one the watchword of whose life had been Obedience. He left Annecy on the 9th of November, never to return. His reception at Avignon was such as might have been given to an Apostle; but he was glad when his duties were discharged, and he was free to commence his homeward journey. He got no further, however, than Lyons, where he lodged in a small room in the gardener's house attached to the Visitation Convent. Here Madame de Chantal had a farewell interview with her friend and Director; while persons of all ranks and ages waited upon him to obtain the inestimable benefit of his advice. He still continued to preach and to celebrate Mass, though his physical sufferings were severe, and never were his sermons and his conversation more instinct with the ardour of love or more impressive in their calm sweet eloquence.

When he rose, on the Feast of S. John, he noticed that his sight was failing, and to his attendants he remarked that it was a sign of his departure, for which he blessed GOD, since the enfeebled body dragged down the soul. He dressed, made his confession, said Mass, communicated the Sisters, and heard the Superior's confession; but on returning from the church he was visibly worn, and so exhausted, that it was necessary to put him to bed. Some kind of seizure followed, but it did not affect his faculties. After receiving the Sacraments of Penitence and Extreme Unction, he fell into a great lethargy, from which the doctors were very anxious to rouse him. The Grand Vicaire of the Jesuits thereupon asked him:—"What think you, Monseigneur, of the Catholic Faith? Does your heart secretly incline towards Calvinism?" The question was a cruel one; but it roused the dying saint; and he exclaimed:— "GOD forbid! I have never tampered with heresy: it would have been too grave an act of unfaithfulness." And he made the sign of the Cross on his breast and forehead. The Grand Vicaire next asked him if he feared death, quoting the words:—" O mors, quam amara est memoria tua!" The Bishop replied:—" Yes, but only to the man whose happiness lies in his possessions" (*homini pacem habenti in substantiis suis*).

Francis lingered throughout the night. Next day the drowsiness returned; and the doctors struggled against it by applying blisters to the head and hot irons to the spine, torturing the gentle, unrepining, dying saint, who murmured amid all his pain, "Do what you will with the sick man." Many came to receive his last blessing and exchange a few farewell words; to all he spoke with his customary serenity and patience. The Père Ferrier asked him if he remembered him. "Si oblitus fuero tui," faltered Francis, "oblivioni detur dextera mea" (Ps. cxxxvii. 5.) "You must say with S. Martin," continued the Father, "Domine, si adhuc populo tuo sum necessarius, non recuso laborem" (LORD, if I am necessary yet to Thy people, I do not refuse any labour). "Necessary," exclaimed Francis; "no, no, I am an altogether useless servant." And thrice he murmured the words:—"Servus inutilis, inutilis, inutilis!" He was asked whether he was not sorry to leave his Order of the Visitation incomplete. With a glow of faith he answered:—"Qui cœpit opus, ipse perficiet" (He who began the work, He will finish it), and he added, emphatically, "perficiet, perficiet!"

Some one idly inquired of the dying Saint whether he feared the last struggle. "My eyes," he said, "are ever looking unto the LORD, for He shall pluck my feet out of the net." Said another—with strange inappropriateness:— "There was one traitor among the Apostles." "I waited patiently for the LORD, and He inclined unto me, and heard my calling. He brought me also out of the pit," was his only answer. To which he added, after a moment's pause:—"Qui cœpit, ipse perficiet." A silence followed. The light of life flickered more and more feebly. Pressing the hand of a friend who tenderly watched over him, he whispered:—"It is toward evening, and the day is far spent." These were his last words, except that he was heard now and again to breathe the beloved name of JESUS. That he was conscious of all that passed was shown by the movement of his eyes and lips as prayer after prayer was sent up on his behalf to the Throne of Grace. About eight o'clock in the evening, that greyness passed over the countenance which tells that the last moment approaches; and the priests and others in attendance, falling on their knees, raised the litanies of prayer and praise which the Church prescribes for the consolation and commendation of the dying. At the words, " Omnes sancti Innocentes, orate pro eo," Francis de Sales fell asleep in JESUS.

It was the Feast of Holy Innocents, 1622, and the Bishop was only 55 years of age.

According to his own request, his remains were removed to Annecy, and interred in the Church of the Visitation. In the year 1665 he was solemnly canonised by Pope Alexander VII.

The lesson taught by the exalted character and holy life of this saintly priest and bishop seems to me best embodied in his own words. Speaking of the saints, martyrs, and confessors, whose memories are the precious inheritance of the Church, he says :—" What may we not achieve with such patterns before our eyes? They were but what we are; they wrought for the same Almighty FATHER; they sought after the same graces : why may we not do as much in our own conditions of life, and according to our several vocations, on behalf of our most eager resolutions and holy profession of faith?" May not we, who belong to a different communion, strive at least to imitate the humility, the tender charity, the gentle moderation, the unquestioning obedience, and the deep, true, simple faith of Francis de Sales?

> " Dear soul, be strong;
>   Mercy will come ere long,
> And bring her bosom full of blessings—
>   Flowers of never-fading graces,
> To make immortal dressings,
>   For worthy souls whose wise embraces
> Store up themselves for Him Who is alone
> The spouse of virgins and the Virgin's Son."
>   CRASHAW.

NOTE.

Since the foregoing pages were written we have read a pamphlet by Mr. Willis Nevins, entitled "The Persecution of Protestants by S. Francis de Sales," which seeks to prove him guilty, in his mission in the Chablais, of acts of extreme cruelty. Mr. Willis Nevins certainly shows that the Duke of Savoy banished a large number of his subjects who refused to embrace Romanism, but he does not seem to us to connect Francis de Sales directly with this unjust exhibition of arbitrary power. At the summons of the Duke of Savoy he undoubtedly visited him in Turin, and consulted with him on the measures necessary for the extirpation of Protestantism; the measures he recommended would now-a-days shock our idea of religious tolerance; but they were scarcely severer than those which obtained in Ireland down to the epoch of Catholic Emancipation; and they were really of a moderate and even gentle character for that age of religious bigotry. And it is only fair to remember that S. Francis, when he undertook his evangelistic labours in the Chablais, was a young man of twenty-eight. In his later life he steadfastly denounced the employment of force in "spiritual warfare."

It has also been objected to him that he practised some deception upon his father in adopting the sacerdotal profession when he was intended for a secular career. We do not see that S. Francis can rightly be censured for shrinking from a life for which he did not feel himself fitted; but as a matter of fact he was guilty of neither deceit nor fraud. He pursued the studies that M. de Boisy had marked out, and actually took his degree in civil and canonical law; and when at length he felt compelled to realize his earliest hope and ambition, he spoke frankly and earnestly to his father. The Provostship of Geneva was not obtained through his own solicitation, but, unknown to him, through the intervention of friends, who thought it would reconcile the father to his son's ordination. The Rev. L. W. Bacon, another assailant of the Bishop of Geneva, charges him with duplicity towards the young lady, Mademoiselle de Vigy, whom his father wished him to marry. He says that though he had taken a vow of celibacy, Francis visited her as a suitor and a lover. It is difficult to see how such a charge can be maintained, when we know that his father chided him for his coldness and reserve with the young lady! On the whole, we see no reason to modify the estimate we have ventured to form of the sweetness and purity of S. Francis's character. We will not pretend that he was perfect, or that in his earlier years he never committed a mistake; but he seems to us to have realized, as nearly as mortal man may do, that ideal of a Devout Life which he has set forth in his own inimitable pages.

S. VINCENT DE PAUL:

THE RELIGIOUS PHILANTHROPIST.

"It is true that S. Vincent de Paul rose to great distinction, and played a very prominent part in his generation, and has left an honoured name behind. Nevertheless, they were not what are accounted extraordinary or brilliant gifts which brought him to such honour. His life is the triumph of unworldliness, humility, a constant recollection of the presence of GOD, and a single eye to His glory."—R. F. WILSON.

[*Authorities:*—The materials for the following sketch will be found in the Abbé Maynard's "S. Vincent de Paul, sa Vie, son Temps, ses Œuvres, et son Influence," which has been agreeably summarised by the author of "The Life of S. Vincent de Paul," edited by the Rev. Prebendary Wilson. See also Jervis's "History of the Gallican Church," Sismondi's "Histoire des Français," and Miss Kavanagh's "Women of Christianity."]

S. VINCENT DE PAUL.

CHAPTER I.

THE preceding chapters have been records of the work done by men and women who have largely influenced the history of their time, and even of the world; Heroes of the Cross, whose lives have had in them a remarkable, almost a miraculous element, and whose genius or force of character compels the admiration or wonder of posterity. We have now to deal with a man who, though he rose to high distinction and effected some notable achievements, stood out less conspicuously from his fellows, making no pretension to any rare intellectual gifts; a man who invites our notice by those virtues of humility, single-heartedness, abundant charity, and unpretending piety which are or should be the ordinary virtues of the Christian. S. Vincent de Paul did not belong to that high order of great men which claims a Columba, a Bernard, and a Francis. He could not excite the enthusiasm of multitudes or control the destinies of nations. He did what he had to do simply, quietly, diligently. His life was not illustrated by any startling events, any dramatic scenes. But for this very reason it is the better adapted for our imitation. The monk of Clairvaux, the founder of the Franciscan brotherhood, the great Florentine reformer—these men stand on a height to which most of us cannot attain. Like the peaks of lofty mountains they soar into an atmosphere in which we could not breathe.

Their gifts and graces are alike beyond our grasp. But in S. Vincent de Paul we have a pattern that we may hope to copy. Not that, like him, we can originate great institutions; but that in our various avocations, and as Churchmen generally, we may practise the same sanctity of life, the same honest Christian industry, the same modest self-denial and unaffected devotion to duty. Like him, into all that we do we may put our best. It has been well said that from the beginning to the end his life was made up of "ordinary actions done extraordinarily well—of ordinary opportunities never impetuously grasped at, never hastily seized, but never let pass, and, when once laid hold of, followed out carefully and perseveringly with eminent common sense, and what may be called worldly wisdom." This is the life that English Churchmen may study with advantage. The opportunities of doing something for CHRIST and His Church come to all of us; but do we make use of them?

"Doing the Church's work in the Church's way" is a phrase of frequent occurrence on the lips of Churchmen; but, unfortunately, it too often remains a phrase and nothing more; the principle which it embodies, admirable as it is, not being very readily transmuted into action. It is true, indeed, that people sometimes profess to be working in the Church's way, when, on examination, it is found that they are deceiving themselves, and that the "way" in question is simply their own self-willed and presumptuous way. For, in truth, if we all of us steadily pursued the lines laid down for us by the Church; if, like Vincent de Paul, we loyally followed her counsels with zeal and yet discretion, energy and yet moderation; we should cease to give the world occasion for ridicule by our variances, and to rend "the body of CHRIST" by our unhappy divisions. The Church demands of us oneness of spirit as *her* way; we reply by separating further apart from one another. The Church demands of us a constant fidelity to her cause; we reply by a sham liberality which ignores the radical difference of creeds and forms of government. The Church demands of us a reasonable service; we reply by plunging up to the neck in worldly business or social pleasures. And all the while we profess to be working in the Church's way. Rightly exercised, the influence of the Church, acting through her children, should infuse a new purity of tone, a new elevation of thought, a loftier and more serious view of life, into what is called Society; but most of us turn our faces away from the Church when we leave her sanctuaries, and in our daily labours allow her no share however small. The Church's way is, that all who take up the name of Churchman should be proud of her standard, devoted to her religious system; that religious system which rests on the broad immutable foundations of Evangelical Truth and Apostolic Order; that religious system which, from generation to generation, has transmitted the precious legacy of the Faith first delivered to the saints. But, too often, we seem to hanker after other systems, putting forward the excuse that a firm adherence to our own standard is bigotry; that the "progress of the age" inclines towards an universal charity, which is to recast dogmas and formularies in its wonder-working crucible, and present them to an enlightened world in one homogeneous mass. This may be very fine and very liberal; it may be the best way, but it is not the Church's way. She insists that in our life, in our habits of thought, in our modes of speech we should be true and faithful, clustering like loving children around her venerable knees. She asks of us that unquestioning devotion which Vincent de Paul gave to the Roman Communion. We see sometimes in a George Herbert, a Keble, and a Patteson, what manner of men this great and glorious Church of ours can rear, when *her* way is zealously followed to the end; and we know that nobler types of Christian manhood have never been presented. But yet a vast number of so-called Churchmen apparently disown such types, and desire something "broader"—for that is the favourite word!—something which shall marvellously blend "sweetness and light" with modern religious radicalism. An American bishop has happily characterised the present tendency to a spurious liberalism as the effort to be half one thing and half another thing; to "cross the breed;" to sow the field with doctrinal statements which are mingled seed; to clothe ourselves in a religious garment half-linen and half-woollen. No good can come of this, either in one direction or the other; and we do not believe it is the Church's way. Rather, like Vincent de Paul, would we keep within the limits of our own communion, and avail ourselves of its opportunities to further the advancement of the truth as it is in CHRIST.

> "Like watchmen true
> Waiting to see what GOD will do,
> As o'er the Church the gathering twilight falls."

Vincent de Paul was born on the 24th of April, 1576, in the little village of Pouy, near Dax, that lies on the high ground at the foot of the Pyrenees. His father was a small farmer, owning the land which he cultivated; and Vincent, in his early years, was employed in the work of the farm, and in taking charge of his father's flocks. The seeds of piety sown by a devout mother quickly ripened in his heart; and while watching his sheep he resorted to a hollow oak that overlooked the pastures, and sheltered there from rain or sun, gave himself up to frequent prayer. His devoutness and gravity of character, and the proofs he gave of considerable intellectual capacity, led his father to withdraw him from the sheep-field and educate him for the priesthood. At that time he was eleven years old. In the Franciscan convent at Dax he made rapid progress in his studies, and acquired so good a repute for proficiency that the chief magistrate of Pouy received him into his house as the tutor of his children; a position which enabled him to continue the work of self-culture without being a burden on his parents. (1591.) He remained in it for five years; years tranquil, useful, and prosperous. In December, 1596, he finally severed himself from the world by receiving the tonsure and the four minor orders; after which he repaired to Toulouse for the purpose of studying theology with adequate completeness. In December, 1598, he was ordained deacon; and on the 23rd of September, 1600, being then in his 25th year, he was admitted to the priesthood.

He did not immediately obtain a charge; and to provide for his support he again undertook the work of a tutor. That this work might not interfere with the theological studies and religious exercises appropriate to his holy calling, he deprived himself of many hours usually given to sleep and recreation. Thus tranquilly passed his life; giving no promise of any distinction or achievement which would be worthy of the biographer's record, yet not without its influence for good in his own immediate circle. In 1605, he had occasion to visit Marseilles, and then occurred the first striking incident in his career. Returning to Narbonne by sea, he was captured by Turkish pirates, robbed of all he possessed, and carried with his fellow-passengers to Tunis to be sold into slavery. "After they had stripped us," he writes, "they gave to each a pair of drawers and a linen coat and cap, and walked us about the town, whither they had come for the express purpose of selling us. Having paraded us round the town with chains on our necks, they led us back to the ship, in order that purchasers might attend and see who ate heartily and who did not, to show them, moreover, that our wounds (Vincent was wounded by an arrow) were not mortal. This done, we were led back to the market-place, where merchants came to inspect us, exactly as men do who want to buy a horse or an ox. We had to open our mouths and show our teeth; they felt our sides, examined our wounds, make us walk, trot, run, lift heavy weights, and wrestle, that they might judge of our individual strength, and they subjected us to a thousand other indignities."

Vincent was bought by a fisherman, who, however, soon disposed of him to a pretended physician and alchemist. At the end of ten or eleven months this master died, bequeathing him, with his other property, to a nephew, who sold the unfortunate priest to a Christian renegade from Nice. The change, at first, was not an amendment of his condition; for he was set to hard labour on an inland farm, where the tropical heat caused him intense suffering, and the work was far beyond his strength. One of the renegade's three wives noticed with some compassion the patient, gentle, humble labourer, in whom she recognised something superior to his condition. She began to talk to him, and their converse naturally turned upon that subject dearest to Vincent, the love of CHRIST. One day she asked him to sing some of the Church's hymns; and with a sad remembrance of the captive Israelites in their Babylonian exile, he began, through his tears, the pathetic psalm, "Super flumina Babylonis;" after which he sang the "Salve Regina;" and many others, which filled her with profound pleasure. That evening she told her husband that he had done wrong in abandoning his religion, of the excellence of which she was persuaded by the account Vincent had given her of his GOD, and the hymns he had sung in her presence. In these she felt such delight, she said, that she could not believe that the Paradise of her fathers, the Paradise of the Koran, could equal in glory and joy the sweet repose and entire satisfaction of soul which she had felt while listening to the Christian's praises of his LORD and SAVIOUR.

Thenceforth the renegade looked eagerly for an opportunity to escape to France, that he might deliver himself from the thraldom of Mohammedanism; his slumbering conscience being keenly reawakened by this opportune message from Heaven. It was not, however, until the end of June, 1607, that the opportunity came; and he and his family, accompanied by Vincent, crossed the Mediterranean in a small boat, and landed at Aigues-Mortes. They repaired to Avignon, where the apostate was received back into the communion of the Church. Vincent went on to Rome, and found favour in the eyes of the Roman Court, so that he was employed to convey a confidential message to Henry IV. This responsible mission placed him on the road to preferment and distinction; but shocked by the profligacy that prevailed in high places, he quickly withdrew into retirement, seeking the rest and peace to be found under the roof of the Fathers of the Oratory. At the persuasion of their Superior General, M. de Berulle, he undertook parochial work in the village of Clichy, near Paris; and his poor and humble flock speedily learned to look up to him as a father, on whose counsel they might rely in all their difficulties, to whose assistance they might look in all their trials. He on his part grew greatly attached to them:—"The good people were so obedient to me," he said, "that when I advised them to attend Confession on the first Sunday of every month, to my great joy no one was absent. Ah, I used to say to myself, how happy thou art to have such good people; the Pope is not so happy as I am! One day, the great Cardinal de Retz asked me, 'Well, Monsieur, how do you get on?' 'My lord,' I answered, 'I am happier than I can describe.' 'Why so?' 'Because I have such good people, people so obedient to all I tell them, that I say to myself that neither the Pope, nor you, my lord, can be so happy as I am.'"

Very reluctantly, at the wish—almost the command—of M. de Berulle, he parted from his little village flock, and as chaplain and tutor entered the illustrious family of Philip Emanuel de Gondi, Count of Joigny, a scion of the great house of De Retz. On taking up these new duties, he little thought that he would continue to discharge them for so long a period as twelve years: still less did he foresee that they would lead him onward to the accomplishment of much precious work for the Church. From what we have already seen of his character, of its humility, simple tenderness, and discreet wisdom, we can understand that he would win the love and reverence of all with whom he came in contact. His was one of those sunny natures in which others seem spontaneously to expand and flourish. He possessed a singular faculty of attraction, a personal charm, that was felt by men of the highest rank as of the lowest, by the cultured as well as by the ignorant. Partly this arose from his self-forgetfulness: he was ready at any time to do any office of mercy or kindness, thinking nothing of the labour it might entail upon himself. For his first thought was how to serve GOD, and his second how to serve GOD's creatures.

Not only did he most unweariedly discharge his duties as tutor and chaplain, his duties to the Count and Countess and their children, but he had always in his mind and heart every member of their large household. He tended them in sickness, he instructed them, he catechized them, he composed their quarrels, he soothed them in their hours of pain and sorrow; while the little leisure left to him he devoted to the care of the peasants and labourers on the great rural demesne of the Joignys. This portion of his work led him to the organisation of that special system of religious instruction which is known as "Missions." One day, he was requested to attend a poor man living in one of the Count de Joigny's villages; he was dangerously ill, and wished to make his confession. By his neighbours he was esteemed as a man of admirable character and irreproachable life, strict in his performance of the ordinary religious duties. But Vincent, on questioning him closely, and probing his wound to the quick, discovered that, with all this fair seeming, he bore a "heavy load of deadly sin" upon his conscience; a load which, but for Vincent's knowledge of the human heart and his power of gaining the unreserved confidence of all who consulted him, he would have carried, without confession or open repentance, into the Presence of GOD.

This incident moved Vincent greatly; and he began to consider whether some means could not be devised for quickening the conscience of the masses, and rousing them to a sense of their religious duty. As a first step in this direction, he held, on the 25th of January, 1607, a special service in the parish church of Folleville, in which he addressed the people in the plainest language on the great truths of the Gospel, and urged them to a general confession. So effective was the appeal, that the hearers flocked in large numbers to his confessional, and he was compelled to call in the assistance of the Jesuit Fathers at Amiens. For three days as many priests were engaged in the work of confessing, preaching, teaching, catechizing. From Folleville they went to other villages, and in all they reaped an abundant harvest. This was the inauguration of that system of "Missions" which, after being for two centuries and a half confined to the Church of Rome, has, with some modifications, been of late years introduced into the English Church.

He continued, with the exception of four months in 1617, which he spent at Chatillon, an honoured member of the family of De Gondi until 1625, when Madame de Gondi bequeathed an annual endowment of 16,000 livres for the establishment of a Society of Mission Priests, whose particular care should be the religious welfare of the peasantry and the rural population of France. Shortly before her death, she and her husband had obtained from the Archbishop of Paris (brother of the Count) an old untenanted collegiate building, called the Collège des Bons Enfants, which they had fitted up as a Home for Mission Priests. The foundation and endowment were made over to Vincent de Paul, who was appointed Superior, and in whom was vested the power of electing and choosing every year as many ecclesiastics as the revenues of the Foundation would bear, whose learning, piety, and holiness of life should be known to him, to labour under his direction, during his life. The conditions attached to the deed of endowment were:—That these ecclesiastics should devote themselves entirely to the care of the poor in country places, and to this end should bind themselves not to preach, nor to administer the Sacrament, in any town where there was a bishop, or archbishop, or a civil court of justice, except in cases of manifest necessity. That they should live in common, under the obedience of the said Sieur de Paul, and after his decease, of their Superior, under the name of the Company or Congregation of Mission Priests (*Compagnie ou Congrégation des Prêtres de la Mission*). And that they should be bound to hold missions every five years throughout the estates of the Count and Countess of Joigny, and also to give spiritual assistance to convicts.

Conjointly with the post of Superior of the Mission College, Vincent de Paul held that of Confessor and Spiritual Guide to the Convent of the Visitation, which had been lately established by Madame de Chantal at Paris, and also that of Chaplain-general of convicts and galley-slaves. In the latter capacity he repaired to Marseilles, to inspect the galleys, and examine into the condition of the poor wretches confined in them, which was probably worse than that of the inmates of the worst prisons in Europe, at a time when prison administration was a synonym for heartless oppression. "Pitiable beyond words," we are told, "was the state of things which he found there. Reckless misery, blank despair, and blasphemy combined, seemed to make of the Bagne a hell upon earth. Touched with feelings of the deepest compassion for these miserable beings, Vincent set himself to comfort and assist them in all ways in his power." Previously, the sole concern of those entrusted with the administration of the criminal law was *punishment;* they never thought of *reforming* the criminal; they cared not whether he repented of his sins so long as he underwent the chastisement ordained for them. But Vincent de Paul endeavoured by his loving tenderness and sympathy to soften their hearts while he revived the dormant sense of right and wrong. He won their confidence by the patience with which he listened to their complaints, and the pity he felt for their sufferings. Frequently he exerted himself to mitigate the cruel severity with which they were treated. He even went further:—Finding among the convicts a young man, in whose innocence of the crime laid to his charge he believed, and who was wounded almost to death by the agonizing thought of the destitution of his wife and young children, he prevailed with the officer of the gang to set him free, and to accept of himself as his substitute. That he might obtain a more exact knowledge of the state of the galleys, Vincent had preserved the strictest reticence respecting his name and position; so that none knew who it was that rose to so astonishing a height of self-sacrifice. For several weeks, it is said, Vincent worked in chains with the rest of the gang, until the Count of Joigny, surprised at hearing nothing from him, instituted inquiries which led to his discovery and release.[1] We are told that he contracted during this extraordinary period of voluntary abasement a disease which weakened him for many years, and that to the end of his days his limbs exhibited marks of the cruel pressure of his self-imposed fetters.

Vincent de Paul was one of those men who are endowed with a genius for organization; who, if they become aware of the existence of an evil, cannot rest until they have found a remedy for it; whose resources seem adapted to every need; and whose plans are so instinct with good sense and so complete in their details, that they are invariably crowned with success. Such men are not so common in the Church as in the World; perhaps, because *in* the Church, Authority too often frowns upon them. Of the facility with which Vincent de Paul provided for every exigency, and of the admirable character of that provision, we may supply an illustration. Returning from Marseilles to Paris he passed through Mâcon, where he found himself hemmed in by a crowd of importunate beggars, who appeared to hold the town *in terrorem*. They were so numerous that the authorities feared to interfere with them, and they lived sumptuously upon the black-mail which they levied from a frightened population. Vincent resolved at once to redress this evil, though as a passing traveller it did not personally affect him. He began by infusing energy and courage into the ecclesiastical and civil powers, and securing their support. Next he formed an association of the more respectable inhabitants, and with their assistance he divided

[1] I confess that this story seems to me almost incredible; but the Abbé Maynard has collected evidence which apparently proves its authenticity.

the beggars into two classes: those shameless mendicants who made a trade of beggary, and those unfortunates who were driven by dire poverty to seek the alms of the charitable. For the latter, assistance was provided in their need and medical advice in their sickness; while to those able to work such help was given as might encourage them to secure an independent position. To the former, regular donations were made, but only upon certain conditions; they were every Sunday to attend at the service at a particular church, and receive religious instruction; misconduct was held to disentitle them to relief; and they were forbidden to ask for or to receive private alms. In organizing this well-conceived system, which effectually extirpated a frightful abuse, Vincent spent three busy weeks; at the end of which he quitted Mâcon secretly, to avoid the ovation its grateful citizens desired to give him.

When Vincent de Paul gave up his chaplaincy in the Count de Joigny's family, and entered upon his duties as Superior of the College of Mission Priests, he was about forty-nine years old. He is described as a man of middle height, well proportioned and robust, rather bald and with a large head; his forehead broad and commanding; his eye keen, his demeanour grave but gentle. By constant self-discipline he had so conquered a natural austerity of manner, and so acquired that easy and winning grace of which I have already spoken, that it was difficult, men said, to find any who made religion more attractive, or possessed a greater power of attaching hearts. He was not a man of genius, of original intellectual force, or bold imagination; yet his mind was large and liberal; it could conceive lofty ideas, and carry them into execution. In judgment he was cautious, in deliberation slow; never committing himself to any enterprise of which he had not carefully studied the particulars; never offering an opinion upon a subject which he had not examined from every possible standpoint. No pressure of affairs could disturb his serenity; no difficulties embarrass, no obstacles discourage him. He knew how to listen as well as how to speak; but he did not speak often, and he never spoke at length. As firmly as the great essayist and thinker of our own time, he believed that speech was silvern, but silence golden. When he *did* speak, he went straight to the point with words deliberate and weighty, which fell like blows from a hammer.

As a Christian, he disliked innovations of all kinds; the Church's way, and that way the way of the early fathers of Christianity, was all he cared for. He mistrusted the sanguine philosophy which is so prone to change things that are well in the hope of some impossible better. His affections were strong and quick: but he could control them if GOD's service made such control necessary. His deep humility was very beautiful to see, and was entirely unaffected; springing from his sense of his unworthiness of the gifts and graces which the HOLY GHOST had bestowed upon him. All his conduct was guided, all his character moulded, by two maxims which he seized every opportunity of inculcating in his conversation and illustrating in his actions:— First, That all true love of GOD must be an active love, showing itself in good works. Second, That in our neighbours we should ever behold the LORD JESUS CHRIST, and so beholding, for His sake and in His name render them the services of charity. On the first point he would say:—To delight in GOD and to long for Him are very excellent and desirable in themselves, yet where and when they do not lead us into the exercise of an active love, they must be regarded with suspicion. "Herein," said CHRIST, "is My FATHER glorified, that ye bear much fruit." There are many who pride themselves on their glow of feeling, and are content with the sweetness of their communings with GOD in prayer. Of these things they can speak with the tongues of angels; but, oh, if there be occasion to work for GOD, to suffer, to mortify themselves, to instruct the ignorant, to seek the lost sheep, to dispense with personal comforts, to welcome sickness or other misfortune, their courage fails them, their love loses its power! Let us not be deceived: all our work consists in doing. (*Totum opus nostrum in operatione consistit.*) On the second point he would say:— That we must learn to see our LORD in all persons, whosoever and whatsoever they might be; in kings as the King of kings; in rulers and magistrates as the supreme Judge; in artisans as Joseph the carpenter's Son; in the poor as the peasant of Galilee. And thus acknowledging the LORD in all sorts and conditions of men, and in each individual contemplating (so to speak) a separate image of the SAVIOUR, we shall learn to serve, honour and love each in our LORD, and our LORD in each.[1] Thus from our love of CHRIST radiates our love of our neighbours; while our love of our neighbours stimulates and maintains our love of CHRIST. In this way love becomes the fulfilling of the law; binding us by its golden bond to one another, and to Him Who is the Source of Love.

CHAPTER II.

THE institution of Mission Services and Mission Priests was the chief work of the first period of Vincent de Paul's active religious life. At first he had only two assistants, and they and he confined their ministrations to the diocese of Paris; but as their numbers increased, they widened the sphere of their operations. In 1627 and 1628 six more priests were added to the little Society, while a Bull of Pope Urban VIII. formally constituted a religious body, under the title of " Prêtres de la Congrégation de la Mission." In the first seven years of Vincent's experiment, 150 missions were held. Its success was complete; and the numerical strength of the Society had so augmented that the old College no longer afforded sufficient accommodation. Opportunely, and one may surely say, providentially, in 1630, the Prior of S. Lazarus felt a desire to turn to some useful and sacred purpose the large conventual buildings, occupied by himself and a few monks, which had at one time been the Leper or Lazar house of Paris. The thought came to him that he could not more effectually fulfil his desire than by installing in the Priory Vincent de S. Paul and his Mission Priests. His proposal, so rich in possibilities of good, greatly surprised Vincent; it had the same effect upon him as an unexpected thunder-clap which breaks upon a man suddenly, and leaves him stunned. The Prior perceived his confusion :—" Eh, what, Monsieur, you tremble?" "It is

[1] "Life of S. Vincent de Paul," ed. R. F. Wilson, pp. 73—75.

true, Monsieur," replied Vincent, "that your offer startles me; it seems so far beyond us that I dare not think of it. We are poor priests, who live in great simplicity, with no other object than that of being of service to poor peasants and country people. We are deeply obliged to you, Monsieur, for your good will towards us, and we very humbly thank you." The Prior, however, charmed by Vincent's sweet and affable ways, would not accept the refusal, and gave him six months to reconsider his offer.

At the expiry of that period, the Prior, along with M. Lestocq, Doctor of the Sorbonne, earnestly solicited Vincent to accept the Priory; but he insisted "that their number was too small, their society only just born, that he did not wish to be the theme of public talk, and that he and his priests did not deserve so astonishing a favour." The Prior would not be denied, and for another twelve months pressed Vincent with as much vehemence as the woman of Canaan cried after the Apostles; until it was agreed to refer the matter to a certain André Duval, a man of special holiness. Acting upon his advice, Vincent withdrew his declinature; and on the 7th of January, 1632, signed an agreement which, with some exceptions during the lives of the then Prior and Monks, placed him in possession of the buildings and endowments of the Priory of S. Lazarus. "And thus," says Lestocq, "did Monsieur Vincent yield at last to the importunate appeals that were made to him, amongst others by myself, who can truly affirm that I talked myself hoarse, '*raucæ factæ sunt fauces meæ.*' I would gladly have taken this Father of Missionaries upon my shoulders, and carried him to S. Lazarus, to compel him to accept it; but he took no thought of the material advantages of the place and of all its income, and never went even to see it all this time, so that it was not the grand position which drew him there at last, but only the will of GOD, and the hope of the spiritual good it might enable him to do."

In the period of seven years preceding the removal to S. Lazarus, as already stated, one hundred and fifty missions had been held, either by Vincent himself or his priests; and from 1632 to 1660 no fewer than seven hundred missions were held, by priests from S. Lazarus alone, while branches of the

Society were established in no fewer than six and twenty of the French dioceses.

The *modus operandi* in these Missions was as follows :—

A written mandate from the Bishop of the diocese was first obtained; next, the consent and blessing of the parish priest. Then one of the company opened the Mission, on a Sunday or other Feast-Day, by a sermon, designed to prepare the people for the coming of the Mission Priests. Another sermon was usually delivered after Vespers, with special instructions as to self-examination, explanations of the Commandments, and exhortations to repentance. A few days afterwards the Mission began : this consisted of preaching and catechising, hearing confessions, reconciling those at variance, visiting the sick, correcting public abuses, and generally performing " all the spiritual works of mercy and charity which lay in their power, or for which Divine Providence found them opportunity." Then public instructions were given daily : a sermon early in the morning, for the benefit of the labouring poor; teaching in the lesser Catechism at one o'clock in the afternoon, and in the greater Catechism in the evening. The Mission Priests also prepared children for their first Communion ; held conferences with the schoolmaster or mistress of the place, and with the parochial clergy.

The second great work of Vincent's life was the institution of a system for the better training and preparation of candidates for Holy Orders. The necessity of such a system was brought home to him by his observation of the carelessness, coldness, and irregularities of the clergy of his time. " He used to say that, as a conquering general, if he would keep possession of the towns which he has taken, must leave strong garrisons behind him ; so, after Satan had been driven from his strongholds, it was very necessary for faithful soldiers of CHRIST to occupy the ground ; and that, unless good and earnest priests could be provided to care for and help on the souls which had been won for GOD, it was almost certain that they would fall back again, and their last state be worse than the first ; and yet he was well aware, from his own acquaintance with the clergy in country places throughout the length and breadth of the land, as well as from the complaints which reached him from all sides, how few such were to be found." To remedy this deplorable state of things became Vincent's earnest desire. He saw that with the existing generation of clergy, men who had grown grey in the old bad order, nothing could be done; his work must be prospective; he must look steadily towards the future. The object to be kept in view was to rear a better class of men as the successors of those who so shamefully desecrated the altars of GOD; and this he proposed to accomplish by providing that none should be received as candidates for Holy Orders who were not adequately instructed and animated by a true spirit of devotion, and by endeavouring that those admitted as ordinands should undergo such a training as would fit them to fulfil successfully the obligations of their sacred calling. His plan was at once adopted by the Bishop of Beauvais, and with results so satisfactory, that it was taken up by the Archbishop of Paris. "Monsignor the Archbishop," says Vincent, "conformably to the ancient practice of the Church, when the Bishops caused all who desired to receive Holy Orders to be carefully instructed for many days beforehand, has ordered that henceforth those in his diocese who have this desire must spend ten days with the Mission Priests, in order to make a spiritual Retreat, to exercise themselves in meditation, which is so needful for ecclesiastics, to make a general confession of their past lives, to go through a course of moral theology, particularly with regard to the use of the Sacraments, to learn rightly to perform the ceremonial of all holy offices, and all other things needful for the clergy. During this time they are lodged and fed, and, by the grace of GOD, such good is the result that all who have gone through these exercises have been found afterwards to lead a truly priestly life; and indeed the greater number have given themselves with special devotion to works of piety, so that their profiting has begun to appear unto all."[1] As the movement extended, Vincent established Retreats for Ordinands at S. Lazarus, receiving five times a year, for eleven days at a time, as many as from seventy to ninety men, who were received as welcome guests, and lodged and boarded free of expense.

[1] "Life of S. Vincent de Paul," ed. by Wilson, pp. 107, 108.

The great blessing which attended the establishment of these Retreats was acknowledged by Vincent with a heart of gratitude; but he was conscious of the weakness of human nature, and fearing that the good impressions and resolutions acquired and made during the Retreat might afterwards be effaced by contact with the world, and the worldly clergy, he meditated some means of strengthening and confirming them until they assumed a permanent character. For this purpose, after much reflection, he instituted a weekly Conference; and every Tuesday the young priests assembled at S. Lazarus to discuss the nature of their solemn duties, and the graces necessary for their due discharge. Out of these meetings grew a confraternity or guild, the members of which were made mutually helpful by certain rules and regulations: thus, they visited one another in sickness, and in case of the death of any of the number, the survivors followed him to the grave. They were also bound to rise at a certain hour, to spend at least half an hour daily in mental prayer, to say Mass, and daily to read, kneeling and bare-headed, a chapter of the New Testament.

The Retreats for Ordinands, by a natural law of progress, developed into Retreats for all classes; so that, at S. Lazarus, soldiers and ecclesiastics, noblemen and artisans, might be seen making their Retreat together, to the number, it is computed, of seven or eight hundred annually. The good that was thus accomplished, who shall attempt to estimate? What a leaven of spiritual fervour must the souls purified and strengthened by these periods of spiritual meditation have diffused among society generally! The soldier went back to his regiment, the artisan to his fellow-workmen, the peasant to his village, to shed around the light of a holy example, and to lead others to a participation in the good which they themselves enjoyed.

We now come to the third, and, in some respects, the most lasting of the great achievements of Vincent's tranquil life, the institution of Sisters of Charity. His first movement in this direction was as early as 1617, when at Chatillon, struck by the poverty around him, and the want of definiteness and order in the attempts made to relieve it, he organised what he called a "Confraternity of Charity," with the design of promoting the care and nursing needed by the sick poor, at their own homes, through the practical sympathy of their neighbours. Any devout women, married or unmarried, were admitted, who, for the love of GOD and His poor, were willing to enter upon the work, and to pledge themselves to a regular and systematic discharge of it. By degrees, these Confraternities spread over all the land, and they almost invariably sprang up in places where Vincent and his Lazarists had held a Mission; so that, in time, their supervision grew into an onerous duty, which for a man burdened with so many good works was almost beyond his power. He looked around him, therefore, for some intelligent, capable, and zealous person to whom he could entrust the delicate task of visiting the various sisterhoods, and seeing that they remained faithful to their original principles. Such a person he found at last in Louise Legras, a lady in opulent circumstances, who, after twelve years of married life, had been left a widow (1625), and had resolved to dedicate herself wholly to the service of GOD. "From her youth," says Miss Kavanagh,[1] "she had been of a serious and philosophic turn of mind; so much so, that her father gave her a classical education, as the only one worthy of her gravity and intellect. But her soul soared beyond the things human learning professes to teach: she longed to enter a religious order; and would have done so, but that her health proved too delicate for the austerities of the cloister. Even in the world she led a life of retirement, charity, and self-denial; and from the first years of her marriage, she belonged to the poor and to the sick of her parish. She visited them in their illnesses, gave them medicines and relief, attended on them, made their beds, consoled or exhorted the sorrow-stricken or the dying, and shrank from no task, not even from the laying out of the dead. In the fervour of her zeal, Madame Legras wished, in placing herself under the spiritual guidance of Vincent, to take a vow of devoting herself henceforth to the poor; but, with his cautious dislike of anything resembling precipitation, he forbade her to do so for four

---

[1] Julia Kavanagh, "Women of Christianity," p. 185.

years; during which he put her zeal and charity to repeated trials."

To this lady Vincent eventually proposed that she should undertake the supervision of his Confraternities of Charity. She gladly assented, and every summer went from village to village, wherever they were established, carefully examining into their progress, and encouraging and instructing their members. Originally they were confined to the rural districts; but as the need for them was as great in towns, and especially in the capital, several Parisian ladies obtained Vincent's permission to form themselves into an association governed by the rules which prevailed in the Vincentian sisterhoods. But it was found, after awhile, that full reliance could not be placed upon ladies of rank and position; that in some cases their husbands objected to the work they had undertaken; that in others the ladies themselves grew weary of its monotony; and that then they were led to devolve their duties upon their servants, who did not always obey their mistresses' orders, and when they did, did not show that love and sympathy and tenderness more eagerly coveted by the poor than any material relief. To meet this difficulty Vincent sought for some pious women who would give up their whole lives to the care of the sick, who would look upon it as an honourable vocation, and a service unto GOD; women whom no social ties would call away from their duties, but in whose faithfulness and intelligence a full confidence might always be placed. It was in 1635 that his search proved successful, and he had the happiness of enrolling three or four "Sisters of Charity" under the charge of Madame Legras. He caused them to undergo a careful training in nursing the sick, in preparing and administering medicines, and other useful and necessary details; and, further, he trained them assiduously to habits of obedience and devotion. The work grew rapidly. The small germ planted by Vincent flourished forth into a noble tree, with branches that extended into many lands. To women—such women as felt no vocation for a married life, but were nevertheless indisposed to enter on the seclusion of the cloister,—women sensible of a capacity for usefulness if they could only find an appropriate channel for their energies,—this new organisation proved almost as great a boon and blessing as it proved to the sick and poor for whose benefit it was set in motion. How many lives it brightened! How many souls it rescued from a dull and dreary lethargy!

In the following century, there were no fewer than four and thirty establishments of Sisters of Charity in Paris alone; and they were to be also found in Italy, and Spain, and Poland, and the Netherlands, in America, and even India. Neither Vincent nor Madame Legras had any conception of the grandeur of the enterprise they had, with so rare a sagacity and so wise a benevolence, initiated. Every great reform outgrows the idea of its author. Columbus, when he revealed the Western World to the investigation of Europe, never, in his most sanguine dreams, anticipated the vast results that would flow from it. In every noble work the increase comes from GOD. Vincent did what he had to do, what lay close at hand to be done, without any thought of the future; and it is only in this way that the best work can be achieved. Let it be owned, however, that he did it admirably; with rare prudence, good sense, and a careful adaptation of means to the end he had in view. He did not attempt too much, nor did he ask too much of the instruments he employed. By degrees he enlarged his design and extended his sphere of action, until almost every branch of philanthropic effort fell within the range of his Sisterhood, but all was done gradually and only after careful consideration. The regulations which he laid down were eminently practical. The sisters took the vows of obedience, chastity, and poverty, after a probation of five years; but they took them only for one year, so that if at any time they became a burden, relief might easily be obtained. Nor could they be renewed without the permission of the Superior. He took every opportunity of impressing them with a sense of the loftiness of the vocation on which they had entered. "A Sister of Charity," he would say, "has need of a higher degree of virtue than the members of the austerest religious order. There is no Order of religious women which has so many duties to perform; inasmuch as the Sisters of Charity must in themselves discharge almost all the offices of other Orders. In the first place, they must labour after their own perfection, with as much earnestness as the Carmelites; next, they nurse the sick, like the nuns of the Hotel Dieu and other hospital sisters; and lastly, they undertake the education of young girls, like the Ursulines. . . . . . They must remember," he would add, " that although they are not nuns, that condition not being suitable for the works of their vocation, for that very reason,—because they are more exposed than those who are cloistered and shut out from the world, they require a loftier and severer virtue. Their monasteries are the homes of the sick; their cells are hired rooms; their cloisters, the streets of the city or the wards of the hospitals; instead of a gate, they have the fear of GOD; and for a veil, holy modesty. Hence they must endeavour in all places to behave with at least as much reserve, self-control, and edification as regular nuns use in their convents; and to obtain of GOD this grace, they must labour to acquire all the virtues commended to them by their rules, and particularly a deep humility, a perfect obedience, and a great detachment or separation from their fellow-creatures. Specially must they take every possible precaution to preserve perfect purity of body and soul."

He continued, in the instructions which he addressed to the Sisters :—" Lest the spiritual offices they render should interfere with the bodily services they are bound to give, —a thing which might easily happen if, by too long staying with one patient they allowed others to suffer, through neglecting to give them their food or medicine at the proper time,—they must be very careful in the management of their time, and the arrangement of their work, according to the number and needs of their patients, great or small. And since in the evening their duties are not generally so urgent as in the morning, they may choose that time for the instruction and exhortation of their patients, particularly when giving them their medicines.

" In their attendance upon the sick they will make GOD their only object, and thus will be indifferent alike to the praises they may receive, or the hard words that may be dealt out to them, except that they will turn both to good account; inwardly rejecting the former, and humbling themselves in thought of their own nothingness ; and welcoming the latter, in honour of the revilings of the SON of GOD upon the Cross by those very men who had received of Him so many favours and graces.

"No gift, however small, must they accept from the poor whom they assist; and they must beware of thinking that the poor are in any way obliged to them for the services they render; seeing that, on the contrary, it is they themselves who are indebted to *them*. For through that small charity which they bestow, not of their substance but only of a little care, they make to themselves friends, who shall one day have a right to receive them into everlasting habitations. And even in this life they receive, through the poor on whom they wait, greater honour and truer satisfaction than they could have dared to hope for in the world: of this they must be careful to make no improper use, but rather to abase themselves in the consciousness of their own unworthiness. . . .

"They will remember that they are called Sisters of Charity, that is, Sisters whose profession it is to love GOD and their neighbour; and, therefore, that, beside the sovereign and supreme love they must have for GOD, they ought to excel in the love of their neighbours, and especially of their companions. Accordingly, they will avoid all coolness and dislike towards any; and, at the same time, all special friendships and attachments to some above others; since these two vicious extremes are sources of division, both in communities and among private persons, if they dwell upon and entertain them. And should it happen that they have given one another any annoyance, they must ask pardon of one another, at the very latest, before they retire to bed.

"Moreover, they will bear in mind that they are called 'servants of the poor,' which, in the eyes of the world, is one of the lowest conditions, to the end that they may always have a low opinion of themselves, and reject immediately the least thought of vain-glory which might arise in their minds, if they hear any good said of their works, remembering that it is to GOD that all the glory is due, because He is the only author of them.

"They will be very faithful and exact in following their Rule, and all the praiseworthy customs which have hitherto been observed in their manner of life, particularly those which concern the perfecting of holiness in themselves.

"But not the less must they remember that, whenever necessity or obedience requires it, they must always prefer the service of the poor to their own practices of devotion, bearing in mind that, in so doing, they are leaving GOD for GOD."

Vincent, however, did not enjoin upon the Sisters those fasts, vigils, and other austerities which are enjoined upon the Cloister. To rise all the year round at four in the morning; to pray twice a day; to live with the greatest frugality; to drink no wine except in illness, to attend on the sick even in the ghastliest diseases, to watch all night long by the bed of the dying, to live immured within hospital walls, and breathe air thick with infection; to endure with calmness, nay, to welcome gratefully, sickness, and weariness, and danger, and death; those were the obligations imposed upon the Sisters of Charity.

This heroism of the Cross commanded the admiration of all thinking minds and excited the wonder even of the thoughtless. To Vincent de Paul himself, who had called it forth, animated, and sustained it, it was ever a matter of deep rejoicing as well as of loving respect. His feelings are best described in his own words, which he addressed to his Mission Priests, in 1658. At the request of Anne of Austria, he had sent four Sisters to attend upon the wounded soldiers at Calais, and two of them had succumbed to fatigue:—
"I recommend to your prayers," he said, "the Sisters of Charity whom we sent to Calais to assist the wounded. Four went, and two, the strongest, have sunk beneath the burden. Imagine what four poor girls can do for five or six hundred sick and wounded soldiers! Is it not affecting? Do not you consider it an action of great merit before GOD that women with so much courage and resolution should go amongst soldiers to relieve them in their need; that they should voluntarily expose themselves to so much fatigue, and even to disease and death, for the sake of those who braved the perils of war for the good of the State? We see how these women were filled with zeal

for the glory of GOD and the succour of their fellow-creatures! The Queen has honoured us by writing and asking for more Sisters to be sent to Calais, and four leave to-day for that purpose. One of them, about fifty years of age, came to me last Friday at the Hôtel Dieu, where I was then staying. She said that, having learned that two of her sisters had died at Calais, she came to offer herself to go in their place, if I would allow it. 'Sister,' I replied, 'I will think about it.' Yesterday she called here to receive my decision. See, my brethren, the courage of these women, thus to come forward like victims, willing and glad to render up their lives for the love of JESUS CHRIST and the good of their neighbour. Is not this admirable? In truth, I know not what to say, except that they will judge us on the great day of the LORD. Yea, they will be our judges, unless we are as ready as they to expose our lives for the love of GOD."

The reference to the Hôtel Dieu reminds us that another of Vincent's good works was the reform of this great Parisian hospital. He also established, in conjunction with Madame Goussault, an Asylum for Foundlings, between 300 and 400 of whom were, at this time, miserably exposed and abandoned in the streets of Paris and its suburbs. It was supported by a small grant from the Crown and by large voluntary contributions; and the King gave up to it the old castle of Bicêtre. There is no exaggeration in saying that every work of philanthropy, every scheme for the improvement of the condition of the poor, the feeble, and the oppressed, was either initiated by Vincent de Paul, or owed its success to his practical energy. Shortly after the accession of Louis XIV., he succeeded, with the help and encouragement of Cardinal Richelieu, in founding a Seminary or Theological College, for the reception and training in all that appertains to the ecclesiastical office of young men desirous of assuming Holy Orders. The first was established in the Collège des Bons Enfants of Paris, in February, 1642; and proved the forerunner and type of similar institutions in most of the dioceses of France. Thus it will be seen that from Vincent de Paul the Church of England has borrowed both her "Missions" and her "Theological Colleges." To some extent she has also adopted his system of Retreats for Ordinands, and Clerical and lay Retreats.

The estimation in which his calm wisdom and unaffected piety were generally held is strikingly illustrated by his appointment, under the regency of Anne of Austria, to be one of a council of six charged with the administration of all ecclesiastical patronage. The other members were Cardinal Mazarin (who had succeeded, on the death of Richelieu, to the reins of government), the Bishops of Beauvais and Lisieux, the Chancellor, and the Grand Penitentiary of Paris. Vincent was not fond of positions which dragged him into the glare of publicity, or involved a waste of precious time in attendance at Court. The Queen, however, would not accept a refusal, and for ten years Vincent was compelled to discharge the only one of his duties which he ever felt to be a burden. He discharged it with a faithfulness which sometimes brought him into collision with his fellow-councillors, and, at least on one occasion, with the Queen Regent, but increased the love and respect felt towards him by all good men.

The Civil War known in history as the Insurrection of the Fronde, which cost France so much blood and treasure in 1648 and 1649, was a source of bitter grief to his gentle soul; and when the royal army, under the Prince de Condé, blockaded Paris, he made a strenuous effort to effect a reconciliation of the contending parties, the Queen and the Parliament (January, 1649). In this he failed; and he then departed on a visitation of some of his houses of Mission Priests and Sisters of Charity. At Richelieu he fell ill; and though he recovered sufficiently to return to S. Lazarus, from that time forward the infirmities of old age crowded rapidly upon him. He was no longer able to move about on foot or on horseback, but was compelled to use a little carriage. It grieved him sorely to resort to this indulgence, but a greater grief was his inability to kneel. He still continued, however, to say Mass daily, and he showed no failure of zeal or energy in the discharge of the multifarious works of mercy, charity, and devotion that devolved upon him. Never was there greater need of his spirit of enthusiastic benevolence and his power of organization; for the war had swept with fire and sword the provinces of Champagne and Picardy, and the Mission Priests, under his direction, were taxed to their uttermost in self-denying efforts to feed the hungry and clothe the naked, shelter the homeless and bury the dead. For upwards of three years the enterprise of relieving the terrible distress in the ravaged districts fell almost entirely to Vincent and his people. And when it was happily brought to a conclusion, there remained yet another loving and charitable work for this unwearied Hero of the Cross to accomplish. In the year 1653, a wealthy Parisian citizen sought his advice how best to employ a large sum of money which he desired to dedicate to GOD's service. It was to be entirely at Vincent's disposal, on condition that the donor's name was never revealed. Such a trust Vincent could not decline; and after due reflection and prayer, he proposed that it should be laid out in founding a Hospital or Almshouse for aged and necessitous artisans. The donor approved of the plan; and accordingly Vincent purchased and fitted up suitable premises for the reception of twenty men and twenty women, under the title of the Hospital of the Name of JESUS.

In May, 1658, being in his eighty-third year, and foreseeing that the hour of his departure could not be long delayed, Vincent prepared for his congregation a code of rules, by which they might be guided in all time to come. The summer passed, and he began to fail very rapidly. Ague, rheumatism, ulcerated and swollen legs, and general debility afflicted him severely, but he did not intermit the exact performance of his duties; his manner preserved its gentleness, his voice its sweetness; and no sigh or murmur escaped his lips. One day, a brother entering his room when the wounded legs were being dressed, was unable to repress the exclamation:—"O, Monsieur, how grievous are your sufferings!" "What," said Vincent, with a serene smile, "do you call that grievous, which is GOD's will, and ordained by Him for a miserable sinner such as I am? GOD forgive you, brother, for your hasty words; but it is not so we should speak in the language of JESUS CHRIST." The same priest, on another occasion, observed that his pains seemed to increase daily. "It is true," he answered; "from the crown of my head to the sole of my feet I feel them increase; but, alas! what an account I shall have to render at the judgment-seat of GOD, before whom I must soon appear, if I do not make a good use of them."

But before he was called away, GOD saw fit to summon three of his dearest friends: the first was M. Portail, his earliest companion, his life-long assistant, his secretary and Assistant Superior. He was followed by Madame Legras, who had been S. Vincent's right hand in organizing the widespread ramifications of the Sisters of Charity. The third was a certain Abbé de Chandenier, who for about seven years had lived at S. Lazare, under the same discipline as the Mission Priests, though not actually a member of the brotherhood, and had been to Vincent a very great joy and comfort by his Christian friendship. The aged Superior yearned to follow these beloved ones to their rest, and was often heard to murmur:—" For so many years, O LORD, have I abused Thy grace! Alas, I live too long, since there is no amendment in my life, and my sins are multiplied according to the number of my years." And again, when he heard of the death of any of his Mission Priests:—" Thou leavest *me*, O GOD, and callest to Thyself Thy servants. I am one of those tares that spoil the good grain Thou gatherest, and here am I still uselessly cumbering the ground. Well, well, my GOD, Thy will be done, not mine."

But to him, as to all, the supreme hour came at last. About noon, on the 25th of September, he fell into a deep sleep. So deep was it and so calm, that, on his awaking, an attendant commented upon it. "Ay," said Vincent, "it is the brother who has come beforehand, while we are waiting for the sister."[1] Next day, Sunday, after hearing Mass in the chapel, and communicating, as was his custom, he was seized with a stupor and drowsiness, from which it was impossible to wake him, except for brief intervals. The physician affirmed that no remedies could further avail, and advised that the Last Sacraments should be administered. He revived sufficiently, however, to utter a few words of benediction on the members of his congregation, absent as well as present. In the evening he received the Sacrament of Extreme Unction. His weakness was so extreme that

[1] The reader will be reminded of Shelley's lines:—
"How wonderful is Death,
Death and his brother Sleep."

no attempt was made to undress him, and he spent the night in his chair, communing peacefully with his GOD in his moments of wakeful consciousness. Among the ejaculations repeated to him he showed most pleasure in the "Deus, in adjutorium meum intende," and whenever he heard it, would answer, "Domine, ad adjuvandum me festina." A Retreat was at this time being held in the Home, and the priest who conducted it, an old friend of Vincent's, obtained permission to take leave of him. He sought his blessing on all the Associates of his weekly Conferences, and his intercession to obtain them grace, so that the fire of holy zeal which his words and example had kindled and fostered might not die out after his departure. Vincent softly answered :—" Qui cœpit opus bonum, ipse perficiet." These were his last words, and they embodied the principle of his whole life; an entire forgetfulness of self, and an ascription of all honour and all glory to his Almighty FATHER.

A few minutes later, at half-past four o'clock on Monday morning, the 27th of September, 1660—"the very hour at which, for forty years, he had been accustomed, every day of his life, to invoke the Presence of GOD in prayer,"—Vincent passed away—still sitting in his chair, in his usual dress, without sigh or struggle—as a child falls asleep. It is profitable to contrast this beautiful picture with that of the old sea-king, who, when he felt the hand of death upon him, caused himself to be clothed in his armour, and placed on his throne, sword in hand, to meet the dread Destroyer, —defiant to the last, because ignorant that, to the saints of GOD, and to all penitent trustful souls, the dark Angel comes with healing on his wings, and throws wide the gates of the Everlasting City! Who would not wish to live and die like Vincent de Paul?

HENRY MARTYN:

SCHOLAR AND MISSIONARY.

" A bright and brief trail of light."
                    MISS YONGE.

"Oh, what a lively life, what heavenly power,
   What spreading virtue, what a sparkling fire!"
                    SIR JOHN DAVIES.

[*Authorities:*—"Journals and Letters of the Rev. Henry Martyn," edit. by the Rev. S. Wilberforce (afterwards Bishop of Oxford and Winchester), ed. 1837; and "Memoir of the Rev. Henry Martyn, B.D.," (by the Rev. John Sargent), edit. 1829. A sketch of Martyn's life and labours at Dinapur and Cawnpur occurs in Mrs. Sherwood's Works. See also Miss Yonge's "Pioneers and Founders;" and Holme Lee's (Miss Harriet Parr's) "His Title of Honour."]

HENRY MARTYN.

CHAPTER I.

HENRY Martyn was born at Truro, in Cornwall, on the 18th of February, 1781. In his eighth year he was sent to the grammar school of his native town, where his lively affectionate temper made him a favourite with his companions, and his docility and diligence with his instructors. Even at this early period, however, he seems to have suffered from an inherited weakness of constitution, which rendered him averse, we are told, to the pastimes and exercises of boyhood. From the Grammar School of Truro he removed, in 1797, to S. John's College, Cambridge. There it was that he first gave indications of the real extent of his intellectual powers; and there, too, his thoughts were first determined towards the things of GOD by the influence of a devout friend, which was confirmed and strengthened by his intercourse with his sister, a woman of gentle spirit and earnest piety. The sudden death of his father helped to fix his inclinations, and he began to study his Bible with a new interest, as a book which not less closely concerned him in the next world than in this. "I attended more diligently," he says, "to the words of our SAVIOUR, and devoured them with delight: where the offers of mercy and forgiveness were made so freely, I supplicated to be made partaker of the covenant of grace with eagerness and hope; and thanks be to the ever-blessed Trinity, for not leaving me without comfort." He was a constant attendant on the ministry of the Rev. Charles Simeon, one of the chief leaders of that Evangelical Renascence in the Church which preceded and paved the way for the great Oxford Revival; and in his later life he was always ready to acknowledge the benefit he derived from his pastoral guidance.

His university career was singularly brilliant. When he entered at S. John's, he was ignorant of the very elements of mathematics; yet, such was the force of his intellect and such the strenuousness of his endeavour, that, in four years' time, and before he was twenty, he won the great and coveted distinction of the Senior Wranglership. Great was his astonishment, however, that the honour when gained brought him so little satisfaction. He felt a yearning in his heart which no external successes could gratify, and soon discovered that the repose he craved could be found only in communion with his heavenly FATHER. His design had been to enter the legal profession; but his newly-awakened distaste for worldly concerns induced him to listen to Mr. Simeon when he discoursed on the high excellence and glorious opportunities of the Christian ministry; and he resolved on dedicating himself to it. He was led to choose the most arduous but the noblest branch of this vocation by hearing Mr. Simeon comment on the services of Dr. Carey in India; soon after which he met with the Life of David Brainerd, the Apostle (as he has been called) of the North American Indians; and, warmed by his example, he decided, not without solemn consideration and frequent prayer, to become a Missionary. Accordingly, he offered himself to the "Society for Missions to Africa and the East" (now known as the Church Missionary Society), which, in 1800, had been established by some members of the Church who were disinclined to co-operate with the older "Society for the Propagation of the Gospel." Thereafter he held himself prepared, "with a child-like simplicity of spirit and an unshaken constancy of soul," to go whenever he was called, and wherever he was directed.

But he was only twenty-one, and too young to take Holy Orders. He had therefore to learn the lesson of patience; and for the next two years he acted as a tutor at Cambridge, while applying himself laboriously to the study of theology.

At this time and throughout his life he kept a journal of his spiritual experiences and daily work. It abounds in evidences of the depths of his piety and the sincerity of his resolutions; but also, as it seems to me, in an excessive self-introspection and self-consciousness which might probably have developed into morbidness, had not GOD mercifully arrested the tendency by calling him to a life of Christian action. Of the severity of the judgments he passed upon himself, the following extracts will give a sufficient idea:—" Pride shows itself every hour of the day; what long and undisturbed possession does self-complacency hold of my heart! what plans and dreams and visions of futurity fill my imagination, in which self is the prominent object. . . . In my intercourse with some of my dear friends, the workings of pride were but too plainly marked in my outward demeanour; on looking up to GOD for pardon for it, and deliverance from it, I felt overwhelmed with guilt. . . . Mr. Simeon's sermon this morning, on 2 Chron. xxxii. 31, discovered to me my corruption and vileness more than any sermon I had ever heard. . . . Oh, that I had a more piercing sense of the Divine presence! How much sin in the purest services! If I were sitting in heavenly places with CHRIST, or rather with my thoughts habitually there, how would every duty, but especially this of social prayer, become easy:—' Memoria tua sancta, et dulcedo tua beatissima, possideat animam meam, atque in invisibilium amorem rapiat illam.'"

On the 23rd of October, 1803, when still within five months of the full canonical age, he was admitted to the diaconate, became Mr. Simeon's curate, and took charge of the neighbouring parish of Lulworth. His diary now multiplies its instances of the extent to which his habit of self-examination cramped his powers and narrowed his views of duty. The emotional side of Evangelicalism had an undue attraction for him, and he suffered himself to believe that the healthy and legitimate cultivation of the faculties he had received from GOD was a sinful employment of his time. " I read Mitford's History of Greece, as I am to be classical examiner. To keep my thoughts," he writes, "from wandering away to take pleasure in those studies, required more watchfulness and earnestness in prayer than I can account for. . . . Did I delight in reading the Retreat of the Ten Thousand Greeks, and shall not my soul glory in the knowledge of GOD, who created the Greeks, and the vast countries over which they passed? I examined in Butler and in Xenophon; how much pride and ostentatious display of learning was visible in my conduct; how that detestable spirit follows me; whatever I do." Happily, the force of events opened out to him a wider sphere of thought and action, which brought with it enlarged and more liberal views. He had formed a strong attachment to a young lady of Cornwall, named Lydia Grenfell, who returned his affection, and this in itself was sufficient to awaken and foster the broader sympathies. But his design of leaving England in the service of the Church Missionary Society was frustrated by pecuniary misfortunes, which involved the loss not only of his own patrimony, but of that of his younger sister, and rendered her to a great extent dependent upon him for support. In these circumstances his friends recommended him to a chaplaincy under the East India Company, and he was promised the first vacancy. He then went down to Cornwall to spend the long vacation, and take leave of those he loved before setting out on his long and lonely voyage. The trial was severe, especially in parting from his sisters and the young lady to whom he had given his heart. For many days after the farewell had been said, "his mental agony was extreme; yet he could speak to GOD, as to one who knew the great conflict within him: he was convinced, that as GOD willed his happiness, He was providing for it eventually by that bitter separation: he resolved through grace to be His, though it should be through much tribulation; he experienced sweetly and solemnly the excellence of serving Him faithfully, and of following CHRIST and His Apostles; he meditated with great joy on the end of this world, and enjoyed the thought of walking hereafter with her, from whom he was removed, in the realms of glory."

On the 27th of August, 1804, he writes in his Journal:—

"Walked to Marazion, with my heart more delivered from its idolatry, and enabled to look steadily and peacefully to GOD. Reading in the afternoon to Lydia alone, from Dr. Watts, there happened to be among other things a prayer on entire preference of GOD to the creatures. Now, thought

I, here am I in the presence of GOD and my idol. So I used the prayer for myself, and addressed it to GOD, Who answered it, I think, for my love was kindled to GOD and divine things, and I felt cheerfully resigned to the will of GOD, to forego the earthly joy, which I had just been desiring with my whole heart. I continued conversing with her, generally with my heart in heaven, but every now and then resting on her. Parted with Lydia, perhaps for ever in this life, with a sort of uncertain pain, which I knew would increase to greater violence afterwards, on reflection. Walked to S. Hilary, determining in great tumult and inward pain, to be the servant of GOD. All the rest of the evening, in company, or alone, I could think of nothing but her excellences. My efforts were, however, through mercy, not in vain, to feel the vanity of this attachment to the creature. Read in Thomas à Kempis many chapters, directly to the purpose; the shortness of time, the awfulness of death, and its consequences, rather settled my mind to prayer. I devoted myself unreservedly to the cause of the LORD, to Him, as to one who knew the great conflict within, and my firm resolve through His grace of being His, though it should be with much tribulation."

Returning to Cambridge he continued to work there until he received his appointment in January, 1805. In the following March he was admitted to Priests' Orders at S. James's Chapel, London; after which the degree of B.D. was conferred upon him by mandate from the University. While preparing for embarkation he applied himself to the study of Hindustani, in which he made considerable progress; and that he might correct some defects in his speech, he attended several lectures on pronunciation. On the 17th of July he sailed from Portsmouth in the *Union;* but on the 19th an accident which befell one of the vessels composing the fleet, led to their putting into Falmouth harbour, where they remained for three weeks. Thus he was afforded an opportunity for a brief visit to his friends, which comforted him greatly. He found his sister engaged to be married to one not unworthy of her; and was led to form a hope that after he was settled in India he might be joined by his Lydia. On the 18th of August the *Union* weighed anchor, but for two or three days longer continued to linger on the coast, and the sight of each well-known landmark and familiar scene awoke in Martyn's breast a crowd of conflicting emotions. By constant prayer and meditation he subdued his natural regrets; and after he had overcome the physical discomfort attending his first experience of the sea, he applied himself zealously to his duties on board. While continuing his study of Hebrew and Hindustani he acted as chaplain, though permitted only to hold one service every Sunday; but he laboured unremittingly to improve the spiritual condition of the crew by private exhortation and reading. Scarcely a day passed but he went between decks; where, after assembling all who were willing to attend, he read, and commented upon, some suitable religious book. Describing his congregation, he says:— "Some attend fixedly,—others are looking another way— some women are employed about their children, attending for a little while, and then heedless: some rising up and going away—others taking their place; and numbers, especially of those who have been on watch, strewed all along upon the deck fast asleep—one or two from the upper decks looking down and listening." He found little encouragement among the officers and better class of passengers, who, resenting the stern and uncompromising character of his addresses, would sit drinking and smoking and jesting while he was holding his Sunday service. Young and inexperienced, he endeavoured to startle them out of their thoughtlessness and profanity by denunciations of the wrath to come and lurid pictures of Hell; but they retaliated by declaring that they would not come to his sermons. On the 22nd of September, he writes:—" Was more tried by the fear of man, than I have ever been since GOD has called me to the ministry. The threats and opposition of these men made me unwilling to set before them the truths which they hated; yet I had no species of hesitation about doing it. They had let me know that if I would preach a sermon like one of Blair's, they should be glad to hear it, but they would not attend if so much of hell was preached. This morning again Captain —— said, 'Mr. Martyn must not damn us to-day, or none will come again.' I was a little disturbed; but Luke x. 1, above all, our LORD's last address to His disciples, John xiv. 16, strengthened me. I took for my text Psalm ix. 17. 'The wicked shall be turned into hell, and all the nations that forget GOD.' The officers were all behind my back, in order to have an opportunity of retiring in case of dislike. B—— attended the whole time. H———, as soon as he heard the text, went back, and said he would hear no more about hell; so he employed himself in feeding the geese. —— said I had shut him up in hell, and the universal cry was, 'We are all to be damned.' However, GOD, I trust, blessed the sermon to the good of many. Some of the cadets, and many of the soldiers were in tears. I felt an ardour and a vehemence in some parts which are unusual with me." Whatever we may think of Martyn's discretion, we must admire his courage; but he exhibited greater wisdom in endeavouring to gain the confidence of the cadets by helping them in their studies and lending them books.

Putting in at the Cape, the *Union* disembarked the 59th regiment to assist Sir David Baird's army in the struggle against the Dutch, and it shared in the great victory which gave South Africa to English enterprise (January 8th, 1806.) Martyn went on shore the next day to minister among the wounded, and he accompanied a party of the Company's troops to the field of battle. "Mournful as the scene was," he says, " I yet thanked GOD that He had brought me to see a specimen, though a terrible one, of what men by nature are. May the remembrance of this day ever excite me to pray and labour more for the propagation of the Gospel of peace. Then, shall men love one another. Nation shall not lift up sword against nation, neither shall they learn war any more. The Blue Mountains, at a distance to the eastward, which formed the boundary of the prospect, were a cheering counterpart to what was immediately before me; for there I conceived my beloved and honoured fellow-servants, companions in the kingdom and patience of JESUS CHRIST, to be passing the days of their pilgrimage far from the world, imparting the truths of the precious Gospel to benighted souls. May I receive grace to be a follower of their faith and patience. . . . I marched back, the same evening, with the troops. The surf on the shore was very high, but, through mercy, we escaped that danger."

While the ship remained at Cape Town, Martyn found

time to form some pleasant friendships with the Dutch clergy; but in the middle of February, she put to sea again, and he was subjected to a renewal of his former trials. He suffered much from illness, but more from the hostility evinced towards him by the passengers and the indifference to divine things shown by the crew. "I go down," he says, "and stand in the midst of a few, without their taking the slightest notice of me; LORD, it is for Thy sake I suffer such slights—let me persevere notwithstanding." To the very end of the voyage this opposition continued; and while we may admit that it was provoked by his faults of manner, and the Calvinistic character of his teaching, we cannot but feel surprise that none of his more educated and intelligent adversaries recognised the moral beauty of his life and his constancy and courage as a soldier of the Cross. His example should have weighed with them, if they scorned his precepts or rejected his doctrines.

As they were rapidly approaching their destination, Martyn, on the 20th of April, preached his farewell sermon. The occasion was one which might have solemnised the most thoughtless; but those who had ridiculed him at first, continued to ridicule him to the last. "It pained me," he remarked, "that they should give a ridiculous turn to anything on so affecting an occasion as parting for ever in this life. But such is the unthankful office of a minister. Yet I desire to take the ridicule of men with all meekness and charity, looking forward to another world for approbation and reward."

Two days later the ship dropped anchor in the Madras roads, and Martyn went ashore to enjoy a brief repose on land before the fleet resumed its voyage to Calcutta. Early in May he was again at sea. While ascending the Hugli, he suffered severely from the climate, which produced a most painful relaxation of the frame, and seemed to unknit his nerves as well as his energies. He looked forward sadly to an idle, worthless life spent in India to no purpose. Exertion seemed to him like death; or indeed, an absolute impossibility. "But it pleased GOD at length to give him deliverance, by enabling him to exercise faith, and to remember that, as a sinner saved, he was bound to evince the most fervent gratitude to GOD."

Almost immediately after his arrival at Calcutta, he was seized with a violent attack of fever, during which he was nursed with devoted sympathy by a brother-missionary, the Rev. David Brown. On his recovery, his friends, and he soon numbered many, would fain have kept him among them at Calcutta; but his enthusiasm yearned for labour among the heathen, and it was stimulated by the sights and sounds of idolatry which met him on every hand. In a dark wood near Serampur, he heard the clash of drums and cymbals, summoning the poor natives to the worship of hideous idols; and before a black image, throned in a pagoda, with lights flaming around it, he beheld the worshippers prostrating themselves, with their foreheads to the earth; a spectacle which thrilled him with overwhelming compassion, and made him shiver as if he stood "in the neighbourhood of hell." In concert with Mr. Brown, Dr. Carey, and other missionaries, he purchased a heathen pagoda, which was devoted to the worship of GOD. He still continued his Hebrew and Hindustani studies, and began to work at Sanskrit, while he seized every opportunity of promoting the great cause he had at heart. His stipend as chaplain proved to be liberal enough to justify him in inviting Miss Grenfell to come out to him as his future wife. No answer could be received under sixteen or seventeen months, and throughout that time he lived in a state of happy expectation, which, perhaps, rendered him all the less fitting to bear the heavy blow of her refusal.

The station to which he was appointed chaplain was Dinapur; and on the 15th of October he began his journey thither. It occupied him, such was then the slow rate of travelling, until the 26th of November. His objects there were threefold; to open native schools, to attain such readiness in speaking Hindustani as might enable him to preach in that language the Gospel of the grace of GOD; and to prepare religious tracts and translations of the Bible for distribution. With the assistance of his munshi, he undertook to translate the Parables into Hindustani; a task of considerable difficulty, as each district had its peculiar dialect. While thus engaged with his munshi, a Mussulman, he had numerous opportunities for study of the Mohammedan arguments. Upon showing him the first part of the 3rd chapter of S. John, he instantly caught at those words of our LORD, in which He first describes Himself as having *come down* from Heaven, and then calls Himself the Son of Man which *is* in Heaven. He said this was what the philosophers called *wickal*, or impossible; impossible even for GOD to make a thing to be in two different places at the same time. As soon as his effervescence had a little subsided, Mr. Martyn explained to him that the difficulty lay not so much in conceiving how the Son of Man could be in two different places at the same time, as in comprehending that union of the two natures, the Divine and the Human, which made this possible. That he could not explain this union Mr. Martyn admitted; but he dwelt on the design and wisdom of GOD in effecting our redemption by this method. Again, the munshi, who seems to have been an admirable specimen of the self-sufficient Mohammedan, expressed great contempt for the Epistles of S. John; so far above the wisdom of the world is their Apostolic simplicity! When he came to the part about the angels " separating the evil from the good," he said, with some surprise, that there was no such thing in his Shaster; but that, at the end of the world, the sun would come so near as, first, to burn all the moon, then the mountains, then the devtas, (inferior gods,) then the waters; and lastly, GOD, reducing Himself to the size of a thumb-nail, would swim on the leaf of the peepul tree.

At Dinapur the arrangements for public worship were at first very unseemly; and Martyn had to read prayers to the soldiers on the long drum by way of desk, and to omit the sermon, because there were no seats. But afterwards a room was provided and decently fitted up, and the families of the English residents began to attend, though as they were not easily reconciled to the innovation of an extempore sermon, he found it prudent to conciliate them by returning to the old orthodox practice. It must be confessed that with all his wonderful ardour and Christian philanthropy, he lacked "sweetness and light"—that discretion and reasonable consideration for the small prejudices and partialities of others which is included in the Pauline precept of being all things to all men; and he was unquestionably better fitted to succeed as a missionary among the heathen than as a priest and pastor among his own people. He had been bred up in a narrow school, and he never emancipated himself from its narrowness. Thus he held strictly to the Judaic interpretation of the Fourth Commandment, and one Sunday, having translated the Prayer Book into Hindustani as far as the end of the *Te Deum*, he abruptly terminated his labours from a fear "that they were not in perfect harmony with the solemnity of the day." Beyond all praise, however, was his courageous sympathy with the natives, whom he frequently interfered to protect from the grossest injustice and oppression.[1]

While at Dinapur he made the acquaintance of Mrs. Sherwood, author of "Little Henry and his Bearer," and other once popular tales. She has left on record a description of his person and manners at this period.[2]

"He was dressed in white, and looked very pale, which, however, was nothing singular in India; his hair, a light brown, was raised from his forehead, which was a remarkably fine one. His features were not regular, but the expression was so luminous, so intellectual, so affectionate, so beaming with Divine charity, that no one could have looked at his features and thought of their shape or form; the outbeaming of his soul would absorb the attention of every observer. There was a very decided air of the gentleman, too, about Mr. Martyn, and a perfection of manners which, from his extreme attention to all minute civilities, might seem almost inconsistent with the general bent of his thoughts to the most serious subjects. He was as remarkable for ease as for cheerfulness. He did not appear like one who felt the necessity of contending with the world and denying himself its delights, but, rather, as one who was unconscious of the existence of any attractions in the world, or of any delights which were worthy of his notice. When he relaxed from his labours in the presence of his friends, it was to play and laugh like an innocent child, more especially if children were present to play and laugh with him."

He had not much time for such relaxation; his labours were arduous and incessant, and his keen sense of duty

---

[1] Sargent, "Life of Henry Martyn," p. 238.
[2] Yonge, "Pioneers and Founders," p. 80.

permitted no suspension of them, no imperfect or half-hearted performance. For baptisms, marriages, and burials he had often to travel great distances; he attended on the sick in the hospitals; he taught in the schools which he had established for the children both of the English and the natives; he preached frequently; he conversed with Hindu and Mohammedan, with all who sought instruction or counsel; and he toiled at his versions of the Prayer Book into Persian and Hindustani. In his Persian work he was assisted by a certain Nathanael Sabat, a converted Arab, a man of wild and varied experiences, great natural ability, and a violent temper. His outbreaks of arrogance caused Martyn great anxiety; but about this time he endured a deeper sorrow in having to abandon all hope of an union with Miss Grenfell, who was induced, for family reasons, to refuse to join him as he had hoped, in India. He writes in his journal (November 23rd, 1807):—" I am filled with grief: I cannot bear to part with Lydia, and she seems more necessary to me than my life; yet her letter was to bid me a last farewell. Oh, how have I been crossed from childhood, and yet how little benefit have I received from these chastisements of my GOD! The LORD now sanctify this, that since the last desire of my heart also is withheld, I may with resignation turn away for ever from the world, and henceforth live forgetful of all but GOD."

The year had also been overshadowed by the death of his eldest sister, so that it passed away in a thick cloud and amid sore tribulation, brightened only by that faith in GOD, that love of CHRIST, that resignation to the Divine Will in which the young missionary never failed. On the 1st of January, 1808, he writes :—" The events which have taken place in the past year, most nearly interesting to myself, are, my sister's death, and my disappointment about Lydia; on both these afflictions I have seen love inscribed, and that is enough. What I think I want, it is still better to want: but I am often wearied with this world of woe. I set my affections on the creature, and am then torn from it; and from various other causes, particularly the prevalence of sin in my heart, I am often so full of melancholy, that I hardly know what to do for relief. Sometimes I say :—' O that I had wings like a dove, then would I flee away and be at rest;' at other times, in my sorrow about the creature, I have no wish left for any heavenly rest. It is the grace and favour of GOD that have saved me hitherto; my ignorance, waywardness, and wickedness would long since have plunged me into misery; but there seems to be a mighty exertion of mercy and grace upon my sinful nature every day, to keep me from perishing at last. My attainments in the Divine Life, in this last year, seem to be none at all; I appear, on the contrary, to be more self-willed and perverse, and more like many of my countrymen, in arrogance and a domineering spirit over the natives. The LORD save me from my wickedness! Henceforth let my soul, humbly depending on the grace of CHRIST, perfect holiness in the fear of GOD, and show towards all Europeans and natives the mind that was in CHRIST JESUS!"

The year 1808 was one of great tranquillity. Martyn continued his ministrations at the hospital, and daily, when his feeble health permitted, received the more religious members of his flock at his own house. He revised the sheets of his completed Hindustani version of the New Testament, and carefully supervised the Persian translation which he had entrusted to Sabat. And he undertook the study of Arabic that he might fit himself to prepare another rendering of the Testament into that tongue.

In April, 1809, he was removed to Cawnpur, where the Sherwoods were then residing, and his intimacy with that agreeable family rendered the removal very pleasant. The time of the year was specially unfavourable for travelling; but with his usual eagerness to respond to the call of duty, Martyn travelled day and night across the hot sandy plains between Chunar and Cawnpur. On his arrival at his destination, Mr. Sherwood had barely led him into his bungalow before he fainted away, and for some days he lay very ill. Himself describing the journey, he says:—" From Allahabad to Cawnpur how shall I describe what I suffered! Two days and two nights was I travelling without intermission. Expecting to arrive early on Saturday morning, I took no provision for that day. Thus I lay in my palanquin faint, with a headache, neither awake nor asleep, between dead and alive—the wind blowing flames. The bearers were so unable to bear up, that we were six hours coming the last six *kos* (twelve miles). . . . Even now the motion of the palanquin is not out of my brain, nor the heat out of my blood."

His life at Cawnpur borrowed a brief sweet sunshine from his acquaintance with the Sherwoods. They conversed together and sang together; and he delighted in petting and fondling Mrs. Sherwood's baby daughter. A welcome was always ready for him in his seasons of weariness and despondency, and in his attacks of illness kind hands provided him with the necessary comforts. Otherwise he lived at Cawnpur as at Dinapur, studying laboriously, and earnestly discharging his pastoral duties. A glimpse of the moral courage which marked his conduct and character is afforded in the following extract from one of his letters (Sept. 18, 1809) :—[1]

"To-morrow the Commander-in-Chief is to be here, and I must let you know whether I can get the promise of a church from him. His family are all at General S.'s, where I breakfasted with them this morning, and baptized a child of Mrs. C., his daughter. Mrs. H. and her three daughters joined with exemplary piety in the Baptismal and Churching services; and they read the responses aloud, and knelt as if they were accustomed to kneel in secret, from the manner in which they bow their knees in public prayer. The Miss ——s are remarkably modest and correct; a great deal of pains seems to have been taken with them by their mother. General —— has never been very cordial, and now he is likely to be less so; for while we were walking up and down together, I reproved him for swearing; though it was done in the gentlest way, he did not seem to like it. It was the first time he had been called to order for some years I suppose. 'So you are giving me a private lecture,' said he. He then went on in a very angry and confused manner defending the practice of swearing. 'GOD judges of the heart, and sees there is no bad intention,' &c. Against all this I urged Scripture."

Of his simplicity, his ignorance of the ways of household management, Mrs. Sherwood records some agreeable anecdotes. Late one evening he observed :—" The coolie (a native porter and messenger) does not come with my

[1] *Journals and Letters*, ii., 255, 256.

money. I was thinking this morning how rich I should be, and now I should not wonder in the least if he has run off and taken my treasure with him." Upon inquiry the Sherwoods found that, not having drawn his stipend for some time, he had sent a note to the collector requesting him to forward it by bearer. It was sent accordingly, silver coin, tied up in bags; but no one expected Martyn would ever see it. However, before the evening was over, the coolie arrived with it in safety. Another time, when both he and the Sherwoods had ordered a pine apple cheese, it was remarked that "the cuts" in the two cheeses were curiously similar; and no wonder! For it appeared that the servants made one cheese do duty for both tables, and this the more easily because Martyn supped always on limes and other fruits, and produced his cheese only when the Sherwoods came to supper.

The close of the year 1809 was marked by the beginning of his public ministrations among the Heathen. A crowd of Togis and Fakirs, and other mendicants, assembled in his garden every Sunday evening to receive alms, and after some trembling of spirit, arising from excessive humility, he resolved to preach to them the truths of CHRIST. It was on the 17th of December he made his first essay. The appearance of the congregation was very striking; no dreamer in the delirium of a raging fever could picture forth a wilder, a more fantastic scene. Four hundred beggars stood or crouched before the earnest, pale-faced preacher: some clothed in abominable rags, others almost without covering, or plastered foully with mud and cow-dung, or with long matted locks streaming down to their heels; every face grim and ghastly with evil passions; the lips black with tobacco or crimson with lecana. One man, in a cart drawn by a bullock, was so bloated as to resemble an enormous frog; another had held his arm above his head with his fist clenched till the nail had come out at the back of his hand; a third had all his bones traced on his dark skin in chalk, so that he looked like the skeleton figure of Death himself. After requesting their attention, Martyn told them,[1] that he gave with pleasure the alms he could afford, but wished to give them something better, namely,

[1] Sargent, "Life and Letters," p. 325.

eternal riches, or the knowledge of GOD, which was to be had from GOD's word; and then, producing a Hindustani version of Genesis, he read the first verse, and explained it word by word. "In the beginning, when there was nothing, no heaven, no earth, but only GOD. He created, without help, for His own pleasure. But who is GOD? One so great, so good, so wise, so mighty, that none can know Him as he ought to know: but yet we must know that He knows us. When we rise up, or sit down, or go out, He is always with us. He created heaven and earth; therefore, everything in heaven, sun, moon, and stars. Therefore how should the sun or the moon be GOD? Everything on earth, and therefore the Ganges also: how then should Gange be a God?" In this strain he continued, and his strange audience heard him with interest and not without marks of approval.

Sunday after Sunday he persevered in these addresses; though the British authorities regarded them with much anxiety, and the natives sometimes interrupted them with howls and threats. The number of his congregation increased every week until as many as nine hundred were present. At last, pulmonary disease, the sad inheritance of his family, revealed some of its worst symptoms, and the physicians ordered him to desist from work (the hardest sentence that can be passed upon a true worker!) to take a sea-voyage, and visit England. With much reluctance he yielded to the mandate; and then, reviving his old sweet love-dream, he entered in his journal a pathetic fancy:—
"Was walking with Lydia; both much affected, and speaking on the things dearest to us both. I awoke, and behold it was a dream. My mind remained very solemn and passive; shed some tears; the clock struck three, and the moon was riding near her highest noon; all was silence and solemnity, and I thought with some pain of the 16000 miles between us. But good is the will of the LORD, if I see her no more." Meanwhile, he learned from the critical authorities at Calcutta that the translation Sabat had made, under his supervision, of the Gospels into Persian, was not simple enough "to be understood of the people," that it was too full of Arabic idioms. Thereupon he resolved to spend the leave of absence he had obtained in travelling through

Arabia and Persia, for the purpose of collecting the opinions of learned natives and improving himself in the language.

On the last day of September, 1810, he took leave of Cawnpur, preaching for the first time in the church which had been raised chiefly by his exertions. "He began," says Mrs. Sherwood, "in a weak and faint voice, being at that time in a very bad state of health; but gathering strength as he proceeded, he seemed as one inspired from on high. Never was audience more affected." After the morning service was over, he returned home, nearly fainting, and was laid upon a couch in the hall of his bungalow. As soon as he revived, he begged his friends to sing to him, and they raised that grand hymn of consolation :—

> " O GOD, our help in ages past,
> Our Hope in years to come,
> Our Shelter from the stormy blast,
> And our Eternal Home."

After an early dinner, and afternoon repose, he preached, on a hot, sickly, lurid evening, to his wild Hindu congregation; preached with a melancholy heart, for of all the seed he had flung abroad he feared that not a grain had fallen upon propitious soil. In this, however, he was mistaken; for it is known that at least one brand was plucked from the burning,—Sheik Salah, the son of a Delhi pundit, who became a faithful Christian.

On the 1st of October, Martyn embarked on the Ganges, and descended the river to Calcutta, where he arrived on the last day of the month. Notwithstanding his excessive weakness, he preached every Sunday but one during his sojourn in the Anglo-Indian capital; he could not rest and be silent, so long as an opportunity offered of proclaiming the message of the SAVIOUR. On the 7th of January, 1811, he took final leave of his friends; and, sick and friendless, departed on his adventurous journey.

CHAPTER II.

MARTYN went by sea to Bombay, and there obtained a passage on board an English ship which had been ordered on a cruise in the Persian Gulf, against 'the Arab pirates. On the 22nd of May he landed at Bushire. As a protection against insult on his road to Shiraz, the Persian capital, where resided the British ambassador, Sir Gore Ouseley, he was advised to assume the Oriental dress; and accordingly provided himself with a tall conical cap of black Tartar lambskin, very wide Zouave-like blue trousers, long red boots, and a chintz coat. He allowed his beard and moustaches to grow, and learned how to eat rice dexterously by handfuls from the common dish. An English officer joining company with him, a muleteer undertook to carry them to Shiraz; a terrible journey, under a glaring brazen sun, and up steep, rugged mountain-paths; no clouds to temper the heat of heaven, no verdure to refresh the parched barrenness of earth. They travelled only by night, and encamped by day; sometimes without the shelter even of a tree; wrapping the head in a wet cloth, and the body in all the heavy clothing possible, to prevent the waste of moisture; but even thus Martyn describes his condition as "a fire within my breast, my skin like a cinder, the pulse violent." In the middle of the day the thermometer often rose to 126°; in the evening sank seldom below 100°.

On the 9th of June Martyn arrived at Shiraz, where he was cordially received by Sir Gore Ouseley, and presented to the heir to the throne, Prince Abbas Mirza. He thus describes the ceremony :—[1]

"Early this morning I went with the Ambassador and his suite to Court, wearing, agreeable to custom, a pair of red cloth stockings, with green high-heeled shoes. When we entered the great court of the palace, a hundred fountains began to play. The Prince appeared at the opposite side, in his talar, or hall of audience, seated on the ground. Here our first bow was made. When we came in sight of him, we bowed a second time, and entered the room. He

[1] Sargent, pp. 377, 378.

did not rise, nor take notice of any but the Ambassador, with whom he conversed at the distance of the breadth of the room. Two of his ministers stood in front of the hall, outside : the Ambassador's Michmandur, and the Master of the Ceremonies, within, at the door. We sat down in order, in a line with the Ambassador, with our hats on. I never saw a more sweet and engaging countenance than the Prince's; there was such an appearance of good nature and humility in all his demeanour, that I could scarcely bring myself to believe that he would be guilty of anything cruel or tyrannical."

Martyn worked with his usual energy on his new Persian translation, deriving much assistance from the co-operation of an accomplished Sufite, Mirza Said Ali Khan. It was completed by the 24th of February, 1812, and in six weeks more he had translated the Psalms. On the 14th of May, one year after entering Persia, he set out, with another English clergyman, to lay his translation before the Shah; but finding, that without a letter of introduction from the British Ambassador, he could not be admitted into the royal presence, he determined to proceed to Tabriz, whither Sir Gore Ouseley had removed. The journey from Shiraz to Tabriz occupied eight weeks, including a rest of six days at Ispahan, and another delay at the Shah's camp; and the latter portion of it was fraught with great suffering and danger. Both Martyn and his companion were attacked with fever, and were almost in want of the necessaries of life. He writes on the 25th of June:—" We have now eaten nothing for two days. My mind is much disordered from head-ache and giddiness, from which I am seldom free; but my heart, I trust, is with CHRIST and His saints. To live much longer in this world of sickness and pain seems no way desirable; the most favourite prospects of my heart seem very poor and childish, and cheerfully would I exchange them for the unfading inheritance."

He reached Tabriz in a wretched condition; and an illness of nearly two months' duration baffled his intention of presenting in person his translation to the Shah. His disappointment, however, was much lessened by the kindness of Sir Gore Ouseley, who, together with his wife, nursed the sick scholar with assiduous attention; and, in order that nothing might be wanting to the favourable acceptance of the result of his labours with the Shah, undertook himself to present it at Court.

As soon as Martyn had recovered from his fever, he decided on making his way to Constantinople, and thence to England, where he hoped to regain his health and strength, so that he might resume his missionary work in India, accompanied, perhaps, by his beloved Lydia. To this lady his last letter was written from Tabriz on the 28th of August, and he refers in it to the possibility of their meeting :—" Do I dream," he says, " that I venture to think and write of such an event as that! Is it possible that we shall ever meet again below? Though it is possible, I dare not indulge such a pleasing hope yet. I am still at a tremendous distance; and the countries I have to pass through are many of them dangerous to the traveller from the hordes of banditti, whom a feeble government cannot chastise." He set out from Tabriz on the 2nd of September; on the 10th, arrived at Erivan; on the 25th, at Erzeroum. This town he left on the afternoon of the 29th, but immediately after was attacked with his old complaint of fever and ague, which he was in too enfeebled a condition to resist. He still pressed forwards, however, though met with the news that he was advancing into a district ravaged by the plague. "Thus," he writes in his Diary, "I am passing inevitably into imminent danger. O LORD, Thy will be done! Living or dying, remember me!" He met with much discomfort from the insolence of Hasan Aga, the Tartar engaged to escort him; and he felt it the more as his weakness hourly increased. The last entries in his journal bear date the 5th and 6th of October, and are very affecting :—

" *October 5th.*—Preserving Mercy made me see the light of another morning. The sleep had refreshed me, but I was feeble and shaken. . . . The manzil, however, being not distant, I reached it without much difficulty. I expected to have found it another strong fort at the end of the pass, but it is a poor little village within the jaws of the mountains. I was pretty well lodged, and tolerably well till a little after sunset, when the ague came on with a violence I never before experienced. I felt as if in a palsy, my teeth chattering, and my whole frame violently shaken. Aga Hosyn and another Persian, on their way here from Constantinople, going to Abbas Mirza, whom I had just before been visiting, came hastily to render me assistance if they could. These Persians appear quite brotherly, after the Turks. While they pitied, Hasan sat with perfect indifference ruminating on the further delay this was likely to occasion. The cold fit, after continuing two or three hours, was followed by a fever, which lasted the whole night, and prevented sleep.

"*October 6th.*—No horses being to be had, I had an unexpected repose. I sat in the orchard, and thought, with sweet comfort and peace, of my GOD; in solitude—my company, my friend, my comforter. O, when shall Time give place to Eternity! When shall appear that new heaven and new earth wherein dwelleth righteousness! There—there shall in no wise enter in anything that defileth: none of that wickedness that has made men worse than wild beasts—none of those corruptions that add still more to the miseries of mortality, shall be seen or heard of any more."

Ten days later Henry Martyn was dead. On the 16th of October, at Tocat, the struggle was ended; but whether he succumbed to the plague, fever, or exhaustion, was never ascertained. He lies in an unknown grave, with no memorial to distinguish his last resting-place.

In the judgment of the world, no doubt Martyn's life was a failure. But was it really so? Did he accomplish nothing for CHRIST and his fellow-men? Oh, infinitely better and nobler such a life of self-sacrifice and devotion even with such an end, than that of the drawing-room idler, immured in frivolities, or of the man of business, with "gain" as the pole-star of all his efforts, or of the warrior who rises to power and glory at the cost of infinite human agony and suffering!

In Holme Lee's " Her Title of Honour," which is founded on the story of Henry Martyn, two characters are introduced as conversing thus :—

"No man," says one, "ever more literally fulfilled the Divine command to forsake all, take up the Cross, and follow CHRIST."

"If self-renunciation," says the other, "be the first of Christian virtues, he practised it, and also he imposed it upon others. He was holy, just, and true—but what profit was there in his life? You call him *missionary*—where are his witnesses? He held disputations with several learned Eastern scholars—did he convert any? With the help of native scholars he made translations from Holy Writ. I believe he baptized one poor old Hindu woman. I know he bore much ridicule, scoffing, mockery; I know he suffered a martyrdom of sorrows; I know he died alone—in a strange land—alone. If GOD accepted his sacrifice, where is his witness?"

"His witness," rejoins the first speaker, "is the loving admiration of all good men. His noble example has drawn many after him. The seed he sowed is springing up a hundredfold. His name will be a light to the world for many generations."

"Well, then, take his journals—let the world know how he laboured and sorrowed, and saw no fruits of his labours."

"It is not true," is the answer, "that success makes the hero. Some day you will be satisfied that what Henry Martyn did was well done; you will not call his journals only a pathetic record of a disappointed life. He was happier than you or I, for he fulfilled more perfectly the will of his heavenly FATHER."

"The sweet peace in his SAVIOUR that he felt when dying, worn out in His service, is, I suppose, the moral of his story."

"It is a beautiful story," concludes the first speaker, "a noble story, look at it as you will. Yes—take that for the moral of it. So GOD giveth His beloved sleep."

A beautiful and a noble story, for it shows to what heights religious enthusiasm may attain, how it may consecrate intellectual gifts, how it may elevate and purify the character, how it may make a man broader and higher than the system in which he has been bred. The weakness of Martyn in his character and work came from the narrow theology in which he was nurtured; his strength came from his absolute devotion to the service of CHRIST. His mind and heart glowed with a pure and holy enthusiasm that beautified all it touched, just as the sunshine gilds every object on which its transforming light is poured. An enthusiasm, like in its kind if different in degree, to that of our

LORD and SAVIOUR, which, as the Jews supposed, perished miserably on the Cross of Calvary. An enthusiasm like that of the martyr Stephen, over whose death as over a great victory his persecutors rejoiced and were glad. An enthusiasm which of apparent failure makes real success; because, fed by the fire that burns on the altar of GOD, it cannot be dimmed or put out by any worldly trial or sorrow or disaster,—looking ever for its reward, and the fruition of its effort, to the Eternal Rest which is in CHRIST JESUS.

JOHN COLERIDGE PATTESON:

MISSIONARY BISHOP OF MELANESIA.

"Ever as earth's wild war-cries heighten,
The Cross upon the brow will brighten,
Till on the very scorner's gaze
Break forth the Heaven-reflecting rays,
Strange awful charms the unwilling eye compel
On the Saints' light to dwell."

KEBLE.

[*Authorities*:—The following sketch is necessarily founded on the "Life of John Coleridge Patteson," by Charlotte Mary Yonge (2 vols., 1874). Some memoirs of the Bishop which have appeared in Reviews and Periodicals add no new facts of interest to those collected by Miss Yonge, whose book derives a peculiar interest from its copious selection from the Bishop's letters and journals. The reader may refer, however, to the essay by Mr. W. E. Gladstone, reprinted in his "Gleanings," Vol. ii., pp. 213—261.]

JOHN COLERIDGE PATTESON.

CHAPTER I.

AT a time when Philosophy seems returning to its ancient symbols, and endeavouring to drive back the full streams of life, thought, and feeling into the old channels; when some of our public teachers are engaged in the effort to erect a vague theism or still vaguer pantheism on the ruins of the faith once delivered to the saints; it may not be useless if we attempt to place before our readers a portrait of the Ideal Man such as philosophy is able to mould him, and contrast it with that of a modern English Churchman, who in life and death showed himself a true Hero of the Cross. The character of a religious creed or an ethical system may, to a certain extent, be estimated by the character of those who proclaim or profess it; and its claims upon human acceptance may be gauged by its ability to satisfy human aspirations. Hence the argument we have in view may be simply stated; that, since the loftiest philosophy fails in developing those higher and purer faculties of our nature which are educed and cultivated by the religion of CHRIST, therefore that religion, apart from all other evidence of its authenticity, presents to us an *à priori* and irrefragable evidence of Sufficiency. We say that this evidence no other code of morality, no other confession of faith has been able to afford; and here we may find an additional reason, if such were needed, for living the Christian life whilst wearing the Christian name, in order that we may bring no undeserved dishonour on the religion of which we boast. How often do our missionaries tell us that the greatest obstacle to the diffusion of Christianity is the conduct of so-called Christians who depart altogether from its standards and disobey its laws? How frequently the Cross suffers opprobrium through the unfaithfulness of those who pretend to bear it! Surely we should each one of us live more purely and more truthfully if we reflected that in the person of each one of us Christianity is on its trial. The world judges of the Master by His disciples: a fact which fixes upon every Christian an individual responsibility of the weightiest and most solemn kind.

The perfect man, so far as Philosophy can make perfect, we take to have been that great Roman Emperor, the last and best representative of Roman Stoicism, Marcus Aurelius Antoninus. Both in his actions and his writings, in every aspect of his character and relation of his life, as statesman, ruler, thinker, friend, he shines pre-eminent. From the calm pen of Gibbon he has extorted the eulogium that "he was severe to himself, indulgent to the imperfections of others, just and beneficent to all mankind." Dr. Farrar declares that he knows not whether the whole of heathen antiquity, out of its crowded gallery of stately and royal figures, can furnish a nobler, or purer, or more loveable picture than that of this crowned philosopher and laurelled hero, who was yet one of the humblest and one of the most enlightened of all ancient "seekers after GOD." Mr. Lecky is not easily warmed into enthusiasm, but his contemplation of the character of Marcus Aurelius awakens all his sympathies. He pronounces him, as in truth he was, the purest and gentlest spirit of the Pagan world, the most perfect model of the later Stoics. He showed nothing of the hardness, asperity, and arrogance of that sect of philosophers. Free from fanaticism, from superstition, from illusion, his whole life was regulated by a simple and unwavering sense of duty. In him the contemplative and emotional virtues, which it was the tendency of Stoicism to repress, regained their place, without detriment to the active virtues. He presented an ideal type, in which the heroic qualities were not lost sight of, while gentleness and tenderness acquired a new prominence. It is the fate of most great men to be underrated by their contemporaries, and few prophets are ever honoured by their own nation. But such was the superiority of his character, that it profoundly impressed the minds of the Roman people, silenced the satirist, and warded off the arrows of calumny; so that, fully a century after his death, his image was preserved by many among those of their household gods. The spontaneous voice of his subjects proclaimed him a god rather than a man; and this, though for nineteen years he ruled with inflexible justice over a city 'notorious for its licence,' and lived with unsullied purity in the midst of a society distinguished by its corruption. "Quod de Romulo," writes Aurelius Victor, "ægre creditum est, omnes pari sensu præsumserunt; Marcum cœlo receptum esse."

The fullest particulars of his outer life are preserved by the historians. He was a successful and laborious general, and though he would never wage a war of aggression, he conducted eight winter campaigns on the frozen banks of the Danube in defence of the empire over which he had been called to reign. He was the sovereign master of the whole civilised world, and yet he was never betrayed into an unjust or despotic action. The benignity of his disposition is illustrated by the regret he experienced that one Avidius Cassius, who had excited a rebellion against him, had, by his self-inflicted death, deprived him of the pleasure of converting an enemy into a friend. He was not without severe trials; but he bore the misconduct of his wife Faustina, and the evil youth of his son Commodus, with a noble patience. To all his duties, and those of the Lord of the Roman World were overwhelming, he paid the most serious attention; he thought nothing trivial which he knew it was right and necessary should be done. As he was foremost to brave the perils of war, so was he ever ready to accomplish the tasks of peace; and though these frequently occupied him from early morning until long after midnight, he still found time for reflection and self-examination. To the pomp and splendour of his imperial rank he was utterly indifferent, yet on fitting occasions he knew how to maintain the dignity of his position. It is a characteristic trait, which shows the depth of his philanthropy, that throughout his whole reign he dedicated but one temple, and that was to Beneficence. After living a pure and blameless life, he died a serenely peaceful death;[1] a death which was very welcome, because to the weary though conscientious ruler it signified Rest; and Rest seemed to the wisest heathens, unprovided as they were with any key to the problems that perplexed them on every side, the highest reward the human soul could desire. Who will not wish that the blessed shadow of the Cross had fallen holily and happily on the deathbed of Marcus Aurelius?

The inner life of this remarkable man is faithfully revealed in his book of "Meditations;" a kind of common-place book, in which he recorded from time to time his desultory reflections; seizing his leisure moments, amid the cares of government or the turmoil of the camp, to lift his mind to the contemplation of higher and better things. A more truthful and transparent image of a human soul was never presented: it records, as Lecky says, in accents of unmistakable sincerity, the struggles, doubts, and aims of a spirit of which, to use one of his own images, it may truly be said that it possessed the purity of a star, which needs no veil to hide its nakedness. We observe with admiration his profound sense of the value and obligation of personal purity; his solicitude to avoid all ostentation, mannerism, and affectation; his gratitude to every teacher from whom he had borrowed any important moral lesson; and his desire to conciliate whenever and wherever conciliation was possible. In these "Meditations" we see at once the strength and the weakness of humanity; its strength as shown in its noblest types, its weakness when unsupported by faith in CHRIST. Some of them upon the surface seem bright and luminous as the precepts of a Christian Apostle; and it is only after an analysis and comparison that we detect in them the absence of a true vitality. Here are a few passages which shine with crystalline clearness :—" Be just, be temperate, and obey the gods; but be all this with simplicity, for of all false prides the pride of modesty is the worst."

[1] Almost his last words were :—"Quid me fletis, et non magis de pestilentia et communi morte cogitatis?" (Why weep for me, and not rather on account of the pestilence [then raging] and the general mortality?)

" Men are made for men; chastise them then or support them."

" It is right that man should love those that have offended him; and he will do so when he remembers that all men are his brethren, and that it is involuntarily and in ignorance that they sin ;—and then, *we all die so soon.*"

What can surpass the pathos of these last words? How plainly they show the weakness of the reed on which the Imperial philosopher rested! He returns again and again to the sinfulness of man, and what he supposes to be its excuse :—

" If men do evil, evidently it is in spite of themselves, and through ignorance."

" It is without its own volition that the soul is deprived of justice and temperance and goodness, and all other virtues. Keep this ever in thy mind, and the thought will make thee more considerate to all mankind."

Of religious feeling, the " Meditations" show us how Marcus Aurelius could attain to nothing more than a cold acquiescence in the supremacy of a mysteriously vague and undefinable Power :—" Willingly surrender thyself to Fate; allowing her to spin thy thread even as she pleases." The keynote of the Christian teaching is Self-sacrifice; it resounds through all Christian history, through the lives of saints and martyrs, from S. Stephen to Bishop Patteson ; the keynote of the Antonine philosophy is Endurance. Man is here : how or why he knows not; let him accept with composure the conditions he cannot alter. How different this frigid submission to an unavoidable Destiny from the passionate enthusiasm with which S. Paul recognises the Fatherhood of GOD, the love of CHRIST, and runs with glad patience the race set before him, because looking unto JESUS the Author and Finisher of his Faith ! " Either thou livest here," says the imperial thinker, " and hast already accustomed thyself to it; or thou art going away, and this with thine own will; or thou art dying, and hast discharged thy duty. *But, besides these things, there is nothing.* Be then of good cheer." Compare with this calm expression of self-satisfaction, and yet of absolute despondency, the humility, combined with the confident hope of the Apostle :—" Shall we not much rather be in subjection unto the FATHER of

Spirits, *and live?*" "Seek those things which are above, where CHRIST sitteth on the right hand of GOD." "This one thing I do, forgetting those things which are behind, and reaching forth unto those things which are before, I press toward the mark for the prize of the high calling of GOD in CHRIST JESUS." "Thanks be to GOD, which giveth us the victory through our LORD JESUS CHRIST." It is a part of the contention of some of our modern teachers that Christianity contains nothing which is not contained in the heathen morality; but nowhere do we find the heathen morality more nobly expressed than in the "Meditations," and nowhere do we more plainly see its signal inferiority to the Christian doctrine. And one special defect is this: its failure to speak a single word that can carry hope or consolation to the average mind. The stoic might wrap himself up in it as in a shroud, and with passionless eyes and irresponsive heart look coldly on, as the thousands and tens of thousands of mankind passed down into the dull oblivion of the grave; but what did it offer to the widow, the weeping orphan, the distraught mother watching by the deathbed of an only son? Could *they* find comfort in the maxims of an impassive philosophy, which was based upon the nothingness of the world?—Everything that belongs to the body flows away like a stream; all that belongs to the soul is a dream and a vapour. Life is a warfare and the sojourn of a stranger; and after fame comes "Oblivion." "Pass through thy little space of time conformably to nature, and end the journey in content: even as an olive falls off when it is ripe, blessing nature which produced it, and thanking the tree on which it grew."

Is it not apparent, then, that the highest morality advances no further than the threshold of religion? In many important respects,—in the charity that hopeth, and beareth, and believeth, in humility, in consciousness of sin, in love and trustfulness, in a clear apprehension of the ends and aims of life,—Marcus Aurelius was far and away beneath the lowliest Christian. The martyr's death of Bishop Patteson he would never have understood; it would have seemed to him the veriest foolishness. His was knowledge without faith; alas, the imperfect, the unripe knowledge which leads Humanity to the brink of a precipice, and leaves it there, confronted by clouds and shadows! His was knowledge without happiness; for with all his enlightenment, and it was great—with all his purity, and it was admirable—with all his elevation of thought, and it was wonderful—he was conscious of a darkness impending over his life, which he could not dissipate; of an aching void in his heart, which he could not satisfy. His was knowledge without hope; he was as one who has taken up his position on the lonely shore of the ocean, and gazes listlessly across the vast and melancholy waste of waters without any clue to the existence of "the under-world." The fret and ferment, the roar and roll of the rushing tide :—nothing more! "Wise," he was, as Matthew Arnold says; "wise, self-governed, tender, thoughtful, blameless; yet, with all this, agitated, stretching out his arms for something beyond—*tendentemque manus ripæ ulterioris amore.*" For something beyond? Yes; for that "peace of GOD which passeth understanding," which rises so immeasurably above all the arrogant self-reliance of an austere Stoicism. Let not the reader be deceived by the false idealism which invests with an empty grandeur the character of the philosophers and moralists of antiquity. The humblest believer is adorned with graces which they never conceived of. Rather let him consider how much beauty and warmth and nobleness the life and teaching of Marcus Aurelius would have gained if, instead of being only a seeker after GOD, he had been a follower of JESUS CHRIST. Let him compare this great Roman emperor with a Christian missionary,—his inferior, it may be, in intellectual power, though not in force of character,—John Coleridge Patteson; and see what a dignity and heroic elevation the latter gains through the intensity of his faith, the brightness of his hope, the completeness of his love!

John Coleridge Patteson was the eldest son and second child of the late Justice Patteson, by his second wife, Frances Duke Coleridge. He was born at 9, Gower Street, Bedford Square, London, on the 1st of April, 1827, and baptised on the 8th. At an early age he gave evidence of exceptional strength of character; but though generous and deeply affectionate in disposition, he was of a wayward passionate temper, which it needed all his mother's firmness and patience to bring under control. Reverence and devoutness, however, seem to have been natural to him. When he was only six years old he expressed a wish to be a clergyman, because he thought saying the Absolution to people must make them so happy; a belief he must spontaneously have gathered from the Prayer Book, as in those days the doctrine was by no means generally taught. It is recorded of him that hearing of the noble exertions of his cousin, the first Bishop of Barbadoes, during the hurricane that devastated that island in August, 1833, he exclaimed :—"I will be a Bishop! I will have a hurricane!"—an indication of that broad humanity and strong love of his fellow-creatures which determined the current of his later life. Two years later, when eight years old, he began his school-life at the Grammar School of Ottery S. Mary; but as a schoolboy he gave little promise of his future distinction. He was not unruly, nor specially idle; but he was indifferent, and worked, not from a sense of pleasure, but at the prompting of conscience. In all games and sports, however, he delighted; and in all he attained to excellence; so that he grew up a happy and active lad, much cherished by his comrades for his courage, patience, and unselfishness. When nearly eleven years old, he was sent to Eton, being boarded in the house of his uncle, the Rev. Edward Coleridge, one of the most popular and successful of the Eton masters. There he made a very considerable progress. The atmosphere of the place seemed peculiarly congenial to him, and his intellect developed rapidly. His bias for art and music began to be displayed; and a contemporary says,—"I well remember how he used to sing the Psalms with the little turns at the end of the verses, which I *envied* his being able to do." This, however, had a devotional feeling as well as a love of music at the bottom of it. He had daily readings of the Bible in his room with his brother, cousins, and two or three friends; but the boys were so weakly ashamed of their religious cravings, that they kept an open Shakespeare on the table with an open drawer beneath, into which, when any person was heard at the door, the Bible was immediately hurried.

The year 1841 is described by Miss Yonge as bringing with it the dawn of Patteson's future life. In that year George Augustus Selwyn (the late deeply lamented Bishop of

Lichfield) was appointed to the bishopric of New Zealand. Soon afterwards a farewell service was held in New Windsor Church, Archdeacon Wilberforce (since Bishop of Oxford and Winchester) preaching in the morning, and the newly made Bishop in the afternoon. Says Patteson, then a boy of fourteen :—" I heard Archdeacon Wilberforce in the morning, and the Bishop in the evening, though I was forced to stand all the time. It was beautiful when he talked of his going out to found a church and then die neglected and forgotten. All the people burst out crying, he was so very much beloved by his parishioners. He spoke of his perils, and putting his trust in GOD ; and then, when he had finished, I think I never heard anything like the sensation, a kind of feeling that if it had not been on so sacred a spot, all would have exclaimed, ' GOD bless him !'" Thenceforth the wish dwelt ever strongly in the lad's heart to go forth, like his friend, to labour in GOD'S name among the heathen. He was at his father's house when the Bishop of New Zealand came to take leave ; and, half earnestly, half playfully, said :—" Lady Patteson, will you give me Coley ?" She started, but did not refuse ; and when her son, in one of their mutual confidences, told her that it was his greatest desire to go with the Bishop, she replied that if such were his desire when he grew up, he should have her consent and her blessing.

The unusual seriousness of the boy, and the solemn light in which he looked at his religious obligations, may be understood from his account of his Confirmation (in May, 1842) :—" You will know," he writes, " that I have been confirmed to-day, and I dare say you all thought of me. The ceremony was performed by the Bishop of Lincoln, and I hope that I have truly considered the great duty and responsibility I have taken upon myself, and have prayed for strength to support me in the execution of all those duties. I shall of course receive the Sacrament the first time I have an opportunity, and I trust worthily. I think there must have been 200 confirmed. The Bishop gave us a very good charge afterwards, recommending us all to take pattern by the self-denial and true devotion of the Bishop of New Zealand, of whom he spoke for a long while. The whole ceremony was performed with the greatest decorum, and in the retiring and coming up of the different sets there was very little noise, and not the slightest confusion. I came up with the first set, and the Bishop came round and put his hands on the heads of the whole set (about forty), and then going into the middle pronounced the prayer. The responses were all made very audibly, and every one seemed to be impressed with a proper feeling of the holiness and seriousness of the ceremony. After all the boys had been confirmed about seven other people were confirmed, of whom two were quite as much as thirty, I should think."

The death of his mother in the following November greatly added to the gravity of Patteson's character, and deepened the impression he had already received. He left behind him at Eton an unstained record—a high repute for truthfulness, purity, and moral excellence—when he went up to Balliol College, Oxford, in the Michaelmas term of 1845. He is described at this time as (on the surface) "a thorough public schoolboy, with a full capacity for enjoying undergraduate society and undergraduate amusements, though with so fond a recollection of Eton that to some of us he hardly seemed to appreciate Oxford sufficiently." He did not allow his "undergraduate amusements" to interfere with his studies or his religious exercises, and he joined in none which bore a taint of dissipation. He soon came to be known and loved for his many unassuming virtues, and for the steadfastness with which he advocated all that was true and honest and pure. As a scholar he was diligent and conscientious, but he won no brilliant distinction. After taking a second class in 1849, he went on a tour in Germany and Italy, which refreshed both his artistic sympathies and his feeling for nature. In 1852 he returned to Oxford as a fellow of Merton College in order to prepare for Holy Orders, and devoted himself with assiduity to the study of Hebrew and theology, while at the same time extending his knowledge of general literature. He also developed a taste for linguistic acquirements. A letter written to his sister early in 1853 will give the reader an idea of what he was doing at this period of his life, and throw some light on his peculiarities of character :—

"My temptation," he says, "consists perhaps chiefly in the love of reading for its own sake. I do honestly think that for a considerable time past I have read, I believe, nothing which I do not expect to be of real use, for I have no taste naturally for novels, &c. (without however, wishing to deny that there may be novels which teach a real insight into character). Barring 'I Promessi Sposi,' which I take up very seldom when tired, I have not read one for ages: I must except 'Old Mortality,' read last vacation at Feniton; but I can't deny that I like the study of languages for its own sake, though I apply my little experience in it wholly to the interpretation of the Bible. I like improving my scholarship, it is true, but I can say honestly that it is used to read the Greek Testament with greater accuracy; so of the Hebrew, Syriac, Arabic. I feel, I confess, sometimes that it is *nice*, &c., to know several languages, but I try to drive away any such thoughts, and it is quite astonishing how, after a few weeks, a study which would suggest ideas of an unusual course of reading, becomes so familiar that I never think of myself, when pursuing it, *e.g.*, I don't think that after two hours' grind at Arabic, the stupid wrong feeling of its being an out-of-the-way study comes upon me now, it is getting quite natural. It comes out though when I talk or write perhaps with another, but I must try and get over it.

"I believe it to be a good thing to break off any work once or twice a day in the middle of any reading, for meditating a little while and for a prayer. This is more easily done at College than elsewhere; and is I hope, a preventive against such thoughts. Then, as I jog on I see how very little I know, what an immense deal I have to learn to become ordinarily well acquainted with these things. I am in that state of mind perhaps when Ecclesiastes (which I am now reading) puts my own case exactly before me. I think, what's the good of it all? And the answer comes, it may be very good properly used, or very mischievous if abused. I do indeed look forward to active parochial work; I think I shall be very happy so employed, and I often try to anticipate the time in thought, and feel with perfect sincerity that nothing is so useful or so full of comfort as the consciousness of trying to fulfil the daily duties of my situation. Here of course I need do nothing; I mean there is nothing to prevent my sitting all day in an arm-chair and reading 'Pickwick.'"

At the long Vacation of 1853 Patteson finally quitted Oxford, and repaired to Alfington, a hamlet in the parish of Ottery S. Mary, to undertake the pastoral charge during the severe illness of its curate. On September 14th, he received the Diaconate, in Exeter Cathedral, at the hands of the venerable Bishop Phillpotts; and on the 22nd of October he preached his first sermon; of which the late Sir John Coleridge has left a pathetic description:—[1]

"October 23, 1853.—Yesterday morning Arthur and I went to Alfington Church, to be present at Coley's first sermon. I don't know when I have been so much delighted and affected. His manner of saying the prayers was exceedingly good: his voice very sweet and musical: without seeming loud, it was fully audible, and gave assurance of more power if needed; his manner quite unaffected, but sweet and devout. His sermon was a very sound and good one, beautifully delivered; perhaps in the early parts, from the very sweetness of his voice, and the very rapid delivery of his words, a little more variety of intonation would have helped in conveying his meaning more distinctly to those who formed the bulk of his congregation. But when he came to personal parts this was not needed."

At Alfington Patteson continued to labour as young clergymen do when their heart is in their work, and the labour had its usual effect in elevating the character and deepening the spiritual life. He was himself conscious of this process of growth, and wrote:—" My reading becomes less discursive; but the teaching of the Bible will, I trust, open upon me in more of its depth and fulness. I feel it does, thank GOD, in a measure, and the coming in contact with so many different minds all helps to make religion more real and to substitute substantial realities for words." It is necessary for the reader to understand and remember this period of developement: for it changed the average young curate and parish priest into the fervent missionary Bishop, who might well be entitled, not indeed for length of career or extent of operations, but for the abundance of his zeal and the entirety of his self-devotion, the English Xavier. He resembled Xavier too, in the direct personal influence which he exercised. He was not a great or a popular or an attractive

[1] Quoted by Miss Yonge, vol. i. p. 151.

preacher; yet in his little sphere of action he was a wonderful power for good. It was as if a virtue went out from him; a sweet scent and savour from his daily life. We are told that the impression he made was "really extraordinary;" that many, by the force of his teaching and example, became " new men."

Yet Patteson himself felt, what now we all know, that a quiet English parish was not the field he was best fitted to cultivate. He was content, like a faithful servant, to do the work that lay at his hand, until he was called elsewhere in the good providence of his Divine Master; but his thoughts often strayed to shores and islands beyond the seas where the darkness of heathendom had not yet been lighted up by the radiance of the Gospel. The missionary fire still glowed in his heart of hearts. This was apparent enough when in the August of 1854, the Bishop of New Zealand, during a year's rest and holiday in England, paid a visit to the Pattesons at Feniton. The Bishop and the young curate had much confidential intercourse together. The former pressed home the question : Was he satisfied with his present work? Only so far as it enabled him to remain near his father; but at a future time he hoped to serve GOD in some great manufacturing town; or, still better, to go out as a missionary. Then, replied the Bishop, if such be your wish, you must not defer it until you are getting on in life; Missionary work should be done with your full strength and vigour.

The result was, that Patteson bared his heart to his father; and Sir John, after a natural struggle with his affections, consented that he should go. "I give him wholly," he said to the Bishop, "not with any thought of seeing him again. I will not have him thinking he must come home again, to see me." He knew that GOD'S service requires a complete renunciation of self, and that the missionary, when once he puts his hand to the plough, must not look back to any human love or friendship or interest. It was soon arranged, therefore, that the young volunteer, after receiving ordination to the priesthood (in September), should accompany the Bishop of New Zealand on his return to his Antipodean diocese, but the arrangement was not made without much quiet, though deep suffering at home, and much openly expressed regret and reluctance in Alfington; where, indeed, the parishioners, looking upon Bishop Selwyn as the immediate cause of their loss, could not refrain from uttering many bitter reproaches. Yet, in the face of all this grief, it was right for him to go. His faculties, as Miss Yonge justly remarks, were not those most requisite for work in large towns. He could deal with individuals more successfully than with masses. "His great and peculiar gifts of languages, seconded by his capacity for navigation, enabled him to be the builder up of the Melanesian Church in so remarkable a manner that one can hardly suppose but that he was marked out for it, and those endowments would have found no scope in an ordinary career." No: the voice which called him away was the voice of GOD; not less distinct than when in the night-watches, it summoned Samuel.

CHAPTER II.

ON the 28th of August, 1855, John Coleridge Patteson sailed from England in company with Bishop and Mrs. Selwyn; and on the 6th of July he landed at Auckland, New Zealand. After resting for a couple of mornings, and familiarising himself with his novel duties, he set out with the Bishop on a coasting expedition in the Bishop's missionary schooner, "The Southern Cross," which extended over one hundred and six days, and included the Chatham Islands, as well as the coast as far as Wellington. On his return he applied himself to master the Maori tongue, which he did with great rapidity, and in the intervals of his pastoral labours, he pursued his studies in theology, Church history, and the critical interpretation of the New Testament. In converse with congenial friends he revealed his general knowledge and refined culture, talking with eloquence and feeling of the great musical composers and the pictures of his favourite masters. In 1856 he was again at sea. Writing to a friend, he says:—"You ask me where I am *settled*. Why, settled, I suppose, I am never to be: I am a missionary, you know, not a 'stationary.' However, my home is the 'Southern Cross,' where I live always in harbour as well as at sea, highly compassionated by all my good friends here, from the Governor downwards, and highly contented myself with the sole possession of a cosy little cabin nicely furnished with table, lots of books, and my dear father's photograph, which is an invaluable treasure and comfort to me. In harbour I live in the cabin. It is hung round with barometers (aneroids), sympiesometers, fixed chest for chronometers, charts, &c. Of course, wherever the 'Southern Cross' goes I go too, and I am a most complete skipper. I feel as natural with my quadrant in my hand, as of old with a cricket bat. Then I do *rather* have good salt-water baths, and see glorious sunsets and sunrises, and star-light nights, and the great many-voiced ocean, the winds and waves chiming all night with a solemn sound, lapping against my ear as I lie in my canvas bed, six feet by ten and a half, and fall sound asleep and dream of home. Oh! there is much that is really enjoyable in this kind of life: and if the care of the vessel, management of men, &c., do harass me sometimes, it is very good for me; security from such troubles having been anxiously and selfishly pursued by me at home."

Home! The word was one that sounded often in Patteson's ear, that touched many a chord of responsive sentiment and emotion in his heart; he loved to talk of Home and think of Home; and his gaze strayed far back over the world of waters to the picturesque Devonshire village where he had passed the happy years of his early manhood. But, like a true soldier of the Cross, he never repined; never regretted the resolve he had taken; and for one wistful glance backward took many a brave look forward into a future in which he should be the messenger of glad tidings to heathen ears. His education was still proceeding; he was learning to be stronger, less fastidious, more humble; his whole nature was gaining in consistency and vigour. And in this way he was rapidly rising to the height of the work that lay before him.

On the 1st of May (Ascension Day), he sailed with Bishop Selwyn for the islands of Melanesia, among whose inhabitants he was intended to labour. The first point, however, was Sydney, where the Bishop hoped to obtain leave to make Norfolk Island the head quarters. In this expectation he was at first disappointed. From Sydney they proceeded to Pitcairn Island, the home of the descendants of the Mutineers of "the Bounty,"—a kind of ocean-Arcadia, in which the homely virtues seem to flourish vigorously; and thence to Anaiteum, which is in charge of a Scotch Presbyterian Mission. Passing Erromango, the scene of John Williams' martyrdom, and Fatè, the abode of a tribe addicted to cannibalism, they came to the beautiful mountainous isle of Espiritu Santo (so named by its discoverers because sighted upon Trinity Sunday), where Patteson first made acquaintance with the great scourge of Melanesia, the kidnappers. "We espied a brig," he says, " at anchor close on shore. Manned the boat and rowed about two miles to the brig, found it was under the command of a man notorious among the sandal-wood traders for many a dark deed of revenge and unscrupulous retaliation upon the natives. At Nengonè he shot three in cold blood who swam off to his ship, because the people of the place were said to be about to take his vessel. At Mallicolo but lately I fear he killed not less than eight, though here there was some scuffling and provocation. For the Nengonè affair he was tried for his life at Sydney, Captain Erskine and the Bishop having much to do with his prosecution. He is now dealing fairly (apparently) with these people, and is certainly on very friendly terms with them. We are glad to let these men see we are about in these seas, watching what they do; and the Bishop said, ' Mr. Patteson is come from England on purpose to look after these islands,' as much as to say, Now there will be a regular visitation of them, and outrages committed on the natives will probably be discovered."

To enumerate the islands successively visited by these Christian voyagers would be almost to trace a chart of Melanesia. In the middle of August they reached the beautiful Santa Cruz group, discovered by Alvaro de Mendana, the Spaniard, in 1594. We like the names those old Spaniards gave to the lands they rescued from the shadow of the Unknown; names dear to Christian hearts, and associating the places that bore them, as if by anticipation, with the future presence of the bearer of "good tidings." Names of good omen, which, to the seaman, should recall many a sweet memory of sacred lessons learned in childhood! Espiritu Santo, Santa Cruz, Santa Fè, how much pleasanter to the thoughtful mind than those every-day names of obscure officials, or royal princes, or forgotten nobles with which our English navigators have so lavishly bestrewn the map of the island-world of the Pacific!

One of the islands of the Santa Cruz group bears the name of Nukapu; Patteson describes it as "completely encircled by a coral reef." He adds:—"The natives soon came off in canoes, and brought bread-fruit and cocoa-nuts. They spoke a few words of Maori, but wore their hair like the people of Santa Cruz, and resembled them in the character of their ornaments and in their general appearance. They had bows and clubs of the same kind, tapa stained with turmeric, armlets, earrings and nose-rings of bone and tortoiseshell." This was Patteson's first visit to Nukapu: unhappily it was not his last.

Tubua was the next island: a gem of verdure within a ring of shining coral, and that again encircled by the sea. The Bishop and Patteson waded through the surf, to find thirteen men assembled on the beach. Patteson went up to the first, tied a bit of red tape around his head, and made signs of his willingness to exchange a fish-hook for a cocoanut. Plenty of the fruit was forthcoming; but the Bishop, to his companion's surprise, suddenly beckoned him away, and when they had regained the boat, said:—"I saw some young men running through the bush with bows and arrows, and these young gentry have not the sense to behave well like their parents." They landed at Vanikoro, the scene of the shipwreck of La Pérouse and his companions in 1788; but saw nobody. Here Patteson came into indirect contact with cannibalism, much to his horror; for a frightful odour attracting notice, close search was made, and the ground having been turned up, human bones were found with flesh hanging to them. A few paces distant was a native oven, namely, a pit lined with stones.

After touching at Banks Island and the Torres group, the "Southern Cross" sailed for Norfolk Island, where it arrived on the 3rd of September, and where its passengers were heartily welcomed by the white settlers, including some families removed, a few years before, from Pitcairn Island. Ten days later it reached Auckland, and Patteson resumed his duties at S. John's College. Thence he wrote a letter to his uncle, from which we select the following passages as full of interest :—

"Here I am on shore again for seven or eight months, if I live so long—my occupations most interesting, working away with twelve Melanesians at languages, &c., with the highest of all incentives to perseverance, trying to form in them habits of cleanliness, order, decency, &c.

"Last night (Sunday), after explaining to the Solomon Islands boys, seven in number, the nature of the LORD's Prayer as far as my knowledge of their language would carry me, I thought myself justified in making them kneel down round me, and they uttered with their lips after me (i.e., the five most intelligent) the first words of prayer to their FATHER in Heaven. I don't venture to say that they understood much—neither does the young child taught at his or her mother's knee—neither do many grown persons perhaps know much about the fulness of the Prayer of Prayers—(these scenes teach me my ignorance, which is one great gain)—yet they knew, I think, that they were praying to some Great and Mighty One, not an abstraction—a conscious loving Being, a Father, and they knew at least the name of His SON, JESUS CHRIST.

"Their first formula was :—'GOD the FATHER, GOD the SON, and GOD the HOLY GHOST, only one GOD.' I can't yet explain that our Blessed LORD came from heaven and died *for our sins;* neither (as far as human thought may reach) does the power of GOD's Spirit as yet work in their hearts consciousness of sin, and with that the sense of the need of a Redeemer and SAVIOUR. I asked in my sermon yesterday the prayers of the people for the grace of GOD's HOLY SPIRIT to teach the hearts and enlighten the understandings of these heathen children of a common FATHER, and I added that greatly did their teachers need their prayers that GOD would make them apt to teach, and wise and simple in endeavouring to bring before their minds the things that belong unto their peace. You too, dear uncle, will think, I know, of those things, for my trust is great. In this cold climate, 26° or 27° south of their own island,

I have much anxiety about their bodily health, and more about their souls.

"The four youngest, sixteen to eighteen, sleep in my room. One is now on my bed, wrapped up in a great opossum rug, with cold and slight fever; last night his pulse was high, to-day he is better. I have to watch over them like a cat. Think of living till now in a constant temperature of 84°, and being suddenly brought to 56°. New Zealand is too cold for them, and the College is a cold place, wind *howling* round it now.

"Norfolk Island is *the* place, and the Pitcairners themselves are most co-operative and hearty; I trust that in another year I may be there.

"Thank you for all your kind wishes on my birthday. I ought to wish to live many years, perhaps, to try and be of use; especially as I am so unfit to go now, or rather, I ought not to wish at all. Sometimes I feel almost fainthearted, which is cowardly and forgetful of our calling 'to fight manfully under CHRIST's banner.' Ah! my Bishop is indeed a warrior of the Cross. . . ."

It soon became apparent to all capable of judging of such things that Coleridge Patteson had found his proper work; as I suppose all of us would do, if we were content to listen to the voice of GOD, and did not mistake for it our own headstrong inclinations, or refuse to be governed by anything but our self-will. The Bishop, who had a keen insight into character, pronounced him "the right man in the right place, mentally and physically." The multiplicity of languages drew out that linguistic gift which he possessed, like S. Francis Xavier. The warm climate suited him constitutionally; and his broad sympathy and genial temper won the hearts of his pupils and secured their confidence. Already Bishop Selwyn, in his own mind, had destined him to be the first holder of a Bishopric of Melanesia; and his supreme qualification for such a post seemed daily to become more conspicuous.

In Easter, 1857, he sailed in the "Southern Cross" on another "missionary cruise." It was of brief duration, and he was soon back again at S. John's College. In the opinion of his accomplished biographer, this was the brightest period (1856—1860) of his life. He had given up all for CHRIST's sake and the Gospel's, and was reaping the blessing in its freshness. "His struggles with his defects had been successful, the more so because he was so full of occupation that the old besetting trouble, self-contemplation, had been expelled for lack of opportunity; and he had become far more simple, since humility was ceasing to be a conscious effort." His residence at S. John's was diversified by expeditions in the "Southern Cross" which familiarised him with the chief geographical features of what was to be his Melanesian diocese. In the early summer of 1858 he and his Bishop made a visit to Lifú, which was productive of much good; and it was determined that Patteson should remain there for awhile as resident missionary. He was accompanied by his twelve Melanesian pupils, and the native chiefs received him and them with great cordiality. He mastered the language with his usual facility. Writing to his father on August 2nd, he says:—

"Yesterday I preached my two first Lifú sermons; rather nervous, but I knew I had command of the language enough to explain my meaning, and I thought over the plan of my sermons, and selected texts. Fancy your worthy son stuck up in a pulpit, without any mark of the clergyman save white tie and black coat, commencing service with a hymn, then reading the 2nd chapter of S. Matthew, quite new to them, then a prayer, extemporary, but practically working in, I hope, the principle and much of the actual language of the Prayer Book—*i.e.*, Confession, prayer for pardon, expression of belief and praise—then another hymn, the sermon about forty minutes. Text: 'I am the way,' &c. Afternoon: 'Thy Word is a lantern unto my feet.'"

Still writing from Lifú, he states his idea of the practical qualifications essential to the success of a missionary working in a new field and among a savage race:—

"I can hardly tell you how much I regret not knowing something about the treatment of simple surgical cases. If when with W—— I had studied the practical—bled, drawn teeth, mixed medicines, rolled legs perpetually, it would have been worth something. Surely I might have foreseen all this! I really don't know how to find the time or the opportunity for learning. How true it is that men require to be trained for their particular work! I am now just in a position to know what to learn were I once more in England. Spend one day with old Fry (mason), another with John Venn (carpenter), and two every week at the Exeter Hospital, and not look on and see others work—there's the mischief, do it oneself. Make a chair, a table, a box; fit everything; help in every part of making and furnishing a house, that is, a cottage. Do enough of every part to be able to do the whole. Begin by felling a tree; saw it into planks, mix the lime, see the right proportion of sand, &c.; know how to choose a good lot of timber, fit handles for tools, &c.

"Many trades need not be attempted; but every missionary ought to be a carpenter, a mason, something of a butcher, and a good deal of a cook. Suppose yourself without a servant, and nothing for dinner to-morrow but some potatoes in the barn, and a fowl running about in the yard. That's the kind of thing for a young fellow going into a new country to imagine to himself. If a little knowledge of glazing could be added, it would be a grand thing, just enough to fit in panes to window-frames, which last, of course, he ought to make himself. Much of this cannot be done for you. I can buy window-frames in Auckland, and glass; but I can't carry a man a thousand miles in my pocket to put that glass into those frames; and if it is done in New Zealand, ten to one it gets broken on the voyage; whereas, glass by itself will pack well. Besides, a pane gets broken, and then I am in a nice fix. To know how to tinker a bit is a good thing; else your only saucepan or tea-kettle may be lying by you useless for months. In fact, if I had known all this before, I should be just ten times as useful as I am now."

The world is fond of disparaging the results of missionary enterprise. It professes to believe that they are really infinitesimal, and asks for proofs that the work done by our evangelists is either lasting or extensive. We fear it must be conceded that our Missions are not as successful as we could desire; that though they gather in many sheep into the fold, the number is less than might be expected; so that at times a feeling of despondency takes possession of our hearts. But why is this? Is it not because the world is continually neutralizing our efforts? The great enemy of the missionary is our boasted European civilisation. What avail his teachings when his hearers see them contradicted by the unchristian lives of the official, the trader, the seaman, the settler? The larger success of the early missionaries is to be attributed, in no slight degree, to their freedom from this antagonistic influence. Their field of labour was not intruded upon by the "white man;" they themselves were the pioneers of civilisation as well as of Christianity, and their example illustrated and confirmed what their doctrine taught.

On this point it is worth reading Patteson's earnest remarks. "A man in apostolic times," he says, "had the lessons of the Apostles and disciples practically illustrated in the life of those with whom he associated. The Church was an expression of the verbal teaching committed to its ministers. How dearly the beauty of this comes out when one is forced to feel the horrible blank occasioned by the absence of the living teachers, influencing, moulding, building up each individual professor of Christianity by a process always going on, though oftentimes unconsciously to him on whom it operates.

"But how is the social life to be fashioned here in Lifu according to the rule of CHRIST? There is no organized body, exemplifying in daily actions the teaching of the Bible. A man goes to chapel, and hears something most vague and unmeaning. He has never been taught to grasp anything distinctly—to represent any truth to his mind as a settled resting-place for his faith. Who is to teach him? What does he see around him to make him imperceptibly acquire new habits in conformity with the Bible? Is the Christian community distinguished by any habits of social order and intercourse different from non-Christians?"

In November the "Southern Cross" called at Lifú, took on board the missionary-priest, and conveyed him back to Auckland. But in the autumn of 1859 he was again at sea; he and his Bishop, with a zeal that never wearied, and an enthusiasm that took no count of labour, visiting the Loyalty Islands, the Southern New Hebrides, the Banks Islands, the Solomon Islands, and the Santa Cruz group. The voyage terminated on the 7th of December; it is notable as the last made under the direction of Bishop Selwyn.

In 1860, Coleridge Patteson entered on a more independent course of action than had hitherto been his; S. John's College, which was under his charge, being removed from Auckland to a healthier site at Kohimarama, where new and suitable buildings had been erected with money provided by Miss Yonge, from the sale of her " Daisy Chain," and by Sir John Patteson. Here is a description of them :—

"The buildings at present form three sides of a quadrangle, but the south side is only partly filled up. The large schoolroom, only eighty feet long, with three sets of transepts, has been removed from the College, and put up again so as to form the east side of the quadrangle. This is of wood; so is the small wooden quadrangle which serves now for dormitories, and a part of which I occupy; my house consisting of three little rooms, together measuring seventeen feet by seven. These dormitories are the southern side of the quadrangle, but do not reach more than half way from the east to the west side, room being left for another set of dormitories of equal size, when we want them and can afford them. The west side consists of a very nice set of stone buildings, including a large kitchen, store room, and room for putting things in, in daily and immediate use; and the hall, which is the northern part of the side of the quadrangle, is a really handsome room, with simple open roof and windows of a familiar collegiate appearance. These buildings are of the dark grey scoria, almost imperishable I suppose, and look very well. The hall is just long enough to take seven of us at the high table (so to speak), and thirty-four at the long table, stretching from the high table to the end of the room.

"At present this is used for school also, as the carpenters who are making all our fittings, shelves, &c., are still in the large schoolroom. We take off the north end of the schoolroom, including one set of transepts, for our temporary chapel. This part will be lined, *i.e.*, boarded neatly, inside. The rest of the building is very rough, but it answers its purpose. . . .

"I hope eventually that stone buildings will take the place of the present wooden schoolroom and dormitories; but this ought to last many years. Here we live most happily and comfortably. The climate almost tropical in summer. The beautiful scenery of the harbour before our eyes, the smooth sea and clean dry beach within a stone's throw of my window. The lads and young men have their fishing, bathing, boating, and basking in the sun, which all day from sunrise to sunset beats upon us; for the west cliff does not project more than a few yards to the north of us, and the eastern boundary is low and some way off. I see the little schooner at her moorings whenever I look off my book or my paper, and with an opera-glass can see the captain walking the decks. All is under my eye; and the lads daily say, "College too cold; Kohimarama very good."

Bishop Selwyn, early in 1860, pushed forward his project for creating a bishopric of the Western Pacific Isles, though it was not without much reluctance and misgiving that Coleridge Patteson assented to his desire that he should be the first incumbent of it. While the necessary arrangements were in progress, Patteson paid another visit to the Isles, and remained for some weeks at Mota, planting there a mission station. During his absence the "Southern Cross" was unhappily wrecked on the New Zealand coast, near Ngungurn Bay; and the return voyage from Mota to Kohimarama was accomplished in a hired schooner. On his arrival at the College he found that the consent of the Crown had been obtained to the creation of the new bishopric, and that his consecration as Bishop was fixed to take place early in 1861. The day ultimately chosen was the Feast of S. Matthias, February 24th, and the ceremony was performed in S. Paul's Church, Auckland, by the Bishop of New Zealand, assisted by the Bishops of Wellington and Nelson.

Of the young Bishop as he was at this solemn epoch of his life, Bishop Abraham (of Wellington) has drawn a touching portrait :—

"You recollect"—he is writing to the Bishop's old master at Eton, Dr. Goodford—"You recollect probably that as a boy he was good, pure, and true as gold, but then he was very indolent, and except at cricket or hockey showed no signs of energy or ability, and I fancy his career at Oxford was very similar. After being admitted to a Fellowship at Merton, he seems by his own account to have had his intellectual tastes stimulated by travel; but the repose of a small and pretty curacy in Devonshire called out all his best moral feelings, yet could hardly, I fancy, have developed much energy. All this natural disposition to repose makes the energy and devotedness of the last five years the more remarkable and more evidently the work of grace and duty.

"Anything more conscientious and painstaking cannot be conceived than the way he has strictly directed every talent, every hour or minute of his life, to the one work he had set before him. However small or uncongenial or drumdrudgery-like his occupation, however hard, or dangerous, or difficult, it seemed to be always met in the same calm, gentle, self-possessed spirit of love and duty,—which I should fancy that those who knew well his good and large-minded, large-hearted father, and his mother, whom I have always heard spoken of as saintly, could best understand. Perhaps the most marked feature in his character is his genuine simplicity and humility. I never saw it equalled in one so gifted and so honoured and beloved."

The Bishop was installed on the last day of February, and immediately entered on his duties in the true spirit of a devout enthusiasm. He was one of those men whose growth is slow, but who are always equal to each new position that devolves upon them. Ordinary men apparently, with no brilliancy or romance about them; yet men who, somehow or other, can be depended upon to stand any test, however sudden and severe. It was the lofty view he took of his mission that, no doubt, strengthened him to its adequate discharge. He was not unaware of the dangers that waited upon it; but what of these? To carry one's life in one's hand, he said, was no more than other soldiers besides those of the Cross habitually did. He would have to go among savage peoples, embittered by the wrongs they had sustained at the hands of the white men—of the kidnappers and men-stealers who infested the Polynesian seas; but would not the providence of GOD precede him like a cloud by day and a column of fire by night? And what bishop in the Church of CHRIST had a diocese of profounder interest? Those blue waters, those bright islands—it was a joy to think of them! And his imagination pictured the shining coral and sandy beaches, with strips of burning sunshine fringing the forest masses that rose into ridges of hills, clothed with luxuriant vegetation; and he saw hundreds of people thronging the curved shores, naked, but armed with envenomed arrows, and making the air horrible with their fierce cries; he could speak to them only by signs; but one sign at least, that of the Cross, he hoped before long to teach them to love and reverence. For were they not his children now?

Children whom he could love with a whole heart; for the death of his father (June 28, 1861) severed the chief tie that had bound his affections to his native land. It was not severed without a bitter pang; but the Missionary Bishop had little time for grief, and he knew that his father's redeemed spirit would not rejoice over a great work interrupted by a private sorrow,—a work which, on earth, he had largely aided and zealously encouraged. So in a hired vessel he had already set out, with two of his clergy and some of his Melanesian converts, for Mota, which he hoped to make a centre of evangelistic and missionary action. In an open boat he made excursions from thence to the neighbouring islands, disarming hostile natives by his bright smile and frank, fearless expression of countenance. There was much to encourage: good augury that the bread thrown upon the waters would return before many days were past; and doubtless this prospect of a glorious harvest helped to uphold him under the deep trial of his bereavement. He felt that he had but one thing to live for—the good of the Melanesian isles; and he abandoned all thought or wish of returning, on ever so brief a visit, to England.

CHAPTER III.

IT is not necessary for me to enumerate the various incidents that made up the record of Bishop Patteson's episcopate. My object in this sketch is simply to dwell upon such points as will help us to understand the development of the character of this great Anglican missionary; a man whom I feel to have been specially fitted for the work he had to do, and who in his qualifications, no less than in that brightly burning zeal of his, I take to have been the equal of the greatest missionaries and evangelists of the Church in any age since the Apostolic. I have shown how he rose to the height of each fresh responsibility that was thrust upon him. I have shown, too, how completely he was absorbed and inspired by his saintly enthusiasm, though, with true English reserve, he repressed all purely external manifestations. Never was life more wholly given up to GOD, not even by a Columba or a Bernard or a Francis of Assisi, than by John Coleridge Patteson. He lived only to do GOD's will; only to call to GOD so much as he could of the heathendom that still lingered in the desolation of darkness. Whether at Kohimarama, or on board the mission-ship, he gave all his energies to the task of laying broad and deep the foundations of the Church in benighted Melanesia.

A *new* "Southern Cross" bore the mission flag in May, 1863, and accompanied by his clergy, five in number, the Bishop sailed on a three months' voyage, visiting Mota, the Banks Archipelago, and the New Hebrides group, collecting suitable pupils for his New Zealand College. He returned to Kohimarama in August, well pleased with his vessel and his assistants, and not altogether dissatisfied with the work done. Mr. Tilly, his sailing master, supplies a graphic sketch of the Bishop *en voyage*:—

"I saw of course," he says, "a great deal of him, and learned much from him—learned to admire his unselfishness and simplicity of mode of life, and to respect his earnestness and abilities. His conversation on any subject was free and full; and those, on the few nights when quietly at anchor they could be enjoyed more, will be long remembered. Of his manner to Melanesians, others will, no doubt, say enough, but I may be excused for mentioning one scene that very much struck me, and of which I am now the only (white) one left who was present at it. We were paying a visit for the first time to an island, and—the vessel being safe in the offing—the Bishop asked me if I would go with them, as he sometimes did on similar occasions. We pulled in to a small inner islet among a group, when a number of (say 200) natives were collected on the beach. Seeing they looked as if friendly, he waded on shore without hesitation, and joined them; the reception was friendly, and after a time he walked with them along the beach, we in the boat keeping near. After a while we took him into the boat again, and lay off the beach a few yards to be clear of the throng, and be able to get at the things he wanted to give them, they coming about the boat in canoes; and this is the fact I wished to notice—viz., *the look on his face* while the intercourse with them lasted. I was so struck with it, quite involuntarily, for I had no idea of watching for anything of the sort; but it was one of such extreme gentleness, and of yearning towards them. I never saw that look on his face again, I suppose because no similar scene ever occurred again when I happened to be with him. It was enough in itself to evoke sympathy; and as we pulled away, though the channel was narrow and winding, yet, as the water was deep, we discovered the possibility of the schooner being brought in there at some future time."

In the early months of 1864, the Bishop went on a visit to Australia, going to Sydney, and Melbourne, and other great towns, with the view of obtaining pecuniary assistance for his Mission. He was eminently successful; people being struck by the clearness and simplicity of his addresses, their practical common sense, and their entire freedom from sentimentalism or exaggeration. In May the "Southern Cross" again put to sea, and called at Norfolk Island, Erromango, Mota, and other islands, prior to undertaking a cruise among the Santa Cruz cluster. While at Santa Cruz, the chief island of the group, a disaster occurred of ominous significance. The Bishop went off in the boat with Atkin and Pearce, and three Norfolk Islanders, Edwin Nobbs, Fisher Young, and Hunt Christian,—all young men of ripe promise, trained under his own eye. He landed at two places among many people, and after a while came back as usual to the boat. On the third occasion he landed amidst a great crowd, waded over the broad reef (partially uncovered at low water), went into a hut, sat down for some time, and then through the throng of islanders returned to the boat, and re-embarked. They had pulled about fifteen yards from the reef, when the savages (for some unknown reason) began to shoot at the mission-party. The rudder had not been shipped; so the Bishop held it up, hoping it might shield off any arrows that came straight, the boat being " end on," and the stern nearest to them.

" When I looked round after a minute," says the Bishop, " providentially indeed, for the boat was being pulled right into a small bay on the reef, and would have grounded—I saw Pearce, [a seaman], lying between the thwarts, with the long shaft of an arrow in his chest, Edwin Nobbs with an arrow, as it seemed, in his left eye, many arrows flying close to us from many quarters. Suddenly Fisher Young, pulling the stroke oar, gave a faint scream; he was shot through the left wrist. Not a word was spoken, only my ' Pull ! port oars, pull on steadily.' Once dear Edwin, with the fragment of the arrow sticking in his cheek, and the blood streaming down, called out, ' Look out, sir, close to you !' But, indeed, on all sides they were close to us.

" How we any of us escaped I can't tell; Fisher and Edwin pulled on, Atkin had taken Pearce's oar, Hunt pulled the fourth oar. By GOD's mercy no one else was hit, but the canoes chased us to the schooner. In about twenty minutes we were on board, the people in the canoes round the vessel, seeing the wounded, paddled off as hard as they could, expecting, of course, that we should take vengeance on them. But I don't at all think that they were cognisant of the attack on shore."

Edwin and Fisher died of tetanus, the result of their wounds, a week after this sad catastrophe. Their fate was a great blow to the Bishop; it seemed to deprive him of his youthful buoyancy, and impressed lines of care on his face that never were effaced.

In the summer season of 1865 work was resumed at Mota. Arva was also visited, and Ysabel Island, and Curtis Island, where the Bishop had some idea of forming a settlement. Afterwards he came to Sydney, Adelaide, and Melbourne, obtaining a large and welcome contribution to the support of his various schemes, and an offer, from the Governor of New South Wales, of a grant of land on Norfolk Island. This offer was gladly accepted; Norfolk Island, from its position and its climatic advantages, being much better adapted than Kohimarama for the seat of the Melanesian Bishopric. Thither, accordingly, he removed in the spring of 1867, establishing the Mission at S. Barnabas' College; and for the rest of his brief life his time was spent in its organisation and development, and in his usual summer cruises among the isles. The progress made was astonishing, and the more astonishing because it was not superficial, but *real*. Bishop Patteson never asked for immediate results; he knew that the seed, if it were to ripen effectually, must go through a certain process of germination, and he waited patiently until GOD's sunshine in due time gave the harvest. But while he waited, he watched, and was careful to clear away any obstacle that could retard a healthy growth. There were trials, however, *external* trials, which not all his patience and vigilance could abate; chiefly those arising from the cruel dealings of the so-called "labour-ships," whose kidnapping atrocities provoked among the islands an ever-increasing feeling of hatred against the "white men." Another serious check to his happy labours was a severe illness in the early spring of 1870, from which he never entirely recovered. That summer the "Southern Cross" went on her annual cruise without her Bishop; but later in the year he was able to visit Mota, the Solomon Islands, and the Santa Cruz cluster, where he landed at Nukapu. In October he was back at S. Barnabas' College.

But I must draw this sketch to a close. After a seven weeks' sojourn at Mota, in the summer of 1871, the Bishop steered his missionary bark to the Solomon Islands, meeting with some sad evidences of the mischief wrought by the labour traffic. Writing to one of his friends, he says :— "The deportation of natives is going on to a very great extent *here*, as in the New Hebrides and Banks Islands. Means of all kinds are employed : sinking canoes and capturing the natives, enticing men on board, and getting them below, and then securing hatches and imprisoning them. Natives are retaliating. Lately, two or three vessels have been taken and all hands killed, besides boats' crews shot at continually. A man called on me at Mota the other day, who said that five out of seven in the boat were struck by arrows a few days before. The arrows were not poisoned, but one man was very ill. It makes even our work rather hazardous, except where we are thoroughly well known. I hear that a vessel has gone to Santa Cruz, and I must be very cautious there, for there has been some disturbance almost to a certainty."

On the 16th of September, the "Southern Cross" was off the Santa Cruz group, some twenty miles distant. For three days she lay becalmed, making scarcely any progress; but on the 20th, a light breeze carried her towards Nukapu, where four canoes, filled with natives, were seen hovering about its white circling reef. At half-past eleven in the morning, the Bishop ordered the boat to be lowered, and entered it with Mr. Atkin, his faithful and devoted assistant, Stephen Taroniara, James Minipa, and John Nonono. He pulled towards the canoes, whose crews immediately recognised him, and when he offered to go on shore, signified their assent. When nearer the reef, he was met by two more canoes, making six in all. The islanders were anxious that the boat should be hauled up on the reef, the tide being too low for her to cross it : and when this was declined, the men offered to take the Bishop into their canoe. To disarm suspicion and gain their entire confidence, he at once complied. Mr. Atkin afterwards said he thought he caught the word "Tabu," as if in warning, and saw a basket with yams and other fruits presented : and it is said this is a Polynesian stratagem, with the object of inducing an intended victim to touch the tabued object, that it may be lawful to kill him.

A delay of about twenty minutes occurred : after which two canoes went with the one containing the Bishop, these canoes being guided by chiefs who had hitherto been friendly to him. The tide was so low that it was necessary to wade over the reef, and drag the canoes to the inner lagoon. The boat's crew were unable to follow ; but their straining gaze watched the Bishop to the beach, when he disappeared.

For about half an hour the boat drifted to and fro in company with the canoes ; then, suddenly, at about ten yards off, without any warning, a man stood up in one of them, and exclaiming :—"Have you anything like this?" discharged an arrow; whereupon the natives in the other canoes let loose volley after volley, calling out, as they aimed :—"This for New Zealand man ! This for Bauro man ! This for Mota man !" With lusty pulls the boat was backed out of range, but not before three out of the four oarsmen had been struck; John on the head, Mr. Atkin in the shoulder, and Stephen with six arrows in the chest and shoulders.

They contrived to reach the ship, and were helped on board. No sooner was the arrow-head removed from Mr. Atkin's shoulder than he insisted on returning to find his Bishop, nor could he be dispensed with, as he alone knew the passage across the reef when the tide had risen. Accompanied by Joseph Watè, Charles Sapinamba, a sailor, and Mr. Bongarde, the mate, he pushed off; and as soon as the water was high enough, dashed across the reef. Two canoes came out to meet him; one cast off the other, and went back; that other with something lying motionless in the middle, drifted towards the boat. When the mission party came up with it, they lifted out of it a bundle wrapped in matting, and as they did so, the natives on the shore raised a loud cry. The bundle was the Bishop's dead body rolled in a native mat, which was secured at the head and feet. "The placid smile was still on his face; there was a palm leaf fastened over the breast, and when the mat was opened there were *five wounds*, no more." One, given with a club, and probably the first, had crushed in the skull at the back, causing instant death; another was on the top of the head, which had been cloven by some sharp weapon; the body was also pierced; and two arrow-thrusts were visible in the legs. In the front of the cocoa-nut palm were five knots made in the long leaflet, indicating that the good Bishop had been murdered in revenge for five kidnapped natives.

Next day, the Feast of S. Matthew, the body of Bishop Patteson was committed to the deep. He was forty-four years and a half old at the time of his death.[1]

---

[1] He was not the only victim. Joseph Atkin died of his wound on the morning of the 27th: Stephen Taroniara, on the morning of the 28th.

INDEX.

Abelard, his Compendium of Theology, 89; it is denounced by Bernard of Clairvaux, attends Council of the Archbishop of Sens, 91; his sentence and death, 93.
Acheenese, battle against the, 309.
Adamnan, credulity of, 34.
Anger, conversion of, 311.
Arrabbiati, the, revive their power in Florence, 261.
ASKEW, ANNE, her birth, 325; Married to Mr. Kyme, becomes a Protestant, 326; her pious life, 328; her first examination, 329; sent to prison, 331; examined by Bonner, 332; confession of faith, 335; set at liberty, second apprehension, 336; examined by Gardiner, 337; sent to Newgate, her belief, formally tried at the Guildhall, 338; sentenced to death, 339; writes to the king, 340; her song in prison, 341; goes to the Tower, is tortured, 343; letter to John Lascelles, 344; writes her "purgation," 345; is burnt, 346.

Bentivoglio of Bologna, 232.
Belley, Bishop of, 375.
BERNARD OF CLAIRVAUX, birth of, 53; death of his mother, 54; his conversion, 55; his converts, 56; enters Cistercian Monastery, 56; his asceticism, 58; love of Nature, 59; becomes a monk, 60; builds Clairvaux Monastery, 61; visits Bishop of Chalons, 63; his letters, 65; composes Homilies, 65; his miraculous cure of S. Thierry, 66; other miracles, 68; visits La Grande Chartreuse, 69; visits Paris, 70; his influence, 71; the "Apology," 74; Council of Troyes, 75; elects Innocent Pope, 76; accompanies him on his progress, 77; honours at Pisa, 79; refuses Archbishopric, 80; returns to Clairvaux, and rebuilds it, 81; reclaims Count William of Aquitaine, 82; Sermons on the Canticles, 83; defeats the claims of Peter of Pisa, 87; accomplishes the unity of the Church, 88; death of his brother, 89; condemns Abelard, 92; influence on second Crusade, 94; goes to Germany, 96; completes *De Consideratione*, 101; his death, 103.
Borgia, Alexander, elected Pope, 231.

Brescia, 217, 218.
Brothers of Penitence, order of, 142.

CATHARINE OF SIENA, SAINT, her birth, 156; her childish pilgrimage, 158; her self-discipline, 160; becomes a Mantellata, her personal charms, 162; spiritual trials, 163; enters on active life, envy against her, 170; her converts, 173; heroism during the Plague, 175; visits Pisa, her correspondence, 176; encourages Crusades, 177; her illness, 178; writes to the Pope, 180; attempts peace negotiations, 182; reproves the Pope, 183; is visited by the great, 184; induces the Pope to return to Rome, 186; goes to Florence, her life is menaced, 189; sides with Urban against Clement, 191; her death, 195; pictures of her, 195.
Chantal, Madame de, 378.
Christmas Spectacle, origin of, 143.
Church Work, 388.
Cistercian Monastery, the, 57.
Clairvaux Monastery built, 61.
Clement VII. elected Pope, his rivalry with Urban, 192.
Colonies, Monastic, 27.
COLUMBA, SAINT, his birth, 6; takes Orders, 8; his Poems, 9; goes to Britain, 10; Battle of Cool-Drewry, 13; founds Monastery at Iona, 20; his Missions, 22; his Miracles, 24; his Monastic Colonies, 27; last visit to Ireland, 31; his varied knowledge, 38; his vision, 41; his death, 44.
Cool-Drewry, Battle of, 13.
Council of Troyes, 75.
Crusade, the Second, 94; its failure, 100.

Dante, quoted 131—151.

"Devout Life," S. Francis de Sales', 351.
"De Ruina Mundi," Poem by Savonarola, quoted, 203.
Domenico, Fra, 263, 270.
Dominicans, the, of Tuscany, restored by Savonarola, 233.

Eliot, George, quoted, 239.

Foundlings, Asylum for, 410.
FRANCIS OF ASSISI, birth of, 107; early life, 108; his vision, 109; finds his vocation, 111; is imprisoned by his father, 113; his poverty, 114; restores churches, 115; seeks converts, 116; institutes order of *Frati Minori*, 118; sympathy with lepers, 121; enjoins active labour, 124; his social reform, 126; his practical wisdom, 126; visits Rome, 129; Innocent seals the order, 130; holds a chapter and institutes the second order, 133; women-converts, 133; sets out to preach, 135; his gentleness, 135; his poems, 137; goes among the crusaders, 140; institutes third order (Brothers of Penitence,) 142; celebrates a Christmas spectacle, 143; goes into seclusion, 144; miracle of Stigmata, 145; his illness, 147; his death, 150.
FRANCIS DE SALES, his "Devout Life," 351; his birth, 362; early life, 363; studies at the University of Padua, 364; his rules for life, 365; takes Doctor's degree, 365; takes Orders, 366; his early labours, 367; his preaching, 368; undertakes mission to Chablais, 369; his meekness, 371; is made a coadjutor of Bishop Granier, 372; goes to Henry IV., 373; succeeds Bishop Granier, 374; his private life, 374; opinion on fasting, 375; his epigrams, 376; Episcopal labours, 377; success of the "Devout Life," 378;

INDEX. 477

visit to Paris, 380; appoints his brother coadjutor, 380; his illness, 380; death, 382.
FRANCIS XAVIER, birth of, 288; friendship with Ignatius, 289; is converted, 291; travels to Venice, 293; goes to Rome, 294; sets out for the East Indies, 295; his missionary labours, 300; preaches a holy war, 309; converts Anger, 311; arrives in Japan, 312; sets out for China, 318; his death on the journey, 321.
Frati Minori, Order of, 118.

Gaming, Savonarola's denunciation of, 223.
Gregory, Pope, 180; returns to Rome, 186; his death, 190.
Guildhall, Anne Askew's trial in the, 338.

Hallam, quoted, (note) 218.
Hôtel Dieu, Vincent de Paul's reformation of, 410.

Innocent II., Pope, his election, 76; his progress, 77.
Innocent III., Pope, vision of, 129; confirms Franciscan Order, 130.
Innocent VIII., Pope, elected, his vicious excesses, 216.
Insurrection of the Fronde, 411.
Iona, characteristics of, 16; its Monastery founded, 20; its ruins, 48.
Ireland, Columba's last visit to, 31; culture of, 4.

Jesus Christ, Order of, 162.
Joam d'Eyro, story of, 305.

Kavanagh, Julia, quoted, 404.

Lascelles, John, Anne Askew's letter to, 344.
Lee, Holme, quoted, 437.
Legras, Louise, 404.
Leprosy, 114.

Libran and S. Columba, story of, 20.
Loyola, Ignatius, converts Francis Xavier, 291; founds a Society, 292; goes to Venice, 293; goes to Rome, 294; forms the Society into a Religious Order, 295.

Marcus Aurelius, 444; his "Meditations," 446.
MARTYN, HENRY, his birth and university career, 418; becomes tutor, 419; his attachment to Lydia Grenfell, 420; parts from her, admitted to Orders, appointed Chaplain under East India Company, 421; his preaching, 422; takes fever, Chaplain in Dinapur, 425; his appearance, 427; literary work, Miss Grenfell declines to join him, 428; his illness, 429; life at Cawnpur, 430; work among the heathen, 431; is ordered rest, 432; departs from Cawnpur, 433; journey to Persia, 434; his illness, 436; his death, 437.
Medici, Giuliano de'. See Lorenzo.
—— Lorenzo de', 209, 211; attempt to assassinate, 210; his objection to Savonarola, 226; tries to gain him, his interview with him, 227; his death, 229.
—— Piero de', 231, 234, 260.
Mirandola, Pico della, attends Lorenzo de' Medici's deathbed, 227.
Mission Priests, Society of, 394.
Missions, S. Vincent de Paul's, 401.
Monasteries, Columba's, 27.
Montalembert, on Columba, 46.
Myers, Frederick, quoted, 321.

Nicola Tulda, story of, 197.

Oliphant, Mrs., translation by, quoted, 137.

PATTESON, JOHN COLERIDGE, birth of, 449; early life, 450; his confirmation, 451; his studies, 452; his first sermon, 454; becomes a missionary, 455; lands in New Zealand, 456; visits the islands, 457; duties at S. John's College, 460; visits Lifu, 462; S. John's College newly built, 465; consecrated Bishop, 466; his episcopate, 468; his voyage among the islands, 469; visits Australia, 470; disaster at Santa Cruz, 470; removes to Norfolk Island, 471; death at Nukapu, 473.

Pazzi and Medici, the, 209.

Philosopher, the ideal, 444.

Piagnoni, the, recover direction of Florentine affairs, 261.

Pico, Giovanni, Prince of Mirandola, 218.

Pisa, Peter of, 87.

Plague of Siena, 175.

Poor Clares, Order of, 134.

Presepio, origin of the, 143.

Rienzi, 180.

Rome, the evil influence of the Court of, on the Church, 208.

SAVONAROLA, GIROLAMO, born at Ferrara, his parentage, his boyhood, 201; his character, 201, 202; his love for Strozzi's daughter, 202; "De Ruina Mundi," his religious tendencies, 203, 204; goes to Bologna and enters Dominican Convent, 205; his personal appearance, his conventual life, 206; "The Ruin of the Church," evil influence of Rome, 208; the Pazzi and Medici scandal, 209, 211; his progress in his position, 211; anecdote of, goes to Ferrara, 212; to Florence, enters Convent of S. Mark, letter to his mother quoted, (note) 213; his delight in art, his hopes and disappointments, appointed preacher, 214; his delivery, his unpopularity as a preacher, his asceticism and visions, 215; devotes himself to the Purification of the Church, his "Song of Praise" (quoted), election of Innocent VIII., his wickedness, distress of Savonarola, he repairs on a preaching mission to San Geminiano, sympathy of his hearers, his war-cry, 216; denounces the corruption of Rome, goes to Brescia, 217; the turning-point in his career, spread of his fame in Italy, his humility, his faith in his mission, his ardour, his friendship for Pico, 218; attends chapter of Dominicans, 218, 219; returns to S. Mark's, his eloquence, 219-221; his sermon, his career in Florence, 220; the mixed character of his preaching, 222; sermon on the Epiphany quoted, 224; deputation to, predicts the end of the Pope and Lorenzo de' Medici, elected Prior of S. Mark's, refuses to pay homage to the Medici, 226; Lorenzo's illness, 227; his interview with Savonarola, 228; his death, 229; increase of Savonarola's popularity in Florence, Alexander Borgia elected Pope, 231; his vision, goes to Bologna; his conduct towards the wife of Bentivoglio, 232; returns to Florence, his work for the Tuscan Dominicans, 233; his objects, his reforms, 234; his habits, his denunciations of the great, 235; his Lent Sermons, 238; effect on the multitude, 240; preserves the peace of Florence, 242; recommends establishment of the Great Council, 243; his system of government, 245; his remarkable influence, 246, 247; Florentine reform, 247; conversion of Bertuccio, 248; his interview with De Commines, 250; desists for awhile from preaching, 251; his social reforms, 252; resumes preaching, 253; his patriotic appeal, 256; he defeats the Pope's attempt to fetter the liberty of his Convent, his Advent Sermons, his authority, his increased contention with Rome, 257; his moral influence, and the Carnival observances, 258; his Lent Sermons, increase of the opposing party, Piero's advance, 260; his excommunication, his defiance, relapse of Florence, struggles between the Pope and Savonarola, 261; he recommences his work, prohibited from preaching, his last sermon, 262; his prediction, endeavours to call a General Council, attacked by a Friar of Puglia, and challenged to prove his doctrines by the ordeal of fire, 263; Fra Domenico's action, 263; plots against him, 264; his doubts, agrees to the ordeal, the preparations, 265; disputes, 267; interdiction of the ordeal, fury of the populace, his trouble, 268; is sentenced to exile, assault on his Convent, 269; his address to the Monks, 271; his surrender, 272; rage of the multitude, his imprisonment, 273; his tortures, examinations, and depositions, 276; his last hours and execution, 280.

Scholastic Philosophy, the, 202.
Selwyn, Bishop, 450.
Sens, Archbishop of, his Council, 91.
Sherwood, Mrs., quoted, 427.
Single Life, opportunities of the, 164.
Sisters of Charity, instituted, 403; duties of, 406; courage of, 409.

Six Articles, Act of the, 327.
Sixtus IV., Pope, 209, 211, 216.
S. Mark, Convent of, 213.
"Song of Praise," (Savonarola,) quoted, 216.
Stigmata, Miracle of, 145.
Strozzi, the, 202.

Troyes, Council of, 75.

Urban VI., Pope, 192; rivalry with Clement VII., 192.
Usury and excessive gains, Savonarola's condemnation of, 223.

Villari, quoted, 229.
VINCENT DE PAUL, SAINT, his moderate intellectual gifts, 387; Church work, 388; birth of Vincent, 390; becomes a tutor, 390; ordained, 390; robbed and sold into slavery, 391; converts his renegade master, 392; is liberated, 392; becomes tutor and chaplain, 393; inaugurates a system of Missions, 394; Society of Mission Priests founded and endowed, 394; work among criminals, 395; organizing genius, 396; his character, 397; receives the Priory of S. Lazarus, 400; establishes Retreats, 402; institutes Sisters of Charity, 403; their duties, 406; and courage, 409; his philanthropy, 410; his illness, 411; his death, 413.
Virgin Mary, exaltation of the, 126.
Visitation, Order of the, 379.

William of S. Thierry, his account of Bernard of Clairvaux, 63; miraculous cure by Bernard, 66.
William of Aquitaine, conversion of, 82.

www.ingramcontent.com/pod-product-compliance
Lightning Source LLC
Chambersburg PA
CBHW051234300426
44114CB00011B/730